THESE ARE
OUR VOICES

THESE ARE OUR VOICES

The Story of Oak Ridge 1942-1970

Edited by James Overholt

Children's Museum of Oak Ridge
Oak Ridge, Tennessee
1987

Graphic design by Kent Brown

The publication of this book is a project of the Regional Appalachian Center of the Children's Museum of Oak Ridge.

The findings, conclusions, and points of view expressed in *These Are Our Voices: The Story of Oak Ridge 1942-1970* do not necessarily represent the views of the Children's Museum of Oak Ridge.

The editor gratefully acknowledges permission to reprint from "The Prophet," by Marilou Bonham Thompson, in *Abiding Appalachia: Where Mountain and Atom Meet*, by permission of Marilou Awiakta (Bonham Thompson); from "Genesis," by Marilou Bonham Thompson, in *Abiding Appalachia: Where Mountain and Atom Meet,* by permission of Marilou Awiakta (Bonham Thompson); from "From Bulletin to Broadside," by June Adamson, in *Tennessee Historical Quarterly*, V. 38, No. 4, by permission of the Tennessee Historical Society; and from "Mother's Advice While Bandaging My Stubbed Toe," by Marilou Bonham Thompson, in *Abiding Appalachia: Where Mountain and Atom Meet*, by permission of Marilou Awiakta (Bonham Thompson).

Children's Museum of Oak Ridge, Tennessee 37830

© 1987 by the Children's Museum of Oak Ridge

All rights reserved. Published 1987.

First Edition

Printed in the United States of America at Kingsport Press

Library of Congress Cataloging-in-Publication Data

These are our voices.

Bibliography: p.
Includes index.
1. Oak Ridge (Tenn.)—History. I. Overholt, James, 1947—
F444.03T48 1987   976.8'73   86-26921
ISBN 0-9606832-4-0

CONTENTS

PART I
WARTIME OAK RIDGE

PROLOGUE

DISPLACEMENT

BUILDING A SECRET CITY

THE ARMY'S EFFORT

COMMUNITY LIFE

PART II
THE POSTWAR YEARS

MARGARET MEAD COMES TO TOWN

RESEARCH AND PROGRESS

EDUCATION

COMMUNITY LIFE

CONCLUSION

FOREWORD

It is especially fitting that the Children's Museum of Oak Ridge compile this community history during "Homecoming '86." Following the guidelines set down by Governor Lamar Alexander—to recall, celebrate, and reflect upon our heritage—this project is the culmination of a two-year effort to gather historical data and memoirs about the growth of the Oak Ridge community from 1942 to 1970.

This work is *not* a list of technical achievements about a science community, but rather a look at the town's social and cultural fabric. It is an attempt to recount the early years and the long-range impact of those years upon its citizens and its region. It presents a look at the people in terms of their past, and does so through individual lives.

It is appropriate that the Children's Museum Regional Appalachian Center undertake this project. The Center evolved from a successful three-year learning-museum project funded by the National Endowment for the Humanities from 1978 to 1981, and now houses an Appalachian library and resource center with programs for adults and secondary students.

The Museum itself has been in existence since 1973 when it was conceived by local senior Girl Scouts who saw the need for creating a place where young people and adults could learn together and enjoy being together. Since that time the Museum has seen remarkable growth, and is today considered a major educational and cultural institution in the Southeast. Moreover, it has been singled out as a significant force in the awakening of interest in the cultural heritage of southern Appalachia.

The present Children's Museum was preceded by a two-room

exhibit center maintained for twenty years by teachers who were members of the Association for Early Childhood Education. From 1948 to 1968 (part of the time period covered in this volume), teachers worked hard providing students with enrichment beyond the school curriculum and envisioned that someday Oak Ridge might erect a full-fledged Children's Museum. Two superb educators who had the foresight and wisdom to know that this could indeed become a reality, and who were involved in the project at the grass roots level, were Marg Wait and Julia Moore. *These Are Our Voices*, with its look at the forties, fifties, and sixties, is a memorial to them.

Today the Children's Museum of Oak Ridge is one of hundreds of youth musuems in cities and towns across the United States offering exciting interactive, hands-on exhibitions in the arts, history, and natural sciences. What makes this learning center unique are the thousands of donated artifacts representing the culture of the Appalachian region, and the tireless effort for innovative projects such as the publication of *These Are Our Voices*.

Jim Overholt, Regional Appalachian Center director, is commended for a job well done—as are the hundreds who have written and proofed and designed and indexed and typed and generally supported the project. This has been a true community effort.

Selma Shapiro,
Executive Director

Children's Museum of Oak Ridge

INTRODUCTION

INTRODUCTION

I f you had driven into the East Tennessee communities of
Wheat or Robertsville in the spring of 1942, you would have
seen a gentle, pastoral setting, populated by old American
families. Fields and pastures, croplands and wooded areas, hollows and fence rows would have filled the good-sized Clinch River
valley. You would have seen farmhouses bordered by barns and
sheds and clusters of trees. Cows may have grazed lazily in pastures, or trace chains echoed from fields where farmers did the
spring plowing. Nothing would have seemed farther from the roar
and boom of world war than that quiet setting. Yet, within
months, that scene had given way to probably the most turbulent
sight the natives had ever witnessed. It gave way to the overnight
construction of a heavily guarded, constantly growing, fenced-in
town on Black Oak Ridge. Within months, bulldozers were rooting in the earth at every turn. Dormitories and houses and huge
plants went up overnight. Spiderwebs of roads were built where
before only pastures had been. Noise was constant, night and day,
a ceaseless, disruptive hammering and banging. As one woman
remarked, "I knew something was wrong when I first came, but I
couldn't figure it out right away. Then, I realized ... there were no
birds. The noise had driven them away." Here, no one seemed to
sleep. Illuminated as much by night as by day, the town labored
under a burdensome twenty-four hour schedule, the sounds of
work spilling over the whole valley. Buses filled the roads, their

engines grunting. On some days, a drive to Clinton—a mere ten miles away—took well over an hour. Lines upon lines of people gathered in Townsite each day, standing and waiting for their mail, groceries, clothes, books—whatever they needed. "I remember when I opened the post office window in the morning," said Zora Penland, a mail clerk in 1943, "they were lined up so far down the street I couldn't see the end. And it stayed like that the rest of the day." In damp winters, mud stuck to everything; in burning summers, mouths and nostrils and eyes were filled with dust. And maybe worst of all was the frantic search for housing. A growing town that never quite met its citizens' needs, this mysterious place was inundated by swarming thousands, many homeless at times. They slept in cars, tents, barns, anyplace they could put their heads.

It was something unlike anything before: one culture replacing another, a new people taking the land of an old. Yet it was something very much American, unfolding into many parallels of form, character, and direction as had the experience of the early American settlers. This place beckoned mysteriously, intriguingly, much as the New World had beckoned the English settlers. It held vast, far-reaching, and unknown possibilities.

This was the scene of Oak Ridge, Tennessee between 1942 and 1945, when America was at war with Germany and Japan. It was, in the words of Secretary of War Henry L. Stimson, "the largest, most extraordinary scientific experiment in history." Built by the army, Oak Ridge was one of the three sites of the Manhattan Project, along with Los Alamos and Hanford; its purpose was to extract uranium 235 from the raw ore to fuel an atomic bomb. Originally designed to house a community of only a few thousand, it eventually grew to over 75,000. It was a town built for the moment, but a town that has become a permanent place in East Tennessee, the nation, and the conscience of the world. In fact, the name Oak Ridge has become synonymous with a new age, the post-1945 atomic age. As Gunther Anders has noted, since that time "all history is now reduced to pre-history.... Although we are unchanged anatomically, our completely changed relation to the cosmos and to ourselves has transformed us into a new species."

These Are Our Voices, published by the Children's Museum of Oak Ridge, is an effort to focus upon those wartime events, the birthing of that new age, and to look at what Oak Ridge has become since—as well as how it has changed all of our lives. It is a "community history," written in large measure, though not exclusively, by Oak Ridgers themselves, and spoken in many and various voices. This volume includes sixty-six essays, the hard labors of forty-four writers, and spans the history of Oak Ridge from 1942 to 1970.

I think of this volume as a "life-history" book, a work closely akin to oral history. From the beginning of the project, our writers were encouraged to tell their own personal experiences about Oak Ridge, as both participants and observers, while relying upon whatever primary and secondary sources would illuminate their stories. I wanted them, in other words, to call upon their memories as much as the hard facts of history—ever conscious of the fallible faculty of memory, but reassured by recent and accomplished works in oral history. For it is through their stories, I believe, that we the readers are drawn so close to the events. History, in that way, becomes a direct expression of an event, rather than an abstraction. It gives the readers an opportunity to experience vicariously the lives and experiences of the participants of the time.

Still, however, I wanted more voices than just Oak Ridgers. I wanted anyone who had something important to say about the city. The aim was to gather the collective wisdom of a whole community and anything beyond if possible. And in this, it seems we did succeed in part; for essays have come to me from Memphis, Bowling Green, Asheville, Atlanta, Buffalo, and San Francisco, to name but a few places. *These Are Our Voices*, then, is a diverse collection of essays, eclectic in nature, presenting a blend of scholarly research and personal recollections. In editing the papers, I always kept in mind that scholarship should not overload them, that they should assume an informal, personal tone, and yet contain the insights of scholarly, analytical minds. I focused on blending these two ways of *seeing* into one volume, unifying them chronologically and tying them into one texture without giving the impression that this is more than one book. Moreover, I always kept in mind that this was a "life-history" book. Even in the scholarly papers, our writers were encouraged to utilize oral interviews.

The pattern of this book, then, is set in such a way as to give structure and direction to the essays, letting the story of Oak Ridge unfold from beginning to end. But I believe, too, that each of these essays can stand on its own, with its own voice, and that readers can dip into the book at any point and come away with a better understanding of Oak Ridge.

As a final word, it should be noted that deficiencies do exist in this volume, and I apologize for them. Several topics were not included that should have been, and certain interpretations were no doubt omitted that were important; but circumstances dictated this. In some cases, I simply could not find the right person for the topic. In others, the right person was there but was too busy with family or work to assume the task. Time also played its menacing role. Given more time, I'm sure some of the deficiencies could have been avoided. Yet, on the other side, it should be stressed that from the beginning I never saw this manuscript as a comprehensive work, and certainly not a definitive one. This was a community history, a "life-history" book, written with the insider's perspective in mind; written to evoke the mood, impressions, and personal experiences of an age; written by persons from a wide array of vocations and professions, attempting to "save from death's dateless night" many of the ordinary happenings of an extraordinary time and place. The aim, in this sense, was to record those personal stories that historians sometimes overlook in their sweep of the great human drama.

The wonder to me is that the work took the final shape that it did. For there were moments at the beginning when I wondered if we would have a book at all. I remember vividly that after eight months of soliciting essays, I had received a grand total of seven. *Despair* was the only word to describe my feelings then. It seemed an endless, impossible quest. In trying to organize this project, I quickly discovered what an imperfect and difficult undertaking a community history is. My sensation was one of great defeat. But then, almost miraculously, when I felt ready to quit, an excitement about the project was suddenly born. All at once, writers started working at a furious pace, calling me, submitting ideas to me, and giving an assistance that I had never expected. They began talking about it among themselves, and spreading word of it to others. Before I knew it, my desk was flooded with papers. My only problem after that was finding time to read and edit them. And really, the credit for this book goes to those faithful people, those writers (and nonwriters), who worked so hard and who did it all free of charge. This is their book. Now it is for you the reader to take that book and read it with the same fervor, imagination, and vigorous commitment with which they endowed it.

James Overholt

Oak Ridge, Tennessee
October 1986

ACKNOWLEDGEMENTS

The completion of this work would not have been possible without the help, assistance, and collaboration of a number of people. First, I wish to thank Selma Shapiro and the Children's Museum for giving me the opportunity to work on this project, and for encouraging me over the rough spots. Thanks go also to the Oak Ridge Library staff for their patience and commitment to our writers as they researched their topics.

Three other people are due a special thanks. They are Jane Alderfer, who typed most of the manuscript, assisted writers in their research, wrote an essay for the book, and provided me with the wisdom of her counsel; David Booker, who graciously took off time from graduate school to help in editing, and who spent endless hours discussing with me the design, organization, and total makeup of the book; and Kent Brown, the Children's Museum designer, who spent months pasting and laying out the five hundred pages within these covers.

Finally, other collaborators who worked periodically and who gave invaluable and unstinting support were Marion Garber, Anne Adamson, and Mary Ann McBride. Whenever I needed them, they almost always dropped what they were doing and came to assist me.

Thanks go to all of them.

James Overholt

PART I

WARTIME
OAK RIDGE

PROLOGUE

To the frontier the American intellect owes its striking characteristics. That coarseness and strength combined with acuteness and inquisitiveness; that practical, inventive turn of mind, quick to find expedients; that masterful grasp of material things, lacking in the artistic but powerful to effect great ends; that restless, nervous energy; that dominant individualism, working for good and for evil, and withal that buoyancy and exuberance which comes with freedom—these are traits of the frontier, or traits called out elsewhere because of the existence of the frontier.

— Frederick Jackson Turner,
The Significance of the Frontier in American History.

THE FRONTIER EXPERIENCE

Jim Wayne Miller

John Hendrix's vision of a city rising on Black Oak Ridge in East Tennessee was couched in the conventions of Old Testament prophecy. But the establishment of a city where nothing was—instant community, a human place built up out of wilderness and mud—is also a typically American experience. As the frontier moved westward across the North American continent—and we must remember that the frontier was always moving—towns were often established much as a carnival, arriving in trucks, sets up in the parking lot of a mall. Towns had a temporary, provisional look—and for good reason. In the west, where timber was scarce, mining towns were sometimes dismantled and moved *in toto* to another site. There were tent cities in the Dakotas as late as the 1880s.

While its purpose was unique, Oak Ridge was typical of town building in a frontier situation in America. The town's establishment involved the dislocation of local people (just as the coming of settlers involved the dislocation of the Cherokee in the 1830s). The people who came were not so much pushed from other places as they were pulled to the new place. The undertaking required a practical, no-nonsense state of mind (heightened in this instance by the urgency of the World War II atom bomb project). The undertaking required a willingness—characteristic of Americans from the colonial period on—to sacrifice the present and past to the future. In many ways Oak Ridge represented the most recent

1

location of the nation's moving frontier. But it was the nation's frontier in a double sense of the word: the frontier of mud and dirt; the frontier of futuristic science.

In earlier frontier situations, it must be remembered, the progression from rude cabin to mansion, from unlettered stump-grubbing settler to elegant orator was not always orderly. The American frontier has always been a place of incongruity, with both cabin and mansion in place simultaneously, with the unlettered and the lettered jostling in raw new places. In the American frontier experience there have almost always been two frontiers. Donald Davidson, in his history of *The Tennessee: The Old River: Frontier to Secession*, identifies an old frontier, consisting of traders working out of Charleston, South Carolina, who frequented the area of western North Carolina and East Tennessee long before there was any settlement, and a second frontier associated with the rapid influx of settlers.

The old frontier had on it knowledgeable, sophisticated people—traders and geographers who often advised the crowned heads of Europe. James Adair was a part of this old frontier. Adair's *History of the American Indians*, the first book written west of the Appalachians, is based on his experience of living among the Cherokee and Choctaw for about forty years. Written while he lived in the Indian towns, Adair's book was published in 1775—in Dublin, Ireland.

Judge John Haywood was a member of an antiquarian society that flourished in Tennessee when the state was still in its frontier phase. Haywood wrote the state's first history, *Civil and Political History of the State of Tennessee*, in 1823—almost before the state had a history! The image of Judge Haywood working on his book, as it is reported, while sitting on a bull's hide spread underneath a tree, his books and documents stacked around him, suggests the incongruities of the frontier experience.

Cragfont, a fine home built near Gallatin, Tennessee in 1802, and identified today by an historical marker as "Grandeur on the Frontier," is another example of civilization set incongrously in the wilderness on the American frontier.

The *Journal of the Reverend Francis Asbury* (1821), the Methodist bishop who traveled extensively thoughout the region, comments repeatedly on the contrasts and incongruities of frontier life. Asbury often deplores the harshness of wilderness conditions, the near-savagery of some of the settlers, the generally "unimproved" conditions and lack of civilization.

While Oak Ridge was certainly different from past America frontiers, the frontiersmen and women of Oak Ridge, not unlike Bishop Asbury, saw themselves as the bearers and guardians of culture, thrust into what they called the "wilds" of East Tennessee. And indeed they were bearers and guardians of culture, as is indicated by photographs of their homes and apartments, photographs that reveal pianos, art, oriental rugs.

Not unlike Asbury, the philosopher William James deplored a landscape in western North Carolina when he visited there in the late nineteenth century. James commented on a large number of "coves" that had been newly cleared and planted. The charred stumps, the trees left standing girdled and killed in newgrounds, the zigzag rail fences presented a scene of "unmitigated squalor." The natural beauty of the place had been destroyed while the "improvements" struck him as "hideous, a sort of ulcer." But in his essay "On a Certain Blindness in Human Beings," James relates how he came to see the scene from the standpoint of the residents. A mountaineer told James, "Why, we ain't happy here unless we are getting one of these coves under cultivation." James came to understand that while the scene appeared ugly to him, to the settlers the stumps and girdled trees and fences represented honest sweat, the fruits of persistent labor, and personal victory. The settlers loved their place not as it was, but as it would be. Like other Americans, they saw not so much the present as the future.

In this respect, Oak Ridgers probably differed from Americans in previous frontier situations. Oak Ridgers necessarily saw the present, not the future. The present demanded their entire attention. The uniqueness of the early Oak Ridge frontier was—at least from the perspective of the war years—that it had no future.

Nevertheless, Oak Ridge, a city rising out of mud, presented contrasts and incongruities similar to those noted by observers of earlier frontier situations. J. H. Rush, a physicist who worked on the Oak Ridge project from 1944 to 1946 recollects the provisional appearance of downtown Oak Ridge in those years: "The downtown shopping area centered around a nearly vacant block that served as a local bus terminal, and great numbers of people in the

Courtesy Department of Energy

At first glance, wartime Oak Ridge resembled the scene of other frontier towns in the American experience. It was a place where the natural beauty was destroyed so that the modern pioneers could fulfill their mission.

Courtesy James E. Westcott

Though living under the frontier conditions of mud, crowds, and shortages, many Oak Ridgers still considered themselves the guardians of culture.

car-scarce town gathered to wait for transportation home.... The sun was hot, and the familiar mud had given way to stifling dust." Rush remembers the diversity of people who converged on Oak Ridge. The project that brought construction workers and nuclear physicists together was "a continual study in contrasts. Pleasant, roomy houses on the ridge for key scientists and officials, and the walled compound of huts in which the Negro women lived; futuristic atomic energy laboratories adjacent to crude farm houses, now abandoned; dedicated men preparing ultimate destruction while their dedicated wives produced a bumper baby crop—all of these anomalies were physical and obvious. More interesting was the undertone of cultural conflict that pervaded this half-military, half-civilian city."

In a presentation at the Children's Museum in 1985 early Oak Ridgers Jane Randolph, Waldo Cohn, and June Adamson characterized the anomalies of the place with the phrase "Brahms and Bombs."

The simultaneous preparation of "ultimate destruction" and the establishment of families, dedication to Brahms and to bombs, is only superficially incongruous. The early Oak Ridgers "studied war" because they wanted peace, built bombs in order to be able to enjoy Brahms. The distinction between the immediate necessity and the ultimately desirable was expressed by John Adams in 1780 when he wrote to his wife Abigail: "I must study politics and war that my sons may have liberty to study mathematics and philosophy. My sons ought to study mathematics and philosophy, geography, natural history, naval architecture, navigation, commerce, and agriculture, in order to give their children the right to study painting, poetry, music, architecture, statuary, tapestry, and porcelain." Americans, from pioneer settlers to presidents, have shared this attitude toward work, its relation to life; this tacit understanding of the difference between what is obligatory and what is desirable; this devotion to the future. Settlers grubbed stumps and broke ground, immigrants labored in mills and factories so that eventually they might enjoy some of the "finer things of life." And if more ease and leisure were not to be theirs, then certainly their children and their children's children would be better off as a result of their labor.

We often misunderstand the significance of the frontier in the

American experience. On the one hand, like Bishop Asbury and William James, we fault the frontier and people on the frontier for what they obviously lack, unable to see the situation from the perspective of those caught up in the frontier experience. On the other hand, we romanticize the frontier and the frontiersman and assume that the frontier life is an option as a permanent "lifestyle."

But frontiersman and pioneers seem to have understood their situations better than we have. They viewed the frontier as a necessary but *temporary* phase. Frontier towns are always built by people who, like Goethe's Faust, have two souls within their breasts: they have the urge to go, but that very urge contains its opposite—the urge to settle (somewhere else).

As surely as settlers brought seed corn to their frontier farms, they brought also the seeds of community—in the hope of the husband to have a road, of the wife to have a window, better clothes, and one day a piano. Except for a few hunters, trappers, and adventurers who were in no way representative of the mass of the population, settlers, frontier people, and immigrants generally in America have not lived with a view toward perpetuating the immediate circumstances of their lives. They expected to do better. Maldwyn James, in his history of *American Immigration*, says immigrants to this country have always tended to be not the most abject and wretched, but those who wanted to better their lives. (And certainly many Oak Ridgers fit this pattern.) They have wanted a better house, better clothes, more of the comforts and amenities, if not for themselves, then for their children.

And for the most part our forebears succeeded. But they did not live close to the land because they thought it a good thing to do; they did so out of necessity. They did not weave and spin, and ply rustic crafts because this was part of their chosen "lifestyle;" they employed the technology available to them in their time, place, and circumstance. No more than a lot of people nowadays expect to live out their lives in mobile homes (the contemporary folk housing), settlers on the frontier never expected to remain long in the frontier and settlement phase. And they did not. (Many old houses in America contain the original log structure, which has been added to over the years, just as in Oak Ridge many contemporary homes contain the old, unattractive, boxlike cemesto structures of the wartime period, altered today almost beyond recognition after forty years of improvements and remodeling.)

In many of its aspects, the establishment of Oak Ridge represents the replication of a fundamentally American experience, which over the years has been lived in the context of a moving frontier. (James Fallows, in "America's Changing Economic Landscape," published in *The Atlantic Monthly*, finds throughout our history the same "churning of people" as is recollected by many Oak Ridgers.) And this American frontier experience is rooted in ideas and attitudes that have characterized the western world since the Renaissance. This complex of ideas and attitudes we understand as the notion of "progress." The German dramatist and critic Lessing wrote in the eighteenth century that if God should place at his right hand all truth, and at his left the desire constantly to strive to discover truth, he would choose constantly to seek truth over truth itself. Goethe's creation, Faust, the paradigm of western man, makes it a central part of his pact with Mephistopheles that he will always strive: "If ever I rest on a bed of sloth, you may take my soul then and there," Faust says to Mephistopheles. "If ever I say to the moment, 'Stay, you are so beautiful,' then take my soul." Tennyson, in his poem "Ulysses," has his idle king say: "'Tis not too late to seek a newer world." The restless veteran of the Trojan Wars, desires always "To strive, to seek, to find, and not to yield."

These are memorable expressions of the modern mind and temperament, and they are shared by Americans on the frontier, wherever that frontier happens to be at any given time—the frontier of self-government in the eighteenth century, or the frontier of nuclear fission in East Tennessee in the mid-twentieth. The people who established Oak Ridge in the 1940s were more genuinely frontiersmen than those who, in the 1960s and 1970s, affected the trappings of the American frontier by hewing logs, drying vegetables, spinning and weaving. The young people of the counterculture were more nearly antiquarian in their interest; the early Oak Ridgers worked in the spirit of Goethe's Faust and Tennyson's Ulysses; they sought a new world, whereas participants in the counterculture often sought an old one.

Marshall Berman, in his book *All That is Solid Melts in Air: The Experience of Modernity*, demonstrates that the frontier experience, whether literal or figurative, is a *modern* experience.

7

Prologue

The "frontier" and "pioneer" situations we associate with settlement and pre-settlement in the United States are not old-fashioned situations, but the result of modern thinking. Frontiers are created by modern ideas and attitudes. The frontier experience is not only a modern experience, but is now itself a *tradition*. Oak Ridge is a part of that tradition of the frontier experience in America.

DISPLACEMENT

Courtesy James E. Westcott

THE PROPHET

Marilou Awiakta (Bonham Thompson)

Cherokee paths were overgrown and pioneers had long plowed the land when the atom came to East Tennessee. It came suddenly and with faint warning in 1942. But forty years before, near the turn of the century, the thought of it had moved along the lonesome mountains and valleys. Like the most gentle breath of wind it moved and stirred the deep.

And on Pine Ridge, in the woods near his home, John Hendrix lay on the ground, looking at the sky. He was a hardworking mountain man, a man who took the Bible to heart, a stern-souled man. But on this day he was steeped in grief. His step-child was dead. He hadn't known she was so sick—never would he have scolded her for such a trifling thing if he had known. Now she was gone and John was old beyond his fourscore years. The stern heart cracked and the deep lay trembling ...

And John heard a Voice from the sky, loud and sharp like thunder. He obeyed its command. Leaving home and kin behind, John went into the wilderness. Forty days and forty nights he stayed to meditate and pray. And the Voice proved faithful to its word. A strange light moved upon the land. And in that light, this man saw a vision.

Then John came out of the wilderness and stood in the crossroads store and spoke solemnly before his neighbors:

I've seen it comin' ...

11

Displacement

Bear Creek Valley some day will fill with great buildings and factories and they will help win the greatest war that ever will be.

There will be a city on Black Oak Ridge and I say the center of authority will be middleway between Tadlock's farm and Pyatt's place.

A railroad will spur off the main L & N, run down toward Robertsville and then branch off toward Scarbrough. It will serve the great city of my vision. This I know.

Big engines will dig big ditches ... Thousands of people will run to and fro. They will build things and there will be great noise and confusion and the earth will shake.

I've seen it. It's comin' ...

His neighbors shook their heads. "Maybe so, John, maybe so. But, you know, this here's mighty solid ground, and 'til that town you speak of comes, we'll keep right on plowin' ..."

Reprinted from *Abiding Appalachia: Where Mountain and Atom Meet*, by Marilou Bonham Thompson.

THE WHEAT COMMUNITY

Patricia A. Hope

L ike the small village of Anatevka, made popular in the musical, *Fiddler on the Roof*, the Wheat community is also a place
remembered for its traditions.

In the fall of 1942, the U.S. Government purchased some
56,00(acres of land in eastern Tennessee for the development of
Oak Ridge, which included sections of both Roane and Anderson
Counties. Wheat lay in what is now the westernmost part of Oak
Ridge, or what is generally referred to as the K-25 area.

The people of Wheat, like the Jews of Anatevka, were forced
to leave their homes for other sanctuaries. Unlike the Anatevka
people though, who left because of political and religious oppres-
sion, the people of Wheat gave up their homes and businesses for a
patriotic cause—to help put an end to World War II. And they
kept something far more sustaining than the material possessions
that they relinquished. They kept their pride, their memories, and
above all their traditions.

As the Nashville *Tennessean* noted in 1950, the Atomic
Energy Commission (AEC) had "decided that a corner of the Oak
Ridge security curtain shall be lifted once a year," so that former
Wheat citizens could celebrate "Homecoming" the first Sunday of
each October. What was probably unknown to the AEC officials,
though, was that the Wheat community had been enjoying homecoming events for over a decade before the government removed
the residents in 1942. The evacuation of the community only

14

served to turn the event into a more prominent celebration.

Indeed, there were other communities on the reservation besides Wheat, communities faced with a similar fate. At the east end of the reservation lay Elza, named for the German families who had migrated to the area in the late 1700s. And in between lay Robertsville and Scarboro. This was the area made most famous by John Hendrix, the prophet who had roamed the woods in the early 1900s and had seen visions of the coming of Oak Ridge: "Bear Creek Valley some day will be filled with great buildings and factories and they will help toward winning the greatest war that ever will be," he had proclaimed. But just beyond the government area lay other communities, too—Solway, Blair, and Edgemoor.

Though settled by a variety of peoples, such as the Dutch, the Swedes, and the Germans, the vast majority of settlers who came to the Roane-Anderson County area had been Scotch-Irish. As George Robinson has noted in his *The Oak Ridge Story*, they had "followed the Quakers into Pennsylvania, then pushed down into Virginia and North Carolina. Later, they followed the mountain gaps ... into the new, promising, free land in the West." Thus all of these communities were similar in roots, religion, and rural developments. They all shared a common history and had known the same closeness to the land.

As for Wheat, its earliest residents date back to the mid-1790s, before Tennessee became a state. A treaty with the Cherokees in 1798 opened up whole new territories for settlement—including parts of what are now Roane and Anderson Counties. At the turn of the eighteenth century, a Revolutionary War soldier, Nicholas Nail, settled on the East Fork of Poplar Creek. This runs parallel with much of the western portion of what is now the Oak Ridge Turnpike. Nail's daughter, Esther, married William Gardenshire, who had bought 150 acres of Poplar Creek. He later purchased, in December 1807, 3,000 acres at approximately where Blair Road and Gallaher Road (Highway 58) now intersect. This would later become the heart of the Wheat community.

It is believed that Elias Roberts was the first settler to live where the Oak Ridge Gaseous Diffusion Plant (K-25) now sits. He and his wife, Rebecca, immigrated to Roane County from South Carolina in 1794. He leased and later bought some 500 acres of land in this vicinity.

By 1796, a grist mill had been built on the East Fork of Poplar Creek. It wasn't long until the lumbermen came. For years the area was referred to as Bald Hill, because virtually all the timber was stripped from the area.

By the late 1800s, however, the trees were growing back, and in 1881, when a post office was built to serve this whole eastern section of Roane County, the community was renamed Wheat, for its first postmaster, Henry Franklin Wheat.

The central part of the Oak Ridge Gaseous Diffusion Plant is built on the old "Maple Hill" homesite of David Houston Gallaher. David supposedly fought with Robert E. Lee for the southern cause in the Civil War.

David's brother, William, was also an early settler and a prominent force in Wheat history. He owned some 1,800 acres, raised cattle and cultivated thousands of peach trees in the 1920s and 1930s, when Roane County was the "peach capital of the United States." In the early 1930s, an exceptionally late cold spell ruined the peach crops of East Tennessee, and left many area farmers, including Gallaher, in financial distress.

At his height of financial success, though, Gallaher had gone to Texas and bought cattle and shipped them to Harriman, the nearest rail depot. One of Gallaher's three sons, William Thomas, recalls helping his father drive the cattle from Harriman to their farm, and when the cattle were ready for market, reversing the process, and shipping the cattle to markets for slaughter.

Probably no facet of Wheat tradition sparkles more than the community schools. The first one was in a tiny log house, established by a Methodist minister, Reverend John F. Dickey, in the 1870s. It was a "loud" school, where most lessons were recited out loud. It was called Bald Hill School. This "loud" school lasted only two years before the community began to outgrow it and wanted a school of higher learning.

Operated much as our high schools are today, the Poplar Creek Seminary was founded at Bald Hill in 1877. Reverend W. H. Crawford, a Presbyterian minister, was its founder, president, and teacher. By this time, another reverend, George W. Jones, a Baptist minister to the Mt. Zion Baptist Church (today known as the George Jones Memorial Baptist Church) was also becoming inter-

A Gathering at the George Jones Memorial Baptist Church in 1947.

The old Wheat High School, built in 1919.

ested in furthering the educational process of the area. In 1879, along with his wife, Lucinda, Jones presented 200 acres to the seminary. This left the Joneses only fifty-three acres for their own use.

Because of a few building stipulations, this gift turned out to be one of the most unique building programs in East Tennessee. Wheat residents who had children enrolled in the seminary could build on and use one-acre lots of this gift without payment. If the child no longer lived at home or if the householder or student did anything detrimental to the school, the resident was obligated to sell his house to a qualified person. Many families and pupils were attracted by this unusual building policy.

The Joneses' generosity extended to their church also. When the congregation began to raise money for a new church building, they agreed to match dollar for dollar any sum the congregation could raise. The new church was named in their honor.

George Jones apparently obtained his wealth "through industry and prudent business ability," and by purchasing much of his wife's estate. He also received a war pension around the turn of the century for having served as a second lieutenant in the 11th Tennessee Cavalry.

By 1886 the educational barometer of Wheat reached an all time high. Poplar Creek Seminary became chartered as Roane College, which offered a four-year liberal arts program for either a B.A. or M.A. For twenty years the college flourished and attracted students from all over the South. After the turn of the century, however, the barometer began to fall, attendance began dwindling and finances fell to an all time low. In 1908 the Roane County Board of Education assumed responsibility of the college and changed the name to Wheat High School. Wheat High School continued in the same building until a new building was constructed in 1919 about a fourth of a mile from the college site.

Today, on the first Sunday of October each year, some 400-500 people return to the Wheat community. No sign marks the way. No banner portrays the event. Only a gate normally closed, now open, leads reunioners to the site.

People still come dressed in their Sunday best, filling the tiny churchyard and spilling over into the nearby cemetery where tombstones silently reflect the names of most of those present.

Names like Gallaher, Jones, Christenberry, Hembree, McKinney, Arnold, Rather, and Magill are on the lips of the living and the tombstones of the dead. Harold McKinney, official custodian of the church, is the grandson of E. W. McKinney, who taught at Wheat High School until its closing in 1942.

Unlike the poor villagers of Anatevka, who can never recapture the "traditions" so important to them, Wheat residents can walk the grassy slopes of childhood, reminisce with the living, remember the dead, and keep the traditions of their past alive.

NEW PLACES, STRANGE PEOPLE

John Rice Irwin

I t was in the fall of 1942. I was only twelve years old, but I
knew something awful was about to happen. We had heard
that the railroad at Elza had started building a spur line off
their main track. About the same time the area was overrun with
land surveyors. Some of our neighbors were notified by the federal
authorities that their homes and farms were being purchased and
that those who were in the so-called hot spots were given only
fourteen days to vacate. No one knew how much land the government would need, and no one knew how many, nor which, families
would be affected. Everyone speculated, and everyone hoped they
would escape.

The answer for our family came suddenly, stunningly. We
returned home late one Saturday afternoon from our weekly trip
to McWayne's corn mill and Nash Copeland's store to find a notice
tacked on our front door. I don't remember its precise wording,
but I do remember the essence of that message, written on the
flimsy paper that fluttered and flapped in the chilly autumn breeze.
I remember, too, the anguish of my father and mother when they
read it.

We had barns filled with hay, thousands of bushels of wheat
and oats, over seventy head of cattle, and numerous other farm
animals. There was tobacco curing in the barns and corn not yet
gathered from the fields. We had only a few days in which to gather
up all our chattels and possessions and move from our Gamble
Valley farm—to a yet unknown destination.

Our farm contained a large, impressive antebellum home where my grandparents lived, two tenant houses and the five-room framed house where my younger brother and I lived with our parents. There were numerous barns, outbuildings and other improvements. The government's offer was a total of $10,500 for the property in its entirety. For this amount we soon found that we would not be able to acquire half as many acres in the surrounding area. This was due to the inflated prices caused by the increased demands, brought on by families who were forced off their land.

This sudden intrusion into our otherwise quiet and peaceful Bethel Valley became the singular topic of conversation, and it burdened everyone, young and old, night and day. People couldn't decide whether to use those few days the government alloted them in gathering their corn and grading their tobacco, or to spend the precious time looking for a new home. Trucks for moving the families were next to impossible to hire, and those that were available were often in poor condition and bore shoddy tires that had to be constantly changed and repaired.

But the economic and technical problems inherent in such hurried-up moving, monumental as they were, did not compare to the mental trauma. One has to understand the cultural and ancestral roots to which rural folk become attached to the land after a few generations in order to understand the shock which results from such uprooting.

Our family had moved into the area only a few years before, when the building of nearby Norris Dam flooded what had been the home of our family since 1784. So, while we knew well the distress of our neighbors, we ourselves were not as adversely affected.

My personal attachment to that Robertsville area home, however, was deep and strong. There was not one foot of those three hundred acres that my brother and I hadn't explored, mostly with our grandfather Irwin. We had gathered wild salad greens along the meadows in the early spring, fished for red-eyes in the creeks, and picked blackberries from the pastoral knobs in midsummer. We gathered hazel nuts in the fall, hunted rabbits in the winter snow, and we tapped the sugar maple in February. Every day was an adventure and every field, hollow, ridge, and swimming hole, was an old friend. It was inconceivable that we soon

21

would be leaving, forever, those many friendly haunts of our childhood.

But young folks could look toward the future with enthusiastic optimism and quickly adjust. Old folks couldn't. They were, to some extent, living in the past, among the familiar hollows and ridges they had known all their lives. They lived among their relatives and neighbors and lived in their memories among their ancestors—their people. This would not be the case when they moved to new places, and among strange people.

No one knew the certainty of the swift and drastic action of the government, and an effort was commenced to thwart the move altogether. I remember hearing that there was to be a "big meeting" at the schoolhouse at Robertsville. Everyone was urged to attend and to the best of my memory everyone did. The word was spread that Congressman John Jennings would be there. I assumed that there was no higher, more powerful and influential person in the nation, except maybe the president. I think most of the people felt the same way.

I have vivid recollections of that meeting. It was not unlike the testimonial services I had heard in church revivals and at the tent meeting. I especially remember one old white-haired lady who spoke in tones which wavered between anger and pathetic beseeching. Her great-grandfather was one of the first settlers there, she said, having brought his family and all his possessions from North Carolina there in an ox cart. She said he, along with all her people, lay in a little cemetery on their farm. And she said, "Four of my babies are there, too. We don't want to leave them."

An old man in faded and patched overalls took the floor and spoke maybe for the first time in his entire life in a public meeting. He stated that he had plowed the same fields, hunted the same woods, and fished the same streams as had his father, and his father's father, and on back to his great-grandfather's day. His son, he pointed out, did most of the work on the old farm now, and his grandson would hopefully take it over some day. He said, according to nature, he didn't have much time left, and that he just wanted to till his farm and spend his last days among his friends, neighbors, and relatives. He looked around the room with tears in his eyes, trying to think of a good way to end, and as he struggled for words, the entire audience broke into applause. The old man nodded awkwardly and sat down.

I don't know if the congressman knew the inevitability of the government's move to acquire the land from the people or not. If he did, he didn't advise them of the futility of their pleas.

The meeting adjourned and a crowd gathered around Congressman Jennings, pointing out how long they had known him and how ardently they had supported him in his elections. Small clusters of people gathered outside the building and wondered if the congressman could stop the government from taking our land—some wondered if he really wanted to.

Whether or not he petitioned the president to terminate the project, or to place it elsewhere, we never knew. What we did know was that the acquisition of the land continued, surely and swiftly.

The surveyors converged on the entire area like flies after honey, and the drone of heavy equipment, tearing the countryside apart, was our constant companion. It reminded us of the seventeen-year locust which had appeared shortly before.

In the meantime we worked literally night and day gathering corn, grading tobacco, sacking wheat and oats, and otherwise preparing for the prodigious move. My grandfather was a lay minister and believed in the most strict observance of the Sabbath. But for the first time in his life he consented to our working on Sundays. The ox was in the ditch.

My father bought another farm about twenty miles up the valley, in the Glen Alpine community. The transfer of all the crops, machinery, livestock, and household items on a single truck (which often broke down) took weeks. At one point it occurred to my father that we had half of our possessions at the new farm, unlocked and unguarded. And while thievery and pillaging was not a great problem in those days and in that area, the concern for security increased as more of our possessions were hauled there.

Late one afternoon, as Roy Edmonson's truck was leaving our Robertsville farm, piled high with lespedeza hay, my father instructed me to go with him and spend the night at the new place. My uncle and aunt, Frank and Sophia Atkins, had moved nearby in a tiny, temporary house, and I was to sleep there (on the floor) when I was not on guard duty. The plans were that I would return to our Robertsville home in a couple of days—when I was relieved.

But more loads of hay and corn came in, then the cattle, hogs,

Displacement

John Rice Irwin and his brother riding a cow on their Robertsville farm.

Reverend and Mrs. John G. Irwin lost their Robertsville farm in 1943 with the coming of Oak Ridge.

mules, and chickens; and they all had to be cared for. After a few more days, the moving was almost completed, and I realized, suddenly and joltingly, that I would never return to that beautiful, rolling farm-home in Bethel Valley. Soon my family came to join me, and quite soon after that the "project" area was closed to visitors. Years passed and a city of some 75,000 was built and when I finally did return to the old home place, as a young man, I found nothing of the tranquil and nostalgic countryside of my childhood.

In 1969 I became director of the Tennessee Appalachia Educational Cooperative, and spent thirteen office years in Oak Ridge, almost within sight of our family's former home. But when I reflected back on those happy and carefree childhood days, spent roaming through the lush meadows and over the familiar hills, I never thought of them as being nearby. They were far away and long ago, and their physical closeness did nothing to change that.

I sometimes saw boys exploring the old knobs where my brother and I trudged every summer afternoon in search of the milk cows. I was reminded of the buckeyes we found along the streams, the muscadines and fox grapes we gathered, and the rabbit tobacco we chewed along the way. I wondered if those boys enjoyed themselves as much, or loved the land as intensely as we had. I wondered, too, if they ever wondered what that land and those hills were like before their time—before their grandfathers came there in the early 1940s.

A FAMILY'S SEARCH

Ruby Daniel

My parents, Pearl Dempter Castleberry and Lois Adora Fischer, were married July 15, 1908. They had fifteen children: ten boys and five girls. The first two boys, George and Hershel, were born in Rising Fawn. Then my parents moved to Kentucky where my father worked in coal mines in Kentucky and Tennessee: High Splint, Peabody, Jellico, Black Mountain, Red Bud, Harlan, and many other places. Eleven children were born in Kentucky. I was born May 3, 1921 in Jellico, Tennessee. I was the seventh child by about five or six minutes, for I had a twin brother. We only lived in Jellico a few months. Since my dad worked in the mines, we moved very often, sometimes living at one place a single month. I remember my mama saying that she had moved thirty-eight times in her married life.

In 1929, though, my brother Hershel was injured in the mines, and as a result my parents decided that mining was too dangerous and that they must find another life. That year we moved to a farm on the Powell River to work as tenant farmers. Mr. Rufus Jones owned the farm. As tenant farmers, we got fifty percent of the crop. We did all the work, sold all the vegetables, and only got half of the earnings. It didn't seem fair, but it was an improvement over the mines.

It was a great change from the mining camp to the farm: no electricity and no ice boxes. Mama and Papa made a place down by the river where there was a big spring in which we could keep our milk cool. All our water was carried from the spring. We still had our barrel of water, though, for washing clothes.

The house we lived in was very big and must have been a hundred years old. The logs in it were hand sawed. It was sturdy, but cold and rather bleak in the winters. In some places it had dirt floors. There were rats in it the size of cats. In fact, one bit my hand one night while I slept. Moreover, we had outside toilets, and all the other buildings—the barn and the sheds—were old and weathered. There were no stores nearby. The closest one, Heatherly Grocery Store, was about three miles away at Walnut Grove. Across the road from the store was Walnut Grove Methodist Church and school, combined. That's where we went to school.

Life on the farm was hard. It seemed that we always worked. Everyone who could carry a hoe went to the fields to work, chopping weeds. I prayed for rain, but when God answered my prayers he also brought me more weeds. I was eight years old at the time.

It was then that my brother Gus, who had left home the year before, returned. One would have thought the prodigal son had arrived. We had all kinds of things to ask him about the rest of the world. He would sit for hours and tell us children his stories. Some were true, but others were made up. He would tell fantastic yarns, but we didn't know it and we didn't care. We would sit outside at night after the work was done and ask him questions about the stars and the moon, the thunder and lightning. He always had an answer for us. He would tell us how God made it rain. He said there were big barrels of water that rolled over large rocks up in the sky, and sometimes the barrels sprang a leak and down would come the rain. Of course, the rolling caused the thunder.

We lived at the Jones farm for only one year. My parents had heard of a farm across the Powell River from us, owned by Mr. Cal Robbins. Mr. Robbins and my dad had got together and evidently my dad thought it a better farm. The land was more tillable, he said, so we moved to yet another new home. The terms with the crops were still fifty-fifty, though. A house was built for us to live in—the first brand-new house we had ever lived in. It was a great change from the Jones farm. It had a huge fireplace and wooden floors. I remember my dad saying that it was so wide, you could put a rail fencepost in it as a fore log. We only had three rooms, but four full-size beds fit into one room. And in the sitting room we placed two beds next to the fireplace that heated the whole house. The house was built in an L-shape. The kitchen dining room also had two full-size beds in it at the far end.

On the Robbins farm we planted a large crop of cane to make molasses. That was one of our main staples of food. I can't remember when it wasn't on our table. If, by accident, a run turned out too strong or too green (not cooked enough), it was fed to the cattle and they loved it. We always had a get-together of all our neighbors when the last run was cooked off. We called it the "run-off." We would cook the molasses down to a candy and then, with buttered hands, two people would take a batch in their hands and start pulling it. The longer you pulled, the lighter it got. Then we would twist it in a long twirl, stretch it out, and break it into pieces. It was very tasty, like taffy.

Our family was very poor. There weren't many in our community who were poorer. But I didn't feel bad about it. And in many ways it has given me strength and character. I learned early how to deal with life's hard licks. There on the Robbins farm, we only had one pair of shoes, and that was for wintertime and church.

Still, I think some of my fondest memories are of the Cal Robbins place, where we lived for four years. One reason I remember it so vividly is because, in my childhood, I lived there longer than anywhere else. Most of the time, we only lived in a place a year or two. But in 1934, Norris Dam was started and we were forced to find another place to live—as were many other families. Mr. Robbins told us we could go with him if we wished, and my dad chose to do that. Mr. Robbins had bought a farm on Hardin Valley Pike. Thus in that year we moved to Hardin Valley in Knoxville, Tennessee.

The people who were forced out of the Norris area were not allowed to take the lumber from their houses. Our house happened to be left above the water line, and being fairly new it was not torn down. I heard later that it was used for a Boy Scout meeting place. I never returned to the old home place, but some of my brothers did.

Our house in Hardin Valley was an old one—two stories with very high steps leading to a porch on the front. There was a barn

Courtesy Ruby Daniel

The Castleberry family in the early 1930s.

and a shed. The road up to the house was impossible to travel by truck. I don't remember how we got our furniture up there, the gullies were so deep. Maybe a horse and wagon took the larger pieces up. But once we settled down and all the children were given their specific jobs, we once more set our shoulders to the grind— clearing the land and farming it.

One incident that I remember vividly about Hardin Valley was the time Papa bought a cow for $50. He got her from a neighbor. Proudly, he drove her home and turned her out to pasture, talking about what a fine cow he had bought. That night, though, when he tried to get her to the barn for milking, she refused to cooperate. Jumpy and nervous, she ran like a deer all over the place. Finally, Papa gave up. The next day he took the cow back to the man he had bought her from and told him he wanted his money back. But the man gave him only $40. He did milk the cow and give Papa the milk. I remember Papa bringing in the milk bucket to Mama and saying, "Here's you $10 worth of milk."

My memories of Papa are fond ones. He was always pulling tricks on us and playing around. Once he said, "Did you know you can look through the sleeve of my coat and see stars?" My eyes widened with excitement, and I jumped up and said, "I don't believe that." So he had me lie on the floor while he covered my face with his coat. He whispered to someone to get him a dipper of water. I said, "I don't see any stars." And he said, "Keep looking." Then, suddenly, down came the water, everyone laughing but me. There were other times too, special times, like when he gathered the whole family to see the eclipse of the moon. It was a sacred occasion for Papa. I remember he took quilts outside and spread them on the ground and called all the children together. And we all lay down to await the eclipse. Papa set an alarm clock so we wouldn't miss it. As we waited, he told stories, all of us gazing up at the stars.

One day in 1935, when we were eating, Papa got up from the dinner table and said, "I think I'll go get the boys to bring us up some watermelons for the weekend, to put in the spring to keep cool." And he edged over, took his hat, and walked out the door. A short time later, while my sisters and I were washing the dishes, my brother came running to the house and said that Papa was sick, for

Mama to come. In a little while, someone else came and said for all of us to come down to Mr. Robbins' house. It was when we got in sight of the house that I knew something awful was wrong. I was carrying one of the babies, and my sister was carrying the other one. My mother was sitting on the porch, crying. I remember her saying, "My children will be taken from me. I know they will." The doctor had just arrived. I ran out to him and started beating him on the chest, saying, "If you had been here, it wouldn't have happened." He just put his arms around me and let me cry.

I was fourteen years old when Papa died, and there were seven children below me, the youngest being two. It seemed as if the world had come to an end. This was our first death in the family, and I just couldn't understand it. The neighbors began to help us. I heard someone say that my dad had no money, so a basket was put in Claude Robinson's store. I don't know how much they got, but I remember someone giving Mama $15. That was a lot of money back then.

We buried Papa at Lebanon Cemetery, not too far from where we lived.

Not long afterwards, someone told Mama about a place called the Pike place, on Coward Mill Road, that was for rent. It was about five miles from where we were living. Mama went to look at it and finally decided that we would move there. She explained that this was our chance to improve ourselves, for we wouldn't be tenant farmers here. "What we make at this new place will be ours," she said. We paid rent for the farm by the year, and we truck farmed. This was a new beginning. But without my dad, it was terribly hard, and we were not sure at times whether we'd make it or not. I remember that someone in the neighborhood put all of us children and my mother in their car and took us to the Red Cross. They gave each of us some clothes. It was humiliating to be given those handouts. We had not asked for them. All the dresses looked alike, worn and faded, and I remember some girls at school saying, "I know where you got that dress."

The house we moved into at the Pike place was a two-story structure with high ceilings and was difficult to heat. But there was rich ground to farm, and we had another cistern and spring. The people who had lived there before had died from tuberculosis, so Mama went through her ritual of fumigating. The cistern was cleaned out and scrubbed. Then, after we had settled in, came the night that Mama called us all into the kitchen and sat us down. It's a scene that will never leave my mind. I knew she had something important to say, but I didn't know what. Once we all got seated, she began to speak, calmly:

"I want you all to listen carefully," she began. "We are on our own now. Your Papa is dead. What we have is ours, and what we get will be ours, too. But in order to have anything, we will have to sacrifice a lot and do without a lot of necessary things. If we ever expect to own a place of our own, it's going to be hard. We will have to work harder and longer hours than we've ever worked. But some day we will own our own home and never have to move again. It will be ours—the land and the house."

It was a moving talk, and I could see in her eyes that she believed what she was saying. She already had a vision of this place in her mind, this place that would be hers some day. I was fourteen years old. I looked around the room, and I could see by everyone's sober faces that they were determined to give Mama her dream. But how much more could we give up, I wondered? How much harder could we work? It didn't seem possible that we could do any more than we had done.

But my mother was a courageous person, more courageous than my father had been, really. He had been well content to go on as we were, but my mother had higher ambitions. She wanted a better life for us. And she had many skills that I'd never even noticed before. Once, I remember, when we visited my father's grave, my mother said, "Let's go in the church." So we went in. When Mama saw a piano in the corner, she went directly to it and sat down and began to play one song after another. That was the first time that I ever knew she could play. I was just as amazed as the rest of the family. How many more hidden talents did she have, I wondered?

Our year at the Pike place went quickly, and soon we were once more looking for another place. Mama had heard of a farm in Solway and decided that we would move there. But for some reason it wasn't available until after January, so we had to move to a place in Ball Camp, to a building that had been a barn but was remodeled. It wasn't too bad. We were only there a little over a month. The year was 1937. We spent our Christmas there. We children who were in school at Karns went to Ball Camp, then we moved to Solway, and we enrolled in Solway school. Thus, in that one year, we went to three different schools.

After moving to Solway, we liked the community very much. We made friends there that have lasted a lifetime. We lived at the Guinn farm for one year, and then in 1938 we moved over to the Jessie McMillan farm. But it was in that year that something much more important happened, something that had never happened for us before. Mama found a piece of property three miles away, bought it, and had her brother build us a house on it. James Gentry had owned the property, and he let Mama have it for a very reasonable amount, she making monthly payments to him. Very soon, we were going to own our own place.

Thus, in 1939—four years after my dad had died—we moved into our new home. It was a day to be remembered. Finally, we had gotten our own place. Everything was brand new. The house was very large, nothing fancy but well built. We moved the last of December, when the weather was very cold. We didn't have time to build a flue to put a heater in the middle of the house, so a stove pipe was set out of the window until the flue could be built. The lumber had been somewhat green when my uncle built the house. And as the lumber seasoned, the cracks began to spread. But soon stripping was put over the cracks, and later tar paper and weatherboarding was applied. We also had hardwood floors put in, and we were very proud.

In that year and the years that followed, our family underwent many changes. Already my older brothers had married and left home. And when we moved into our new home, my sister quit school and Karl paid her way to take a beautician course at Tennessee School of Beauty. Then my twin brother decided he would quit. It was then that I decided to quit, too. Things were still bad financially, and we knew that if we didn't quit the rest of the children couldn't stay in school. After we went to work we helped buy their clothes, books, and food. I got a job in the Knoxville Glove Company. I didn't make much money and the work was very hard, but it was something anyway. I worked there two years.

In January 1943 I decided to enlist in the WACs with a girlfriend of mine who also worked at the Knoxville Glove Company. My sister went with us to watch us be sworn in, and she decided to join, too. We were sent to Fort Oglethorpe, Georgia for basic training. After six weeks there, we were sent to Denton, Texas to a state teachers' college to learn administrative office work and various jobs. Then we were separated, and I was sent to Michigan and worked as a medical technician for about a year and a half. Then I was sent to Boise, Idaho and worked as a dental technician until the war ended in 1945.

But in 1944 something else was happening back home. For in 1943 they had started building Oak Ridge, and the communities around Oak Ridge began to expand to make room for the new workers. One of the things they did to accommodate Oak Ridge was build roads. And it so happened that one of the roads they built ran straight through my mother's home in Solway. They wrote her and told her that she would have to move, that they needed her land to build the new road. They said she could have her house back after they tore it down and moved it. But they offered her almost nothing for the land. She had nowhere to go and no money to go on. Moreover, she didn't even have a way to get out and look for another place. By then the oldest child at home was only sixteen.

What upset me most about this ordeal was to think how patriotic my mother was—how much she wanted to help the war effort. I remember that when she heard of anything that was needed for the war effort, she gathered it up and sent it in. She had a good Royal typewriter, and when they made a request for typewriters she sent it to them on the bus by one of my brothers. She also gathered up scrap iron and sent it in.

There were also, at that time, seven members of our family who were serving in the military. Of my brothers, one was sent to Alaska, one to Germany, one to Australia, one to Belgium, and the other was stationed in the states. I was in Michigan and my sister in Georgia. It was then that my mother was being ordered off her land. Even before she moved out, the bulldozers had pulled up on her doorstep. And a flatbed truck was sent to get the furniture out. They tore down her house that day, even while she was there. My brother Freeman told me later that they were taking the roof off the house while she was still inside. It must have been heart-breaking for my mother to stand and watch them tear down her house—the first house she had ever owned, the one she had worked so hard for.

A neighbor we used to live beside drove up and told my mother that he had a place for her to live in, and it wouldn't cost her anything. It was, in fact, a rat-infested dairy barn that had been remodeled. But at least it was a roof over her head. Meanwhile, the movers had gathered up all the lumber from our big house, barn, and chicken house and had piled it to the side. But instead of my mother being able to use this again, another neighbor came and helped himself to the lumber, doors, windows, and roofing, using it to build himself a house.

My mother had hardly got settled in the dairy barn when she received a notice that my brother, Howard, was missing in action. That was in November 1944. On December 17, 1944, she was finally told that he had been killed in the Battle of the Bulge in Belgium. She refused to believe it for a while, thinking he would come back. It didn't seem possible. She never received any of his personal belongings, and it bothered her that she did not. Everyone else she knew who had lost a family member had received something back. She wrote to the army asking for some explanation, but never received anything. Later, his body was brought back home and he was buried in the Solway Cemetery with my dad.

Afterwards, Mama learned that there was a $10,000 insurance payment on Howard's death. It was offered to her in a lump sum or in monthly installments for the rest of her life. She chose the monthly payments. It was then that her landlord, who had let her move into the dairy barn, and who had evidently heard about the money, went over to see my mother. He told her that she was behind in her rent. She reminded him that he had offered to let her live there free; but he just laughed loudly and said, "Do you think you can live anywhere for nothing?" He asked for $10 a month. So Mama began, again, to look for property to buy. The piece of ground that was left from her property was on top of a very high hill, and the State of Tennessee didn't make a road up to it, even if she had wanted to build back there.

Finally, Mr. John Sturgill, who lived across the road from us in Solway and who liked Mama very much, came to see her. He told her that he would sell her a piece of land if she would move back over there. The amount being reasonable, Mama decided to buy five acres. And she got Mr. Herbert Holloway to build her a block house. She moved into the house in 1945. It was even nicer than the first home she had built. I don't know exactly how much she paid for it, but having the money from Howard's insurance certainly helped.

Mother was only fifty-four years old then. She lived in that house for eleven years until 1956 when someone offered her $10,000 for the house, which she accepted. Taking the money, she put it in on a house on Beaver Creek Drive, and she lived there until her death in 1959 at the age of sixty-nine from a heart attack. She had outlived my dad by twenty-four years. It had been a hard life for her, but she had always faced it with courage and strength. She canned corn the day before she died and was planning to put up a quilt the very day she died.

A HOUSE STRONGER THAN TIME

Lois M. Kaufman

In 1942 Howard Van Gilder was one of hundreds of Anderson County property owners who lost property to the Manhattan Project. The U.S. Army Corps of Engineers had acquired 56,000 acres, including land tracts, homesteads, and farms. Van Gilder's property loss was nearly 1,000 acres and the log house at Freels Bend.

Today, the log house still stands. It epitomizes the juxtaposition of a newfangled pioneer/nuclear world and an oldfangled pioneer/farming one. The house's sturdy construction and the uniqueness-of-character "saddlebag" design lets us see a glimpse of the long and vibrant tradition from which it comes. The patience, dexterity, and skill of the early pioneers are recorded in the quality of the log house. Children who ran across the knolls, across the slopes to the sheep and cattle barns, or routed their way through the dense forests, took the stability of the house for granted.

The mere fact that the house stands today after hundreds of sister houses have been destroyed by the nuclear age makes it a unique survivor. Perhaps it holds on to the ghosts of those settlers and the children who carried their Clinch River culture from the eighteenth and nineteenth centuries into the twentieth. (Indeed, early twentieth century log-house tenants told "ghost stories" about ancestral residents returning to avenge the killing of a trespasser.) If so, the house brought the spirits of very brave and determined souls to the day when a new age destroyed all that they had known.

Van Gilder, the final private owner of the house and property now owned by the U.S. Department of Energy, was the last of many. Beginning with Annanias McCoy in 1788, then William Davidson in the first half of the 1800s, these families and the Isaac Lowes of later years proudly developed it into The River Farm, known throughout the region.

The pioneers who built it, possibly before 1800, made their way with hand-wrought tools and hand-crafted survival across the northern shore of the Clinch River. They saw yellow pine, tulip poplar, white oak, "sugar trees," poplar, sweetgum, dogwood, and "sauerwood." They chose pine trees to build the original section of the house—possibly selecting from the huge yellow pine, their favorite. The one and one-half foot wide logs of the house are about the size they could have found then. Such large logs would not have been available after the lumber industry took hold in the region, in the 1820s. The pioneers loved huge yellow pine for building because of its softness and resistance to termites and other insects. And indeed, the wood, the "buttermilk paint" traces, and the second-story loft have outlasted the ages.

By the year 1844, probably a combination of prosperity and a growing family led to the decision to add a second section. Adding a room on the opposite side of the chimney from the original house gave it its saddlebag construction. Both the downstairs rooms had fireplaces from the center chimney.

Saddlebag houses, also called double-pen houses because the two sections "hung" on either side of the chimney, haven't been seen anywhere else in this area, according to Dr. Charles Faulkner, a historical archeologist at the University of Tennessee in Knoxville. Faulkner says that the only other instance of this came from drawings of the original layout of the James White house in Knoxville. Its construction was revised before renovators prepared it for the public.

The chimney of the Freels Bend log house was built of limestone. (Hundreds of limestone rocks were gathered, possibly with help from competitive siblings who hauled their best loads for comparison.) The original section of the house was built with V-notch corner log fittings, while the addition was made with one-half dovetail fittings. Care with construction and effectiveness

39

in the corner fittings of both sections tell of the pride taken by fathers and sons or brothers. The improved skill level between those who made relatively simple V-notched corners and those who made one-half dovetail fittings tells a story in itself. Maybe northern families moved into the area and shared their knowledge of Pennsylvania German architecture. Or possibly the eldest son "went to school" when an outsider stopped enroute to the West with willingness to draw a how-to diagram. Wherever the builders of the Freels house derived their know-how, they registered their pride in its completion by carving the year, 1844, on the wood-beam mantel above the fireplace.

The Freels family, who originally settled on Poplar Creek, were, over time, neighbors and then partners in farming The River Farm, though they did not build the house nor even live in it. Isaac Freels and his wife, Nancy, are said to have been among the first settlers of the area. Their close association led to the identification of the Freels name with the 1,000-acre bend. When William Davidson and William Freels were neighbor-farmers in the mid-1800s, they both produced wool and flax and crops of corn, wheat, sweet potatoes, and oats. Davidson produced somewhat larger amounts of these products, while Freels differed by producing impressive amounts of maple sugar, beeswax, and honey. Both farms listed production of 200 pounds of butter and twenty-five pounds of cheese in 1850. Neither farmer grew rice or tobacco.

The children of the pioneer settlers probably had some of the experiences of Donald Holloway, 73, of Clinton, whose family lived in the cabin for several years in the 1920s. Holloway tells of "snaking in the wood." After cutting trees boys would help their fathers drag the logs behind teams of horses or oxen, cattle trained to pull the heavy loads. Children who lived on The River Farm also had to be wary of cut corn stalks after harvest. If, as he did, they ran from the log house to the barn or over the fields to the shoreline there were treacherously sharp, newly cut stalks pointed from the surface of the ground. Holloway told of injuring himself as a child when a newly cut stalk punctured his foot. He said he went running out the back door, heading in the direction of the sheep barn, when the daggerlike point went through his foot.

In time, the thick forest on the north shores of the Clinch River gave way to a vital farmstead landscape with thriving families who were friends to their neighbors. Nearby was the community of Scarboro where children went to school and families worshipped at the churches or traded at the country stores.

Perhaps nowhere in the region is the open-shut door of yesterday and tomorrow more memorialized than by the log house at Freels Bend. The log house is seen today by a new generation, some of whom are surely descendents of that sturdy stock. The Freels Bend cabin serves now as the Oak Ridge Associated Universities employees recreation area, scene of many picnics and outings. Those who sit on the cool porches or climb the ladder to the loft cannot help but feel their link with those other pioneers, those earlier ones who have left a house that is stronger than time.

Courtesy Oak Ridge Associated Universities

The Freels Bend log house, probably built before 1800, still stands today on the Clinch River.

41

BUILDING A SECRET CITY

Courtesy James E. Westcott

GENESIS

Marilou Awiakta (Bonham Thompson)

Settlers sowed their seed.
Then their sons took the plow and in their turn grew old.
And the mountains abided, steeped in mist.
But in the deep was a quickening of light, a freshening of wind ...
And in 1942, as fall leaves embered down toward winter,
     new ground was turned near Black Oak Ridge.
     The natives pricked their ears.
     These descendants of old pioneers
     lifted their heads to scent the wind—
     A frontier was a-borning.
Many had to pack up hearth and home and go.
But others joined the energy that flowed toward Black Oak Ridge
as to a great magnetic power:
     Thousands of people streamed in.
     Bulldozers scraped and moved the earth.
     Factories rose in valleys like Bear Creek
     and houses in droves sprang up among the trees
     and strung out in the lees of ridges.
A great city soon lay concealed among the hills.
     Why it had come no one knew.
     But its energy was a strong and constant hum,
     a new vibration, changing rhythms everywhere ...
It charged the air in Knoxville, where we lived
and when I saw my parents lift their heads,

45

Building A Secret City

I lifted my head too, for even at seven
I knew something was stirring in our blood,
something that for years had drawn the family along frontiers
from Virginia to West Virginia, on to Kentucky and Tennessee.
And now, a few miles away, we had a new frontier.
Daddy went first, in '43—leaving at dawn, coming home at dark
and saying nothing of his work except,
"It's at Y-12, in Bear Creek Valley."
The mystery deepened.
The hum grew stronger.
And I longed to go.
Oak Ridge had a magic sound—
They said bulldozers could take down a hill before your eyes
and houses sized by alphabet came precut and boxed, like blocks,
so builders could put up hundreds at a time.
And they made walks of boards and streets of dirt (mud, if it
rained)
and a chain-link fence around it all to keep the secret.
But the woods sounded best to me.
My mind went to them right away ...
    to wade in creeks and rest in cool deep shadows,
    watching light sift through the trees
    and hoping Little Deer might come.
    In the Smokies I'd often felt him near
    and I knew he'd roam the foothills too.
Woods were best. And if the frontier grew too strange
    my mountains would abide unchanged,
    old and wise and comforting.

So I kept listening to the hum, and longing ...
Mother said we'd go someday, in the fullness of time.
And when I was nine the fullness came,
exploding in a mushroom cloud that shook the earth.

Reprinted from *Abiding Appalachia: Where Mountain and Atom Meet*, by
Marilou Bonham Thompson.

THE BUILDING BEGINS

Martha C. Sparrow

W hen government and army officials selected Black Oak Ridge as one of the Manhattan Project sites, they realized that a community must be built for the operating personnel who would work in the weapons plants. Early investigation had revealed that sufficient housing was not available near the project site. An architectural firm noted that "It was a case of building housing at Oak Ridge for construction and operating forces or not having the manpower to build and operate the plants." Additional reasons for building a community were to keep the major operating personnel under government protection and to make it relatively easy for employees to reach their jobs.

From the beginning the army made a distinction between operating personnel and construction workers. The town proper with semipermanent houses was reserved for operating personnel, while construction workers lived in trailers, hutments, and other temporary facilities. This distinction was further defined by the ruling that only those construction personnel whose homes were farther than eighty miles away were allowed to live in the on-site construction camps. Thus large numbers of workers were brought into the area each day on project-sponsored buses.

In January 1943 the army set aside the northeast corner of the reservation for the town. It lay entirely within the borders of Anderson County in a valley between two parallel ridges. It consisted of a narrow strip of hilly, wooded land approximately one-and-a-half miles wide. Eventually the town stretched for a length of almost seven miles. It occupied 9,000 acres of the 56,000 purchased for the entire project. Black Oak Ridge marked the northern boundary of the town; the Oak Ridge Turnpike, a major east-west artery, formed the southern boundary.

Since the atom project was uncertain, Oak Ridge was developed without a long-range plan. Construction activities were designed to meet only necessary requirements. There was a need to keep the town as simple as possible, to minimize the cost of construction and to use noncritical materials and labor. The industrial plants definitely had top priority. Living quarters were to meet only basic needs.

Oak Ridge, however, did not become simply a cheap housing development. As the army and its contractor progressed with their plans, "something better" became the watchwords. The main reason for this change of attitude was the need to attract and keep necessary personnel for the weapons work, personnel who were essential to the outcome of the project. Dissatisfaction with housing could cause them to leave. An army lieutenant involved in town planning said: "All we wanted to do was take care of the longhairs. You can't expect a high-powered joe like Dr. Compton to sleep with ants." The urgency of doing the job quickly still remained, however, as did the commitment to using noncritical materials. There were also financial limitations to be followed.

One of the most difficult tasks faced by town planners was determining its size. The army frequently changed its estimates. As work on the weapons facilities grew, the demand for personnel also grew. In the earliest stages, project officials believed that perhaps only 500 residents would live in the new community. Later, the figures were revised upward and continued to be revised upward at approximately six-month intervals for the next two years.

Once actual construction got underway, the revisions went through three main phases. The first called for a city of 12,000 people whose residential area would extend from the turnpike on the south to the crest of Black Oak Ridge on the north. Oak Ridge would be a well-planned, integrated community consisting of three neighborhoods, a central high school, and a main business district — all designed to meet the needs of 3,000 families. Long before this first phase was completed, expansion of the plants created a need

49

for more housing. The second phase began in the fall of 1943. This plan called for a town of 42,000 residents. In the fall of 1944, builders stopped construction temporarily only to resume their work in January 1945. This time the estimated population had grown to 66,000. And even this figure was too low as Oak Ridge's population exceeded 75,000 when the first atomic bomb exploded over Japan.

The general contractor for the construction of the plants and the preparation of the town was Stone and Webster Engineering Corporation. Its employees appeared on the scene in the summer of 1942, starting work on "the Castle" (the administration building) and the roads. By the time construction ended there were approximately 100 miles of roads within the reservation. In order for the roads to be constructed as economically as possible, the main arteries were laid out to follow the contours of the land. Several thoroughfares called avenues connected the ridge with the valley. These avenues were named for states beginning at the east end of town and moving west with new construction. Secondary streets had names starting with the same letter as the avenue from which they ran and were in alphabetical order moving from the valley toward the ridge.

There were three types of secondary streets: roads, circles, and lanes. Roads were short secondary loops off the main avenues, circles came back to the point where they began, and lanes were dead ends. During most of the war years, the secondary streets were not paved. In the earliest days of the town, they were dirt or mud depending on the weather. Later they were surfaced with oiled, crushed stones, which was not much of an improvement. The dust from this surface was so thick that residents sometimes watered their streets, using garden hoses. Sometimes calcium chloride was used, but was not much help either since it caused cars to rust.

Curbs, gutters, and concrete sidewalks were nonexistent in Oak Ridge, except in the shopping area. In residential areas the army revived the use of boardwalks as substitute sidewalks. Made from scrap lumber, these walks wound through wooded areas behind houses, and both children and adults enjoyed walking through areas of town on these substitute sidewalks.

Construction plans for the houses and the town were done by

the architectural firm of Skidmore, Owings, and Merrill. With offices in Chicago and New York, this firm adopted a contemporary style for its buildings and was always searching for new ideas and applications for modern architecture. The firm's architects had been working for several years to develop low-cost, prefabricated housing panels of cement asbestos, or cemesto board.

Early in 1943, before coming to Oak Ridge, the company had received what could be termed an ideal assignment. The architects were told that the government wanted them to design a new town for about 12,000 residents. This small city, it was said, would be a totally planned community, and the architects could design the facilities to their own tastes. Moreover, they were told that most of the residents would be technically trained professionals accustomed to living well. These residents would require pleasant houses, good schools, complete shopping facilities, and recreational opportunities. The streets ought to be planned to accommodate buses that would take residents to work in nearby plants. This job should also take top priority. The army had nothing further to say and told the architects not to ask any questions.

The one obvious question the architects did ask, before coming to Oak Ridge, was, "Where is this community to be built?" The army would not answer. They merely referred the firm to some aerial photographs and to a few topographical maps that had had the identifying names removed.

Thus Skidmore, Owings, and Merrill set forth making plans. The main concept of their plan was one that revolved around the notion of a neighborhood community. Groups of houses would be clustered near small neighborhood shopping centers, and each neighborhood would have its own elementary school. Down at the bottom of the ridge, not far from any of these residential neighborhoods, would sit the central business district. There, ample parking facilities would be provided for the shopping area, and the town's one high school would sit near the central business district.

In addition to the main shopping area, other centrally located facilities would include a library, a hospital, and a dental clinic. There would be several recreation centers and cafeterias throughout the area. One of two army chapels would sit just north of the main business district, and the other at the east end of town.

The secrecy of the project was revealed in the manner that

51

Skidmore, Owings, and Merrill received its orders. When the company presented its plans to the army, they were accepted immediately. But after the army accepted the plans, six architects headed by John Merrill were told by army officials to go to Pennsylvania Station at a certain time and not to ask questions. Only after they boarded the train did they learn that their destination was Knoxville, Tennessee. This group of architects was soon joined by a large staff of officials at the Oak Ridge site and there they were given more instructions—however brief and secretive. John Merrill personally supervised the Oak Ridge operations for eighteen months. The architects worked from dawn to dusk seven days a week. They had very little office space, cramped housing, and no telephone at first. While Merrill was in charge of on-site operations, Skidmore and his New York staff continued to draw plans and forward them to Tennessee.

This tremendous effort produced an attractive town. Writers in architectural publications have heralded the building of Oak Ridge as "one of the most skillful jobs of town site planning to be seen anywhere."

Construction difficulties did arise, however. Each house had to be individually staked along newly built roads, and the architects adjusted each house to fit contours of the land to avoid time consuming grading. Road construction, too, presented problems since project officials did not want the roads to have a steep grade. Moreover, all roads had to be faced on both sides by houses. (The houses in Oak Ridge had an unusual feature. Most of the kitchens faced the street, thereby shortening the distance for plumbing and utility lines. Another advantage of arranging houses in this manner was that the picture windows faced the woods and provided a very attractive view. The view from the houses located on the ridge was spectacular.)

The original homes designed by Skidmore, Owings, and Merrill played a central role in determining the character of the town. They were built of the prefabricated cemesto board. There was a variety of sizes beginning with an A and a B which were fairly small two-bedroom houses. The C-house had an extra bedroom, and the D had the luxury of a dining room. The A, B, and D-houses were ranch-style while the C was L-shaped. The F-house came along a little later when army management requested the architects to design a larger L-shaped house with a dining room for top project officials. A small number of houses labeled G and H were also built.

All of the houses had picture windows in the living rooms, fireplaces, hardwood floors, and blower systems of air circulation. They were equipped with stoves, refrigerators, garbage cans, and venetian blinds or shades at all windows. They were heated by coal furnaces, which made coal dust one of the miseries of Oak Ridge living. One resident laughingly recalled that Oak Ridge was probably the only town where the babies' diapers were black from crawling on floors.

Apartment buildings consisted of four dwellings. The E-1 apartments were one-bedroom while the E-2s were two-bedroom townhouses. The E-1s were on the ends with the E-2s in the middle. There were also groups of efficiency apartments in larger buildings and dormitories for single people.

The rental rates for all the houses and dormitory rooms were quite reasonable. The dormitory rooms rented for $15 a month for a single room and $10 for a double. Monthly rates for houses ranged from $38 for an A-cemesto to $68 for a D. Apartment rental was $38 for a one-bedroom apartment, and $40 for a two-bedroom, two-story apartment. Rent included coal for heating, water, electricity, and garbage collection.

Despite inconveniences, Oak Ridgers were generally pleased with their cemesto homes. Housewives found the floor plan convenient and the wooded surroundings attractive. Of course, no one liked the mud or the coal furnaces which "blew up" periodically. Coping with these annoyances, though, was made more bearable by the fact that everyone faced similar circumstances.

It was perhaps easier for those modern pioneers to adjust to Oak Ridge because they were reasonably young. Many of the young couples had never lived in a house since marriage. Consequently, their Oak Ridge house looked good compared to the apartments they had been living in. Moreover, they were keenly aware that this was wartime, and that families throughout the country were separated because of it. The fact that their family could be together under one roof was extremely important. Oak Ridge housewives were thankful to have their husbands at home rather than overseas.

Housing for construction workers was considerably more austere and drab than that provided for the operating personnel. The reasoning behind this was that the construction phase of the project was, by nature, temporary; and more importantly, construction workers were not as difficult to find or as essential to the technical phases of the project. Many of these workers lived in one of the several trailer camps adjacent to the main Oak Ridge residential area. While the large construction companies provided their own trailer camps, the army arranged for thousands of trailers to be brought in from other government installations throughout the country. These trailers were considerably less comfortable than today's modern ones, with central bath houses and central laundry facilities for the camps. They were painted a drab olive green which did nothing to enhance the landscape. Like the rest of Oak Ridge the trailer camps were unbelievably muddy.

Despite these primitive conditions the pioneer spirit apparently thrived in the trailer camps as well. One factor which made hardships easier to bear was that the construction workers were well paid. Also, a number of these people had worked in the construction industry for some time. They were accustomed to living near their job sites in less than ideal conditions. They, too, were bolstered by the knowledge that their families were together.

Another form of housing was the hutments, the most spartan of Oak Ridge housing. These hutments provided minimal housing for construction workers. They were sixteen-foot-square buildings made from two inch by two inch studs. The walls were one-fourth inch plywood with no insulation and no interior finish. There were no windows and only one door. Generally, four people lived in a hutment, with a bed occupying each corner, and a potbellied stove in the middle of the room. One resident recalled that in the summer officials moved the stove out and put a fifth person in the center of the room. There were hutment areas for both men and women. Even families sometimes lived in hutments. Family units were made up of two hutments put together.

The only excuse project officials offered for such grim accommodations was that housing shortages were so acute that hutments provided the only means to alleviate the problem. The hutment camps did have bath houses and minimal recreational facilities, but life there was still unpleasant. During the peak of construction,

54

32,000 workers and their families lived in barracks, trailers, and hutments.

In addition to the cemestos, trailers, dormitories, and hutments, a number of other semipermanent dwellings soon dotted the Oak Ridge landscape. As the Oak Ridge population swelled, the number of cemestos for operating personnel became inadequate. Planners then decided to use a house designed by the Tennessee Valley Authority—referred to as TVAs or flattops. These prefabricated houses, used by TVA for its construction, were brought into Oak Ridge in sections. A one-bedroom unit consisted of two sections; a two-bedroom, three sections; and a three-bedroom flattop, four sections. These houses were put together on the site and came complete with furniture. But even these units did not meet the huge housing demand and additional substandard houses, called victory cottages, were therefore constructed for operating personnel.

By the summer of 1945, the army and its contractors had provided 10,000 family housing units for Oak Ridge, consisting of both houses and apartments. About 13,000 residents were housed in ninety dormitories. Another 16,000 lived in hutments and barracks. And there were over 5,000 trailers on the Oak Ridge reservation. Of the total population, fifty percent lived in houses or apartments, twenty-one percent in dormitories, another twenty-one percent in trailers, and eight percent in hutments.

Skidmore, Owings, and Merrill also had the responsibility for building the commercial facilities. As Oak Ridge's population grew, the size of the main shopping area (Townsite) doubled in size. Another large center was built, and additional neighborhood centers were added to the three originally planned. There were more temporary shopping centers in the trailer camps and hutment areas. By 1945 Oak Ridge had 165 businesses, including thirteen supermarkets, nine drug stores, seven theaters, a department store, and seventeen major eating establishments.

In addition to residences and commercial facilities, a hospital, dental clinic, and schools were also built. Construction of the Oak Ridge Hospital, a fifty-bed unit, began in June 1943. The first phase of the hospital opened on November 17, 1943. Because of the growth of Oak Ridge, three additions were made between June 1944 and April 1945. By the time the atomic bomb was dropped

Courtesy Department of Energy · Westcott Photo

A-House

Courtesy Department of Energy · Westcott Photo

Dormitories

Trailer Camp

Hutments

By the summer of 1945, the army and its contractors had provided 10,000 family housing units for Oak Ridge consisting of both houses and dormitories. Another 16,000 lived in hutments and barracks. And there were 5,000 trailers on the Oak Ridge reservation.

the Oak Ridge Hospital could accommodate over three hundred patients. Moreover, a dental services building was completed in the fall of 1944, adding to the overall health care provided to city residents.

The design of the school buildings, as much as anything, reflected the burgeoning growth of Oak Ridge during the war years. The well-planned high school and the first elementary school were part of the original town plan. But as Oak Ridge grew, the additional schools were of less permanent construction. The schools that the children in the trailer camps and hutment areas attended were of a minimum temporary construction. Except for the high school, all schools were one-story buildings. They were either of weatherproof insulation board on wooden frames, or of prefabricated panels.

The army realized that Oak Ridgers also needed recreational facilities. Thus six recreation halls were spaced throughout the city. Other recreational buildings provided soda fountains, a miniature golf course, a skating rink, four movie theaters, and a drive-in theater. The Oak Ridge Welfare and Recreation Association, a nonprofit organization operating many of these facilities, provided the townspeople with bowling alleys and a 65,000 square foot swimming pool. Tennis was also a very popular activity in Oak Ridge largely because of the twenty-one concrete and two clay courts available. Twenty playgrounds were also built throughout the town and trailer areas.

Thus the army and its contractors succeeded in providing Oak Ridgers with the necessities, if not the luxuries, of daily life. There seemed to be a genuine concern to make the residents as comfortable as possible. By early 1945 the town of Oak Ridge was firmly established in the East Tennessee hills. People continued to move into the area in droves, sometimes as many as 5,000 a month. Hastily constructed living quarters, shopping, and service facilities, as well as the muddy landscape, dismayed many of the new residents. Many left in disgust. Others stayed for the duration of the war, but spent their time complaining bitterly about the hardships they faced in their daily living. There were others, however, who stayed to make up the nucleus of the Oak Ridge community. They accepted both the challenge and the opportunity to make Oak Ridge the type of place they wanted it to be.*

* Some of the material in this article was used in Martha C. Sparrow's master thesis. *The Oak Ridgers*, copyrighted in 1980.

AN APPALACHIAN SEEKS WORK—1943

Connie Bolling

Katherine and I had had a restless sleep that night, and as she poured my second cup of coffee at breakfast, she said, "Connie, I can't see why in the world you wanna go way down to Knoxville to take a job you know nothing about."

"Well, you know what Earl and Arnold said," I responded. "Since leaving teaching, they've made twice the money at their new job down there. I wanna give this a try."

"You mean to go off and leave me and Sandy and our nice stone house that's paid for? Besides, you have fifteen years teaching toward a pension. You'll lose all that," she reasoned.

Katherine continued in a level but firm voice, "Connie, you've been very restless the last two years. You went to Baltimore and got that shipbuilding job last summer and were back home within a month. Your eyes were burned, welding. Your arms and hands were cut and bruised. Now, if you go off down there, the same thing'll happen again. I just know it."

"Well," I said, "I wanna do something for the war effort, and you know I don't wanna go to war and get shot up and maybe even get killed. Besides, Earl said this work could end the war. And he said they were especially looking for teachers to hire. I've got to go."

I kissed my little Sandy's cheek while she lay asleep, and when I turned to kiss Katherine she was crying. "At least will you be home for Christmas"? she sobbed.

"Yes, I'll be home with lots of gifts," I said consolingly.

In 1943 the Tennessee Eastman Corporation was recruiting teachers and engineers to work at the Manhattan Project in Oak Ridge, Tennessee. The city that was to be, was as yet unnamed. Since it was said that the finished product of our work would possibly end World War II, I had eagerly resigned my Coeburn, Virginia teaching job, earning $139.00 per month, and planned to make my way to Knoxville to hire in with Tennessee Eastman and Clinton Engineer Works. I was also lured by the prospect of higher wages.

To reach Knoxville, I traveled south on State Highway 11-W. As I neared the city, traffic slowed to a honking and shouting snail's pace. I was unaccustomed to such hurly burly. When I finally entered Magnolia Avenue, I was frightened to see four lanes of traffic with a street car line in the middle. All lanes were clogged and traffic was being directed by soldiers. Thus, fearful, I parked my 1941 Chevy and set out on foot to find the Daylight Building which was located only God knew where. All hiring was, at first, done in this building, and I knew only that it was near Gay Street.

Shortly I saw an old man leaning against a stone wall, ogling the hubbub. I leaned over to him and shouted above the noise, "Do you know how far is it to the Daylight Building?"

"Eh?" he asked. I came closer to him and yelled my question again. He squared himself and, looking down Magnolia Avenue, he directed, "Yes, yes, I do. You jes' go all the way to the end of Magnolia and turn left on Gay, and I'd say that it's about three mile."

It was a freezing cold November day, and I began running down Magnolia, dodging people and traffic. Soldiers were everywhere. The frenzied activity frightened me because, farm boy that I was, I was used to more tranquil settings. I felt as if I were in a battle zone. Huffing and puffing, I reached Gay Street and turned left to see if I could find the Daylight Building. After about a twenty-minute hike, I came onto a milling mob around the front of a building one block south of Gay Street. Needless to say, that was it.

There were several lines outside the building, and I chose the shortest, shivering in the cold. A large sign on the front door read: "Wanted: engineers and teachers." I was in the right line. I was surprised to see that there were no women in line—and no blacks. Once on the inside and warmed up, I was happy and excited.

I soon approached the man, a Mr. Biggers, at the employment counter. I remember him because he had a great wart on the side of his nose. After shuffling out an application form, he began asking me questions and filling in the blanks. My life's history was condensed onto that sheet. He kept the application and handed me a card, reading, "Supervisor Trainee"—*if* I qualified. The card gave me directions to the Clinton Engineer Works, to what is now Oak Ridge, and I was to show up there at nine the next morning.

By this time it was dark and cold, and I was very worried about where I would stay the night. I walked back to Gay Street and looked to the east at the towering Andrew Johnson Hotel. Boy, I thought, I should be able to find a bed at such a big place as that. My car was locked and my suitcase was in the trunk. But, goodness, I thought, I won't have any pajamas! Oh, well, I decided, I'll just sleep in my long handles.

When I reached the hotel, I made my way to the desk clerk and asked if I might have a room for the night. He just pointed to the corners of the lobby where there were knots of men, some lying on the floor, and some lounging on the stairs with their suitcases under their heads.

He said, "That's all I've got, but you're welcome to sleep there on the rug." I was too flabbergasted to thank him. I left in a high trot to the ritzy Farragut Hotel in the center of town.

On arriving there, I found a lobby overflowing with weary men clamoring for a bed for the night. The floor was covered, except for walkways, with slumbering people. Now I was worried in earnest and began dashing from rooming house to rooming house. All of them displayed the inhospitable sign, "FULL." I was so dejected I wished to be back in my warm bed in Coeburn.

It was nearing ten o'clock when I reached my car. I was tired and hungry, even though I had gulped down two hotdogs, a hamburger, and a Nehi pop before I left Gay Street. On a bank above my car was a three-story house bearing a sign that read, "Rooms and Massages—Lady Heidelberg." Could I find shelter for the night in this unlikely establishment?

I leaned heavily on the door bell. At length, a large Germanic woman came to the door and boomed, "I know, I know; I haff no

bed for you, but you can haff my massage cot down in the basement ven I'm through vith it. Vere are your clothes? Haff you no
suitcase? Chust bring it in and you may stay for one dollar."

I hastened to gather my belongings and trotted obediently
behind her as she headed back to the basement and her patrons. I
waited behind a screen while she pummeled and thumped her last
grunting customer.

The next morning, bright and early, I headed out Magnolia
Avenue, turning west on Clinton Pike. Once again it was stop-and-
go traffic. I just followed the crowd, knowing that we all were on
our way to the same destination.

Soldiers were also present in Clinton. I yelled out my open
window to one of them. "Which way to the Clinton Engineer
Works?"

He pointed his finger westward and called, "That way," as I
rolled by. It was then almost nine o'clock, and I was shaky and
uneasy. I had had no breakfast, I hadn't shaved, and I looked and
felt awful.

Finally the line of traffic brought me to present-day Oak
Ridge up to "The Castle-on-the-Hill," where the Department of
Energy Building is located today. Signs reading, "Clinton Engineer Works," hung on each of the four yellow-tile buildings just
south of the administration building. Those structures, still standing today, were referred to then as Elza College.

I trotted into the first building and a nice lady at a desk
scanned my card and instructed, "Sir, you're scheduled to be in the
third building over."

When I arrived, an instructor was speaking to a large group
of men. He was lecturing on security and reminded us that one of
every four persons was FBI. We were never to utter one word
about what we saw or heard in the course of our work. If we did, we
would be in deep trouble. The hair on my head bristled. God, what
was I getting into? I wished I was home.

I felt a little easier when he asked us to introduce ourselves
and relate our "pedigree." I was surrounded by big-brains, I knew,
when many rattled off degrees from Harvard, MIT, UCLA, and
Georgia Tech. My little alma mater, Emory and Henry College,
paled in significance. Could I make my way with such a brainy
bunch?"

Our teacher informed us that we were to have three weeks of

intensive training in physics and electronics. Then, if we passed the tests, we would be sent to Y-12. (What in hell could that be? I wondered.) I struggled through three weeks of study, trying to work problems the likes of which I'd never seen, and as it turned out I'd never see again. Nearly everyone failed the tests, but we were sent on to Y-12 in drab army-green trailer buses.

We traveled through a heavily guarded gate and were put off in the center of the plant. Stone and Webster workers were thick as ants, busy constructing the nine huge buildings that would house the 1,800 calutrons that would produce material for the first atomic bomb. To my knowledge, the ordinary worker had never heard of U-235 or U-238, the refined uranium that we would spend the next two years feverishly producing, much less calutrons. Every unit, piece, and even dial readings were in code names, letters, and numbers.

During our training period, we worked in the Alpha One Building doing hands-on operations with simulated cubicles and calutrons. It was then that everybody was disturbed because they had lost the Z—a term that was mysterious to me then, but which I later learned was part of the process of refining the raw uranium.

Then came the flow of operators and support workers that we teachers had to train. We were called training foremen.

During all this time, we were temporarily housed in a large army barracks in Oak Ridge. There was row after row of bunks, very close together. I never heard so much snoring in all my life. Little did I know then, living in this muddy frontier camp, that I would one day make this my home.

A SCIENTIST
AND HIS SECRETS

Chris Keim

Christmas Day in 1943 was a day that changed my life and that of my family. We were living quite contentedly in Pittsburgh, Pennsylvania where I had been chosen as a research fellow at the Mellon Institute of Industrial Research. Of course, at that time we were deeply concerned about the Second World War. I was seriously considering joining the navy in anti-submarine warfare. The choice was mine since I was over draft age.

As we were gathered around the Christmas tree enjoying the day, the telephone rang. The voice on the line was a familiar one, an acquaintance of more than fifteen years with whom I had studied physics in undergraduate and graduate school. He was in Oak Ridge. He suggested that I come there as soon as possible "to see what was going on." Obviously something important. I had never heard of Oak Ridge, but he instructed me to come by train and someone would meet me at the L&N Depot in Knoxville.

Two days later I checked into the Guest House in Oak Ridge. The following morning I was escorted in the company of a uniformed guard through the Y-12 area where I saw huge buildings under construction and mounds of packing cases—supplies of some kind. Some of the components appeared to be huge magnets. I was taken around the area and I met several important persons in the fields of physics, chemistry, and engineering.

By the end of the day I had drawn my conclusions, though I was told nothing. I thought to myself, "It looks like atomic energy." I had known of the discovery of uranium fission in 1939, and it was only logical that practical applications should be seriously investigated.

I returned to the Mellon Institute and applied for a leave of absence for the duration of the war. How long that would be, no one knew. My request was granted. In fact, the director of the Institute told me, "You are making the right decision. I would go there, too , if I could." He then asked me questions that indicated to me he knew much more about what was going on than I did, and that he knew the overall purpose of the Manhattan Project. I learned later that he was chief chemical consultant on the War Production Board, an all-important government agency with far-reaching authority in making decisions affecting military needs.

Early in February 1944, I hired in with Tennessee Eastman Corporation, operator of the Y-12 area for the Manhattan Project. This area was the site for the electromagnetic separation of the uranium isotopes, U-235 and U-238.

Processing in, I received the customary smallpox innoculation and my assignment to a dormitory. It was WV-13, West Village 13. I had some difficulty finding the dormitory since the guards, scattered along the roads, had no idea where it was. I found it in a sea of mud across from a hillside of trailer homes. West Village 13 was near what is now the YWCA. Others in the dormitory included construction workers and new technical types like myself. Since it was rainy, the floors had a thick layer of dried mud up and down the corridors.

Over the next few days, as time permitted, I selected my future B-cemesto house on Outer Drive. I observed its construction with high hopes. It appeared, in fact, that it would be completed within a month, certainly no later than the first of April. It was, however, not released to me until June, three months later than promised. I learned later that the contractor was using it as his field office and would not release it. In cooperation with the builder, in all probability, the housing office had conveniently misplaced any record of the house's existence or its allocation to me.

After hiring in, I was directed to a row of yellow-tile buildings near the Manhattan Project headquarters building—the Castle— where we would receive supervisory training. Eastman was well known for its personnel training program. During this brief training period, we learned that military intelligence was running its security investigations on those of us in the training program. We did not know for sure just what was going on in Y-12, and we were warned not to speculate or even think out loud. It was sufficient to complain about our dormitory accommodations, the food in the cafeterias, and the endless rain. In fact, we swore that we had rain and mud and dust all at the same time.

There were those who did not survive this screening period. For example, one prospective employee was an expert locksmith, and he looked forward to proving he could open any lock that might challenge him. He boasted how he would open safes and doors once he reached the plant area, thus proving to military security the vulnerability of their system. He never got the chance. One day he failed to appear in class, and we never saw him again. He had been quietly removed.

Another candidate told us he had come to Oak Ridge to get away from his wife, with whom he was having marital problems. One day she appeared at Elza Gate searching for him. Security personnel located him in the training class and released him into her custody. I presume they returned home somewhere.

One young man had been promised a new car by his mother should he secure employment and no longer be a burden to her. His immature attitudes evidently did not qualify him as a good security risk. One day he, too, did not appear in class.

After ten days of supervisory training, we who had survived received our Q-clearances and were sent to Y-12 for more training—technical training this time. Many of my earlier suspicions were confirmed when we received lectures on basic atomic physics, a good review of my college courses. One day I ventured to ask the instructor a question since I did not understand one of his explanations. This had been normal college procedure. I was firmly told, however, that I would be informed of what I needed to know, and that if I showed needless curiosity by asking too many questions I might not be wanted.

Our badges, always worn on our lapels, carried our pictures and a Roman numeral indicating the level of information we were entitled to receive. Roman numeral V was for the top level personnel, numeral I was for the lowest. We wore our badges all the time within the gates of Oak Ridge. Even adult family members not employed within the city had to wear resident identification. One day, as I was getting off a bus, I was grabbed by the MPs (Military Police) in the townsite. They took me aside and pointed to my badge. I was unaware of it, but my badge had been partially hidden by my turned-up overcoat collar. Wearing badges became such a habit, in fact, including showing them to guards at every gate and doorway, that I found myself showing my badge to the minister on Sunday mornings as I left the church.

In Y-12, I was assigned to Building 9731, a pilot plant for the Process Improvement Division for the electromagnetic separation of U-235 from U-238. A succession of experiments went on in 9731, a building about 100 feet wide and 300 feet long, and it was divided into two distinct areas. These areas, separated by a high wall with security guards protecting the doorways, were known as XBX and XAX. XBX had a higher level of security than XAX. Both had two large vacuum tanks in them, positioned between large magnets generating strong magnetic fields. In these vacuum tanks were production scale mass spectrographs, capable of separating U-235 from U-238. In natural uranium there is only one atom of U-235 to every 140 atoms of U-238.

XAX constituted the first stage—the alpha stage—of the enrichment of U-235 from its natural abundance of 0.7 percent U-235 to approximately twenty-five percent. In XBX—the beta stage—the product from the alpha stage was enriched to approximately ninety-five percent.

It was interesting to learn that the direct-current generators which supplied electrical current for the magnets had been salvaged from an inactive sugar cane mill somewhere in the South. Later, when these motor-generators failed, similar ones were found in a former lumber mill of the Ford Motor Company where they had once been used in making wooden bows for the collapsible tops of Ford Model T's. This machinery had been maintained in perfect condition; even the brass was polished. We brought three such generators to Y-12.

Everything we were doing was secret, and we respected this need for secrecy, especially when we considered the end use of enriched U-235. We were working with precious metals, and extreme precautions were followed to prevent losses of any kind.

69

Building A Secret City

Courtesy James E. Westcott

The Y-12 plant in 1945. By the spring of 1945, almost 22,000 workers were required to keep Y-12 in operation. Workers were not allowed to have metal objects on their persons due to the strong magnetic forces of the huge electromagnets in the plant. Due to the shortage of copper, 14,700 tons of silver were used to wind the coils for the magnets.

Since our equipment was washed after every experimental run there was the possibility of accidental spillage of wash solutions containing uranium. The floors were designed to provide total containment of liquid spills, preventing any flow out of the building and making complete recovery possible. We had to walk carefully because there were concrete curbs in the least expected places.

Most personnel were scheduled to work around the clock and all days of the week. Top management, those on monthly payroll, could be expected to work any time their job required it. We all felt the urgency. We were preoccupied with the unanswerable question: Would Germany produce the atomic bomb first? After all, with their discovery of uranium fission, we knew of their progress in nuclear physics.

We had frequent visits and discussions with high level technical and military personnel who came in unexpectedly to check on the improvement of the electromagnetic process and to keep abreast of U-235 production. Among these visitors were General Groves, head of the Manhattan Project; Colonel Nichols, director of all Oak Ridge operations; Professor E. O. Lawrence of the University of California; and key people from allied countries such as England and France. The Y-12 electromagnetic process was the technical offspring and responsibility of Professor Lawrence. He and his staff designed the large mass spectrographs which they named "calutrons." They also initiated continued improvements in the refining process.

One evening Professor Lawrence came by the XBX operating cubicle to observe an experimental run. We had already started and everything was going smoothly. The collection meters on the U-235 collectors indicated a steady reception of the desired isotope. We were quite content to let the run continue without interruption. Seeing this, Professor Lawrence sat down at the controls. He began working the knobs, turning up the accelerating voltages, increasing the temperature of the oven containing the uranium tetrachloride charge material. As we watched him, he gently increased reception at the collectors, edging it higher and higher. The run changed from one of smooth, low productivity to one of sparking unsteadiness, one requiring continual attention. But the production rate of U-235 increased greatly. Professor

Lawrence personified a more aggressive approach to our experiment, attempting something we should have been trying. He then prepared to leave, but not without first admonishing us to do everything possible to increase production, even to the destruction of the equipment. We were deservedly humiliated.

Shortly after Professor Lawrence left the building, the equipment in the vacuum tank literally erupted; vacuum was lost and the run automatically terminated itself. We followed the customary procedure: removing all equipment from the tank, examining it, and determining the cause of the failure. It was obvious: wild sparking had broken heavy ceramic insulators supporting the high voltage ion source which propelled the uranium ions from source to isotopes receiver. Our next job was to try to find a way to prevent this heavy sparking or, at least, to protect the insulators from being bombarded. This is what we should have always been doing, and through experimental failure we could and did find improved methods.

One night when General Groves came in, we were testing some new collectors for U-235, trying to increase the retention of the high energy ions as they struck the collector pockets, sometimes bouncing out. General Groves studied our logbook and asked questions of everyone, supervisors and operators alike. He asked if this new equipment was ready for the production buildings. Would we assume responsibility for endorsing it? he asked. (Equipment in the newest beta production building had to be firmed up the very next day.) We boldly said that this new equipment was not ready, that it would not hold up more than a few hours—which was not acceptable in production runs. The next morning, word came to us that the next Beta Building would be equipped with equipment similar to that used in previous buildings. General Groves, too, was not ready to take chances on unproven equipment. We received a great boost in morale to know that General Groves had listened to our opinions.

One Sunday morning in 1944, we were alerted to a scheduled visit of General Groves, Colonel Nichols, Professor Lawrence, top Tennessee Eastman officials, and others to the pilot plant. They would be accompanied by a distinguished visitor, Professor Baker. We had not known Professor Baker, but we suspected it was a fictitious name which was not unusual under the policies of military security.

As our visitors entered the building, the identity of Professor Baker became clear. We had seen his pictures in our physics textbooks. We had studied his concept of atomic structure; we remembered he had received the Nobel Prize in Physics. "Professor Baker" was Professor Niels Bohr of Copenhagen, Denmark. He was a gracious man, visiting with everyone who was on duty at the time, and his visit would not be forgotten.

Many of us who worked at the Y-12 pilot plant had interesting security experiences. Yet probably my most interesting ones came on my customary visits to Berkeley, California. I had to go there from time to time to visit Lawrence Radiation Laboratory where continued cyclotron development was going on, providing new information and ideas. I traveled across the bay from the San Francisco side to Oakland in an interurban streetcar, then transferred to what was called the K-car, a small trolley which took me to the Berkeley campus. Imagine my surprise when, one morning, as I boarded the K-car, the motorman said, "Good morning, Dr. Keim. How is everything in Oak Ridge?" Fortunately I was so shocked I didn't respond. After taking my seat, I began trying to figure out who this man was and how he knew my name and where I worked. Finally, after some thought, I decided he was probably a representative of military intelligence trying to trap me. Had I acknowledged his remarks, I probably would have been taken into custody and my security clearance withdrawn. I did not know until many years later that other Oak Ridge scientists, who had made the same trip with me, had experienced similar encounters. At the time none of us mentioned it to each other.

Another time in Berkeley, I was browsing among the shelves in a campus bookstore. Much to my surprise, I located several copies of the science fiction story *The World Set Free* by H. G. Wells. I purchased a copy, then told my colleagues at the cyclotron building of my find. They, too, went to the bookstore and bought all the remaining copies. They bought them so quickly that the manager became curious and began asking why the interest in this book. Military intelligence learned of his interest and silenced him. Without success they tried to find out who had bought the books.

Why such concern with *The World Set Free* written in 1914. After exciting discoveries were made in radioactivity, Wells had predicted in this book the atomic bomb, an atomic-powered airplane, and atomic warfare. In fact, in the story, the world situation becomes so serious that a one-world government is proposed. I still have my copy.

At the Oak Ridge site, we had nothing but the highest respect for all those in top management. The pressure sometimes bore heavily on all of us, and we were frustrated by not getting answers to many of our questions. But we did receive the information necessary to do the work. We had to remind ourselves that we needed only Roman numeral IV on our badges, not Roman numeral V, which would have entitled us to know about Los Alamos, Hanford, and all the rest of the Manhattan Project. Many times, we knew very little about activities even in the X-10 and K-25 areas of Oak Ridge. And probably we didn't need to know.

We in the electromagnetic separation of U-235 were aware of the continued improvement at K-25 in the gaseous diffusion process. After the high priority shipment of U-235 from Y-12 was made in July 1945, we were confident that the use of this isotope would soon be demonstrated. General Groves had told us repeatedly that "the use of your material is in abeyance." The Hiroshima bomb was not a total surprise, but the release of all the information we had so carefully protected was nothing short of astonishing. We were shocked. Yet we knew it was the American way. The Smyth Report, in mimeographed form, was distributed to us within a few days after August 5, 1945. We now had the overall picture.

A fitting epilogue to my wartime experiences in Oak Ridge came a few weeks before Hiroshima. In the Y-12 plant, we had been working particularly hard the last six weeks, making a last-gasp push toward high production. The needed amount had to be delivered on a certain day in July 1945. Finally the schedule was met. The next day, when things had let up and production was relaxed, I casually remarked to one superior, "I expect the U-235 is on its way." The answer came back, "It's already there!" That was confirmed at Hiroshima on August 5, 1945.

WORK AT Y-12, 1944

Connie Bolling

It was nearly six a.m. when our small Oak Ridge bus arrived at the Jackson Square Terminal. Traffic was bumper to bumper—mostly buses since gas rationing reduced the number of cars.

The large, drab-green army trailer bus was pulling out of the terminal for the Y-12 plant. I jumped from my bus, ran over, and began pounding on the cab door, the driver slowing to a stop. As he rolled the window down, he yelled, "What do you want?"

"I've got to get to Y-12," I said. "I'm already late."

"Maybe you can scrounge in," he replied. "The expediter gave me the signal that I was loaded; but maybe you can get on." He opened the door, and I made my way inside.

Cigarette and cigar smoke hung in the air, and foul, hot, sweaty body odors struck my nostrils. One man said, "We're packed in here like sardines."

A woman yelled back, "And we all smell about as bad, too." There was a cackle of laughter. Then all was still as the sweat trickled down our miserable bodies as we rolled toward Y-12.

A big, fat man boiled out his cigar smoke over a neatly-dressed lady standing behind him. The angry lady tapped him on the shoulder and said, "For God's sake man, put that cigar out, you're killing me."

He rolled his bloodshot eyes back toward her and answered, "Oh! Excuse me," as he ground the burning cigar with his boot heel on the floor of the bus.

Finally, at six-thirty a.m., our creaking bus lumbered in the north portal of the Y-12 plant, and took its turn disgorging about one hundred passengers. I remember this day especially because it was July 4, 1944, my first day as supervisor over the operation of one-fourth of the machines in the 9201-1 Alpha Building. Until then I had been a foreman on night shift. Upon arriving I could see that many problems had arisen with the overall operation. Comments were made that we had "lost our Z,"—that meant production was down, though we had no idea what we were producing.

I was nervous. I trotted past the large number one cafeteria, smelling bacon frying and coffee brewing. The cafeteria was jam-packed with people eating, smoking, and some waltzing to Fats Domino's "Blueberry Hill," coming from the jukebox. Many remained at the cafeterias, canteens, and change houses and were never missed. Thousands of employees rotated shifts with nothing to do but attend training classes, go to movies, play checkers, or to rendezvous with lovers on rooftops. But I had a job to do.

When I entered the basement floor of the Alpha Building, the two huge generators that powered the mysterious machines that we called "D's" (which later we learned were calutrons, machines that separated uranium 235), were screeching like two powerful planes taking off. Also, the giant exhaust fans and vacuum pumps put out such a noisy din that it was impossible to hear one speak. Technicians and operators were milling about, hugger-mugger, talking hastily to one another and writing on pads and making adjustments on the huge, noisy machines. All this uproar made my nervousness worse.

The whole Y-12 valley was filled with a mighty roar that could be heard back in Oak Ridge, four miles away.

As I hurried upstairs. I passed by heater and vacuum operator stations where I saw sleepy-eyed workers leaning on their telephones—trying to hear beyond the din—and watching for their relief workers to arrive. The noise, not the work, had worn them out. A group of people, fifty or more, sat asleep at the clocking station.

As I turned the corner near cubicle forty-eight, a teary-eyed young lady, half-asleep and with her hair fluffed over her eyes, mumbled to her foreman, "This damned cubicle has been kicking off all night. Every time I start to raise the M or G voltage, the pressure and drain goes off scale. See there how it does, it kicks off every time."

"Let it go," her foreman advised. "Turn it off 'its shift change' now, and turn down the heaters."

It was seven a.m., and all of my operators had arrived and many trainees were looking on. They began checking the log books for their cubicles and began making adjustments and pushing up production.

I looked at the round production meter on the wall at the end of the cubicle room and saw that the line on the chart had risen quite a bit. I was pleased for the gain.

Courtesy James E. Westcott

One tract of an Alpha Building that held ninety-six calutrons. Each calutron was operated by one powerful cubicle located in an adjoining area. These two operations together accomplished the separation of uranium.

After greeting all of my operators, I turned my attention to stubborn cubicle number forty-eight, where my technician was already struggling.

He said, "This is the strangest operation I ever saw. Look, when I raise the M one thousand volts, the pressure goes off scale. You know we can't get innage until the M is on thirty-five thousand volts." ("Innage" was our word for production.)

I looked through the night-shift logbook.

"Well, you know," I said, "I think something's wrong in the

M unit. Let's cool it down and pull the unit out and see if we can find the trouble."

From my cubicle, fifty feet away, I telephoned to the handler foreman on the track to pull M (a unit of the calutron). I then walked from the cubicle to the track. After tank forty-eight had cooled, we let it "down to air" and pulled the M. Just as it was pulled back, clearing the tank, I saw what the trouble was: a booklet was lying on the edge of the M unit. This had pulled the fiery hot production molecules and mass into a short arc down onto the booklet which caused outgassing and caused the cubicle to kick off.

The handlers bolted the unit back in place and in about two hours, cubicle forty-eight was in good production.

Courtesy Department of Energy   Westcott Photo

One of the cubicle rooms that operated the tracks containing the calutrons. The cubicles were generally operated by young women, most of them natives of the region.

The heat that was given off by the cubicles caused the whole working area to become deathly hot and everybody suffered greatly, even though two large three-foot fans ran constantly, one at each end of the room.

A scorched odor of burned insulation and copper issued from the highly energized cubicles all the time. The cubicle that housed all of the rectifying tubes, breakers, cables, and capacitors was made of heavy sheets of metal, eight feet high, ten feet wide, and fifteen feet long. Each cubicle used an enormous amount of electricity. It was stated in a statistical report that at the peak of production, there was as much power used by the 1,728 cubicles in Y-12 as was needed to operate the city of New York.

My lady cubicle operators were always keeping the best production by carefully adjusting the M, G, K, and J voltage, symbols that meant nothing to us at the time beyond the technical task at hand.

The lady operators tried to have good production when the hourly spot-checker came along to record meter readings. If they couldn't keep their cubicle on, the checker gave them zeros, and sometimes the ladies cried.

Along about eleven a.m., I noticed that one of my new operators was having trouble getting production. As I approached her she said, "I've lost my Q and R readings and I've raised my heater all the way and I've lost my J's."

I took the logbook, looked through it and said, "It seems that you can cut if off since it's been operating five days. The charge is exhausted. We'll terminate the run."

I went over to the track when my handlers pulled the "D" from the tank, and I said to the process engineer, "Let's follow this unit into the chemistry area and look into the E box 'bird cage,' and see just what we are making. Let's get there before the two 'secret fellows' put the black hood over the E box. I'm anxious to see what the stuff we're making looks like. What do you reckon we're making?"

My engineer looked at me with open mouth and big eyes and said nothing. He turned and walked away.

Soon the secret workers came with their black hood and step ladder. I quickly grabbed a step ladder and climbed up to watch, but they tried to shield it from me. I stretched around them and saw the dark, brown sootlike material that we were making there in the E's bird cage. There might have been one teaspoon of the stuff.

One of the workers said, "Get down from here now, buddy, you're not supposed to even be in this area."

I hustled back to by cubicle room with my added knowledge. Three o'clock was approaching, and my shift was almost ended. Soon, I had left the vast confines of Alpha Building and stood at the corner waiting again for a bus to return, dreading the wretched, crowded ride back.

An Alpha 1 calutron with a cutaway, showing the E unit on the lower left where the refined uranium was received. During the war, these machines were never referred to as calutrons but as D's.

A close-up of the E unit which was the receiver of the U-235 and U-238. During the secret war years, men came with "black hoods" to collect the refined uranium.

The days that followed bore much the same routine, riding the bus to work, standing before huge machines, prodding the operators, pushing for higher production, and wondering all the time what this mysterious operation meant, and what these thousands of workers were doing each day, coming and going through these huge, shiny buildings.

I think I always tried to guess, however unconsciously, what in the world we were making that could end the war. I thought, "Could poisonous gas be made from it? Could heavy water be made from this sootlike, brown, black material?" I had heard that the Germans were trying to build a bomb somehow with the heavy water method. And I wondered what that meant, the question consuming me with curiosity.

During those days, even though my attention was glued to the production numbers on the cubicle meters, and my daily routine was a hurried one, I continued to search, to wonder what we were doing. One night, around three a.m., when I was on night shift, I slipped into a highly secret laboratory and pulled a glass cork from a bottle of some sort of liquid and quickly put my nose to the open bottle. Suddenly I found myself staggering backwards. I lost my breath and almost lost consciousness. I collapsed to the floor, rolling around, coughing and gagging, feeling my head expanding out like a balloon.

I had learned the valuable lesson of putting my nose into pure ammonia.

A little later when I became building process engineer, I was given an identification badge which gave me the privilege of seeing many other things. Now secret and classified documents came across my desk daily. And I perused them with the greatest curiosity. But these papers were so coded, so clouded in mystery, that they only served to befuddle me. I simply couldn't make any sense of them at all.

It was about this time that a strange United States Engineering Division (USED) man began to follow me. It seemed that wherever I went, he appeared, watching me. A bit jumpy, I became convinced that he was an FBI man, and that he had discovered me peeping at some coded papers, snooping into areas where I didn't belong, or going to places where guards had turned me away because I had the wrong badge number. For a couple of months,

October and November 1944, I was afraid to show my face anywhere. I simply went to work and did my job, trying to show in my
actions what a model worker I was. Finally, the USED man
disappeared.

One day, a month or so later, all process engineers were called
into an urgent meeting in the main administration building at
Y-12, where the brains of the project had gathered. Now, I
thought, "they will tell us something special. They'll tell us what
we're doing." My speculations again began to rise. I was eager for
the meeting to begin, but I was sorely disappointed when Dr.
Conklin, who was over everything in Y-12, began his spirited
speech on our production quotas, without any suggestion that he
would inform us of our mission. He told us that General Groves
was less than pleased with our output. In his thirty-minute speech,
he pointed out several areas in which we were failing. He was angry
because we were allowing material to be thrown all over the inside
of the tank instead of into the E bird cage. Then with a strong
admonishment, he let us go.

I was very disappointed that I had learned nothing, but near
Christmas time a new scientist appeared in our building. I had met
him in the late thirties at Emory & Henry College when he came
there and gave a commencement address. Renewing our acquaintance we became good friends. His office was on the second floor
above mine, and we often had lunch together, talking and discussing events of the past. Our families became good friends; we visited
in each other's homes and even took trips to the Smokies together.

During our friendship, he said very little about the operation
at the Y-12 plant. Once when I spoke about the way I had to prod
the foremen and technicians under me, he quickly turned the
subject to something else. It was obvious to me that he didn't want
to talk about his work at all.

I really believed, however, that he knew what we were producing. After all, he wore one of the highest badges in the plant.
Moreover, personnel from the administration building often frequented his office, briefcases in hand.

One day, in 1945, I happened to cross paths with him in a
small restroom. He was subdued, wearing a rather fatigued expression. Then, all at once, he began to talk about our work. We were
alone, and he seemed to want to confide something in me, to get

something off his chest. But I had no idea what he was going to say.

He leaned his back against the stall door, and with a quizzical half-smile, he said, "What do you think we're making in this plant? Remember you are a good friend of mine and I want to know."

I must have turned pale at this question, struggling to make some response. I didn't answer, however. I was afraid that he was trying to trap me. I wanted to leave the restroom, to get away, but he kept his back against the door. There I was facing what I knew was a friend and a great scientist, but I was afraid to mention any ideas that I had about the project. In fact, I couldn't speak, I was so frozen with astonishment.

Finally, after what seemed an eternity, he said in a whisper, "Atomic bomb ... and you will soon hear about it because it will be tested." He seemed relieved.

We pushed the door open and wended our way down the winding spiral steel stairs to our work area and in among the workers. I never answered him in any way because I was too scared. But what he said was true, and I discovered it a few months later with the successful explosion of the atom bomb. Afterwards, when we talked of such things, it was not hidden in the shadows of a bathroom, cloaked under the weightlike feeling of wartime secrecy, but in the open, among friends and acquaintances.

IMPRESSIONS OF EARLY OAK RIDGE

Joanne S. Gailar

In 1945 I was an immature, unworldly bride of twenty from New Orleans, Louisiana, a very old, well-established city, a city steeped in traditions, with a garden district of beautiful old homes, lovely parks, historical monuments, and gracious live oak trees with Spanish moss along St. Charles Avenue. I was a fifth generation New Orleanian, whose wedding dress rested in the Cabildo (the New Orleans museum), along with the four wedding dresses of my great-great-grandmother on down. Coming to Oak Ridge—new, raw, frontierlike—I felt that I had left civilization behind me. When my husband and I arrived at the Guest House to spend our first night in Oak Ridge and he told me that this was the most beautiful building in town, I sat down and cried.

My first impressions of Oak Ridge had started at Elza Gate, where the MP inspected our passes. Once our bus was given the "go ahead" sign, it zoomed forward in a cloud of dust. Sensitive passengers reached into pockets or purses for handkerchiefs; others, hardened to the dust through habitual exposure, breathed in without change of expression. I merely coughed slightly and regarded it in a detached way, hardly knowing that it would help to produce in me later a bad case of "Oak Ridge croup," as the doctor so aptly termed it. ("Honey," he told me as I entered his office thinking I was dying, "What you have is the Oak Ridge croup.") As I sat on the bus, it was just "dust." After I had been in Oak Ridge for a short time, I realized that dust was one of its integral characteristics. Oak Ridge might be dedicated to manufacturing bombs, but Dust and Mud were the physical elements that went into its making. In the summer, there were long, hot days during which the inhabitants went about all day with parched throats from dust. In the fall it turned into sloshy mud that persisted in sticking to shoes and dirtying up houses. I feel certain that if anybody ever gets around to writing the annals of Oak Ridge, they will include Dust and Mud just as surely as the pioneer days include covered wagons and buffalo and Indians.

Another thing one noticed on first coming to Oak Ridge was buses. When our bus pulled into Central (Bus) Terminal, I was at once reminded of my arrival at Grand Central Station. The terminal resounded with the zoom and rattle of big impersonal buses pulling in and out in a hurried fashion.

There were three kinds of buses: off-area buses, which ran between Oak Ridge and other cities or towns such as Knoxville, LaFollette, Oneida, Chattanooga; area buses, which carried people about the residential and commercial sections of town; and work buses, which transported people to the plants. One could hardly help being impressed with the atmosphere of rudeness and hurry that prevailed at the bus terminals. Everybody rushed to get a seat, men and women alike. A "gentleman," who in his home-town would have stood politely and tipped his hat while a woman entered the bus, in Oak Ridge was merely part of a mob of elbow-pushing fiends.

I believe one of the reasons for the impatient scramble for seats on the buses had to do with cumulative frustration from standing in line. Not only did you stand in line for transportation, you stood in line for food and recreation. You even stood (or sat) in line for medical attention. (I might add that you had no choice of doctors; you got whoever could see you.) Only at the bus terminal, however, did you get jostled and elbowed and kicked. A certain amount of decorum existed at the cafeterias, movies, and hospital. There was a bit of pushing at the meat counter of the grocery, but public disapproval was sufficiently strong to keep every jostling-Tom in his place. If someone dared to step out of line at the "Vomitarias" (as the fellows so aptly called the cafeterias), he was never allowed to get ahead of anyone.

Breathing in red dust, being pushed around in bus terminals,

Central Bus Terminal in the 1940s. There were three kinds of buses: off-area buses, which ran between Oak Ridge and other cities or towns; area buses, which carried people about the residential and commercial sections of town; and work buses, which transported people to the plants.

Waiting in line was a rude fact of life in wartime Oak Ridge.

and standing in line are fairly unpleasant experiences, but a considerably more unpleasant experience connected with those early days in Oak Ridge was bedbugs. It was at Cove Lake, in fact, where my army husband and I lived, that we became first acquainted with this dreaded insect. I learned—later—that bedbugs were all over the dormitories. It is doubtless from a previous dormitory dweller, whose room we occupied, that we became infested.

We had never seen a bedbug. So when my husband woke up covered with red welts after our first night at Cove Lake, we thought it was hives. The second morning we saw one or two little critters scurrying across the sheet when we turned on the light. "Wood ticks!" I exclaimed innocently. My husband caught one to take to work to see if anybody could identify it. When he came home with a sheepish expression on his face and conveyed the information to me, I was horrified. The following day, he came home from work and conducted a one-man campaign against them. He concocted a mixture of kerosene, gasoline, and Flit (an insecticide) and sprayed it all over the room. No crack escaped treatment. The mattress got particular attention, an all-day sunning along with a thorough spraying, and all our clothes were aired on the clothes line. The campaign, to my relief, was a success.

In writing my early impressions of Oak Ridge, I could hardly omit those made by the houses, especially the flattops or demountables, as these flimsy-looking structures were sometimes termed. They resembled little, rectangular boxes on stilts that had been scattered around as haphazardly as bird seed. They looked as if they had been dumped, and dumped they were! In this early period of rapid construction, one could look down the road at almost any time and see a truck transporting a fully assembled flattop to its destination. The direction in which the flattop faced seemed determined almost entirely by the will of the truck driver, or more aptly, by his sense of humor.

The similarity of the houses gave a certain look of monotony to Oak Ridge. It puzzled me at first how people kept from getting lost in the many labyrinths of similar houses. In 1945 Oak Ridge was not the attractive town it later became. Few felt firmly entrenched enough in the community to start gardens or to take a civic pride in Oak Ridge. The first question a new acquaintance

Courtesy Department of Energy

A sea of monotony in a new frontier town.

would ask you would be, "Where are you from?" So one could hardly expect so unsettled a population to take the pride in its houses or gardens that would distinguish them one from the other.

As much a part of Oak Ridge as its Central Terminal, its gates, and its houses were its signs and posters reminding its inhabitants to be security minded. Everywhere you went in Oak Ridge, you saw security posters—on the buses, on bulletin boards of dormitories, in the Guest House, on big sign boards in the streets, in the cafeterias, and movie and recreation halls—in every place that had a wall. Some signs appealed to your sense of responsibility, some to your sense of humor, and some to your sense of fear, but they all conveyed the same terse message—"keep your mouth shut about project information." The only example that I can remember is a picture of three monkeys with the words, "What you see here, what you hear here, what you say here, let it stay here."

At first these posters had the effect that the "brains" behind them desired them to have: they made me wide eyed and cautious. Then as I was exposed more and more to them, I progressed to the stage of merely noting their quantity and looking for the new brainstorms (posters) that appeared regularly. The final stage was to ignore the signs altogether, just as you learn to ignore the telephone pole in front of your house.

Yet no one could become altogether complacent about security. There were stories of individuals with big mouths who talked on buses or in theaters, who were seized by G-2s (army intelligence agents) and hauled off to the place where suspected spies were taken. But I was never personally acquainted with any such person. As for myself, I knew from my husband that we were working on an atom bomb, but I never said I knew—even two years later in 1947, when I wrote my recollections of the war years in a paper entitled *A Boy, A Girl, A Bomb*. Nor did I know how many others knew. It was not a topic anyone even dreamed of mentioning.

However, a curious thing happened in 1945 before the world at large knew that Oak Ridge existed. One morning a short article about the feasibility of a nuclear weapon—an A-bomb, in fact—appeared in the *Knoxville Journal*. It occupied only about two or three inches and was not conspicuously placed. My husband pointed it out to me very somberly at Cove Lake behind closed doors. He had one finger on his mouth when he did, and we never discussed it.

My own small contribution to the atom bomb project began with an ordeal that figures largely among the first impressions of many early Oak Ridgers: the ordeal of "hiring in." I had no idea when I accepted a job that hiring in was as exhausting as a two-day seige of the flu. To those of us with security clearances today, being fingerprinted and having to fill out security forms are "old hat," but I found having my fingers roughly rocked back and forth on an ink pad rather intrusive back then. I also found it odd to be asked: Would I tell on my husband or father or brother if they revealed any secret information; or whether I got drunk often, seldom, or never; or whether I had ever belonged to any organization that opposed our present form of government. But this phase of orientation proved to be the least strange of the events that followed.

Having been photographed, fingerprinted, and interviewed, I was then joined to the fifty-odd other individuals hiring in on that particular day. We were led to a small auditorium which contained a stage, a motion picture projector, and screen. Some movies were about to be shown. I have seen so many propaganda pictures since that day that the two they showed do not stand out particularly. I do remember, however, that one of them was devoted entirely to depicting to us the treachery and power of the Japanese. It was designed to make us think of our enemy as fiends that were inhuman, cruel, and sadistic creatures who would stop at nothing and who could very conceivably be victorious over us if we didn't put forth our best effort. After we had been supposedly terrified by the power of our enemy, we discovered that we were to be instilled with another sort of fear: the goblin's-gonna-get-you-if-you-don't-watch-out variety.

We were still blinking from the lights that were turned on following the movies when a pale, serious man with a mustache and an undertaker's expression mounted the platform. His was a face from which all traces of joviality had long been removed. The entire purpose of his speech was to scare us into silence about our jobs and about the city of Oak Ridge, the size and scope of which was still a heavily guarded secret. This sober-faced gentleman did not start off addressing us with a series of "don't." Oh no! He was far too clever to antagonize us by using the negative approach.

Instead, he left us with a series of impressions created by little stories and anecdotes. Even today, many years later, I clearly remember many of his tales. It wasn't, "Don't write home about the number of dormitories and cafeterias," but, "I know of a girl who wrote home about the number of dorms, cafeterias, etc., and now that girl is ..." He didn't say, "Don't describe any of the machinery or equipment you see around the plants," but, "Willie described some contrivance in his letter to his friend Mac, and ooh! What's gonna happen to him." There were other tales of "Jack, who confided his duties at work to his wife who played bridge," and "Sue, who kept a diary." These remarks were made even more impressive by the solemn reading of the Espionage Act.

The cumulative effect of the events associated with hiring in was akin to that of being initiated into a secret and highly selective fraternity. The mud and dust, the metropolis-like bus terminals, the lines and lines of people, the helter-skelter houses, and the multitude of posters—all the features of Oak Ridge that formed my indelible first impressions—fell into place, found their reason for being, when I as a low-ranking clerk joined the host of scientists, engineers, secretaries, technicians, craftsmen and others to work on a supersecret project—an atom bomb—the success of which could determine the future of our country.

HAPPY VALLEY

Helen C. Jernigan

In the summer of 1944, Oak Ridge's western edge was a rough-and-ready community with the unlikely name of Happy Valley: the construction site of the K-25 complex. The thousands of people who worked there were also housed there—in trailers, hutments, and barracks. There was a post office, stores, cafeterias, a bank, recreational facilities, and a nearby school for the children: all gone now.

I had a summer job that year in Happy Valley; I was eighteen, and it was an experience I have never forgotten. Yesterday I sharpened some pencils and, thinking to sharpen my memory as well, drove to the visitors overlook at the Oak Ridge Gaseous Diffusion Plant to write a few paragraphs onsite about what it was like to live there.

From the overlook, the contrast between then and now is so great that I was incredulous. I might have thought I only imagined living there, had I not recently talked with two other people who were there at the same time: Tom Mullinix and Jo Ellen Rowan Iacovino.

Today the scene is a picture postcard—the huge, quiet buildings set in green woodlands, the peaceful little lakes with waterfowl—and not a soul in sight. That other summer, forty years ago, there were anthills of visible human activity and huge, ever-moving construction machinery. It was hot, dusty, and noisy. Loudspeakers attached to power poles blared music all day. *Sugar*

94

Blues, Josephine and some Sinatra and Crosby numbers were favorites. There was no night: bright street lights and spotlights illuminated the area as people worked shifts around the clock.

From the overlook I tried to determine where things had been: the movie theater, the bowling alley, grocery and department stores, the barracks where I slept, and Coney Island where I worked. Tom Mullinix had sketched a map when we talked. He reminded me that the post office, laundry, and ice house were on the north side of the dusty road that is now Highway 58; everything else, including the trailers, hutments, and barracks, was on the south side. He had added to my "places" list the recreation hall, the barbershop, drugstore, dispensary, and bank.

Tom came to Happy Valley late in 1943 from Louisville, Kentucky as an engineer for the primary contractor, J. A. Jones Construction Company. He was in his early twenties, and he came because a friend, already here, had written to him about jobs that were available. For the first two weeks he lived in Oliver Springs in a boarding house, then was assigned a room in the "non-manual" barracks in Happy Valley. He worked thirteen-hour shifts, over-lapping an hour with the preceding or following shift workers for briefing purposes. He had plenty of energy left, though, for danc-ing at the "rec" hall, where live bands played several nights each week. Tom won a jitterbug contest there four Saturday nights in a row.

Tom later shared space in a sixteen-foot hutment with a friend for a while, then moved to Knoxville, where he met and married his wife, Johnnie. He now looks upon the Happy Valley experience as a "tour of duty" for the war effort.

For Jo Iacovino, the smell of a hot, dusty day still evokes strong memories of living in Happy Valley as a child. Jo lived with her family in the trailer area and attended the "new" Wheat School as a third-grader. Her parents, James and Bess Rowan, planned to move from Nashville to "the project," but James was prevented from leaving his job with the postal department because it was considered to be essential to the war effort; so Bess, Jo's sister Colleen and brother Brian, came on ahead, leaving seven other children in Nashville with their father. The children sensed that this move was important, but they were embarrassed about their father being a househusband when "he couldn't even cook!"

Because she did not qualify as "head of the household" Bess was not able to get housing in the restricted area. Thus she and the children lived for a while in Harriman with an aunt, until James and the others could join her. The family then moved to a double trailer in Happy Valley. They lived at the back of the trailer camp in a wooded area near the tall security fence, topped with barbed wire. The children often played in the edge of the woods, but did not venture too near this formidable barrier because "we thought the Germans were just over the fence," Jo says.

Life in the trailers had its hardships. Beds were available for everyone only because some people worked night shifts. "We had to put up the beds in the daytime so there was room to *be*," Jo recalls. Toilets were in a central building; at night human waste was collected in "slopjars" for transferring in the morning. There were no telephones, except at a central location, and the names of people receiving phone calls were "blasted out" over the loud-speakers. Many families with sons, brothers, or fathers in the service were fearful of being paged: it might mean bad news.

●   ●   ●

One of the picnic tables among the sycamore trees at the visitors overlook afforded a perfect place to write, but my solitude was soon broken by a carload of picnickers. I wanted to tell them that I used to live there—partly to convince myself—but thought better of it. So I drove home to Oak Ridge proper, ten miles in space and more than forty years in time, and sharpened the word processing program on my microcomputer—to write about my own experience in Happy Valley.

That other summer I had just finished my first year of college at Tennessee Wesleyan and had gone home to Pleasant Hill, on the Cumberland Plateau. I hadn't begun to look for a summer job yet; but met a group of my old high school friends who were part of a team of traveling folkdancers. They were attending the school there, Pleasant Hill Academy, a church school whose faculty was dedicated to preserving the folk arts.

When I arrived home, the folkdancers were rehearsing for a performance "in Clinton, where there's some kind of war plant," they explained, and they needed me. So off we went one evening, traveling in a station wagon, not having the slightest idea that we were going to a secret place called Happy Valley. Somewhere, I still have the poster for the show. I remember it included Grand Ol' Opry stars Sam and Kirk McGhee—"the boys from Tennessee."

After the show Mr. R., the man who managed the theater, bowling alleys, and amusement center, offered me a job, and I accepted. When I reported for work, I was assigned to a room in an H-shaped barracks, with men in one wing and women in the other. There were no locks on the doors, but during the time I lived there I never heard of any thefts or violence in the building. I met the rest of Mr. R.'s staff, most of whom were teenagers from his hometown. Our job was to operate the bowling alley, a duckpin alley, and a large amusement arcade called Coney Island. We started work around noon each day. I kept the books, did the payroll, received and paid for supplies, and hired and supervised the pinboys at the alleys. (One boy was named Edgar Allen Poe; I delighted in paging him.)

Nights, I joined the other young people at Coney Island, where we manned the various game booths. Our customers paid to shoot and throw—air rifles, darts, basketballs, baseballs, and the like. The prizes were not so various: they were either cheap, chalky materials, or cigarettes. In those war days cigarettes were rationed, but we had plenty. Business was so good that I wrote to my cousin and her girlfriend to join us; Mr. R. and I made frequent trips to a Knoxville warehouse for more cigarettes.

We would close Coney Island about two a.m., after which we went in search of our own recreation. The boardwalks were full of people, even at that hour, and I found the variety of people who "followed construction" very exciting, having known mostly WASPs up to this point in my life. There was a large group of young American Indians from Oklahoma, employed as riggers because of their famed balance and fearlessness in high places. They would make playfully aggressive movements toward girls and shout "me scalp 'um!," to the girls' delight.

We paired up with other young people. Sometimes we would sit in the cafeteria and talk over coffee for hours; sometimes we went for long walks; sometimes we sat on the steps of the padlocked churches and drank wine. Occasionally, we would drive to the Plantation Club, a place near Rockwood where we could dance till very late.

At the summer's end, I returned to school—a different world indeed. Only then did I learn that I had been in *Oak Ridge*, for we didn't know that name, and our mailing address had been a post office box in Knoxville. Later that fall, I learned that Mr. R., my former boss, had left Happy Valley following an investigation by the FBI—something about trafficking in blackmarket cigarettes. I never learned what happened to him. I wondered if they would come for me and hoped I could convince them that I was an unwitting accomplice.

But they never found me, and in time I returned to Oak Ridge to work at K-25, in one of the buildings I had watched them build that summer. Happy Valley had served its purpose and had disappeared without a trace.

OAK RIDGE IN CONTRAST

Jane Barnes Alderfer

A s often noted, the secret nuclear cities of Los Alamos, Oak
Ridge, and Hanford shared many common elements. All
were isolated, all were administered by the army, and all
provided recreational and social programs for their residents. All
presented hardships, stemming from underplanned housing, work
stress, and inadequacy of services. And most importantly, all
aspects of their existence were permeated by the need for secrecy.
Yet, even with these common threads, differing purposes did
prevail; each community fostered its own unique characteristics,
and was indeed unlike the others. This can be seen perhaps most
clearly in their technical roles within the Manhattan Project in
which the Los Alamos personnel were commissioned to discover
the explosion requirements for uranium 235 and plutonium 238
and to assemble the bombs while Hanford people were to produce
and separate plutonium and the Oak Ridge workers to enrich
uranium. Beyond these obvious roles, however, other, more subtle
differences can be found in such things as site requirements, land
acquisition, and methods of secrecy.

Los Alamos, because of its role as a scientific laboratory for
the development of the bomb, differed markedly from the industrial complexes at Oak Ridge and Hanford. The site of the Los
Alamos Ranch School for Boys (forty miles northwest of Santa
Fe, New Mexico) was selected and taken over in early 1943. The
land met requirements set down by the Manhattan Project includ-

ing geographic isolation away from both coasts, good railroad and road transportation nearby, a seemingly adequate water supply, space for testing at widely separated sites away from populated areas, and a climate suitable for year-round construction and experimental work in the outdoors.

Condemnation proceedings went smoothly because the school was having difficulty finding teachers due to the war and was eager to sell. In addition, about 45,000 acres of nearby land were already owned by the U.S. Forest Service. The rest was used mostly for grazing cattle and was given up with little resistance. In all, about 54,000 acres were acquired.

At Los Alamos, employment of scientists and technicians peaked at 5,000 persons by 1945. Open communication between scientists was essential to facilitate the extremely intense developmental work being carried out in the facilities there. For this reason security arrangements differed from Hanford and Oak Ridge. The army principle of security was to compartmentalize information so that each person knew only the amount of information needed to do a particular job. This principle was in effect at Hanford and Oak Ridge. At Los Alamos, however, permission was given to form a colloquium for the exchange of ideas. A limited number of higher level persons holding scientific degrees attended these sessions.

External security, though, was utilized to keep information from filtering to the outside. A fence was erected around the project. Only close family members were told that persons were in New Mexico. The address for the site was a post office box in Santa Fe and all mail coming to this box and leaving the site was censored. Professional journals were to be delivered to former work addresses or to a post office box in Los Angeles. The only telephone communication was via a forest service line which was monitored. License plates on project cars were coded and the key to the codes was kept at the project. Income tax returns, drivers' licenses, insurance policies, and other items indicating address and identity were coded as well. Persons were to leave the area only on laboratory work or for personal emergencies. When traveling, many scientists bore fictitious names. Socializing outside the project was forbidden, and shopping visits to Santa Fe were restricted to once a month. While in Santa Fe, Los Alamos residents could usually count upon being followed by security men as they completed shopping in the city.

Oak Ridge (originally called Clinton Engineer Works) had its origins in the decision to locate all plants at one site. Initially it was thought that 80,000 acres would be needed for this purpose. Ultimately, 56,000 acres were taken. The electromagnetic plant (Y-12) and gaseous diffusion plant (K-25) were authorized in 1942, and a thermal diffusion process plant (S-50) in 1944.

The location of a full-scale plutonium production plant at Oak Ridge was not thought to be wise since the supply of water was inadequate for a large plant of this type, which utilized a great deal of water. In addition, the area lay too close to Knoxville and other towns to offer protection to the population if a disaster should occur. However, a small pilot plutonium plant, the training of certain Hanford personnel, and the operation of a small pile (graphite reactor) took place at Oak Ridge.

The urgent need for enriched uranium drove the War Department to rush ahead in acquiring land for Oak Ridge. The site was chosen primarily because of its ample supply of TVA electricity, and also for its location away from both coasts, and convenience for travel to Manhattan Project headquarters in Washington and to experimental laboratories in New York and Chicago. Additional site requirements were: relatively undeveloped land which was not expensive to purchase, a large supply of water, a large pool of local workers, and a climate which allowed building to proceed year round. The Y-12 and K-25 plants were to be located in separate valleys seventeen miles apart so that contamination would not spread from one plant to the other in the event of an accident.

Oak Ridge, however, being the most populated of the sites, presented certain problems in working with the people of the area. Landowners were disgruntled because of the wide variance between government appraisal values and the values they had expected for their land. Over 1,000 families were forced to relocate at a time when land values were rising and few farms were available in the area. Moreover, because of war shortages, few vehicles were available to move household possessions, farm implements, harvested crops, and farm stock. Clinton, Knoxville, and other surrounding communities were presented with problems, too. For construction workers crowded into these towns in search of housing. The new project seemed to drain the area of its labor force, its resources, and its supplies which were scarce because of wartime rationing; moreover, rumors concerning the work being done created curiosity and uneasiness.

A large work force was needed to build and operate the Oak Ridge plants. Peak employment involved a work force of 82,000 people. Involvement by this many people, however, presented significant security concerns. This may be indicated by the fact that the Manhattan Project intelligence and security division was headquartered at Oak Ridge after July 1943. The plant areas and the town were surrounded by a security fence. It was impractical to completely isolate workers from the general population since many lived outside the reservation. Therefore, the military procedure of handling security concerns by compartmentalizing knowledge was utilized by officials. Workers knew only what was needed to know to perform their particular job. Different letters showed the part of the plant where the worker was employed, badge numbers signaled the amount of knowledge which each worker possessed, and various colored work clothes showed the type of work performed. In addition, at hiring in, it was made clear that dire penalties would befall persons who shared knowledge with unauthorized persons or who took information outside the workplace. This principle was reinforced by frequent reminders from supervisors, by billboards throughout the site, by searches conducted at the gates, and by badge checks. In addition, employees and residents knew of the presence of security agents operating in civilian clothes and of employees and residents acting as security informants in their midst.

At Hanford, unlike either Los Alamos or Oak Ridge, over 400,00 acres of land were taken. The acquisition of so much land seemed essential to protect the population from possible danger resulting from large quantities of radioactive materials. Consequently, no town with more than a 1,000 population was allowed closer than twenty miles to the chosen site. Plants and piles were to be widely separated so that in the event of an accident, the reaction could not spread easily from one area to another. The center of the site was reserved for the plants and their operators, while the outlying land was needed to provide a safety zone. The hazardous manufacturing area was to be no closer than ten miles to the nearest railroad, main highway, or residential area. Richmond, at that time a town of 250 people, was purchased to serve as a residential area for operating personnel, housing 6,500 persons. This housing was later expanded to 17,500 people when a large number of plant workers were unable to find housing off the site.

In addition to size and isolation, the Hanford site met other important requirements. Most crucial to the operation was an ample supply of water which the site supplied—25,000 gallons per minute from the Columbia River, one of the largest in water flow in the nation. Also important was the potential of utilizing 100,000 kilowatts of electrical power from the Bonneville and Grand Coulee Dams. In addition, the topography of this semiarid area was suitable for supporting large structures, and the sand and gravel soil suitable for mixing concrete for construction. Acquisition of the major part of the land was fairly routine and was completed by 1944. The entire population of the area acquired was only about 1,500 persons. Most residents were involved in farming and ranching. Seventy-one thousand acres of land were already owned by the government. The remaining land had to be bought, leased, or covered by restriction agreements. The isolation of the area can be seen in use statistics which indicate that farmland composed approximately eleven percent of the total land, grazing eighty-eight percent and towns less than one percent.

Forty-five thousand workers flooded the Hanford construction camp until 1945 when it was abandoned. By 1945, 15,000 residents—largely operating personnel and their families—remained in Richland. Workers here were also governed by security restrictions. Recruited from DuPont facilities and from nationwide posters and newspaper ads, they were told only that they were going to a facility in eastern Washington to do important war work. They were not to discuss their jobs. In addition, many other restrictions in effect at Oak Ridge applied to their activities. These included the censoring of mail and listening in on long-distance calls, as well as strong admonitions when workers hired in.

Each site shared the common elements of haste in construction of facilities and in carrying out duties. Personnel raced against time to aid the war effort, trying to complete the project as soon as possible; but few knew its ultimate purpose. Personnel at all three sites carried out their duties using the most modern machinery, but at the same time lived their personal lives under extremely rough pioneer conditions. Personnel in all three areas confronted the vastness of operations in their particular environment, but few knew of the size of the total work of the site, let alone the vastness of the entire Manhattan Project. And, above all, everyone's life was ruled by the need for security.

On the other hand, each site, because of different purposes, varied in the amount and type of land taken, a factor which affected future development. Hanford boasted the largest area because of the hazardous nature of the plants located there. The land taken, however, was sparsely populated and poorly suited to farming. Some land was leased and former residents could use it to graze animals, but not to reside there. Thus, for some, their livelihood was not threatened. The Los Alamos Ranch Boys' School was also in a sparsely populated area and its acquisition affected fewer people. In Oak Ridge, though, the situation was different. The Oak Ridge area boasted the largest population, consisting of farmers who had owned their land in small close-knit communities for generations. The loss of their farms was difficult for these families to accept. This factor would have far-ranging effects upon future relations between Oak Ridge residents and the surrounding areas, since a larger proportion of the local population perceived these newcomers as intruders and aliens, coming in and taking up their land and resources. In later years, the local people would still find it difficult to accept this new municipality.

Oak Ridge, ironically, was the site most dependent upon local labor. Some of these workers lived off the site and commuted to their jobs. Most workers in Hanford and Los Alamos moved to their work sites from other places and left these sites primarily for shopping in Pasco and Santa Fe, respectively. Since almost all of them came from other areas, they did not have the personal ties to the region. Consequently, they, unlike the Oak Ridgers, were exposed to much less outside contact. It is to the credit of the Oak Ridge workers that the secret of the operations there was kept, since they interacted more extensively with the outside world.

All three secret atomic cities grew under wartime conditions and were shaped by the purpose of their mission—to maintain the secrecy of the development of the bomb while carrying out the work necessary to bring the project to fruition. Secrecy shaped every action of those involved, from relocation, to workplace, to interaction with the outside world, to living arrangements, to leisure time pursuits. Even the amount of food and beer consumed was classified in order that population statistics could not be deciphered by the enemy. Differences arose between the sites because of local topography, climate, and population density, but the secrecy remained paramount—with the most obvious variation seen in the Los Alamos scientists' colloquium which allowed a free, open, and intellectual exchange of ideas, to help accelerate bomb development. All three communities shared a subordination of individual to national purposes—a typical wartime phenomenon. What remains impressive is the scope of the total Manhattan Project—the amount of land and resources expended, the total budget involved, the numbers of people contributing to the work, the immensity of the facilities created, and the sense of wartime mission.

THE ARMY'S EFFORT

Courtesy James E. Westcott

MY WORK IN OAK RIDGE

K. D. Nichols

In June 12, 1942, General Wilhelm Styer, representing General George Marshall, chief of staff of the United States Army, agreed with Dr. Vannevar Bush, the top scientist on military work, to issue a report recommending the construction of the plants necessary to produce atomic weapons. One week later, on June 18, President Roosevelt approved Dr. Bush's recommendations (fast action in those days). This important decision made the U.S. Army responsible for construction of the fissionable-material production plants necessary for development and production of atomic weapons.

On June 20 I received a call instructing me to attend a meeting in Syracuse, New York on Sunday morning. At that meeting my boss, Colonel James C. Marshall, sat at the head of the table with a large envelope in front of him. He informed me that he had been designated as district engineer of a new district that would carry out a secret project of great importance. Furthermore, he said that I had fifteen seconds to volunteer for the position of deputy district engineer—or be drafted for the job. I volunteered.

After a hectic ten days trying to find out what the project was about and taking the initial steps to get an organization started, and a contractor—Stone and Webster—to assist us, we went to Knoxville on July 1, 1942, for the purpose of inspecting a proposed site for the production plants. A group of scientists from the University of Chicago had visited the area in April and had recommended a site near the farming community of Elza.

Thus I first came to what is now known as Oak Ridge on a hot July day. I was then thirty-four years old and eager to get started. We decided to locate the town and production plants there because it was an isolated area. It was located away from both coasts, not too densely populated, and individual plants could be located in the separate valleys included in the site. Furthermore, the land was inexpensive, suitable for building the plants, and more importantly, TVA provided the electric power required, while the Clinch River afforded a boundary on three sides and also a good water supply. The mountain ridge called Black Oak Ridge formed part of the boundary on the fourth side. The site was approved for acquisition in September. Construction of the administration building started in November 1942.

When I succeeded Colonel Marshall as district engineer of the Manhattan District in August 1943, the district headquarters was moved from New York City to Oak Ridge. I reported directly to General Groves, the commanding general of the Manhattan Project, who had a small staff in Washington, D.C. As district engineer, I was responsible for: all design, construction, and operation of the U-235 and plutonium plants at Clinton Engineer Works and Hanford; the feed-material plants located at several sites in the United States and Canada (for the acquisition of uranium ore); the administration of the research efforts (at the University of California, the University of Chicago, Columbia University, and other universities); and also liaison with and support of Los Alamos. The largest of the production projects was Oak Ridge. More than half of the two billion dollars appropriated was devoted to Oak Ridge construction and operation of plants. It became the largest engineering and construction project in history completed in so short a time.

General Groves' responsibilities, in addition to supervising the activities of the District, included international cooperation, intelligence, planning for delivery of the weapon, and in cooperation with the Army Air Force, the actual delivery of the weapons on targets in Japan. He had a clear-cut channel to President Roosevelt for periodic approval of the overall project.

From time to time, I have been asked how we accomplished our objective in such a short time. The primary reason was the high quality of scientific and industrial leadership in various parts of the

Courtesy Department of Energy Westcott Photo

General Leslie Groves looks on while Secretary of War Robert P. Patterson presents Colonel K. D. Nichols the Distinguished Service Award.

111

project, in addition to the determination to complete the project and hasten the end of the war. We inherited from the Office of Scientific Research and Development an absolutely topnotch scientific organization, each component headed by the best scientist in that field. As the scientific effort expanded, each new position was filled by selecting the most highly qualified man or woman for the position.

As the army assumed the responsibility for design, construction, and operation of production plants, the contractors were selected by first determining the best qualified firm and then approaching it. In many cases, firms were relieved of other war projects in order to work in Oak Ridge. Contractors, however, for the houses and dormitories were selected by competitive bidding.

By choosing the best qualified personnel and organizations, there was little need to be constantly reviewing decisions by appointing review committees. In most cases we already had the best experts in charge, and the primary function of the army was to coordinate the effort, to see that the various projects were assigned a clear-cut mission and were completed on time. Several approaches for solving specific problems were frequently started, and selection of the method to be used was determined only after one had obviously been proven.

Looking back, it is amazing how well these various project teams worked together. Occasionally friction was engendered by a sincere difference of opinion, but most differences were solved by getting the right people together and seeing that they threshed out an answer. Cooperation was a major factor in achieving success.

Another thing in our favor was that from September 1942 till the war's end, we had top priority in the war effort. From time to time other war projects, such as landing craft for the Normandy invasion, were assigned equal priority, but never to my knowledge was another project given a higher priority. President Roosevelt never wavered in his determination to achieve the atomic bomb at the earliest date.

A further advantage was that we had a single, clear-cut objective: an atomic bomb that could be delivered by a B-29 at the earliest date. We avoided the temptation to develop a more suitable plane, or to divert effort from the main objective.

Maintaining security of information was not only a wartime

necessity, but it also helped to maintain continuity of effort. Protected by the secrecy, we were seldom bothered by willing helpers who would have liked to tell us how to do the job had they known about our effort. Moreover, there were no attempts to kill the project because of interference with the main war effort, or because individuals thought the project impossible.

We were not hampered by excessive paper work. Financial responsibility, of course, required proper accounting and auditing. But directives were clear and concise. For example, presidential approval of Dr. Bush's recommendation to start construction of plants was endorsed to the new district engineer by the simple words, "For your information and appropriate action." Most directives from General Groves to the district engineer were verbal, in fact there was very little correspondence with Washington. For example, the short, monthly district progress reports were hand-carried to permit the chief and the deputy chief of engineers to read them, and then carried to General Groves to read and file.

A final and major factor was that General Groves was delegated contract and administrative authority almost equivalent to the wartime authority of the secretary of war. Much of that authority was in turn delegated to me as district engineer. Moreover, there was the direct channel to the president. For approval of progress reports and authority to expand or continue the program, General Groves reported through a three-man military policy committee, or through the chief of staff of the army, to Secretary of War Henry L. Stimson, who personally obtained presidential approval.

It was the dedicated and superb effort of the individuals in this wartime organization who made success possible. At Oak Ridge the major effort was made for the production of U-235 for the Hiroshima bomb. The Electromagnetic Plant, the Liquid Thermal Diffusion Plant, and the Gaseous Diffusion Plant all played a part in making bomb-quality material. Tennessee provided a large part of the personnel required. At peak, the total workers for combined construction and operation reached 82,000, and the peak population living on the site reached 75,000. In addition, some 40,000 workers commuted each day. One of the big questions about the feasibility of the Electromagnetic Plant was whether or not we could find the talent to operate it. Many thought it would require Ph.D.'s to operate the control panels. Tennessee Eastman, our contractors for operating the plant, thought otherwise. They set up a training program at Oak Ridge and trained mainly young girls as operators, most of them natives of the region. Our practice at that time, when a production unit called a "racetrack" was completed, was to turn it over to a group of scientists from the University of California for initial operation and to get the bugs out. On one occasion I told Ernest Lawrence, top scientist for the electromagnetic process, that I thought the Tennessee girls were better operators than the scientists because their units produced more material. He laughed and explained that his scientists had the job of correcting errors and were not concentrating on just production. I persisted in my claim and challenged him to run a production contest for a week. He accepted and was surprised when the so-called hillbillies won the contest.

For each of the major plants, either during construction or initial operation, we had at least one serious crisis where we knew something was wrong and had difficulty finding the cause. For example, when we initially started to operate the Electromagnetic Plant, everything seemed to be going well, except no material came out of the spout. It took many tense sessions to get to the root of the problem. In fact, it required an improved chemical process. Another similar crisis had occurred earlier when the magnets shorted out and had to be sent back to Allis-Chalmers for correction. The Gaseous Diffusion Plant was about one-third completed before we found a suitable barrier; this required scrapping our initial preparations for producing a barrier and starting a new process. This crisis caused long hours of work on the part of Dobie Keith, George Felbeck, and others who searched for solutions, but no one gave up. They were determined to succeed. The overall result was that we shipped the last of the material for the Hiroshima bomb to Los Alamos in late July 1945, on the schedule that had been presented to Secretary of War Stimson in May. As an incentive for Tennessee Eastman to make the schedule, I bet a half case of Scotch with Dr. F. R. Conklin and Dr. James G. McNally, of Tennessee Eastman, that they could not meet the schedule that they had set. I bet the Scotch in General Groves' name because I thought that they would have more pleasure winning the bet from

114

him than from me. I told General Groves I thought he ought to cover at least half the amount. He agreed, and it turned out that Tennessee Eastman won and we all got together and shared the Scotch.

The Liquid Thermal Diffusion Plant was built in accordance with an impossible schedule of ninety days from start to initial operation. I collected a bet with Dobie Keith, the designer of the Gaseous Diffusion Plant, who thought it could not be done. But H. K. Ferguson Company did it. (Dobie and I got a real steam bath from leaking valves while checking the operation of the plant. The leaks were ultimately fixed.)

The other major installation at Oak Ridge was the Clinton Laboratories. Early in March 1944, Dr. Arthur H. Compton invited General Groves and me to accompany him to the Clinton Lab where Dr. Martin D. Whitaker handed me a vial containing the first gram of plutonium which was urgently needed at Los Alamos for the design of a plutonium bomb. The plant also served as a semiworks for processes to be used at Hanford.

The town of Oak Ridge itself required approximately $100 million for construction, or about one-tenth of the overall cost of the Clinton Engineer Works. More headaches for me, however, were generated per dollar spent in the construction and operation of the town than for any of the production plants. Handling personnel on a construction job or in an operating plant was one thing, but being responsible for the men, women, and children in a government-owned town of which the best that can be said for the form of government is that it was a benevolent dictatorship, was another matter. Mrs. Nichols was actively interested in the many community organizations and clubs that were formed to help meet the civic and cultural needs of the town. The wives of the more than one hundred military officers living there were united into a service committee that provided volunteers for various organizations such as the Red Cross, scouts, and women's club. Roane-Anderson, the contractor who had charge of the operation of the town, absorbed most of the criticism which naturally resulted from building the fifth largest city in Tennessee in a matter of months. I tried to remain as anonymous as possible. Furnishing all the facilities from scratch, such as schools, theaters, library, hospital, stores, buses, telephones, recreational facilities, restaurants, churches, houses and dormitories, for a constantly growing population, was bound to cause periods of impatience and exasperation among the residents. Also, we had many diverse opinions about how to operate the town. Some wanted to run social experiments, such as establishing a unified church. However, I felt that the more normal the town, the better; and that was the policy finally established.

In regard to religion, however, I did have one crisis—when a staff member assigned a house to a clergyman. I immediately had requests for others, and in view of the number of religions, it would have been an unwise diversion of labor and materials to furnish houses for all. We initially settled on five or six houses to be assigned, and it was decided that the assignment would be based on church attendance. I specified that the church attendance would be determined by a physical count of all those present at each service during the month of August. I then was criticized by my own pastor, of the Episcopal Church, who contended that I should have known that Episcopalians are notorious for not attending church during the month of August. Anyway, the problem was reconciled, at least satisfactorily to the winners.

I also had a problem with the ministers. Generally, I was at Oak Ridge only on Fridays, Saturdays, and Sundays. On one weekend, my executive officer insisted that I see a delegation of ministers who were upset about dormitory life. It seemed that some of the girls in the girls' dormitories were entertaining men in their rooms, and the ministers were asking that we take measures to separate the good girls from the bad. I listened carefully while they explained the problem. Finally, after some consideration, I agreed that I would make separate facilities, provided they submitted to me a list of the bad girls. Happily, they adjourned to their meeting rooms to make out the list, but after fifteen minutes returned to inform me, sadly, that we might as well forget it. Making out such a list was impossible.

Oak Ridge was a city without a past, and it was not designed to have much of a future. We tried to design only for the duration of the war, in order to conserve money, materials, and labor. This scrimping undoubtedly caused some of our problems. The very fact, however, that Oak Ridge is a thriving town today shows that the foundations laid were more lasting than we expected. During the war we produced the bomb successfully, and in spite of our efforts after the war to seek agreement on eliminating nuclear weapons, weapons work is still an important mission for Oak Ridge. However, of equal, or perhaps greater, importance has been Oak Ridge's efforts to develop some of the beneficial aspects of the atom. There have been tremendous improvements in health treatment methods that were by-products of the nuclear research conducted during the war. There are also countless other research and industrial methods of a similar nature. Of course, the chief benefit was expected to be nuclear power for the production of electricity. It is a major benefit when we consider that about sixteen percent of the electricity generated in the United States is produced in nuclear power plants. And even higher percentages are generated in other countries.

Nevertheless, after spending three exciting years of my life planning, constructing, and living in Oak Ridge, I am pleased that this once temporary town has fixed its place, permanently, in the history and future of those other towns that make up Tennessee. [*]

* Portions of the material in *My Work in Oak Ridge* will appear in K. D. Nichols' auto-biography, to be published by William Morrow and Company in early 1987.

SPECIAL ENGINEER DETACHMENT

June Adamson

The Special Engineer Detachment (SED), which brought 1,257 soldiers to Oak Ridge in 1943 and 1944, was by most standards a plush unit. An anecdote from the detachment's mimeographed in-house publication illustrates the point: "We rode in from Knoxville this week with some new men for the detachment who had just finished infantry basic training. We told them all the facts with no embellishments, but would they believe us? Hell no! The thing they found hardest to believe was the inner spring mattresses."

One GI recalled his first night in the SED: "We arrived in the pouring rain, so we were told to sleep late before orientation the next day. Imagine my surprise to be awakened by a group of Negro maids coming into the barracks to make our beds. I couldn't believe this was the Army."

There was no kitchen patrol and no mess halls either. Most of the GIs were glad to be in Oak Ridge. Considering such alternative as the Battle of the Bulge that was building in Europe in the fall of 1944, where some of them knew they were headed, they didn't resent too much that they were working for army pay—$50 a month for a private and a daily food allowance of $2.25 for those who lived in the barracks and ate in the cafeterias. Many of the men stayed on in Oak Ridge after the war. Some married local girls. Some brought wives and families with them and were allowed to move out of the barracks to be with their families—if

118

they could find a room in someone's house, or if their wives could find jobs that entitled them to a house. Men were assigned from all parts of the country to work in Oak Ridge when it was realized that not enough civilians with science and engineering training could be found to do the job.

On May 22, 1943, the commanding general of the Army Service Forces authorized the establishment of the SED. The first district roster consisted of 334 enlisted men and it was thought this would be enough. However, by the fall of 1943, with technical men still scarce, the district began a program of recruiting among colleges and universities. This recruiting extended to the Army Specialized Training program where many young men were receiving their first college training. Not all of it was in science. The late Richard Gehman, for example, was a writer and was sent to Oak Ridge to help edit the town's first army-run newspaper.

Since this program still did not fill the need, the Corps of Engineers was authorized to recruit men from replacement centers as well as directly from such army bases as Alabama's Camp Sibert and Fort McClellan. Men were plucked out of such camps and forts all over the country in twos and threes, right up to V-J Day.

The first enlisted man assigned to Oak Ridge arrived July 19, 1943. The first commanding officer was Captain William A. Fogg. In March 1944 he was succeeded by Captain William A. Barger who held the post until after the war.

The first men who came to Oak Ridge lived in dormitories with civilians, but as the SED grew, it was moved into eight barracks located approximately where Downtown is today. As the detachment grew and grew, hutments were added near the barracks. The hutments were one-room, primitive constructions, each housing four men. As in most army camps, there were separate bathhouses. However, by December 1945, after the war was over and detachment numbers fell, the SEDs returned to dormitories, this time taking over complete buildings remodeled for army use.

WACs served in Oak Ridge, too, but just how many is uncertain. One article in *Yank*, the magazine for GIs by GIs, said "a handful." One SED publication said several hundred. Somewhere in between is more likely the truth. But there were some who served at the SED headquarters and others who worked as clerks, secretaries etc., at the Castle-on-the-Hill where the Corps of Engineers army officers oversaw the work of the town and the plants. Apparently, there were no WACs assigned to Oak Ridge to do scientific work, but in those years of secrecy, it could have been possible.

Before V-J Day, the army bulletin, *SED News,* carried no news or information that was significant. Scores of winning bridge teams, soft ball and bowling teams, and other sports information filled its columns, including news about the movies. Columns were filled with jokes, most of them sexist, some quite "raunchy" for the time. Headlines such as "Girl Found in Barracks" pertained to a skunk named Mabel who had crawled in through a window.

From time to time, there was mention of "The Commandos," a unit that one former SEDer described as "a group of uncoordinated scientists and engineers who practiced for a short time in case such emergencies as riots occurred." None did, and the GI added that it was mainly close-order drill that was practiced, which wouldn't have helped anyway, "but that was the army way."

It seems clear from the *SED News* that the soldiers assigned to Carbide, then K-25 only, received better public relations than those assigned to the other plants. They were feted several times a year at a special buffet supper, with a menu worthy of talking about in times of food shortages. Reports about such occasions never failed to mention that the other two plant operators, Tennessee Eastman Company for Y-12, and DuPont for X-10, should do likewise. The SED had a swimming team too, thanks to the natural spring in the Grove Center area, where a pool had been built. Following V-J Day, more information about the SED began to be printed, including results of a survey conducted by Warrant Officer Nisbett. It was he who noted that the men came from forty-seven of the forty-eight states, "New Mexico being the lone survivor." Perhaps it is reasonable to assume that anyone qualified for such scientific and engineering work from that state had been sent to Los Alamos, although that is not usually the army way. The Oak Ridge GI knew that some men from the detachment were sent there and knew that Site Y was part of the Manhattan District, but most of them couldn't see how the two installations fit together.

The top two states represented in the SED by August 1945 were New York, with 228, and Pennsylvania with 110. The next eight states represented in SED were Ohio with 107; New Jersey,

83; Illinois, 80; Michigan, 58; California, 54; Massachusetts, 53; Indiana, 45; and Wisconsin, 31. Tennessee was eleventh with 30 and Wyoming and Nevada were last with one each.

According to one story in an early *Oak Ridge Journal*, there were six Ph.D.'s living side by side in the SED, but the *SED News* disagreed. On October 12, 1945, it claimed "... there is only one. George Steinberg must have been beside himself that night." The *News* source was "Form Twenties," and it is entirely possible that the *Journal* had been correct and that five of the Ph.D.'s had been sent other places, for some were brought to Oak Ridge very briefly and then sent to Los Alamos and other places. In any case, the *Journal* story got its editor, Frances Smith Gates, called on the security carpet. *Yank* magazine, after the secret of the bomb was out, reported that there were nine Ph.D.'s in the SED at one time.

When it came to degrees and intelligence, however, the SED did all right. There were 607 bachelor's degrees, and forty-five men held master's. Many went on for advanced degrees upon their discharge, most, of course, under the GI Bill. The *SED News* reported that seventy-five percent of the detachment expressed this intention in a survey. SED men were courted by such universities as Massachusetts Institute of Technology (MIT), one announcement explaining that houses had been built near MIT campus for GIs.

Both the *SED News* and the SED Yearbook noted that the men of the detachment represented three hundred institutions of higher learning and the median Army General Classification Test score for the detachment was 133, "undoubtedly one of the highest scores for any single unit in the Army." GIs throughout Oak Ridge chortled with delight when it was announced that the score was higher than the median for the officers stationed here.

Even though GI uniforms were seen all around Oak Ridge, not many residents realized just how large the SED was. At work in the plants, the men wore the protective clothing, coveralls, and the like, and were not necessarily recognized as being in service by their co-workers. The majority were working at K-25, as has been noted, probably the next largest group at Y-12, with a smaller number assigned to Clinton Laboratory. An illustration of this point is found in the September 23, 1945 "Grapevine" column of the *SED News*:

We heard an interesting story from Clinton Lab the other day. As you know, the lab was taken over by Monsanto the first of July. Last week, the new big boss got up before the assembled employees and made a speech in the "big happy family" vein. At the conclusion of the speech one of our detachment boys raised his hand and asked the policy toward GIs. The big boy replied that the company was very thankful to all the boys in service and that they would all get their jobs back. Our boy said no, he meant the GIs working for the company now. The big boy got a blank look on his face, turned to the man next to him, and said, "Do we have soldiers working for us?"

In addition to the "Grapevine" column, the postwar *SED News* began to carry a column, "Hatched and Matched," to tell of births and marriages. Many of the marriages took place at Oak Ridge's Chapel-on-the-Hill, but a great number took place out-of-town with GIs returning to hometowns on furlough for that purpose. News of such weddings were not written in the usual social style, as a column of October 12, 1945, indicated: "T/5 Johnny Farquharson and Lois Ann Amos performed the deed on Oct. 7 at Chatham, Va. T/5 Ray Eby got hitched to Rosemary Booth on Oct. 6 here in Oak Ridge."

During the weeks following the news of the atomic bomb, stories among GIs were many and varied, some of them no doubt apocryphal. The one from a girl back home, for example, who didn't write much: "It has been a long time since I received your letter and when I picked up the paper and read about Oak Ridge and the atomic bomb, I just HAD to sit down and write ..."

One GI claimed to have heard from a friend in the Philippines: "When in hell are you coming over here to relieve us? There you are diddling your stirring rods and shaking your test tubes while I've been working my fingers to the bone over a hot artillery piece!" And the letter from a gunner on a naval cruiser: "How big is the bomb? How many tons of powder do you need to set it off?"

One SED man said his parents wrote: "Is it dangerous? Son, take good care of yourself—don't take any chances." And another said his former professor of physics wrote to ask: "Why the hell didn't you tell me?"

By late fall 1945, the *SED News* carried a serious column called "Berlin Calling" to explain what was going on in occupied

Germany—how hard it would be for the Germans to feed themselves, and quoting Eisenhower that the Americans were there to help them reconstruct, not to do their work for them. Political education was also outlined with a question: "What will the Herrenvolk accept as a fair form of government?" A map showing the break-up of German industry was included. But by December, the most serious thing GIs seemed to be thinking of was a Christmas party—the second Christmas in Oak Ridge, still with scarcities and shortages. However, for most it had been a happy time, a time when the men felt they were contributing to the war effort, using the skills and knowledge they had gained in training and for which they were far more suited than shooting guns. Married men had a chance to be with their wives, and those with children were able to be with their families. Late in 1945, GIs were even allowed to rent shacklike victory cottages, painted drab gray and arranged in duplex fashion, close together. The units were small and cramped, but many couples moved into them. There was no air conditioning anywhere in Oak Ridge then, but the cottages needed it more than most, since the cook stove was coal fired and gave out a lot of heat even when the thermometer was pushing 100 outside. However, there was a lot of sitting outside, "neighboring," and despite complaints, the experience was survived. Some GIs chose to stay where they were, in rented rooms in more normal Oak Ridge housing, or off the area.

The men of the SED took part in the life of the community and contributed to it. In addition to participating in sports, some played in the Oak Ridge Symphony, some acted in plays, and many participated in the various special interest clubs that were started. They also presented two plays, both in melodramatic style. The first, *Gold in the Hills,* was presented in January 1945 for two nights. Admission was something like a quarter, perhaps less, and the auditorium in the first Oak Ridge High School was filled both nights. A second successful melodrama, *The Drunkard,* was presented by the SED men and WACs on November 2 and 3, 1945.

Rumors about early discharge circulated almost from the day the war ended. On September 29, 1945, Secretary of War Robert P. Patterson and Major General Leslie R. Groves were interviewed at a press conference at the administration building. GIs wanted to know about the future of the SED. Secretary Patterson replied that the Special Engineer Detachment would continue as usual, as "long as the contractors feel that they need the men." To this, General Groves added that the men of the SED would be discharged on the same basis as anyone else in the army. Some months later, GIs at the three plants were offered early discharge if they would stay on the same jobs they were doing. Some chose this route, but others chose to stick it out until they had enough "points"—or two years of service so that they could have a greater opportunity for job choice. In September, however, Groves added that the future of the whole project rested in the hands of Congress. "If Congress decides to discontinue the project, the SED will probably be shipped out almost at once." So there was continued uncertainty among the men.

Late in 1945, the "Grapevine" column reported: "This place is getting more like a college every day. We have a musical group, a newsletter, a theater group, and now a yearbook. All we need to make the set-up complete is a few fraternities. And how about a reunion in 1958?" (Actually, the first reunion had to wait until August 1985—forty years later—at the Steiner-Bell Health Resort in Gatlinburg.)

The first announcement that the SED men would have an official yearbook—if they paid for it—was made at the end of October. It was planned to have about 130 pages, with sections on administration, activities, sports, and individual pictures of each man. The cost of the picture was included in the price of $3 for the book. At the time, the price was reprinted rather apologetically, noting that the cover would be of "Marvelleather" to save money. The SED patch in full color was emblazoned on four blue stripes running the length of the book. The letters SED and the year 1945 were embossed on the cover in gold. "Because of the small number of men assigned to Fercleve and Kellex, these men will be included in the Carbide section," it was noted.

Because of all this, the men sometimes forgot that they were, in fact, in the army. And the army, from time to time, had to remind them of the rules. At one point, a notice was served that the pasting of beer labels on the Detachment Exchange (DX instead of PX) ceilings would result in "the loss of stripes." Another time the men were warned that they should not go around without their hats. "The MPs are on your trail," the notice read, adding, "Extra duty on Saturday awaits." However, there were only a few reminders that this was the army. In fact, army "interference" with the SED was kept at a minimum—the emphasis focused on their scientific and engineering work. One major came through early in 1945 and tried to "GI things up." It meant that the SED men had to spend time spit and polishing in their quarters rather than being on the job in the plants. The major was suddenly sent to Panama.

Although beer was the major drink enjoyed by the GIs, Oak Ridge being in a dry county, it was often smuggled in from other places and from short trips to the well-known Oakdale liquor store. One time a group of GIs had their liquor confiscated and, illegal or not, they complained. It was not "officially" returned to them, but word came back that if they could identify their property, it would be restored, and it was.

By January 1946 the lead story in the *SED News* was "Cadre Leave!" explaining that the top ranking enlisted men had joined the mass exodus that was beginning to take place in Oak Ridge. "By Feb. 15, the ranks of the Cadre will have experienced a complete turnover," a *News* article reported. Among those scheduled to leave was Master Sergeant Campbell King, and readers were informed that he would return, along with many others, to work at K-25.

One of the final issues of the *SED News* on March 18, 1946, noted that "The Bikini Boys are off—almost," referring to the group of enlisted men who went to Bikini Atoll for the first major atomic bomb test after the war. There was no reference to how many would go, but some idea is given by the fact that they traveled by train in two Pullman cars and would not have to change trains during the trip.

Early in 1946 the back page of the *SED News* resembled a sheet of advertisements. It was devoted to public service. Each block carried information special to GIs about to be discharged, such as: educational opportunities, available loans for homes, businesses and farms, all on the GI bill. Information about converting government insurance was also given, with necessary names and addresses to contact.

There was one sarcastic note: "For the latest project information, read Drew Pearson every day." For although many GIs loved Oak Ridge and wanted to stay, its future was uncertain.

A SOLDIER-SCIENTIST
IN OAK RIDGE

Robert R. Hentz

In 1944, at the conclusion of a two-week furlough, my orders sent me to Knoxville, Tennessee by an L & N train. A year's course in the army Specialized Training Program at Kansas State had ended. Normandy had been invaded that June, and we were needed urgently for the prosecution of the war. I arrived on a dark, rainy September night at the L & N Station, a railroad station with a fireplace over which was a quotation that I loved from Robert Burns' *A Man's A Man For A'That*. That was, of course, in the waiting room for whites. What quotation might have been in the waiting room for blacks, I could not know. The degrading, depressing aspects of segregation were familiar to me from basic training at a camp in Alabama, but the wound was reopened on arrival in Knoxville and remained raw for the following nineteen months. Jim Crow pervaded the South with a moral stench like the stench of the paper mills hanging over that camp in Alabama. The sight of black and white waiting rooms, drinking fountains, and toilets was not a welcome sight and clouded my first impressions of my home to be.

A noncommissioned officer was at the station to meet us. About a half-dozen of us had arrived on the train. We threw our duffel bags into the rear of an olive-drab army truck covered like a Conestoga wagon with canvas stretched over wooden hoops. We climbed in and sat on the wooden benches that ran along each side. The truck moved off through the city and soon city lights gave way to the blackness of the country. Rain drummed on the canvas roof. Occasionally, through the arched opening at the rear, lights could be seen of a house in the distance or of a cafe or gas station at the roadside, but mostly there was only blackness and the sounds of rain on the roof and tires on a wet road. The truck sped along a winding, bumpy road for about an hour when it was enveloped in a mist suggesting a nearby body of water. It slowed and came to a stop. Voices of the driver and another man were heard, and we were again on our way. Through the rear opening, we saw military policemen at a gate with a guard station, and a high chain-link fence surmounted by barbed wire faded into the misty darkness. We surmised that we had come to another army camp. To do what? For how long? A stopover for battle training before shipment to Europe?

Our conjectures seemed to be confirmed as the truck rolled to a stop before a barracks building, where we climbed out and entered with our duffel bags. We signed in and a soldier led us up a boardwalk into a wooded area where little square huts were scattered. The latrine was pointed out and we each were led to a hut that was to be our home. There was an army cot in each corner of the hut, along with clothes racks and shelves for our personal belongings. A stove occupied the center. Snug quarters for four.

In the morning light we found ourselves in a fenced area that was clearly an army site. The small square huts were distributed among a strand of pines and connected with each other and with latrines by a network of boardwalks converging into a single boardwalk. This led to a collection of barracks buildings that housed the headquarters, supply, a post exchange, and a cafeteria. Outside the fenced area a major road was visible, as was a group of buildings that appeared to be a small shopping center. Beyond the road many small houses looking monotonously alike, were visible at a distance. They were scattered among rolling hills as if the gods had tired of a Monopoly game and swept the board free of its accumulated little houses onto the hills of eastern Tennessee.

We were given an orientation lecture after breakfast. We had been brought to work on a highly secret war project that could make a significant, perhaps vital, contribution to bringing the war to an end. We would use our special talents and training in the laboratories and production facilities of the project. We would be working with civilians who lived in the houses on the hills and in dormitories inside the larger fenced area, and who came from outside to work on the project. We would be subject to army regulations, but would have a greater measure of freedom than customary in an army camp—in some respects approaching that of a civilian. Absolute secrecy about our work was essential and was reinforced in every way possible. Pictures were taken, badges issued for passage in and out of the city and its work sites, and we were assigned our jobs. We were members of the Special Engineer Detachment.

The next morning I boarded an olive-drab bus. The bus wound over hilly roads and through woods until an industrial-like area came into view. The bus stopped at a large terminal into which similar buses deposited people from all over eastern Tennessee, people as far away as Jellico on the Kentucky border. Crowds swarmed through gates showing their badges, and fanned out in different directions, disappearing into buildings. There were frame barrackslike buildings and larger brick or concrete buildings. Everywhere, large steam pipes ran through the area which was largely devoid of trees and hot under the intense late-summer sun. Another soldier and I, soon to become friends, were assigned to an analytical laboratory much like those familiar to chemistry students. There were rows of lab benches; on each side of each bench, a woman performed a particular chemical operation on a sample that was passed to the next bench in an analytical assembly line. There, a final separation of a solid took place, igniting it at high temperature. This solid (unknown to most of us working on the project—including myself) was the substance around which the Manhattan Project was built. The women ranged in age from eighteen to near fifty and had no training as chemists, but were taught to do their specific job which they did well. The laboratory was supervised by a civilian foreman, with a soldier assistant. We new recruits began work on the line and learned each operation from start to finish. We worked on rotating eight-hour shifts—7 to 3 for six days with a day off; 3 to 11 for six days with a day off; and 11 to 7 for six days, with the equivalent of three days off if one could manage to stay awake for about thirty hours after coming off the graveyard shift. My friend and I, both with B.S. degrees in chemistry, worked on the assembly line for several months. Once, on the graveyard shift before taking a Christmas furlough, we decided to set a record for samples processed. We worked across from each other straight through for eight feverish hours, leaving samples stacked up for following benches and shifts to work their way through in succeeding days.

A little later, the lab was moved to a barracks where it occupied a spacious, bright, airy room with stainless-steel trays embellishing the sense of cleanness. The process was then changed to a more efficient and simple solvent extraction. My friend and I were promoted to assistant foremen with responsibility for maintenance of lab equipment, solution preparation, clean-up of spills, making the analytical calculations and reports, and teaching new operators, all of whom were women. Here, I met my future wife who was living then in the little textile town of Loudon about thirty miles away. On our first date she stayed over with a girl-friend in one of the large two-story wooden dormitories which was operated like a college dormitory. We rode into Knoxville in a trailer bus, a long, windowless, stuffy, olive-drab, cattle car. A steak dinner at Regas was followed with conversation and coffee at the USO, a performance of the Knoxville Male Chorus, and then home by bus to a parting at the dormitory.

There were many activities available, including all the usual sports. Some attended churches and became acquainted with the people who lived in the little houses scattered on the hills. There was a crude, makeshift movie theater in the nearby shopping area that looked like a frontier town out of the B westerns that often showed there. Every evening many congregated at the post exchange to drink beer, eat ice cream and snacks, converse, and sometimes dance in a small space to tunes from a jukebox. Some had their own record players and record collections. One hutmate had a radio that provided news and entertainment. I spent much of my leisure time reading my books and keeping up with current events in newspapers and magazines.

I shall never forget an April day when we went to pick up a friend for dinner. We entered his hut and found him and his hutmates sitting with tears in their eyes, listening to a recording of the dirge from Beethoven's *Eroica*. Thus I learned that President Roosevelt had died.

On off days a friend and I often hitchhiked, especially on the long break between graveyard and day shifts. We roamed far afield with the help of our thumbs. Being a college boy from a midwestern city, I was enchanted by the hill people, the rural and rugged terrain of East Tennessee. We went as far south as Chattanooga for a gaze at Lookout Mountain. On the way, in the truck of a gaunt, grizzled farmer who was hauling pigs to market, we passed through Dayton and he pointed out the courthouse where Clarence Darrow and William Jennings Bryan had made history. Once, we got as far into Virginia as Lynchburg. Another time, we hitched a ride into Knoxville for a Thanksgiving dinner, no adequate place being available in Oak Ridge. We saw the Loudon and Norris TVA dams and swam from a civilian friend's boat in Norris Lake. We explored the Smokies and saw Gatlinburg, riding horses down the middle of the main street. After meeting my future wife, I hitched rides to and from Loudon, and she sometimes hitchhiked with me, once riding in the back of a pickup with a farmer's kids, all of us bouncing about on the flatbed.

Things were different then. The people were united by the war and by a common cause, for it seemed to us that this was a war as moral as any war could be. People were friendly and sharing. "Give a soldier a ride," the posters said, and almost everyone did. It was a good way to see the country with a sense of adventure and suspense, not always knowing or caring where you were going or how you would get there.

Later, I acquired a 1932 Chevrolet in which we toured the area—my future wife and I. One midsummer day in the Smokies inspired a poem from which the following fragment is taken:

> Riding the horses in a mountain vale
> Regaled by wildflowers along the trail;
> Sitting by the bank of a pristine stream
> Imbrued in the shade of a mountain glade
> With lunch of fried chicken your mother made;
> Roaming at leisure an upland pasture
> And petting a calf with rustic rapture;
> Then, country ham at a crossroads cafe
> And driving home in an old Chevrolet.

There came an August night when shouts of "Extra! Extra!" were heard from paper boys on the streets of Y-12. We stopped work and dashed from the buildings to learn from large blaring headlines what we had been doing. We were too naive, perhaps, and too immersed in the present to be horrified by the event and its future implications. The general emotion was pride that we had made such a significant contribution to the war effort and a joyful conviction that the war was near an end. And we soldiers anticipated an end to the chafing, often insulting, petty regimen of army life. Within less than a month, the war did end. Marriage followed a week later in a little frame church in Loudon with the letters CP over the door, letters which I appropriately interpreted as "chemically pure," but which my wife informed me signified Cumberland Presbyterian. I left my three male hutmates and the square hut in the barracks area for a wife and one-half of a little furnished square hut—a duplex with a bedroom, shower stall, and kitchen—in the rolling hills of the residential area. Seven more months of a more conventional life were to pass before my discharge from the army. Then, farewells followed and a journey north to resume pursuit of goals postponed for three years of unplanned, unanticipated adventure and romance.

COMMUNITY LIFE

Courtesy James E. Westcott

133

THE SCHOOLS OF
OAK RIDGE

Marion Alexander

Today people who were associated with the early Oak Ridge schools remember them only in a positive sense. The concerted opinion, in fact, is one of praise: "they were fun," "the teachers were wonderful," "the administrators were superior," "everybody learned," "they were the best in the state, maybe even the nation." Building the schools in Oak Ridge was a success story like the building of the atom bomb.

Certainly, the schools opened under the most harried, hasty, and adverse conditions that the devil himself could have devised. There were no buildings, no books, no furniture, and in October 1943, only 637 students.

The magic that got the schools opened on October 4, 1943, only a month after the designated time, was hard work and persistence, part of the character of the frontier town. The first ones to open in the town were Robertsville (an old school that had come with the territory), Elm Grove elementary, and the high school which stood on the hill above Jackson Square. Pine Valley elementary opened in late November 1943, and Cedar Hill elementary in late winter 1944.

One of the main reasons for the success of the Oak Ridge schools was its first superintendent, Dr. Alden Blankenship. Recruited by the army from Columbia University early in 1943, Dr. Blankenship, a former football player, undoubtedly had charisma. He has been described by the teachers he hired as inspirational, reassuring, and supportive. The exact directive his employer gave him is unknown, but evidently his mission was to build a school system that would obtain and hold parents in this rugged frontier town. One of his important qualifications was his ability to recruit good people. One administrator has noted, "he had a kind of antenna that found good people," and in addition, the kind of personal magnetism that kept them. One teacher said, "He listened. After you talked to him, you felt like you could solve your problems."

Problems did arise, too. Obviously when Dr. Blankenship recruited staff, he could not promise them an easy job. Like most people working to win the war, school employees toiled long hours. They performed fatiguing work, confronted dozens of new students each week, and spent much time fashioning a good curriculum. The staff, like the students, arrived from all points of the country, though most of them came from Tennessee and the nearby states. Dr. Blankenship did a lot of recruiting from Peabody Teachers College in Nashville and from the Universities of Tennessee and Kentucky.

One of the first librarians described the scene she came to in 1943: "There wasn't much to be seen but bulldozers and bare earth." Dr. Blankenship pointed out to her the site where the high school would be; they visited the existing Robertsville school of red brick with four rooms downstairs and four rooms upstairs. Dr. Blankenship's office was a cubbyhole in the Castle-on-the-Hill.

While the army engineers were simultaneously building the first schools and the 3,000 cemesto houses, Dr. Blankenship was, in addition to recruiting and overseeing the schools, holding workshops for his new teachers. Sometimes he did this on Sunday evenings at his home.

The first staff in place when school opened has been variously numbered from seventy-five to ninety. Dr. Blankenship requested that by September 1, his employees give him in writing their personal philosophy of education. According to Sarah Ketron, his own philosophy was that every child is unique and important. Curriculum guides from many schools were studied, and the first curriculum coordinator, Mildred Kidd, also from Columbia University, compiled a curriculum guide as large as "the Sears

Roebuck catalog."

From Dr. Blankenship's belief that teachers should improve themselves while they taught, teachers' inservice training was established. Until a Wednesday afternoon inservice time was approved in 1970, teachers and administrators worked one Saturday morning each month. Additional training was added to the faculty meetings in all schools every Wednesday afternoon after the children had been dismissed. Much of the inservice was cooperative: teachers shared their ideas and projects; they initiated enrichment activities for grade levels and for departments; and they worked on solving the building problems. Curriculum guides were changed, added to, and improved. The professional staff was encouraged to attend summer school and to take courses for advanced degrees. Salary increases were incentives for acquiring additional graduate hours and the master's degree.

The attitude that shines through many reminiscences of those days is that the staff had worked hard and long for the love of it: "It was exciting ... Dr. Blankenship was wonderful ... Dr. B. made you feel as though you were an important part." One teacher said, "I'll tell you why the schools were good. It's because the teachers were encouraged to teach and because no one ever questioned your ability to perform in the classroom." Dr. Blankenship, large, energetic, and outgoing, was not dubbed "the pied piper of Oak Ridge" for nothing.

The staff not only built curriculum while they were adding four thousand students to the rolls; they unloaded furniture and carried it into the classrooms. The textbooks and library books had been ordered from the Tennessee Book Company in Nashville, but had not been delivered to the schools by the time they opened. Dr. Blankenship himself hunted for these books and one Sunday found them in a warehouse. Great boxes of them, sealed tight, sat there stored away. When the librarian discovered that a carpenter on the site could not open them because of union rules, she and a group of Pine Valley teachers set about prying open the boxes with their own hands, getting possession of the books they needed.

Some teachers and administrators, always in waiting, worked as substitutes. Since the schools had no telephones, substitutes had to be called for and then delivered to the school by someone on the staff who cooled "his" heels while "she" got dressed.

The first-year teachers were added as enrollment increased. Many of them were single, some of them were scientists' wives, and all of them taught the best way they could in the face of hammering and sawing in the next room, machines raising the dust outside where trailer housing was "sprouting up like mushrooms," or while custodians scraped the mud from the floors.

One incentive Dr. Blankenship could offer was more money than they could have earned elsewhere in Tennessee or in the surrounding states. The salaries were comparable to those paid in New York. Even if supplies were slow in coming, money was not lacking for anything needed. Still, while money can certainly contribute to good education, it was not everything. The exuberance and sense of mission in Oak Ridge seems to have been much more important.

Most students responded to this dedicated work by finding it "wonderful to go to school." Like the teachers and the administrators, the students came from "all over" and had a fine time learning each other's accents and speech patterns. There was no snobbery (everyone was living with shortages), and if there was placement according to ability, the students were not aware of it. For the most part, students did not know what their friend's father did for a living. They came to school on free buses with guards to take care of them.

There were various learning activities on the elementary level. Some students put on skits and plays, others had a shop class and learned to use tools, and others had a fractions class where water was poured from different sized containers. Enrichment classes in art and music were routine, and every student had physical education. "The classes were exciting because there was something new to do all the time." As their talents matured, their dramatic efforts became more sophisticated. One eighth grade class performed "HMS Pinafore."

At the high school, student activity expanded somewhat. On Saturday mornings students went to the local radio station and played records, told stories, acted in skits, and announced the community news. The first graduating class in 1944, numbering twenty-five with seven of them graduating at midterm, published a kind of yearbook entitled *Oak Leaf.*

In addition to starting a school newspaper, the students organized several clubs. There was a Library Club, an Art Club, a Home Economics Club, a Dramatic Club which presented three one-act plays in January, the Band, the Girl Reserves, and a Student Council. The school had no football team the first year, but basketball, track, and boxing teams competed with other schools and in intramural tournaments. Four girl cheerleaders were there to yell them on. Twenty-five faculty members were photographed in a group with Dr. Blankenship, whose office was now in the high school building.

The next school year, 1944-45, the football team, coached by Ben Martin and John Francis, organized and soon became famous. Visiting teams liked to play at Blankenship Field because of its good turf. Before the fences came down, visiting teams created one more problem for the high school principal. Every passenger on the bus had to have a pass and the passes had to be checked at the gates. Invariably a booster or a parent would sneak on the bus without a pass, and then the principal had to go to the gate and attend to the uproar with the security guards. Those first high school principals often worked sixteen-hour days.

Another duty of the principals was to schedule community events. Every organization in town, and there were hundreds, used the school buildings as meeting places. Everything from church to hoedowns was held in the schoolrooms or the gyms. Once some folkdancers were scheduled at eight p.m. to follow a church service, but that evening the minister prayed overlong and the dancers grew impatient—they had only an hour, too. They set up their record player, and the instant the preacher pronounced "amen," the music began.

None of the former students deny that the fun of going to school included working on lessons. Academic excellence was emphasized, and the teachers expected good work from them. High school core classes, in session for two hours—combining studies in language and history—were adopted from a plan used by Berea College, and they became respected for the high level of interest they engendered in the students. Dr. Earl Strobein, director of audio-visual education, filmed the core class taught by Francelle Jarrard (Buckminster) and showed the movie at teachers' meetings in Knoxville and Nashville. The Oak Ridge

139

schools were gaining a reputation in Tennessee and in surrounding states, and envy for their money and accomplishments was not unknown.

The old Oak Ridge High School which sat just above Townsite (later named Jackson Square.)

In the school year 1945-46, after the atom bomb was announced, high school students, under the leadership of Philip Kennedy, an English teacher from West Virginia, organized the Youth Council on the Atomic Crisis. By March 1946, 171 students had joined the council to "promote responsible citizenship in the atomic age." The club's purpose was to "urge responsible men to prevent destructive use of atomic energy." Members of the club with the *Oak Leaf* staff prepared an issue of the paper for national circulation to high schools. The articles promoted "constructive action toward control of atomic energy."

Parents, too, were supportive. Mr. Herbert Dodd recalls how the parents would visit the schools. "They expected a lot, but they treated us with great respect, assuming that we were as good in our field as they were in theirs." The Service Club, organized in February 1944, had for its purpose, "to bring teachers, students, and parents to a better understanding of each other." The 1946 yearbook, the *Oak Log*, noted that the Service Club "has been slightly disorganized by people moving away from Oak Ridge every day." One parent who stayed here said, "Oh, yes, they were good. Blankenship was topnotch and we had so much that other Tennessee schools didn't have, like a good guidance program." Very early

140

Courtesy Department of Energy   Westcott Photo

Students walk up the boardwalk to the old Oak Ridge High School.

141

citizens were elected to a parents advisory council in lieu of a board of education. After incorporation in 1959, when the first board of education was elected, some of the most competent citizens in town ran for the five seats.

Through the years, the Oak Ridge schools have had rather a tumultuous history with schools opening and closing, with enrollment rising and falling. In February 1945, the enrollment was 8,043 students. By September the number had dropped to 7,354, a loss of almost 700 students. In 1950 enrollment fell to 6,354 pupils when St. Mary's Catholic Church opened an elementary school. The school population peaked in September 1954, at 8,117. The largest graduating classes were in the mid-1960s, with well over 600 for several years. Not until 1971 did enrollment again fall below 7,000. Oak Ridgers were young and educating their children was a serious business, the second biggest in town.

Through these up and down years, however, the Oak Ridge schools were always looked upon with envy and emulation. A present administrator, who came in 1947 as a mathematics teacher, put it this way: "It could not be compared to any other place. So much was offered that other schools didn't have. You didn't have to bargain for your salary, there was no nepotism, no old established organization who ran things, no push and pull and jockeying for position. Getting a job didn't depend on who you knew."

It may be that the excellence of the schools resulted from the army's decision to translate the schools into human dimensions: teachers who were free to teach, administrators who trusted their staff, parents who cared about the system, and students who were inspired by all these things. The decision makers obviously loved building a new life in a new town.

FROM BULLETIN TO BROADSIDE

June Adamson

A s in colonial times of early America, amidst shortages, hardships, and censorship, the first semblance of a newspaper in Oak Ridge came into being "by authority." In this case the authority was the Army Corps of Engineers, the government in charge in 1943.

The "by authority" was benevolent, but it was there just the same, and there was strong influence upon the kind of newspaper produced, and upon its service to the town. The first and second War Powers Acts of 1941 and 1942 were enforced at the conception of the town, and any information concerning military activity was forbidden. The code of federal regulations passed in 1943 warned that "some sacrifice of the journalistic enterprise of ordinary times" would be necessary. This applied to newspapers across the country, not just the one started in Oak Ridge.

How does a newspaper grow in an atmosphere of wartime secrecy, amidst security "hush-hush" even when the war is over? What purpose does it really serve when it is completely subsidized and published "by authority" of the military?

The early *Oak Ridge Journal* could hardly be termed a real newspaper as definitions of modern newspapers go. Pages of the bulletin size communication, mimeographed and folded, measured only about seven by eight inches. The four to eight pages were printed on both sides, occasionally upside down. It contained such things as movie reviews, schedules of events at Townsite, and news about other neighborhoods scattered through the hills of Black Oak Ridge—each one hidden from the other. It even told what the army was doing about some things—as much, that is, as army authorities wanted people to know. For the newspaper bulletin had grown out of a need the army recognized—that the thousands who had been brought from the forty-eight states during those years needed some source of reliable information. As in colonial times, early Oak Ridgers were very dependent upon neighbors and newfound friends for many things, including information. But unlike those early colonists, it was not for news "back home" that was needed. That could be read in hometown newspapers and from Knoxville newspapers that residents began to buy. What was needed was information about this community.

Oak Ridge in 1943 and 1944 was one huge rumor factory. Unbelievable rumors ran rampant about what the army was going to do next that affected everyone in this primitive, strange, and hastily constructed town. It was a sprawling, mixed-up, wartime world of superbrains and superbrawn; slide rules and bulldozers. In this bizarre community, a Ph.D. lived next door to a muscle-bound construction worker with a grade school education, and as in my husband's case, a GI next to an army colonel, and the top man on the "project" at that. These were the people this little bulletin began to serve.

The first issue of the *Oak Ridge Journal* appeared in September 1943 and contained a page one editorial written by an army officer expressing the hope that "you will strive to advance the development of the town of Oak Ridge in order that the war effort may go on at full pace."

Sergeant Murray Levine was the first editor. He told how he put a staff of WACs to work gathering the news of the community—the "rec" hall schedules, church services, and other activities being started. He said he wrote some of the editorials—including one advising residents to take a "Pollyanna" view of conditions and to consider Oak Ridge as home. He told how many of those first *Journals* were delivered by horseback, again as the first circulation system in colonial America. Later, when postal service was established in Oak Ridge, newspapers were mailed to all households. And those words, "By authority," had an impact again, as under the masthead read those security-minded words:

"Published For Oak Ridge: Keep it here Please." or: "Not to be taken from the CEW (Clinton Engineering Works) Area."

The first printed issue of the *Oak Ridge Journal* appeared March 2, 1944. It was now nine inches by twelve inches in size. A. Carleton Jealous was appointed editor and general manager by the civilian agency set up by the army to run the town. Jealous assumed editorial duties on a part-time basis in addition to his main job as a chemist at one of the plants. It was a moonlighting job in reverse for him, since he was on the nightshift at the plant and did his newspaper work during the day. He was picked as editor because he had been one of a loyal group of volunteer writers and editors of the first little bulletin *Journal* and had worked hard to produce something more professional. It was with no reluctance that he gave the job up after only a few months because he couldn't do both.

By early 1944 the army powers saw the need for something even more professional, so Frances Smith Gates was named editor and Richard B. Gehman was assistant editor. The new *Oak Ridge Journal*, by now tabloid size, appeared with the issue of June 23, 1944.

Mrs. Gates often said her "taking over" from Jealous was an accident. Widowed when her West Point career officer husband was killed, Mrs. Gates had come to Oak Ridge in a general public relations capacity to "whittle" away at the problems of keeping workers content. She wrote reports on dormitories, quality of milk, shopping facilities, and schools. One report had to do with the need for a better newspaper, one that would give more coverage on the town's activities, more communication with the top brass, more explanation of government decisions and regulations, more plugging of worthwhile opportunities, and as a medium for buying and selling through classified ads. There was fast action on this from Washington, and Mrs. Gates was asked to be the editor. She was reluctant because her professional experience had been limited to public relations. But she became editor, while the professionalism was filled by ordering the late Richard B. Gehman to Oak Ridge.

Thomas Francis Xavier McCarthy was the last editor of the *Oak Ridge Journal* and later the managing editor of the ill-fated first independent newspaper, the *Oak Ridge Times*. He had come to Tennessee as a civilian to handle selective service problems for one of the plants. "I had been turned down by the draft, so I thought why not go to this marvelous project. It'll be a war job and I'll see the world." McCarthy, a native New Yorker, really never got over his wonder of Tennessee. It was a culture shock, but of the best kind, as he discovered the trees and the woods and the whole out-of-doors, as well as the strange mixture of people in this new community. He wrote of his first impressions of Oak Ridge and of many other things in "McCarthy's Corner," a column for the *Oak Ridge Journal* under Mrs. Gates. That's how he got his foot in the door of journalism, through that column. He tells that very frankly: "K-25 officials had decided there should be a plant paper even before the war ended, and I was tapped to edit it. They had me pegged as an 'old newspaperman' because of that column, and I didn't enlighten them." Gehman gave him a few easy lessons, followed by screams every now and then of "Hey, you can't do that"—or—"Maybe you can."

As for what could be printed in those "By authority" days, one *Oak Ridge Journal* told the policy:

> Editorial policy under this regime has been, and continues to be determined by the United States Engineering Department in any controversial issue. However, the editorial staff is allowed a maximum of freedom in reporting the news as they see it. The content of the news has always been limited to Oak Ridge events and personalities. No effort is made to cover outside events and news except in so far as it affects the Oak Ridge Community. An effort is made to concentrate on future events, rather than to report past ones.

Even as the *Journal* grew to something more closely resembling a newspaper, stories were local and generally innocuous. No wire service was used. Great care was given to matters of security, for whereas early bulletins listed such things as the number of doctors in town, no statistics nor demographic information was allowed in the later *Journals*. Army officers were quick to ban anything that might give outsiders the least hint of how many or what kind of persons lived in Oak Ridge.

Fran Gates said, "Yes, we took our copy to be checked by army officers every week, but it was superficial. After all, I was

Frances Smith Gates at her desk. She was editor of the first newspaper in Oak Ridge, the *Oak Ridge Journal*.

pro-army by background and had been hired by the army to do a job. If I was in doubt about the acceptability of a story I usually asked. I didn't try to defy them." She did tell of getting into difficulty a couple of times. "One time we ran a human interest feature on two little boys who produced a comic strip in a home shop and sold it for a neat profit. We even showed one sequence in illustration. One of the characters was 'Atom Man.' I was reprimanded for letting that sneak in. Even if I had no inkling of what was going on in Oak Ridge, that would have been a vital hint."

Another time she got into trouble while doing an interview series on dormitory residents. "We stumbled on the information that there were 17 Ph.D.'s, all soldiers, all scientists, in one dormitory." She told of two other times she remembered being chastized. "I got wind of a big addition being added to the hospital—got the story with dates and figures, got it cleared, printed it, then got bawled out because the story appeared before General Leslie Groves in Washington had approved it."

The kind of information found in those early newspapers was mainly news of stores, of public health clinics, of churches, of new businesses starting. But a careful study of those early papers shows that much can be learned about the city despite restrictions. The fact that early Oak Ridge had a system very close to socialized medicine during its army occupation is indicated in the medical service information carried in one early bulletin. It called attention to eleven highly recommended physicians—six certified in specialities, including psychiatry, "entrusted with the well being of the community."

That the army had a slogan—"An Effort Will be Made"—whenever there was a complaint from any citizen, particularly civilian workers, was also very apparent in those early *Journals.* One of the most famous editorals in Oak Ridge journalism history appeared in September 1943. It has been reprinted many times since then. It began:

"Yes, we know it's muddy—you think prices are too high in the grocery store—coal has not been delivered—it takes six days to get your laundry done ..." and on and on in a similar vein. Then: "But what you want to know is *What's Being Done About It?* Well, roads will be paved—the grocers are obligated not to charge prices in excess of those in Knoxville and a constant check is maintained—coal will be delivered—sidewalks will be laid—a third shift will be started in the laundry as soon as we can get help ..." The editorial concluded, "We would have planned it differently too if we'd thought of it in '33." And finally, "We are at war— Sherman was right."

But what was not printed in those early newspapers? So far as the *Oak Ridge Journal* was concerned, no one was born and no one died between 1944 and 1946. Certainly, the baby boom that occurred at Oak Ridge Hospital during those years would have statistically exaggerated the scope and size of the operation. There were actually very few deaths, the town being one of young and healthy individuals. The town had no mortuaries and no grave-yards except those abandoned by farmers who lived there prior to Oak Ridge, and these were fenced in and seldom used again, although cared for. That there was crime and violence, if only on a very low scale, was also kept entirely out of the newspaper. Sui-cides were kept out of the newspaper too, even one of a prominent army officer's wife.

Mrs. Gates remembered that certain names were also forbid-den. There was one occasion when a picture of a group from the Woman's Club could not be used in connection with a story. The reason was that one of the women in the picture was Mrs. Arthur Holly Compton, wife of the late world famous Nobel prize-winning physicist who played an important role in the develop-ment of atomic energy. The Comptons virtually commuted from Chicago to Oak Ridge during the war years, but when "in resi-dence" in Tennessee were supposed to be known as the Arthur Hollys, a rather thin disguise. It was feared that if her picture appeared in the newspaper, even under that name, that that paper might fall into the wrong hands.

Younger persons who did not live through those times find it hard to understand why more newspapers were not sent to rela-tives in other places, why Oak Ridgers cooperated so fully in matters of security. But it was so, in spite of some leaks that did get out. And it was true that war loan drives were important page one news too, since everyone in Oak Ridge felt and were constantly reminded of the importance of the war effort, even when most of them didn't know what their individual efforts meant. Traffic safety awards made news too, though most Ridgers lived in ignorance of another kind of safety record being made behind the secret fences of the plants, where all sorts of potentially dangerous jobs were being carried out.

One of the biggest national news breaks of the war years was the story of the death of President Franklin Delano Roosevelt. The *Oak Ridge Journal*, being a weekly, could not report the news until several days after it happened. But the news stirred citizens deeply, the more so because a persistent rumor had prevailed again that April that President Roosevelt had visited Oak Ridge. Actually he had not, but the Secretary of War Henry L. Stimpson had. Enough persons had caught a glimpse of Stimpson being helped in and out of cars, always encircled by army MPs, to lend credence to the rumor.

The greatest news break for Oak Ridge—the news of what the city was really all about—the atomic bomb—was also late being printed in the *Oak Ridge Journal*. For though Knoxville papers, along with other papers, printed rare extras on bright-colored newsprint and with double banner seventy-two-point headlines, that Monday in August when Truman revealed that an atomic bomb had been loosed upon Japan, the *Oak Ridge Journal* did not print the news until the following Thursday. Mrs. Gates said, "No, we didn't think of getting out an extra. I was teased about the whole world scooping us on our own story, but there was enough glory for everyone, enough excitement to keep us buoyed up. Our staff was 'used to' briefing the armies of visiting journalists who descended upon Oak Ridge." These included Daniel Land of the *New Yorker* and William L. Laurence, the former *New York Times* reporter and the only newsman to witness the first atomic bomb test. So Ridgers scrambled that Monday, August 6, 1945, to buy the extras of Knoxville newspapers announcing "Power of Oak Ridge Atomic Bomb Hits Japan."

An *Oak Ridge Journal* editorial the following week commented, "More has been written about Oak Ridge in newspapers and magazines of the nation during the past week than in the two years of its existence. The fact that the story of the secret city is now known to the world will not materially affect our editorial policy. We are dedicated to one purpose: to reflect your life here, your activities, your problems, your spirit ..."

From its beginning, whatever the content, the *Journal* was welcomed by news-starved workers, and became even more welcomed as it grew. It gave husbands and wives something to discuss, for as indicated, shop talk was off limits, and women without war jobs were living closed-in, isolated lives. They especially waited for the postman each Thursday and read the *Journal* avidly whatever the content. However, much of it was well written and even clever, even though throughout the war years and immediately following, there was exclusive use of local feature material—no really "hard news." Gates, Gehman, McCarthy, and others contributed regularly to a column called "Oak Leaves," a hodge-podge of miscellany that sometimes included the briefest details of a wedding. Sometimes the catch-all column contained a request for an old mystery novel or two for the Red Cross; sometimes the request was from new organizations. For instance there was the optional riding club wanting to know how many persons would join if horses were available. There were occasional items about such esoteric groups as the African Violet Club and the Music Listening Society.

There was a continuing feature that claimed widespread attention and one that proves the old adage that people are hungry to read about people. Entitled, "You're in the News," it was a weekly personality sketch about some person in Oak Ridge. Mrs. Gates remembered that it was eagerly awaited each week. She said of it, "We tried to keep it well laced with 'little guys' as well as some occasional 'big guys,' the biggest ones mostly after the secrecy was over." She also remembered the development of the letters to the editor department where readers could air their gripes, but this section did not come about without considerable argument with those in authority. The gripes did not get into the national security area. Editors Gates and Gehman—and the army authorities—had the last word.

But back to the growth of that newspaper. George Chandler, the Knoxville printer, recalled that the tabloid size *Oak Ridge Journal* was printed on sheet-fed presses—eight pages on one press, four on another, hand fed and hand folded. "By 1947 they wanted to make the paper bigger and I had gone as far as I could go. I had trouble buying anything—I couldn't get machines—had a hard time getting newsprint." However, Chandler made a deal to buy out a printing company in Knoxville, and he located a press in Kansas capable of printing a sixteen-page broadside. Not everyone in Oak Ridge was happy about the change. The week after the first broadside issue was printed, a story on page one of the *Journal* was headlined, "Journal Expanded Size Stirs Pride With Regret." It was reported, "After seeing the full grown *Journal* last week, Ridgers had mixed feelings of pride and sadness—not unlike that of a mother who first sees her son in long pants." But those "in authority" expressed pride. This was shown in another article noting, "In the administration building everyone held up the eight full-fledged columns of the *Journal* for careful measurement comparison with the Knoxville newspapers."

As for advertising, there was some, but at first not in the usual sense. Since only a few stores had been built when the first bulletin was printed, only a few classified want ads were carried, mostly for such things as a room for rent. As the paper grew, classified advertising was one of its main reasons for being. Mrs. Gates said, "We were subsidized, but the subsidy decreased as time went on, because of advertising. We had a terrific demand for advertising space and could have sold ten times more than we did." She insisted on at least sixty percent news and forty percent advertising ratio, however, and "our advertising manager spent more time mollifying businessmen who wanted more space than she did selling." Mrs. Gates expressed the opinion, "One of the great services of the *Oak Ridge Journal* was its classified ads."

So while at first the army subsidized the newspaper completely, later advertising helped to pay the cost. But how much did it cost to run that newspaper? Mrs. Gates said, "When the Atomic Energy Commission moved in they welcomed a healthy local weekly and cooperated fully with the operation. I had to submit budgets and abide by them, but by that time the subsidy was minor." She also said she had begun plugging for a printing plant in Oak Ridge, and there were a few persons interested in backing that idea privately. But she said in her opinion the AEC was thinking in terms of commercial journalism and was stalling for time.

When quizzed about the paper's financial support, McCarthy shook his head. "I have no idea how much it cost to run that paper. I never saw financial figures. All bills were sent to the AEC. If we wanted a raise for someone, we asked the AEC, and either we got it or we didn't. I don't know anyone's salary except mine—it was around $4500 a year." McCarthy said he did know that the figure $25,000 a year was tossed around. AEC officials kept saying Oak Ridge had to have an independent newspaper—they couldn't go on spending this amount to give a newspaper away. McCarthy agreed that $25,000 sounds low, even for then, and impossible if it included salaries; but he had no idea how much additional revenue was added from advertising income since that was automatically turned over to the AEC when he was editor.

So-called normalcy in journalism was slow in coming to Oak Ridge. But by the spring of 1948, the idea of normalcy was strongly promoted. Newspaper editorials and AEC proclamations were talking "transition" and "a reduction of federal subsidy." It was not mentioned specifically, but the *Journal* was one thing the AEC planned to eliminate. Then the announcement came that there would be an independent daily newspaper called the *Oak Ridge Times*, to be published daily by the Chandler-Waters Company. And for the first time the newspaper would not be "by authority." Chandler wrote then, "There will be no control of its contents except that dictated by good taste and good judgment." Chandler apparently did not have the resources required to keep a newspaper going until it got "out of the red," but he blamed it on a lack of support by advertisers. He also joked that his editors were "used to spending government money and were a bit high-handed about spending mine." But one thing was certain: it was the end of "by authority" journalism in Oak Ridge.

McCarthy, who had been final editor of the *Oak Ridge Journal*, became managing editor of the new daily, the *Oak Ridge Times*. He told of his regrets that that newspaper lasted such a short time. "It was all of a sudden—pow—we quit. I was as shocked as anyone. I wish it had continued. It was literate and it was getting better. It takes time to make money."

From June 22, 1948 to September 20, 1948, Oak Ridge had no newspaper at all. This dry spell again convinced Ridgers of the need for a community newspaper. Rumors flew again about the future of the plants and the future of the town. The grapevine worked overtime, and everyone felt insecure. By September there was another weekly, but not so much a newspaper as an advertising handout. This was printed until January 1949, and it did not fill the need for solid news information even to the extent that the "by authority" *Oak Ridge Journal* had. The final issue of this handout, called *The Mail*, announced the coming of *The Oak Ridger*. The news of a new five-day-a-week newspaper was welcome to everyone and was much talked about.

While scarcity and shortages were key words during the early years of this secret city in Tennessee, so was "serendipity"—even in the printing of the newspaper. As Fran Gates said, "It was a real challenge to produce a paper that was lively, interesting, readable, when we could not mention the thing that interested us most—what we were really doing in Oak Ridge. It was a great adventure."

The *Oak Ridge Journal* often reflected what early comers still remember as the very special flavor of a boom town that was partly army camp and partly college campus in atmosphere—and eventually a hometown for many. The final editorial Dick Gehman wrote for the *Journal*, before going to New York to make his fortune in writing, conveys some of this. Under the title, "Summing up," he wrote: "At first it seemed that Oak Ridge was simply a place where people had come to work—a cheerful, embattled spirit upon the atmosphere, to be sure—but no sense of achievement, no consciousness of the place of Oak Ridge in the affairs of the nation and the world." But he concluded, "such is not the case today...."

"MUSIC MAKING" ON THE RIDGE

Jacinta K. Howard

In the latter half of 1943, the musical life of Oak Ridge began to flourish as enthusiastically as the growth of the new city. People who sang and played instruments were eager to make music. This need was especially felt by dormitory residents who were bored and in search of a way to leave their bleak rooms to play or sing in a "house." As one early Oak Ridger expressed it, "In the beginning, if you wanted music, any kind of music, you had to go out and make it yourself." So those first citizens of Oak Ridge did just that.

There were performers and there were listeners. The performers joined together in various instrumental combinations and vocal groups. The listeners were just as dedicated, and they formed record listening groups that met at each other's homes. People were seen either carrying music stands and music, or records and pillows (the latter being a prerequisite for floor sitting since there was never enough furniture). Record listening, indeed, became so popular that home living rooms soon could not accommodate the increasing number of listeners. That activity then moved to the Community Center (later called Ridge Recreation Hall) across from Town Hall in Jackson Square.

The end result of this togetherness by the performers was, of course, free public concerts by these groups and by the larger groups which grew out of them—the Oak Ridge Symphony, the Oak Ridge Chorus, and the Concert Band.

By spring of 1944, the umbrella for all music groups was an organization called The Music Society, whose aims were "to provide the enjoyment of music making to its members, to present programs of serious music to the residents of Oak Ridge and to co-operate in all respects with the other groups which comprise the Society." These groups were represented by:

Waldo Cohn (director of the Symphony)
Frank Stratton (director of the Chorus)
De Forrest Beers (director of the Band)
John Van Wazer (director of the Small Ensemble Series)
Anne Metcalf (director of the Women's Madrigal Singers)
Edward Bunn (director of the Brass and Woodwind Choir)
Jacinta Howard (representing the String Ensembles)

The Music Society, which in 1947 changed its name to the Oak Ridge Civic Music Association with an elected board of directors, was sponsored by a civilian-run Recreation and Welfare Association, including a representative of the army. This latter association recognized the importance of these musical groups to the cultural life of the city and aided them in solving the problems of equipment, such as pianos and rehearsal and concert space.

For a brief period in the fall of 1944, the chamber music performances took place at the Grove Recreation Hall, but when construction of the Ridge Recreation Hall at the corner of Broadway and Kentucky Avenue in Jackson Square was completed in late 1944, all the chamber music concerts were held there in the formally designated East Lounge. The change from the Grove "Rec" Hall to the Ridge "Rec" Hall prompted a comment by the music columnist in the army-controlled newspaper, *The Oak Ridge Journal*, that "one of the greatest charms of Oak Ridge is the fact that everything is always being reorganized."

At Ridge Hall all kinds of events took place—art shows, club meetings, church services, wedding receptions, dances, bridge tournaments, fairs and festivals—but it was especially the locale for chamber music held in the East Lounge. Concerts were presented there for years.

Soon the name of East Lounge was changed to the more descriptive name of "Green Room" because of its movable and comfortable green upholstered chairs. Its hardwood floors and walls provided good acoustics, and the many chamber music concerts presented here were always well attended. The musicians, in fact, took it upon themselves to provide a living room atmosphere by turning off the cold ceiling lights and providing a floor lamp which shed its mellow light upon the performers clustered around it. This lamp was the responsibility of the husband of one of the players, and he dutifully transported it, along with an extension cord, from home to hall whenever his wife played. It came to be a necessary piece of equipment and was "on loan" for other groups. The home atmosphere was further enhanced by arrangements of greenery gathered from the surrounding woods.

The chamber concerts given there soon became known as "coffee concerts" because of the coffee and cookies served afterwards, prepared by devoted listeners. Cookies were brought in by people who "signed up," and these were placed on two long tables, each with a samovar at one end for use as coffee servers. The coffee was made amidst the brooms and mops of the custodian's utility room, because that was where the water was.

The walls of the Green Room were periodically repainted, but the chairs remained the same until they and the floor took on a patina of age like comfortable old shoes. By the time Ridge Hall was demolished twenty-six years later, to make way for an office building, the old walls and shabby chairs had become old friends exuding warmth and friendliness. The Green Room will always be affectionately remembered by those who spent many happy hours there.

In addition to the concerts in the Green Room, chamber music was also an integral part of dedication ceremonies, anniversary celebrations, and scholarship benefits. The new town was trying hard to become a normal town. New buildings were erected to house the arts and sciences, and there was always inaugural music for the ceremonies and full-length concerts to help the students.

It was fitting then, when Oak Ridge celebrated its twenty-fifth anniversary in 1967, that there be a concert involving and honoring those who had participated in the June 16, 1944 concert of the Oak Ridge String Symphonette.

Listening to records in the Green Room.

In this aerial photograph can be seen the Chapel-On-The-Hill at the top, the Guest House (later called the Alexander) in the middle, and the Ridge "Rec" Hall at the bottom. The East Lounge of the "Rec" Hall was later called the Green Room.

THE SYMPHONY ORCHESTRA

June Adamson

Take one biochemist who loved to play cello and whose background included a great deal of orchestral and chamber music playing in his spare time. Mix him with physicists, chemists, engineers, physicians, secretaries, housewives, and soldiers who were like-minded about music. Plunk them all down in an alternatively muddy, dusty place that was Tennessee's newest city, even if very much secret at the time. And what resulted was good musical vibrations that have continued for forty-two years as the Oak Ridge Symphony Orchestra. The symphony is now the oldest "continuing" orchestra in the state, as noted by Governor Lamar Alexander when he was piano soloist with the symphony November 8, 1980.

The biochemist is Waldo Cohn, who arrived in Oak Ridge in 1943 with his cello as his only companion in the dormitory while he watched the city being built.

Cohn didn't bring along a dream of founding a symphony orchestra, but he did hope that he could round up enough musicians to play chamber music. In October 1943, he saw a small notice in the then mimeographed army bulletin called the *Oak Ridge Journal* asking for musicians to meet at a certain time and place. He went, and there he found Jacinta Howard and Phyllis Cannon, violinists. He still needed a viola player. No luck, but he soon met Herb Pomerance, another cellist, willing to play viola parts. And so a quartet was formed. It wasn't long before Dorothy

Silverman joined Cohn's Clinton Laboratory group as secretary, and he learned that she played violin as did her husband, Mike. This meant a string quartet—plus. More came, including servicemen assigned to Oak Ridge, some of them highly professional musicians, and just-for-fun rehearsals of string music began in the Cohn living room.

Courtesy Waldo Cohn

The Oak Ridge Symphony Orchestra around 1950, with Waldo Cohn conducting.

Both Cohn and Pomerance recalled the very first musical program in Oak Ridge played by the four musical pioneers. It was at the Chapel-on-the-Hill on December 19, 1943, the Sunday before Christmas. The newly formed choir sang Haydn's *Seven Last Words*, and with Pomerance playing the viola part on his cello, Cohn, the cello part, Jacinta Howard and Phyllis Cannon, violins, there was instrumental accompaniment to aid the piano accompaniment by Estelle Keys. Then the quartet played the slow movement of the Beethoven *Quartet Opus 135*, for the offertory. "We agreed that if the Reverend B. M. Larsen spoke too long, we'd just quit playing," Pomerance recalled. But the minister for the town's first organized, interdenominational church intended that the music speak for all faiths. He simply said, "It's better to give than to receive" and sat down.

The number of string players grew and grew, along with the population of Oak Ridge. As the musicians began having difficulty following Cohn's nodding head to keep musical time, he was prevailed upon to take up the baton. By June 16, 1944, the string group, now called the Oak Ridge Symphonette, was ready to present a public concert. The program included Mozart's *Eine Kleine Nacht Music*, Bach's *Passacaglia in C Minor*, and the main feature was the Bach *Concerto For Two Violins*, featuring Jacinta Howard and Sergeant Philip Karp as soloists. Mrs. Howard was the first concertmaster and among the first soloists when the full-fledged orchestra was formed a few months later. Sergeant Karp was among the many GIs assigned to the Special Engineer Detachment (SED) because of scientific or engineering training. Cohn recalled that there were about ten soldiers in the original orchestra and that when the war ended, there was quite a gap to fill.

When Cohn heard Karp "fiddling around" with the Mendelssohn *Violin Concerto in E* prior to one early symphony rehearsal, he asked, "Can you play that?" The somewhat "laid back" Karp answered, "You want Mendelssohn? Sure, I play Mendelssohn," and tossed off a cadenza on the spot. So, with a little discipline under the Cohn baton, Karp was the featured soloist in the symphony's first concert in November 1944. There were enough musicians in the community that no outside help was needed. "We even had four French horn players, including the late John Ramsey, who was among those to encourage the formation of a full symphony orchestra," said Cohn.

As has been pointed out, Karp was not the only soldier in the orchestra. Cohn smiled as he showed one picture in his scrapbook that makes it look as if the army, not musical ability, decided where they should sit in the orchestra. Karp, with his sergeant's three stripes, was at the first stand of violin, behind him a two-stripe corporal, and behind him a one-stripe private first class. There was at least one WAC in the orchestra also—Rita Eringer—who made a professional musical career after leaving Oak Ridge.

Although the army mainly contributed GIs to the symphony, there was one officer, Lieutenant Colonel Donald Williams, who was soloist in the Grieg *Piano Concerto*. That concert was memorable because every brass hat (as all officers were called), turned out "dressed to the nines" as the cliche goes. There was something of a "town-gown" split between those in uniform and the so-called highbrow scientists, so that orchestra members considered the presence of army officers at the concert a real coup.

Even with all volunteer players, creating an orchestra took hard work and money. Cohn was aware that the army had a Recreation and Welfare Department that ran the town's movie houses and bowling alleys. Any money from these endeavors was plowed into recreational activities. Because the great majority of people in town were not in uniform and could not be forced to stay on "the project," the army's slogan, "An Effort Will Be Made," was applied to nearly every form of recreation requested to keep workers happy, and this included music. Cohn had no problem at all when he took his list of music stands, tympani drums, oboes, symphony scores, and other essentials to the captain in charge. "Yes, it was a kind of socialism," Cohn recalled.

It was only socialism at first, however. After the war there was a great exodus; and during the next year the population dropped by half. The population of the symphony dropped too, with many of the most professional musicians taking off for civilian life. "We didn't know whether we'd have a town left, much less a symphony," several members recalled. Cohn was reluctant to try to continue, but was prevailed upon by a group of musicians, notably Alice Lyman, who had come to Oak Ridge as a school music teacher and band director. She formed a committee to help find musicians to fill the vacancies.

Cohn recalled that it became important to draw on Knoxville, and about 1947, when the University of Tennessee formed its first Department of Music and Arts, bringing David Van Vactor to head it, new music affiliations began. Van Vactor brought in George DeVine, bassoonist and musicologist, and William Starr, violinist. The Knoxville Symphony Orchestra, which had faded away during the war years, was revived, and the musical life of Knoxville grew. The late Bertha Walburn Clark began to play violin in Oak Ridge too, as did her husband, Harold. The couple was among the many players who came from Knoxville to play in Oak Ridge, and many in Oak Ridge returned the favor. There was no payment involved. "We needed each other," recalled Mary Cox, violinist turned violist. "A symphony orchestra had not been an easy thing to scare up in East Tennessee," Mrs. Cox added.

With the army having pulled the rug out from under music, Cohn decided that the answer to the audience problem was to sell the entire season in advance. He suggested that an Oak Ridge Civic Music Association be formed to sponsor symphony and chorus concerts, and to bring in outside professionals. With the staunch support of such persons as Dorothy Silverman, it was accomplished. Under the auspices of an organization called The Music Society some rather esoteric programs were heard. Spearheading these programs, later called "Coffee Concerts," were John Van Wazer and John and Myra Stratton, who were particularly interested in playing the ancient instruments they brought with them. Mary Winters, a singer and an early Oak Ridge Chorus member, was another active Oak Ridge Civic Music Association supporter. "So we struggled along for the first season," Cohn recalled.

Ridgers now had to pay for what had been free during the war years. But even during the "free" period seats were reserved. "I wanted concerts to be dignified with no mad scrambling for seats," Cohn said. He personally numbered 600 seats in the old high school auditorium where concerts were held, and those interested had to pick up tickets prior to concert time. Concerts were presented on two nights in those early years, and the symphony played to packed houses both nights. As Cohn chuckled, "After all, it was one of the few shows in town."

Anyone connected with the Oak Ridge Symphony from the beginning can recall the varied repertoire played, geared to what the musicians could play. Cohn had a good sense of the possible, but often challenged players to tackle things some thought they couldn't play. Although the classic three Bs, Bach, Beethoven, and Brahms, were standard fare, it might have been a long time before such music as Rimsky-Korsakoff's *Russian Easter Overture* was heard live in Oak Ridge except for the symphony. It was first played in 1945. Prokofiev's music was new for many players as well as listeners. Symphony members will never forget the performance of the Edward MacDowell *Indian Suite*. Mrs. MacDowell sent a telegram of congratulations to the symphony from the famed MacDowell Colony in New Hampshire. Other American composers whose works were played included LeRoy Anderson, Henry Cowell, Aaron Copland, Samuel Barber, LaMar Stringfield, and Virgil Thompson. David Van Vactor's compositions were played too, and he was flute soloist upon several occasions.

One unforgettable concert featured the premier of Arthur

Roberts' *Overture for the Dedication of a Nuclear Reactor*. Dedicated to the Oak Ridge Symphony, the performance received attention from such national publications as *Time* magazine and the San Francisco *Chronicle*. Its themes were based on the letters, A-E-C (for the now defunct Atomic Energy Commission), as well as letters and numbers symbolizing chemical elements. The discordant Cd chord (for Cadmium), played by nearly the entire orchestra, signified a shutdown of the reactor. Near the end of his eleven-year tenure as conductor, Cohn attended a workshop for community orchestra conductors, sponsored by Eugene Ormandy and the Philadelphia Symphony. After Cohn conducted the Philadelphia musicians in a work "they could play with their eyes closed," he handed them the score for the Roberts' *Overture*. He grinned as he said, "Now that was a feeling of power, watching them sit up and take notice to sight read that. It is a difficult piece."

The single outstanding memory of the symphony members was the Isaac Stern experience. "That was my most memorable moment, certainly," Cohn said. Mary Cox agreed: "I can honestly say that I played violin with Isaac Stern." It was because Cohn had played quartets with Stern that the world-renowned violinist agreed to come to Oak Ridge to help promote the new Civic Music Association for the small stipend that could be afforded.

"He interrupted a four-day vacation early in 1948 as a favor to me and to help," Cohn recalled. The Stern experience meant a marathon dress rehearsal on the afternoon of the concert. "It was a lesson on an individual basis for all of us," Alice Lyman remembered. She said Stern was asked what he thought of the symphony. He replied, "It was an experience." Stern, however, returned the next year to play another concert, and his interest in the symphony grew. In a 1984 letter he wrote that his playing of the Beethoven Violin Concerto in 1948 and subsequent visits were because of, as he wrote, "the enthusiasm and affection Waldo Cohn had for music and musicians. It was clear that he was bringing to Oak Ridge and the surrounding areas a knowledge of living with music as a part of the civilized way of life and giving the area a sense of participation ..."

There was participation, including student musicians from the high school, some of whom went on to make a profession of music. Most notable was the late Rhonda Lee Rhea, who concer-

Courtesy James E. Westcott

In February 1948 Isaac Stern visited the Atomic City and was soloist with the Oak Ridge Symphony Orchestra.

tized on both ancient and modern stringed instruments both in America and abroad.

One of the special memories cherished by Dorothy and Mike Silverman was the appearance of sixteen-year-old Samuel Sanders in the Rachmaninoff *Piano Concerto.* Dorothy had "discovered" the young brother of Mrs. Syndey Visner of Oak Ridge and featured him in an ORCMA sponsored Coffee Concert when he was only twelve. Now the complete professional, Sanders appears in solo recitals with the likes of Stern, Perlman, and other greats.

Then there was the time Percy Grainger, the Australian-born pianist, composer, conductor, appeared with the symphony in 1949. Three of his compositions were played: *Spoon River, Harvest Song,* and *Handel on the Strand.* He came back in 1950 at his own suggestion to perform his *Danish Folk Music Suite.* Mary Cox recalled that Grainger was a "wellness advocate" and a "jogger" before the terms were coined. He ate a whole grain breakfast and jogged around the Alexander Hotel and was ready for practice before most Oak Ridgers were up and about. "His two appearances here added greatly to the city's musical life," said Mrs. Cox, who saw to it that all her piano students had a chance to hear him. He also conducted his *The Merry Wedding* for chorus and orchestra. Old-time symphony players recalled playing with Yaltah Menuhin, the younger pianist sister of violinist Yehudi Menuhin. She was living in Knoxville while her husband was in the army, and again because of an old friendship between the Menuhin and Cohn families in their native California, she agreed to play the *Concerto in A Minor* by Mozart and the *Emperor Concerto* by Beethoven with the symphony.

Alice Lyman, long known as Oak Ridge's Ms. Music, recalled a performance of Dickens' *Christmas Carol*, accompanied by members of the symphony during the war years. The orchestra played in the "pit" in front of the stage for several operettas as well as for the Dickens play, but this time Lyman accidentally struck her violin against the first row of seats in the auditorium, jarred loose the neck of the instrument, causing the strings to lose tension. With every note that Alice played in the number, *Danse Macabre*, the pitch became lower (a real dance of death). Finally she swapped violins with someone behind her in the orchestra. The next day Herb Pomerance, always a kind of jack-of-all-trades and fixer of things for the symphony, came to her rescue by using the glue and clamps from the high school workshop and put the neck back in place.

Herb Pomerance also recalled that his marriage to the former Eleanor Hawk, a nonplaying member who was doing publicity work for the symphony, took place early in 1948 just before Isaac Stern was to play. It was really a symphony event. The late Paul Arow, a tympanist with the orchestra, performed the ceremony and Cohn was best man. The conductor's parting shot to the newlyweds was, "I don't care what you do on your honeymoon— just be back in time for the rehearsals and the concert," Pomerance remembered.

Although Cohn, the founder, was conductor for the longest time, eleven years, there have been seven others. When Cohn went to England for two years of scientific research, he turned the baton over to the late Anthony Raisis, the Oak Ridge High School music

167

teacher who was also a violinist of concert caliber, and who had considerable conducting experience. Although many in the symphony expected Cohn to take the baton again when he returned, he declined to do so and instead took his place in the cello section where he still plays today.

THE OAK RIDGE LIBRARY

Connie J. Green

I poured forth my first love on a strange object—an old army ambulance which rolled to the bottom of Waltham Lane once a week in the 1940s. The vehicle was painted to resemble a circus wagon; the sides were white with red and white tent poles painted on to support the gold-fringed red top of the ambulance. My sisters and I, along with all the other children on the lane, climbed metal steps into its shady interior. Inside, books lined the walls of the small room. A one-step wooden stool allowed us to examine those books beyond what we could comfortably reach. The tiny traveling library was a magic place. At six I was already in love with books, and here they were delivered in an abundance right to my door. I could leaf through the pages and choose what I wanted to keep until the van returned. Picking out books was never a problem for me. I would have kept them all if possible, so I was happy with whatever my eye lit upon.

I thought I had found heaven in the Oak Ridge Traveling Library.

It turned out I was smitten only with puppy love. The real thing bloomed the first time I walked into the library itself—a building whose exterior belied its contents. From its opening on May 29, 1944, until the new Civic Center was constructed in the late 1960s, the library was housed in one wing of an ordinary Oak Ridge recreation building. The building, flat and long, sided with green composition shingles, could have been any other building:

170

Town Hall, the cafeteria, or one of the many recreation halls.

On the outside it looked like all Oak Ridge buildings. Inside it was another matter. It was my traveling library multiplied by thousands. Bookshelves reached to the ceiling. More than a one-step stool would be required to reach all of these books. On my first visit I stood at the doorway in awe. How would I ever look through so many books? A librarian showed me the section for my age level. Life became a little more simple. Instead of choosing from fifty thousand, I could choose from a thousand or so. But I knew that someday I would explore the regions of the other books. Someday I would climb the stairs to the balcony. Then I would truly be grown up.

I considered myself unbelievably lucky when, in third grade, my family moved into a house on Tyson Road—one block from my beloved library. Now on summer days I walked to the library. From the glare of the street, I stepped into the dusky coolness of books. All was soft and quiet. The feelings I had then were akin to my feelings as an adult when I enter an ancient, majestic European cathedral—the sense that I am in the midst of the wisdom and secrets of the ages. I knew not only where books for my age were, but I also knew where my favorite authors were. I could find Elizabeth Enright's *The Saturdays, Then There Were Five, Thimble Summer;* Eleanor Estes' *The Moffats, Middle Moffat, Rufus M.;* Maud Hart Lovelace's *Betsy, Tacy, and Tib,* and *Down Town.* When I was going through a fairy-tale phase, I could march straight to the Brothers Grimm and their ilk. I never cared for the prettified versions of fairy tales, when wolves were converted into pleasant fellows who could get along with everyone. I wanted my fairy tales real—wolves who plunged into pots of boiling water or were slain by a woodsman. And I found them all on those beloved shelves in that drab little building.

My love affair with the library grew more intense with the years. By the time I was in sixth and seventh grades, I would happily have given myself entirely to the library—moved in with the bare necessities and read my way hungrily down aisle after aisle of book-filled shelves. Throughout my elementary and high school days, I haunted the public library. During the school year I used the school libraries, but still I turned to the public library for those books I couldn't find at school or simply for the feeling of a special place where so much wisdom was stored.

But not everyone was as content as I was with the three-thousand-square-foot confines of the wing of that ordinary building. With an Oak Ridge citizenship whose reading tastes ranged widely, the library desperately needed additional room. In August 1950 book space had been enlarged by installing new shelves and opening the balcony. Fluorescent lighting and a modern ventilating system had added to the comfort of the room. But more was needed.

In the summer of 1955 the library moved from its original location into another wing of Ridge Recreation Hall, facing Broadway and the Alexander Guest House. The recreation hall had been constructed more than twenty years earlier as a temporary building, and this move was seen also as a temporary solution to the problem. But it did alleviate the crowded conditions for several years.

The door through which I entered the library was changed with this move, but my love hadn't altered. For one more year, my last year of high school, I continued to take books from the shelves, read them, and return them.

Then I left Oak Ridge for four years of college. The library continued without me. When my husband and I returned, we bought a house. I fell in love with the small B - cemesto with its unpainted brick wall in the living room and the old apple tree in the front yard. But the best thing about the house was its location—up Michigan Avenue just a few blocks from the Oak Ridge Public Library. Walks to the library once more became a way to exercise my body before I exercised my mind. After my son was born, I pushed his stroller, its pocket filled with books, down Michigan and along Broadway. Then I pushed the stroller back up the hill, this time its pocket filled with unread books.

By the time the final move from Jackson Square to the new Civic Center came, I was the mother of three children, all of whom had fallen in love with the library. We lived in the country outside Oak Ridge, so daily library walks were no longer a part of our lives. But the Oak Ridge Public Library still was. I paid for a nonresident card, considering it the best buy I would ever make. And my children devoured books as greedily as I had when I was their age. My own appetite had not diminished either.

In the new building, the children were given not just a few shelves but a large room to themselves. There, wide windows overlook the courtyard where trees and shrubs bloom in the spring or where the winter wind teases branches. Carpeting and low tables invite children for a few hours of reading. Even toys are a part of the welcoming atmosphere of this special room. The new library represents progress which has brought all of us a long way from my first love affair with the little van stuffed full of books.

But the wonder will ever be the same.

Courtesy James E. Westcott

Oak Ridge's first library was an old army ambulance painted to resemble a circus wagon.

AMERICAN RED CROSS NURSES AIDES

Jacinta K. Howard

ot many months after Pearl Harbor, the American Red Cross initiated a new program of training for women to become volunteer Red Cross nurses aides. The purpose of this program was to alleviate the shortage of graduate nurses who left civilian hospitals for service in the armed forces. Women all over the country responded to this program, and after eighty hours of rigorous training were put to work doing the many routine jobs which were formerly done by registered or student nurses. The Red Cross nurses aides pledged 150 hours of work a year after training.

In Oak Ridge the first appeal for Red Cross nurses aides came on October 30, 1943, in an issue of the *Oak Ridge Journal*, two days before the opening of the new hospital. Women who had been trained elsewhere reported immediately for duty, and those who were interested were requested through the *Oak Ridge Journal* to attend Red Cross training. The activities of the Red Cross involved knitters, sewers, preparers of surgical dressings, gray ladies, and nurses aides.

On February 23, 1944, the federal government asked for at least 4,000 Red Cross nurses aides countrywide. This appeal was succeeded by the following editorial in the February 26 edition of the *Oak Ridge Journal*: "The call for women to become volunteer Red Cross nurses aides cannot be ignored. With registered nurses leaving each month for the Army and Navy, the shortage of such nurses on the home front is becoming acute. Many a woman can

174

sacrifice her leisure hours and volunteer as a Red Cross nurses aide. This is the time to make a real contribution to the war effort and to serve your community and your country. Get in the fight."

Soon afterwards the first class of nurses aides graduated on April 29, 1944. A public fashion show held by the Woman's Club on March 2, 1944, emphasized the colors gray of the Red Cross gray ladies, bright blue of army canteen workers, and the work day denim blue of the nurses aides in prominent fashion. The nurses aide uniform was indeed attractive, consisting of a blue pinafore, white blouse, white shoes and blue nurse's cap with the Red Cross insignia upon it.

In Oak Ridge Red Cross nurses aides met one of their greatest challenges when on July 6, 1944, a troop train wrecked near Jellico, Tennessee hurtling into the rugged Clear Fork River gorge. Thirty-four soldiers were killed, and more than eighty were injured, most of whom were taken to the Oak Ridge hospital since it was an army hospital. All nurses aides were called in during the early morning hours of July 7, and worked many hours assisting nurses and doctors in treatment of the injured soldiers. "Arrangements were made," read the *Oak Ridge Journal*, "for emergency aid ten minutes after the hospital staff was called about the train disaster. Nurses aides reported promptly for duty at the hospital, many before they had been called. Nurses aides trainees who [went] on duty after their daily working hours, also reported on schedule and helped with the emergency."

There were not enough available rooms in the hospital, and many of the soldiers lay on cots in the halls. They were young, bewildered, uncomplaining, and grateful for the care given them. Their first thoughts were for their families, and many messages were written for them by nurses aides and gray ladies, then posted to their relatives. They spoke also of the accident, and asked about certain friends who had traveled on the train with them— information nurses aides tried to provide. They remained in Oak Ridge only a few days, but the memory of that event is still vivid to this writer who was a nurses aide at the time.

On August 3, 1944, there was an editorial in the *Oak Ridge Journal* praising nurses aides, saying that the hospital told the Red Cross that it could use fifty a day. The second class graduated on August 10, 1944, and on December 7, 1944 there was a special

Pearl Harbor Day recognition service at the Chapel-On-The-Hill. Thirty-three aides were capped and all Red Cross volunteers from the various Red Cross branches attended in uniform.

Classes continued to graduate through most of 1945, and gradually phased out after the war ended—when the army nurses returned to civilian life. The experiment was one of the most successful in the history of the American Red Cross.

PSYCHIATRY ON A SHOESTRING

Eric Kent Clarke
Edited by Amy K. Wolfe

E ric Kent Clarke, now deceased, was the head psychiatrist for the Manhattan Project. He witnessed the first atomic bomb blast in Alamogordo, New Mexico, and visited all the laboratories participating in the Manhattan Project. Dr. Clarke was based in Oak Ridge during the war years, and founded the psychiatric service there. Unlike many medical professionals in Oak Ridge, he remained a civilian throughout his tenure in the city.

After the war, probably some time between the summer of 1945 and the summer of 1947, Clarke wrote this account of his experiences in Oak Ridge. It is interesting that Dr. Clarke also wrote about many other experiences in his life. From an early age, Clarke was encouraged to keep a journal. Thus, for example, the yellow note pad on which this manuscript was written also contained his recollections of growing up on a farm. Although Dr. Clarke penned many manuscripts, so far as I know, none has been published until now.

Dr. Clarke's manuscript never was completed. Nevertheless, this series of reminiscences captures much of the flavor of wartime Oak Ridge. Those anecdotes dealing with the psychiatric service are particularly revealing. Dr. Clarke's article is important, also, because documents by participants in wartime Oak Ridge written so soon after the war years are rare.

I received a photocopy of E. K. Clark's handwritten manuscript, entitled "Oak Ridge 'An Amazing Interlude'," from his daughter, Joan Holdren, through Nancy and Rich Holdren. The title of the article was changed for this book. The following excerpts from Dr. Clarke's twenty-seven page account have been selected to highlight his unique perspective as a member of the wartime psychiatric service. Excerpts have been edited to enhance the flow of his story. The ideas expressed are solely those of Dr. Clarke.

—Amy K. Wolfe

In the beginning in Oak Ridge, there were no social workers—probably the only community organized in recent times without such services. It was assumed that as everyone on the project had a job and a place to live, there would be no need for social workers—who it was assumed were only concerned with indigents and unemployed. There was, however, a staff of town hostesses attached to the Housing Bureau. Their duties were to welcome each new family on arrival and to help them get oriented to stores, shopping, and recreational facilities. This in itself was a tremendous job. Frequently 200 or more new families would arrive each day who had to be welcomed. It was only natural that, as the town hostess was the only official representative the newly arrived housewife had encountered, the town hostess would be the one sought to help solve any problems that might arise. The town hostesses were a capable group—recruited from wives of men employed in various capacities on the project. There were few other resources upon which they could call for help, except in some real emergency. Our definition of a "real emergency" was on a narrow base as compared to ordinary standards. In case of severe illness, there were the facilities of the public health physicians and nurses and an exceptionally well-organized hospital. The Red Cross had a small volunteer unit that was primarily concerned with "disaster," the welfare of veterans and their families, and dependents of men on active service on or off the post. Later, toward the end of the war period, such auxiliary services as social workers, visiting teachers (school social workers), school counselors, school nurses, and all the other services one would expect in any well-organized modern community were forced by circumstance and demand to come into being.

The psychiatric service at the Ridge came into being as a result of pressure from several sources. The general program of the project developed under pressure, and that engendered much tension. The hospital was one of the first units to develop. From the start it was a highly developed service, with an ever-increasing staff and additional beds. It was originally planned as a fifty-bed hospital. Expansion of its facilities never ceased until the end of hostilities, when it became apparent that the community would not expand further. There were eventually 300 beds, and an additional wing was planned but never built. The medical staff was organized to cover all branches of medicine and its specialities, trying to meet the needs of a growing community.

The high incidence of neurotic manifestations observed by the medical staff in patients, the emotional disturbances occurring in the children in the schools, and the stress among the public health nurses, town hostesses, and the medical officers brought about the early establishment of the psychiatric service. I started in alone in the service in March 1944. By July 1945, it had expanded to five psychiatrists, and a total staff of fourteen. No one ever defined the responsibilities of the psychiatric service, for like topsy it just grew.

There was a minimum sense of competition or rivalry as to what was the prerogative of one division and not of another. It was always potentially there beneath the surface, but was never a major factor. Everyone had more to do than could be accomplished, so a compromise was usually worked out. For instance, a new head arrived to establish a family counseling service. She was a very able woman who had been persuaded to leave a responsible position as head of a well-established unit in one of the large eastern cities, where there was an orderly array of community resources to call upon. Her ambition was to establish a well-rounded, scientific creation of the highest order. She had the idea that, since no previous resource had been there, it should develop, like Venus springing in full adult form from the crest of a wave, into a model of perfection. The goal was ideal. In fact, I think it safe to say that each of us had come with the same idea. Oak Ridge offered the most gorgeous chance to test out in practice the theoretical philosophies in sociology, psychology, psychiatry, psychosomatic medicine, preventive public health, and community nursing that one could seek. Here was a new, highly organized city of substantial size where an ideal of community living could be introduced.

Although the medical group had gone to the project as civilians, they had become commissioned into the Army Medical Corps in December 1943, a few months prior to my arrival. I came as a civilian, and remained one of two civilians in an otherwise solidly military unit. It was a convenient spot to be in. As a civilian I was not expected to know or accept army routine; I was not an army officer. On the other hand, because of my close association with the army, I was not completely accepted as a civilian. So, I had a surprising degree of independence as far as both groups were concerned.

No one ever got around to defining my job, which was probably wise. From the day I reported for duty, life was busy and never dull. My headquarters were in the Oak Ridge Hospital. For a short period, while construction to expand the hospital from its original fifty beds to one hundred beds was being completed, I used whatever space happened to be vacant. The first day we moved into the new quarters was a traumatic experience. Construction was not quite complete, and a continuing chain of workmen appeared and departed.

The building was being checked, and there was a mysterious offstage character named Joe that I never did see. First came an electrical inspector. He switched on each light three times, tried out each wall socket, and then called, "Lights OK in 218, Joe," and departed. Next came a window shade inspector. He pulled down each window shade to the bottom and then let it go with a snap and a bang—each one three times—and then said, "Shades in 218 OK, Joe," and departed. Later came inspectors of door keys and of floor tiles, and all reported back to the mysterious "Joe."

There was one man who appeared with a large box that looked intriguing. But, before I had time to investigate it, another man appeared and picked it up and removed it—without a word. The crowning blow of the morning came when three men appeared and started to remove my desk from between my current patient and me. On that I protested vigorously, as I had just completed sorting out my belongings and placing them neatly in the drawers. One man said, "These drawers will fit your desk when it comes," and proceeded to stack the drawers neatly in the corner. This seemed a senseless move. I had the drawers from the desk; someone else had the desk but no drawers. The next day my desk arrived—identical to the original—and the drawers did fit.

My office was the last on the corridor, a corner room. Late in the first morning I could hear some commotion down the corridor and looked out. A filing cabinet was riding majestically down the hall on a dolly. As it passed each door, the M.D. inside would pop out and say pleadingly, "That belongs in here," and would follow along to see who was the lucky owner. It belonged to me. I had impressed upon the administration that my file had to be confidential, and I got the single filing cabinet available.

It was perhaps a good introduction to the Ridge. Earlier, I had encountered the mud, had become a number, and now had become aware that there would be no tranquility.

Since my office was exceedingly hot, some generous person supplied a much battle-worn electric fan. It was universally known as "Waltzing Matilda." It was a "traveling fan" that took fourteen minutes to wander from the doorway to the radiator, hitting the latter with a loud bang. Once, when the floor had been highly waxed, Matilda cut down her rate of progress to twelve minutes. Usually, it was as good as a clock with quarter hour chimes. Replacing it before it hit the radiator became automatic. And, at the end of the hour one let it hit the radiator as a signal—the hour was up. We never did figure out any satisfactory method of control. Matilda had to remain a floor fan because of its traveling habits. Once we tried it on top of a file cabinet, but it waltzed off that in short order and continued to operate facedown on the floor. It sounded like a buzzsaw and caused no end of confusion to the head of the obstetrical service who had the office directly below. The only thing that can be said for Matilda was that she was sturdily built and practically indestructible.

There were many amusing incidents—viewing them in retrospect—although at the time they did not appear so. Late one Saturday afternoon I received a somewhat desperate call from one of the town hostesses. She asked for advice on the removal of a pig that had become stuck under a trailer and was causing a disturbance. It seemed a strange request to come to the Psychiatric Clinic, but she justified the call on the basis that the trailer was occupied by one of my patients who was becoming hysterical. It was not her pig. I suggested she call the Maintenance Department. She had already done so, but they had only been concerned as to whether the trailer was damaged. They could only come if there was damage. How about the town police? They had been contacted and were interested only in knowing who owned the pig. No pets or animals were allowed on the area. If the town hostess found out who owned the pig, let them know and they would order them to remove the pig from the area. They could not send anyone out since all the available policemen were busy.

My only suggestion was that she try the service station tow truck, which was equipped with a crane for lifting wrecked cars. Although it was irregular, if someone paid for the trip, they would come. Thus she accepted my suggestion, and the end of the trailer house was raised. Interested bystanders prodded the pig, which trotted out. Once again, all was serene. I never knew the outcome of the story beyond that—as to who owned the pig, what became of it, or who paid for the tow truck. My patient suffered no permanent ill effects, and the town hostess was able to keep her dinner date with her husband.

The majority of the dormitory residents were young; many had never been away from home before. The incidence of homesickness was high. The dormitories sometimes had a completely impersonal atmosphere that accentuated the homesickness. The youngsters who had been away at school made a quick adjustment. It took some time to install dormitory counselors in the women's dormitories. Counselors made a big difference. The town was devoid of grandmothers. If grandma came on a visit, it very often happened she stayed on as a counselor. Grandmas seemed to be just what the dormitory needed. Counselors were distinct from the dormitory managers, who were concerned only with maintenance of the building and collection of rent.

The accommodations for married couples without children were slow in developing. Consequently, the husband often was quartered in a different dormitory from his wife. This caused problems. Every effort was made to police the women's dormitories, and visitors were limited to the front lobbies. There was little policing of the men's dormitories. In response to repeated complaints to the police that women had been observed going into the men's dormitories via the fire escapes, one night a raid was carried out by the police on one of the men's dormitories. Many women were found and brought along to police headquarters. There were many red faces amongst the officials, since the majority of the ladies arrested in the raid turned out to be the wives of the men in whose rooms they were caught. Soon afterwards, some dormitories for married couples were established.

There was no unemployment in Oak Ridge, since remaining in the community depended upon having a job. Unemployment led to expulsion, a matter that created problems. One man, a chronic alcoholic, was fired repeatedly from different jobs on the area. He was regarded as a security risk, so he was terminated and excluded, and his badge confiscated. His wife was a sound and capable worker employed in a position of some responsibility. It was desirable that she be retained, for it would be hard to replace her or train someone to take over her work. Her husband, being on the blacklist, could not come to Oak Ridge even for a visit. She, having reverted to the status of a "single employed female," could not retain her house for their family. So, her resignation was to be anticipated. It was quite a hardship, for they had come to the area from a considerable distance with all their belongings and household goods. Because of the circumstances of termination, they were not entitled to transportation of "personal household goods" back home. It was one of the tragedies that was a by-product of any large operation created under pressure. The lack of consideration for those who ceased to be useful to the community was a continuing concern to those of us trained to consider individual needs.

[Dr. Clarke writes a little about the experiences of children who lived in Oak Ridge. He describes what happened when, because of child labor laws, children from eight to twelve years of age legally were no longer allowed to work as pinsetters in bowling alleys.]

The most violent protests against this ruling came from the parents of the small boys who had been employed. What were they to do with the children out of school hours? There was no room for them at home in the small trailers or prefabs. It was rainy, cold, and muddy outdoors. There were no recreation centers for children. The only outlet outside the home was the movie theater. Apparently, many kids were attending from seven to twelve movies per week. An increase of juvenile delinquency and gang activity caused official concern. Hurriedly, recreation centers for school age children were opened, but these never offered much appeal to preadolescents. Scout troops and cub troops did not flourish too luxuriantly. There was a scarcity of trained group recreational leaders who could control or retain the interest of the younger kids. Dancing had some appeal for the adolescents.

There seemed no easy solution for the preadolescents. Gradually they gravitated back to their former jobs as pinsetters, where they probably suffered less harm than from the steady diet of movies and from roving surreptitiously about the townsite. In the employment office there were frequently applicants for work who did not look their stated age of sixteen. I understand that the production of a birth certificate was not pushed too insistently. These young people were usually used in noncertified, unskilled work. They were part of a family group already employed on the area. As the schools were chronically overcrowded, the enforcement of the school attendance law was not too rigorously enforced, particularly where there was no protest from the home.

During the war, a curious attitude of silence rapidly developed in the residents of Oak Ridge. It was totally different from anything I had encountered previously, for the men and women simply did not talk about their work at all. Obviously, the necessity of having to get a permit to leave or return to the area, the omnipresent military police, the wearing of identification badges, and the emphasis placed on silence during orientation, led to much of this attitude. At any rate, there was an amazing lack of curiosity as to what your neighbors worked at, or where.

Every precaution was taken to protect the secret, and it was effective. One was always conscious that there might be supervision, so one acted accordingly and without any particular concern. There were things that were not for discussion, and that was that. One did not discuss them.

Two men, each of whom developed an acute psychosis, showed how deeply impressed the necessity for secrecy had been. Although they were acutely disturbed and agitated, (because of the anxiety growing out of the knowledge of what the process on which they were working would mean in wartime application), both retained the ability to remain silent throughout the acute period. The agitation was the anticipation of the destructive qualities of their product, which was later demonstrated in reality at Hiroshima and Nagasaki. At this late date it is betraying no secret—for I have seen repeated references to it in the daily press—to say one of these men felt compelled to escape from the area and make his way to Japan in a plane he would steal to inform Emperor Hirohito of what was brewing and persuade him to call off the war forthwith. It was a worthy motive, but showed faulty judgment in his method of carrying it through.

There were no facilities for the care of such an acutely disturbed individual. The anxiety that he might talk freely was acute, and spread from the immediate staff of the psychiatric division in Oak Ridge to top administration in Washington. Our facilities on the psychiatric ward were limited. It seemed advisable to arrange for transfer to a larger and better equipped psychiatric hospital elsewhere. Washington authorities were adamant, however, that this man must remain and be isolated and cared for by our psychiatric nursing staff. It was a big order, for it meant setting up a complete psychiatric hospital for one patient. In view of the circumstances, the investment was deemed justifiable. The man was cared for in a single family unit by a staff of three nurses (eight hour shifts). Since he was disturbed and violent, these nurses were augmented by four orderlies, three to cover the days and nights, and one for relief. One psychiatrist was assigned to assume responsibility. And the chief of Nursing Service and head dietician were called upon for assistance in personal supervision of the operation.

Great care was exercised in the selection of this personnel because these people would be in such close and constant contact with a man whose entire drive was to escape. Military intelligence selected the personnel from a hand-picked group. It is doubtful if ever any one acute psychotic was surrounded by such a highly selected group. In due course this man made a complete recovery and returned to work, after the destructiveness of the atomic bomb had been proven at Hiroshima and Nagasaki, and after his mission to warn the emperor of Japan no longer seemed imperative to him.

Courtesy James E. Westcott

The Oak Ridge Hospital medical staff in 1945. Eric Kent Clarke is in the back row, seventh from the left.

WOMEN AND
BLACKS

Courtesy Department of Energy

WOMEN ALSO SERVED

Jane Warren Larson

In 1943 and 1944 women came to Oak Ridge to work on the war project or to follow menfolk who had taken work there. Their attitudes might today be considered naive since they did not come with conscious plans for the future, but counted on the good intentions of their husbands, bosses, and the necessities of war.

Along with the excitement of change and good pay, women did have problems, uprooted from home as they were and transplanted to a raw, one-grocery-store community in the wilderness. Because of secrecy, it was not possible to talk over the day's work with one's husband or to boast a little to the folks back home. Surrounded by mud in unfinished houses, "demountables," and dormitories, they were uncertain about the duration of the project and unable to put down roots. It certainly wasn't a woman's world. There was little beauty except in the far-off mountains. They had friends, however, who had started doing volunteer work in other cities, in organizations such as the League of Women Voters and Planned Parenthood. These women were making a place for themselves in Oak Ridge.

Such a woman was my mother, doctor's-wife Vi Warren, who realized soon after she arrived in November 1943, that Oak Ridge homemakers were having a hard time. As she wrote in 1945:

No one was anxious to have them here except their own men-folks. It would have been so much simpler to leave the

191

women out—to build Oak Ridge without women, without schools or grocery stores or playgrounds or beauty parlors. Just a line-up of dormitories, cafeterias, and production plants. But the men-folks wanted their families and so the founding fathers made provisions for the women and children.

She began talking to other women about what could be done. She talked to Jackie Nichols, wife of the district engineer. She became acquainted with Fran Gates, widow of an army officer killed in the early days of the war. Mrs. Gates had taken the job as editor-in-chief of the new newspaper the *Oak Ridge Journal*. She met other capable women anxious to be useful in the community.

Of course, many women were young, and as early as June 1943 community dances were held in the north wing of the central cafeteria. When the central recreation hall was finished in July 1943, there was a nightly program including dancing, quiz contests, bingo, ping pong, bridge, or Sunday night young people's services. In the first issue of the *Oak Ridge Journal* in the summer of 1943, people were encouraged to organize into groups: "Various buildings in the town center are available for the use of organizations or groups, provided these gatherings are of a public nature."

And many special interest groups were formed. But it was not until April 1944, with the organization of the Woman's Club, that special emphasis was placed on the role of women in Oak Ridge. It was organized with Vi Warren as first president. For a dollar membership fee any woman in the area could join, and meetings were also open to nonmembers. It was a major step towards encouraging all women to banish depression and develop their talents. In a neutral setting the club offered book discussion groups, bridge marathons, teas and luncheons, and was so successful that it has remained a vital organization in Oak Ridge for forty years.

Vi Warren was active in other ways. She wrote a series of columns for the *Oak Ridge Journal* between July and December 1945, articles that helped residents, particularly homemakers, see themselves as the adventurers they were. Her column headings are revealing. Beneath the by-line "As You Remember," topics included: "The Natives Left Their Valley," "Take a Look at Our Town," "Oak Ridge Organized for Fun," "Oak Ridge Enticed Us

All," "We Couldn't Write Home," "Trailers Were Indispensable,"
"Schools Outgrew Their Walls," "The Women Also Served."

She added to this production a radio address or two at the
end of the war, sounding like the true feminist she was. In one of
her radio addresses, she said:

> Good morning friends. The housewives of Oak Ridge are
> speaking to the outside world from behind the barbed-wire
> fence. Yes, we're still here. Did you forget about us? We just
> wondered, because we didn't find ourselves mentioned in the
> Smyth Report. We are the ones who do the chores for the
> men who make atomic bombs, and we bring up their children,
> bomb or no bomb. The kids are two years older now, and we
> are at least ten. That's the way you grow old—fast, when the
> going is tough.

Vi Warren projected a spirit of gaiety-in-adversity that was
typical of much Oak Ridge thinking. It is captured in this bit of
poetry she wrote to a friend about to leave Oak Ridge in February
1945:

When you've ditched your badge and pin,
    When you're outside looking in,
    When you're just a Ridge "has been,"
    Think of us!

When you walk on pavement walks,
    When your plumbing never balks,
    When at last your husband talks,
    Think of us!

We'll we walking on the gravel
    With our cars unfit for travel
    Till our toes begin to ravel.
    Think of us!

We're glad you're going shopping,
    Glad you'll miss the mud a-slopping.
    Lord, how topping, stopping mopping!
    Think of us!

Oak Ridge women weren't just homemakers, however. They
also worked in the plants. At Y-12 where I was assigned, they

worked side-by-side with the men, helping to make the bomb. Some were clerks, secretaries, and information-gathering persons. Others, closer to the stuff of bombs, actually served as operators of the calutrons which separated the U-235 from the raw uranium. They worked forty-eight hours a week, plus overtime. They worked near the secret, eye-catching "racetracks" that hummed while in production around the clock. It should be noted, too, that for the most part the women operators, who sat in front of the "cubicles" measuring the activity of calutrons that separated the uranium, were mostly Tennessee mountain girls, handling thousands of switches with unmatchable skill.

With the assistance of Eastman Kodak's enlightened policies, women worked under fair wage and benefit conditions from the beginning. Unexpected pregnancies did not keep most women from their jobs. Thanks to meticulous planning, an untroubled birth, and a company grace period, a friend of mine successfully made it back to her demanding job within a few months. It was not easy, of course. Later I found myself being considered for a promotion to department head and was quizzed severely on my intentions about having a family. In those days, the more important the job the more necessary not to have interruptions in its execution, which females were thought to cause. On the other hand, several war widows who were employed as executive secretaries were freely given unusual leaves of absence. A top secretary at the plant for a long time was low-keyed, friendly Nell Parks, who managed to be impartial to all. On the whole, then, women found the Oak Ridge working world a fair-minded place in which to seek an industrial job and to do so successfully.

Many fragmented episodes come to mind of adjustment and change in the lives of women working in Oak Ridge. I met a scientist's wife who had written several stories for the *New Yorker* and was now devastated: readers would not understand her war project settings. A young, pretty, black woman came by during the midnight shift with mop in hand to inquire if I might have books she could borrow. (Segregation was still a sorry fact in Tennessee during the war years.) A friend came to Oak Ridge while her husband was fighting overseas, but she was so lonely that she left a good job to go back to her family. Another woman friend, with a B.A. in physics, found the laboratory work boring and exhausting.

Perhaps her capacity was misjudged, for she left physics after the war, earned an M.D. degree and is now a highly placed physician.

One senses in some ways that Oak Ridge women may have had brains they didn't get to use. One cannot, however, forget that men were having troubles, too. And for every dissatisfied woman I think there was at least one who was challenged by her situation and who searched through her job for greater fulfillment. In Oak Ridge, women had the unique opportunity of taking part in a major scientific field which led at the end of the war to stunning success. As Vi Warren tried to point out to her sisters, for women who stayed with it, Oak Ridge became the most memorable adventure of their lives.

Courtesy James E. Westcott

Oak Ridge women played a significant role in the war effort. In addition to homemaking, they also served as clerks, secretaries, and plant workers.

Courtesy James E. Westcott

Women answered the call to duty as operators at the Y-12 electromagnetic plant. They are seen here leaving the change house where they changed from coveralls to street clothes before clocking out at the end of the day.

A NEW HOPE

Valeria Steele

In 1942 recruiters roamed the South in search of Negroes to work on a mysterious project located in the East Tennessee hills. Word spread rapidly among relatives and friends about the new hope that awaited them in this war-born community. Talk of jobs, high salaries, and newly built homes stirred their imaginations and prompted many of them to leave their home places, hoping finally to escape the hardships of the Depression and the longstanding legacy of blacks in America. A job opportunity in Oak Ridge seemed an answer to their prayers.

President Franklin D. Roosevelt's Executive Order 8802, in 1941, had seemingly opened this door of opportunity for blacks when he stated in the order that "there shall be no discrimination in the employment of workers in defense industries of Government because of race, creed, color or national origin ... and it is the duty of employers and of labor organizations ... to provide for the full and equitable participation of all workers in defense industries, without discrimination." This action by the president was taken after threats of a march on Washington, D.C., by fifty to one-hundred thousand black Americans. But to reinforce this executive order, a prohibition-of-discrimination clause was written in all defense contracts; and a committee on fair employment practices was established to function as overseer of complaints about discrimination.

While still in the planning stage, army officials in Oak Ridge expected a population of only 2,500. But as construction began and plant facilities expanded, the population grew, exceeding many times its original estimate. Soon, the number of cemesto houses proved inadequate, with temporary housing and prefabricated homes being brought in by the Tennessee Valley Authority. Because of this miscalculation, the army abandoned plans for a "Negro Village" which was to have been a wonderful community of nice homes for blacks.

The Negro Village would have been located at the east end of town. Though segregated from housing for whites, it would have been composed of the same type of homes. The community would have consisted of fifty houses, four dormitories, a cafeteria, a church, a school, and some stores. But in the end, this plan was completely abandoned. The influx of people into Oak Ridge was so great that East Village became another white community. Since blacks had such low-level jobs, they were not entitled to the better housing. Moreover, it was rumored that blacks did not like the better-type housing.

The black men and women who came to Oak Ridge believed that it was a city of opportunity. They came by the hundreds from Alabama, Mississippi, Georgia, and Tennessee. They arrived with great anticipation of how life could be improved and how they could make a new start. But soon, they realized the hollowness of such a dream. For coming to Oak Ridge only reaffirmed one rude fact: that they still lived in America, in the country that had always denied them freedom and equality. In Oak Ridge, as in other places, segregation would continue to play a central role in their lives.

Still, there was a bright side. Many blacks in Oak Ridge received more pay than they had ever known, their living conditions were in some cases improved, and, indeed, their opportunities for the future were enhanced. For many blacks the ordeal of the Depression years had been a harsh and forbidding one. Life had been a sheer struggle for survival, living on the bare edge of existence. In Oak Ridge some of these conditions were at least alleviated, if far from eliminated.

Those blacks who consented to go to Oak Ridge were provided with transportation—usually by bus—to their destination in East Tennessee. It was an arduous task to leave their familiar homes. Many of the men, for example, had to leave their families and go alone. But the pay of fifty-eight cents and more per hour was a blessing, and difficult to refuse. One early resident of Oak Ridge said, "Everybody was so glad to have a job making some money. We weren't making money back home."

Generally, black workers were unskilled and performed such jobs as common laborers, janitors, and domestic workers. Very few Negroes were hired for skilled labor or technical jobs. But while they did not have the best or most challenging jobs, their contribution to the success of the project was important. Blacks shared with whites an eager desire to help the war effort, and at one point some gave volunteer hours in their jobs. But still, after their day's work, they returned to their segregated and deficient hutments.

Because the federal government allowed segregation to exist in Oak Ridge, it became an accepted lifestyle. Local officials in those days stated government policy as one that conformed "with the laws and social customs of the states and communities in which federal installations are located." Thus blacks and whites lived in almost totally different worlds except when they were working, however vaguely, toward the completion of the war project.

For the black person in Oak Ridge, segregation was total. Blacks lived day in and out under oppressive conditions. They utilized separate facilities such as cafeterias, recreational facilities, bathrooms, drinking fountains, and change houses. They had to ride in the back of buses and suffer other indignities like being served food at the bus station through a pigeon hole. One facility that many blacks appreciated, though, was the washhouse with washing machines. One early resident said, "We were still using scrub boards back home."

In early Oak Ridge black married couples were not allowed to live together. As one person recalled, "We were told before we came that there would be no housing for me and my mate." Though black men and women lived in the same general area, they were separated by a fence five-feet high with barbed wire across the top. The women lived inside this area which was referred to as the "pen." There were guards on duty at the entrance to make sure the women were inside by a curfew time of ten o'clock each night. This was considered a form of protection for the women.

Housing for men and women was in frame buildings, called

hutments, measuring fourteen by fourteen feet. These were primitive dwellings with dirt floor, coal stove, no glass windows, and a single door. There were no bathrooms in these hutments, and each of the four residents living within the unpartitioned room had to use facilities provided in central bathing houses. In this type of housing, provided for blacks and some white men, conditions were worse than anywhere else on the reservation. Not only was it oppressively hot in summer and cold in winter, with little privacy for the occupants, but violence sometimes marked the area. Yet blacks had to live in the hutments until 1950, while white construction workers were moved to better homes by 1945.

Moreover, no black children were allowed to live on the reservation until 1945. In fact, black family life, generally, was nonexistent. Husbands and wives lived in separate huts and if they had no children previously, they were prohibited from doing so afterwards. One early resident recalled that "any black woman who became pregnant lost her job and was put outside the gate of the city to wait for a bus." And for those who had left their children back home with relatives, they had to make a long, arduous journey back to see them.

By 1945, when family housing became available for blacks, black children were finally allowed to live in Oak Ridge. This new development caused concern among parents for the education of their children. For while schools had been established in Oak Ridge in 1943, they served only whites. It was not until 1946, when Mr. and Mrs. Robert Officer organized the first elementary black school, that blacks had their own school. And still, there was no high school for them. Parents concerned about that had to have their children bused to Knoxville, where they attended a black high school.

Oak Ridge blacks did find ways to cope with their situation, however. One of the major forms of recreation was socializing with friends. Many stories were shared as people from various other places began to form a new community. Some blacks used the recreation facilities and played games. The church, though, was the most important institution in the black community. Many attended church meetings that were held in the Chapel-on-the-Hill. "The churches were well attended," remarked one early resident. It was also a place where blacks could enter and feel totally

While over 1,500 blacks came to Oak Ridge during the war years, seeking a new life, they almost always were relegated to such jobs as common labor, domestic and janitorial work.

Blacks were generally assigned to the most primitive and uncomfortable form of housing in Oak Ridge, the hutment. A typical hutment could sleep as many as five workers.

free and welcome. Hence, the church functioned as a vital force among black families.

The black experience in early Oak Ridge was one of many highs and lows. For while a policy of segregation was perpetuated by federal officials, continuing into the postwar years and reaffirming past experience, there were new experiences, too—experiences that did improve their lives. Approximately 1,500 blacks came to Oak Ridge, and most would agree that this was "the city on the hill," hope in the midst of a depressed period in their lives. Though many of their hopes were dashed, most would say that the good outweighed the bad, that Oak Ridge did in fact enhance their lives. Regardless of the bad times, Oak Ridge was a beacon light for a people who needed help and hope in the 1940s.

IMPACT ON EAST TENNESSEE

Courtesy TVA Billy Glenn Photo

NEW NEIGHBORS COME
TO ANDERSON COUNTY

Horace V. Wells, Jr.

The coming of Oak Ridge in 1942 brought exciting and frustrating days for the people of Anderson County, and especially for me, as editor of the county's only newspaper. With a war going on and everything in short supply (all the automobile dealers had gone out of business and gasoline and tires were being rationed), it came as a great shock that the government was buying—or taking, depending on how one perceived it—56,000 acres and requiring the people to move out before their crops were harvested or even before they had found another place to live.

When the word was received that the War Department would create some sort of project in the west end of Anderson County and the east part of Roane County, we made every effort to find out what was coming, but without success. The first suggestion was that the War Department was preparing a "demolition range." The first name given to the project was the Kingston Demolition Range.

More than 1,000 families from the two counties were involved, and as chairman of the Anderson County Rationing Board it was my job to try to provide the farmers, who were being displaced, with gasoline and tires for their trucks. They needed to look for a place to move to and then to actually move, none of which qualified them under rationing regulations. Consequently, I went to Nashville to see General Lytle Brown, head of the state rationing board. He had already informed me that he was unable to find out anything about the project, saying that his superiors in Washington knew nothing about it and had made no provisions for such an emergency. His feeling, like mine, was one of perplexity. After some discussion of this with him, he finally suggested that I go back home and devise rules, with my rationing board, to provide for the situation—and to keep it quiet and be consistent and fair to everyone. He said he would try to supply us with new and recapped tires—mostly recapped, since new tires were going to the armed forces. Anna Belle Clement (O'Brien), his secretary and now a state senator, took care of the details. She gathered the unused quotas of tires from other counties and made them available to Anderson County. In this way, and over a period of several months, we managed to supply tires and gasoline to those who were forced to leave their homes and farms.

By this time the "project," as everyone called it, was known as the Clinton Engineer Works and later as the Manhattan Project, and the War Department people made their presence conspicuously known.

The acquisition of the land was a painful process for the people. The appraisers who were sent in were trying to do a good job for the government, and to them the hills of Robertsville, Scarboro, and Wheat were dirt-poor farms. Apparently, some of them, if not all, were more familiar with the rich plains of the Midwest and could see little value in the scraggly, uneven acres of Anderson and Roane Counties. Judge T. L. Seeber, who owned several farms inside the reservation, had one hundred acres in the Robertsville community on which he had a small lake for swimming and a summer cabin, as well as a large barn. This was in the vicinity of the present Oak Ridge municipal swimming pool. He was paid $8,500 for that, or $85.00 an acre. In addition, he had another 150 acres in the area now known as Emory Valley. On it stood a two-story house and several outbuildings. The government appraiser offered him $1,500 for it—or $100 an acre for the land and the buildings. He called the chief of the land appraisers office in Harriman and said that they "had stolen the Robertsville land and now they were trying to steal an additional 150 acres," and that he was not going to accept the offer. The chief of the appraisers told him that unless an error had been made that offer would stand, but he would check the figures. Later, he called Judge

Seeber and said, "We made a $500 mistake," raising the offer to $2,000.

I heard of an elderly widow who had a small house—probably just a shack in the eyes of the appraisers—but one which she owned and which was her home. With it was a small garden and a well. In those days there were no welfare checks or food stamps, but she was self-sufficient and happy. They offered her $75 for her property and ordered her out. Where could she go and find another house, with a garden and a well for $75? As Judge Seeber said, "Many people were turned out of their homes and paid such low prices that they were unable to buy a house anywhere else," even in 1942.

A group of the landowners protested and there was a congressional hearing, but it was too late for most of the people. Others went into federal court and secured some adjustments, but after paying their attorney's fees and other expenses, they were not much better off.

In 1940 Clinton had a population of 2,761. It had a police force of two men, one on day duty and one on night. There were no car radios in those days. In fact, the police had no cars at all—they walked. If they were needed, the telephone operator switched on a light bulb that hung beneath the town's only traffic light at the corner of Market and Main, and the policeman called in for the message.

With the influx of people to work at the Manhattan Project, things changed rapidly. At one time it was estimated that there were close to 80,000 people in the area, living in patched-up barns, former garage buildings, and even chicken coops. Almost everyone in town took in roomers from the project. In fact, we had six of them in our home for a while, and my wife methodically collected the rent and bought herself a long-wanted piano!

Our public systems, however, faced several difficulties. It was necessary, for example, to beef up the police force, but with most of the desirable men working at the project, the ones hired were often problem people. In fact, we had more killings by policemen than we did by criminals. The shootings came as the result of law violations, public disturbances, and robberies; and they gave the town a black eye.

The schools, too, soon became overcrowded, both in Clinton

and in the county, and appeals to the Manhattan District brought some assistance—though not enough. Clinton got an annex added to the elementary school, and the county got the elementary school at Norwood with government-provided funds. Then, there was the problem of sewerage. Clinton, at that time, dumped its untreated sewerage into the Clinch River. With Oak Ridge drawing its water supply from the Clinch, this became a problem, if not of health then at least one of the imagination. So Clinton had to install a waste water treatment plant, which has been upgraded from time to time since then.

There were many points of friction between the highhanded operations of the War Department and the financially hard-pressed county government. One of these was the old Edgemoor Bridge. The War Department condemned the land to the west side of the bridge, but left the bridge in the county's hands. All county residents, however, had been moved out of the area, and the only people using the bridge were workers going to and from Oak Ridge.

The bridge was narrow and had a wooden floor, and soon became beaten up and dangerous. The War Department insisted that the county repair the bridge, but Judge Seeber (then county judge) felt the War Department should take responsibility. After an impasse was reached, Judge Seeber finally closed the bridge on the grounds that it was "dangerous," which meant the workers had to come through Clinton to get to work. This brought action from the War Department and the bridge was repaired and opened, later replaced with the concrete bridge that now stands there near the Bull Run Steam Plant.

There were other conflicts as well. The county people felt that the project workers were not eligible to participate in local elections or in liquor referendums, because they were temporary residents on a government reservation. There was no voter registration back then and the poll tax had been abolished, so anyone who showed up at the voting places usually was allowed to vote. Finally, a court order was obtained allowing the residents of the Manhattan District, now called Oak Ridge, to vote, and they had to go to the courthouse to cast their ballots since there were no voting places behind the fence.

Later, after the war, provisions were made for voting in Oak

Ridge. There was a memorable election in which World War II veterans, who had returned, formed a ticket of Democrats and ran for all the county offices. Paper ballots were in use back then. The night after the election, when there had been a huge turnout of voters at Oak Ridge High School, the counting went on all night and well up into the next day, with anyone handy being called on to help out the duly appointed officials. Instead of calling the ballots as they were marked, these people called whomever they wished. Later an election lawsuit showed that two county officials had been illegally "counted out" in the process. Only one of the officials filed suit, Miss Mattie Hollingsworth, county court clerk, and she was returned to office with back pay. The other official, Woody Duncan, did not file suit, but when the ballots were counted in court it was found that he, too, was "counted out" in the all-night affair.

We had liquor referendums in which there were other instances of fraud. The names of many Oak Ridgers were listed as voting at Rosedale, but most of them had never been to Rosedale, and some didn't even know where it was. With the backing of the Oak Ridge League of Women Voters, the county bought voting machines, and since then elections have been honest and, although there have been mistakes, no indication of fraud.

But back to the war days. Everything was in short supply. Eleven automobile agencies were closed since there were no new cars. Food became scarce, and people stood in lines to buy bread, cigarettes, and women's silk hose. To get meat one had to have been a long-time customer of the butcher, and bacon was a collector's item. Sugar and coffee were rationed, as were shoes and other such items. This helped provide a more equitable distribution of these things, but the project workers were hard pressed to find some of the scarce items.

At the project area, however, things were a little different. Rationing boards were set up and operated by the contracting companies. Companies like Tennessee Eastman, Stone and Webster, Fairchild, and others saw to it that their employees had gasoline stamps and apparently enough tires to get to work—with approval of the War Department, which put the status of the project ahead of everything else, except fighting the war itself.

People in the county grumbled about this apparent liberal

distribution of gasoline stamps to project workers, who often showed the natives handfuls of stamps, some of which they gave away and others probably were sold. Not knowing what was going on in Oak Ridge made it hard for people to accept what was happening to their food, gasoline, rooms, civic affairs, and other phases of life.

Then came 1945, the dropping of the atom bombs, and the end of the war. East Tennesseans were finally told about Oak Ridge and what had been done there, and their frustrations were diminished. Many were full of pride that this area had taken a hand in bringing this dreadful war to a close.

In an editorial that week, The Clinton *Courier-News* wrote that "Oak Ridge will not only become a permanent place, but it will have tremendous possibilities in the world of tomorrow.

"Not only will it be necessary that the atomic processes, both from a developmental and manufacturing standpoint, be permanent to prevent future wars, but peacetime possibilities are beyond the imagination of man.

"No scientific discovery—not even of electricity nor of the gasoline engine—has such revolutionary effect upon the ways of life of mankind as this.

"Atomic power, when our scientists turn their minds from the military to the peacetime needs, might be harnessed to drive our ships, our planes, our trains, or cars—or even be used to run our factories or light our homes.

"It is staggering just to think about the future.

"We are suddenly caught up in the swirling power of a whirlpool of events and swept along at so rapid a rate it is not possible to see either where we are going or where we can stop."

Then came the postwar years, the opening of the gates, and the movement of Oak Ridgers into the county area. Because they were interested in government and in an improvement of life generally, Oak Ridgers soon became deeply involved in the activities of the communities in which they resided. They offered themselves as candidates for the board of education, the county court, and the various town boards and commissions. Because of their educational background and their previous experience in other parts of America, they have made fine contributions to the county and to the towns in which they live and serve.

The people of Oak Ridge also are residents of either Anderson or Roane Counties, and what affects those counties affects the residents of Oak Ridge, just as it does those of us who live in Clinton, Norris, Lake City, or Oliver Springs. All of us pay county taxes in addition to municipal taxes, and all of us have the responsibility to see that our money is properly accounted for and wisely used. There should not be any conflict between the two areas, for what is good for Oak Ridge is good for the county, and what is good for Clinton also benefits Oak Ridge in a smaller way.

As I wrote in an editorial on August 9, 1945, "Clinton, so close to Oak Ridge, may someday be linked with it physically, for only eight miles separate us now." While this has not yet occurred in the forty years since the war, we are certainly much closer than we were, and our aims, our needs, and our problems are common.

CHANGE COMES TO KNOXVILLE

Ruth Carey

From the beginning, the foremost impact that Oak Ridge had on Knoxville was to create a surge of prosperity. A heady infusion of money began surfacing and Depression-haunted, empty stores along Gay Street began to come alive. Many people without work got jobs; others got better jobs. And people came from everywhere to work on the mysterious project. Growth in Knoxville soon became linked to growth in the "secret city."

"We knew *something* for the war was being made," said a Knoxville businessman, now in his eighties. "We were ready to do anything for the war effort, but the Knoxville-Oak Ridge dichotomy that developed at that time was a natural thing."

Part of this dichotomy, he added, was based on the nearness of the new city, some twenty-five miles away. For however close in geography, it was far away in its secrecy; its fences and uniformed guards set it apart almost wholly from Knoxville, and from East Tennessee generally. And then there were the thousands of people coming from all over the country to work behind the fences, on land that once belonged to East Tennesseans. The local people were told to leave, to give up their family homes, and to make way for new, strange people. "It was only natural to be curious and suspicious."

There were grave apprehensions about these people, these "aliens," but it was "tempered with some admiration, and maybe a little envy too," noted the elderly business man, "because they were

214

involved in some kind of exotic, scientific war work. We would see a lot of men in army uniforms. Others would come to town looking pretty scruffy. But there was an unfamiliarity and mystery about those people in muddy boots. We could not help but think of them as aliens, for they were strangers that we should not question. On the other hand, they were people with money to spend and there were a few who would try to take advantage of them."

As a young boy, a Knoxville attorney remembers delivering meat to the secret city. His father, a butcher, would drive a truck up to one of the gates where armed guards inspected it, then transferred it to a waiting army truck. The guards then signaled the young boy's father to turn around and leave, hurrying them out. "We knew that great big fence was there for a purpose," he remarked, "that something big was going on inside of it, but we knew it was for the war—so that was good enough for us. It was okay. And we didn't ask any questions. But incidents like that gave Oak Ridge and its people an aura of science fiction."

It also had a way of setting Oak Ridgers apart as aliens.

Economics, however, was not the only thing altered by the secret city, by these aliens. "The important impact that Oak Ridge had on Knoxville for me," noted a Knoxville woman who was attending the University of Tennessee at the time, "was the availability of men."

The war had taken away many of the available young men; but suddenly the creation of Oak Ridge brought thousands of unmarried males into the region again. And when these young men came to Knoxville, or the young ladies managed to get passes inside the fence, the ladies sometimes found that at social functions "the boys outnumbered the girls more than ten to one." Some of these girls regained a popularity that they had not known since the war began. Moreover, there were many marriages between Knoxville girls and GIs, as well as civilian men, who worked in Oak Ridge.

My own memories of early Oak Ridge are those of a twenty-two-year-old housewife. Knoxville was my hometown. My husband worked for the Tennessee Valley Authority, and we had a young child. Like most Americans, the war pressed foremost on our minds. Members of our family and friends were serving overseas. Ominous news stories of battles shouted from newspaper headlines and from radios. Gold stars appeared on flags hanging on doors or windows of homes where families had lost sons, husbands, brothers, or fathers.

And then we heard that in Oak Ridge something was being done for the war effort. It was something, the whispers said, that might end the war. Moreover, there were jobs in abundance there—"war work." It was the patriotic thing to do. But we also heard raised-eyebrow talk of "those people—people from New York and all kinds of places. Aliens." They were moving in and buying scarce items: meat, cigarettes, gasoline, nylon stockings. And some Knoxvillians held strong feelings toward these new people. Seeing them at a distance, it was particularly easy to feel harshly toward them. As we got to know some of them, though, the perception of *alien* faded slightly.

One evening my husband returned home and made an announcement. He said, "I've been recruited for a job in Oak Ridge. They recruited me right out of my office." It was war work. Of course, I had learned from meeting the Oak Ridgers that one simply did not talk about their work; now, I could not talk to my husband about his work either. Every day he rode the "stretchout" to work—a long car that appeared to be made of two cars welded together—going back and forth between Knoxville and Oak Ridge. The stretchout came by the homes and picked up the men. What is now a drive of twenty-five minutes took about two hours over bumpy, dusty, or muddy roads.

Meanwhile, I heard that I might help the war effort by working on the "project" in Knoxville, part-time. A recruiting and procurement office was set up in what had been a Ford agency on South Central Street. I was hired as a clerk/typist, and I arranged for my child to be placed in a nursery school or with relatives. Desks and file cabinets sprouted in the garage of the agency. Trucks rumbled through the building next to the desks. All kinds of people—local and alien—came to apply for jobs. The excitement of working on something connected with the war was intense. We did not question the secrecy. Moreover, as a Knoxvillian working on the Oak Ridge project, I felt I had a foot in both camps: local and alien.

My assignments included handing out endless employment applications and typing up appropriate materials. As I typed the application forms, I perused the backgrounds of the applicants. They were a mixture of local people and outsiders, the outsiders coming from practically every state in the union. Many applicants had very little to qualify them for any job; but many who came got a job. Others had what seemed to me astonishing qualifications. As it turned out, both unskilled and skilled (professional) were needed.

"Security clearance" was a new phrase of the times. Each person who worked in Oak Ridge had to be granted a clearance. People throughout the country, and many in Knoxville, were contacted by investigators busy gathering information on the new applicants, exploring their backgrounds and their character. Many of those questioned wondered if the person being checked had done something wrong, and were hesitant to answer.

In mid-1944 my husband was issued a house in Oak Ridge. We moved from Knoxville via a flat-bed truck sent from the project. Our new house was a boxlike, prefabricated flattop on wooden stilts. It had a potbellied, coal-burning stove in the middle of the living room. A few days after the move, I went to Knoxville by bus. It was impossible to wipe the mud from my shoes. I walked into a store and the people looked at me forbiddingly. I knew I was perceived as an Oak Ridger. I had become an *alien* in my own hometown.

Alvin K. Bissell, former mayor of Oak Ridge, was also a Knoxvillian who became an Oak Ridger. He, too, experienced the reversed role of becoming an outsider. "We furnished jobs for them while they insulted us," said Bissell. "They insulted me and I was one of them. Yes, we were aliens in our own hometown. Friends were just as nice as ever, but others treated us with disdain." Bissell took a job in Oak Ridge in 1943, never dreaming it would become his new hometown. "Yes, first the Tennessee Valley Authority, then Oak Ridge, raised the standard of living in Knoxville. I remember before that when people were scrambling for jobs at Brookside or Standard Knitting Mills for $1.38 an hour."

When the bomb was dropped on Hiroshima, the secret was out. Tall, bold headlines proclaimed the secret city to the world. Oak Ridgers became instant heroes everywhere—including in Knoxville. The joy and relief and the hope that the war might soon be over was overwhelming. And soon everybody knew what had gone on in the secret city behind the fence.

Remnants of the dichotomy that had its roots in those early years still remain today, but for the most part the lines have gentled. The fact that Knoxville keeps expanding westward toward Oak Ridge speaks of the economic impact of Oak Ridge on Knoxville, an impact that the once secret city has had on many of its neighbors.

PEOPLE OF THE CUMBERLANDS

Joanne S. Gailar

Having lived in the Oak Ridge area for over forty years now, I have met enough Appalachians to know that they are as individual, as varied in personality and character, as people from any locale. Like the Creoles of my own native New Orleans or the Cajuns of the Bayou Teche country in southern Louisiana, where my grandmother spent her early childhood, Appalachians cover a broad spectrum.

My earliest associations with Appalachians, however, came first in 1945 with the people of the Cumberlands, whom my husband and I met when we lived in Cove Lake, near Caryville, and then in 1946 and 1947 in Oak Ridge, in our victory cottage and flattop days.

On Sundays, when we lived in Cove Lake, my husband and I often took long walks into the sparsely populated mountains surrounding the inn where we lived. These, indeed, were so sparsely populated that we wondered how the school bus or the draft board ever found their way to carry the children to school or to induct the young men into the army. The people we met were extremely friendly, maybe because we ourselves were young and friendly. They greeted us warmly, sometimes telling us what happened to "Aunt Lucille" that morning, as if we knew who Aunt Lucille was.

There were usually casual, single encounters. But the Appalachians we got to know best at Cove Lake were those who rode the bus to K-25 with us. Collectively, they were a friendly group of people, always saying "howdy" and always willing (in fact, eager) to engross anyone in conversation. The men rolled their own cigarettes, probably using Rooster or Garrett snuff, both of which were advertised frequently and enjoyed popularity among these mountaineers. "Crow like a rooster, cackle like a hen. Rooster snuff is just the stuff for women and for men," was the jingle of the Rooster snuff makers.

A few personalities among the people who rode with us stand out particularly in my mind. There was Slim, who lived alone with his mule and wouldn't trade freedom or mule for any wife in the world. There was Gus, the fellow who "made like a train" so realistically that I always looked around to see which direction it was coming from. And there was Clem, who sang hillbilly songs in a nasal twang that jarred you at first, then grew on you, and then even became very appealing after a fashion. Such selections as *Walking the Floor Over You* and *For Tomorrow, I'll be Daid* were his favorites. They all sang but he soloed more than any of the others except Mrs. Turner.

Mrs. Turner was our favorite. A tremendous, white-uniformed woman who worked in the laundry at K-25, she was good natured, massive, friendly, and always ready to sing for anyone who would listen or even for her own pleasure. Her songs were charming. What kind did she sing? Well, hymns for the most part, but hymns that I had never heard on any other occasion. They had a folksy simplicity about them both in melody and in words, and she had a delightful way of singing them. The voice emerging from the depths of her flesh was rich, powerful, and melodious, and the characteristic nasal twang of the locale did not detract at all from the effectiveness of the songs.

The Caryville and Jacksboro women who rode the bus were oh-so-different from us city "flowers." From the city, Sue complained of sore hips, Alice of an internal infection, Dotty of intestinal upset, and I of a heart flutter. The Appalachian women, however, who rode with us always appeared healthy, uncomplaining, and strong. They were long used to a life of hard work, but we Cove Lakers, fresh out of college, found the combination of holding down a six-day-a-week job and cooking and washing a very laborious undertaking.

A few years after we left Cove Lake, we bought a record of Dorothy Shay, the Park Avenue Hillbilly. Her song, *Feudin' and Fightin'* brought back recent memories of Cove Lake. One morning when the bus with our one-eyed driver pulled up to our stop, we noticed that the windshield had been shattered by bullets. I don't remember any of the details except the question that Clem eagerly asked at the end of the tale: "Hey, Jack, did y'git him back?"

Nor was this our only contact with violence. In our flattop on West Washburn Circle, our usually taciturn, hen-pecked, and mild-mannered neighbor got into an argument one day with another neighbor when they were drinking beer together. All of a sudden we saw them break off the top of their bottles and go after one another with the jagged edges.

This man, Jerry, and his wife, Mabel, came from the Kentucky Cumberlands, but in many respects they were very much like the people who lived in the hills above Cove Lake in the Tennessee Cumberlands. They were illiterate, superstitious, friendly, colorful, generous, talkative, and independent. All five of them— mother, father, and three boys, aged four downward—lived in a tiny two-bedroom prefab, a flattop as they were called. After we moved, I heard that a baby girl arrived to live with them. Mrs. Smith was a woman who had wanted a girl all her life. When Harry Lee, the youngest, turned out to be a boy just like the other two boys before him, it was too much for her. So she put dresses on Harry Lee and let his hair grow, calling him "Lee." I shudder to think of little Lee's future had not a sister come along before he reached three.

The little boys were winsome fellows with blue eyes, dirty mottled blond hair, and pale, pasty complexions. They played in the yard happily and were well behaved as little boys go. They were usually naked to the great chagrin of the woman across the street who didn't want her little girl to see "such terrible things" and complained regularly to the Welfare Bureau of Oak Ridge. The boys' unclad state never disturbed my husband and me. In fact, we practically split our sides laughing one brisk, September day. As they were playing happily outdoors in the weather, unclad from head to toe, we heard their father call out to them, "Harry Lee, Tommy Ray, and Johnny James, come in here this minute afore

Courtesy James E. Westcott

"The Appalachian women ... who rode with us always appeared healthy, uncomplaining, and strong."

223

you catch a death o'cold out thar without no shoes on."

It was Mrs. Smith, the mother of these boys, a woman of twenty-six who looked forty-six, who cautioned me when I became obviously pregnant, "Don't lay in too much for the fust un, because the fust is always born daid." We were concerned, in fact, about the survival of Harry Lee, her youngest, when he had a festering wound from having stepped on a rusty nail, and she showed no signs of taking him to a doctor. But remembering the savage fight with the broken bottles and Mr. Smith's nasty temper when aroused, we decided it was best not to meddle—a decision that troubled me until it was clear that little Harry Lee would recover.

One of the things that stood out about these and our former East Tennessee neighbors was their strong sense of pride, their refusal to be "beholden" to anybody. The first time I encountered it, I was taken aback. This was when I invited a new victory cottage neighbor in to have a Coke on the day he moved in. He accepted with pleasure and drank it at the table in the front room. As he talked to me about his army experiences and about reenlisting as an MP, he nervously fingered a nickle. When he was ready to leave, he placed the nickle on the table and murmured as he approached the door, "That's for the Coke."

We soon learned that nobody would willingly accept anything for nothing. Before leaving for a two-week vacation in New Orleans, we brought our leftover milk, eggs, and other perishables to our flattop neighbors. "How much we owe you?" snapped Jerry. It wasn't so much ungraciousness as it was poverty, pride, and independence that prompted his reaction. After the birth of my first child, when my husband made only $270 a month, we visited New Orleans in our Oak Ridge clothes. When my mother-in-law insisted on giving me one of her dresses to wear to a luncheon to which she was taking me and would have to be seen with me, I came to better understand how these neighbors felt.

Some of the adjectives that come to mind about our East Tennessee neighbors are uncomplaining, good, spare, independent, and proud. Having come to East Tennessee from New Orleans, there was much that I missed at the beginning. I missed the oldness, the stability, and the culture of New Orleans. I missed my family and the St. Charles Avenue street car and Audubon

Park. And I missed the live oak trees—called "live oaks" because they always have leaves. The new leaves come as the old leaves die. Somehow these stately oaks with their outspread branches, bedecked with Spanish moss, were associated in my mind with the expansiveness and gracious living of the old South. But that I learned to love another kind of oak and to appreciate and respect the spare, independent Tennesseans I found as neighbors became more evident to me in passing years.

THE AFTERMATH

Courtesy Department of Energy

227

ATOM BOMB DAY

June Adamson

Excitement. We couldn't believe it. The secret was out at last, and we couldn't wait to share it. There was bustling about, telephone calls, and busy signals. Goose flesh made us shiver even on this hot day. There were moments of deep concern, a feeling of awe at the power released. But there was pride too, even exaltation, relief, celebration. World War II would surely end, and Oak Ridge had had a hand in its conclusion.

It was about ten a.m. as I remember, when the first news flash came over the radio about the dropping of the first atomic bomb on Hiroshima, Japan. I have been asked many times since what Oak Ridge was really like on that day.

For me—for most housewives in Oak Ridge—this Monday started just like any other humdrum Monday during those grim war years. For plant workers who hoped their jobs would win the war, but didn't always understand how, the same was true. In those days of the forty-eight-hour weeks, working in shifts around the clock, there hadn't even been a weekend in which to let down.

Monday morning meant coping again with the problems of day-to-day living in what at the time seemed a temporary place. We were harrassed by shortages of food and lack of gas coupons— and by doing laundry over a scrub board because it was impossible to buy a washing machine even if you had the money. But that morning laundry became a forgotten word in Oak Ridge. No one worried about lunch or dinner, and I even wasted whatever it took in gas coupons to drive to Townsite (now Jackson Square) to find someone to talk with about the news—anyone.

Oak Ridge was a friendly place during those years, and talking to strangers was a thing everyone did. That was how friends were made during the difficult months, since most of us didn't have families nearby. Neighbors were immediately friends, of course, but as we sat on buses or shopped at the A & P, it was the practice to introduce ourselves to each other. Many close friendships began that way. Thus, on this day particularly, people headed for Townsite to talk about the event.

My memories of that morning are vivid for various reasons. I was a member of a two family household, a common practice then, particularly among army-connected couples without enough rank to qualify for housing. Our particular household included the editor of the *Oak Ridge Journal*, Frances Smith Gates, her two sons, ten-year-old Sam, and seven-year-old Dick, my husband George, and our son, Stanley. Since our son was too young for nursery school when we came to Oak Ridge, and Mrs. Gates needed someone to look after her children, the arrangement was made.

That day I had no one but my young son to share the news with. For although vacations were practically unheard of, Mrs. Gates had taken a much-needed few days to go to the New York area for a family visit, and her boys were in camp near Gatlinburg. That morning, however, she was due to return. About eight-thirty a.m., before news of the bomb had been announced, the phone rang and Fran Gates on the other end said, "Hello, I'm back. I'm at the office, but I'll be home in just a little while to tell you all about New York. Do you have some coffee left?"

The little while passed, then a little longer, with the coffee getting too strong. I was getting just a little exasperated as I set about to finish up the flurry of early morning chores. More than an hour passed, and the phone rang again.

This time Mrs. Gates sounded breathless as she said without preliminaries, "Turn on the radio and you'll find out what we're doing in Oak Ridge."

I tried to question her, but the receiver clicked abruptly. I then turned on the radio in time to hear President Harry Truman intone: "It is an atom bomb. It is a harnessing of the basic power of the universe, the force from which the sun draws its power has been loosed against those who brought war to the Far East."

This could not be grasped all in a moment. After all the secrecy, I had almost stopped believing any answers would be known. I nearly exploded with excitement and awe. Without fully comprehending all of the implications of this announcement, I dialed my husband's number at Y-12 hurriedly, a thing no wife did except in cases of extreme emergency during those years. My husband wasn't particularly patient when I told him in the voice of the canary-swallowing cat, "I know what you're doing."

Thinking it was simply another trick to get him to reveal something about his work, his answer was completely non-committal... I then smugly quoted President Truman's radio announcement, "It is an atomic bomb," and could almost hear the double-take as he turned to tell his fellow workers that the big secret was out. He then asked me if anything had been said about the material used, the material he had been working with at Y-12. When I said it hadn't, he clammed up again.

That afternoon I drove to Townsite again, the largest shopping center in the Clinton Engineer Works area, to find board-walks swarming with people, all talking excitedly and earnestly. "The war can't last now ... Japan can't hold out in the face of this ..." were some of the words of the day.

I don't remember talking with anyone in particular, but just feeling the need of people—adults with whom the excitement could be shared.

In front of the post office on Tennessee Avenue, extra editions of area newspapers were being sold. Later in the day, newsboys were swarming up and down the streets, an unheard of practice previously in the secret city. Headlines read: "Power of Oak Ridge Atomic Bomb Hits Japs: Truman Reveals Use of World's Greatest Bomb; World's Biggest, Best Kept Secret Hidden at CEW; Atomic Super Bomb Made at Oak Ridge Strikes Japan; Story of Secret City Officially Told; 20,000 Ton Atom Smashes Japan; Allies Tell Japs Hirohito Must Obey Our Commands; Bomb Staggers Nips." Note that the words "Japs" and "Nips" were in common use all through the war years.

By late afternoon reporters and photographers were swarming over Oak Ridge. I remember that one of the first arrivals was

Daniel Lang, of the *New Yorker* magazine, whose first impressions of Oak Ridge and the work done here subsequently appeared in the magazine, and then later in his first book, *Early Tales of the Atomic Age.*

I never did see Mrs. Gates that day. For a small town weekly newspaper editor, it was a field day—a day unsurpassed in excitement, even though she was badly scooped by every other newspaper in the country. The *Oak Ridge Journal* was published each Thursday and there was no effort to get out an "extra" sooner. But the August 9, 1945 edition carried its own banner headline: "Oak Ridge Attacks Japanese." The front page story explained the workers' thrill at hearing the news of the atomic bomb. The article also described how the "fantastically powerful" weapon would undoubtedly save many lives by bringing the war to an early end.

By dusk everyone knew the meaning of such words as "atomic" and "uranium," though many, even those working in the plants, had never heard them before. Those who had known and had kept them secret shouted the words from their office windows. These same people who knew may have occasionally referred to uranium as "tea," or more likely as "the stuff."

By dusk too, telephone wires were hot—not only locally, but for long distance calls as well. Ridgers telephoned friends and family, or were telephoned by them, again such calls not being an everyday happening. Ridgers could hardly wait to hear the reaction of others and to shout out personally the part played by their atom-splitting town.

The excitement carried over even to young children. The favorite question was, "Did your daddy work on the atomic bomb?" I still remember the crestfallen disappointment of one child who had to announce, "My daddy is only a dentist."

For many families, the celebration of the evening was quiet. I remember my surprise when a knock came to the door and I opened it to find Colonel Kenneth D. Nichols—district engineer for Oak Ridge—standing there with his wife, Jackie. They had stopped to see Fran, who wasn't home yet. They said they had been taking a peaceful walk on Olney Lane (probably their first calm moment of the war years). They spoke quietly about their hopes that this meant no more wars—ever. But they were both smiling.

Some families got together to toast each other with illegal

liquor. We toasted Oak Ridge with a long-hoarded bottle of sherry. But many celebrations throughout the town were more elated. Many groups gathered in the town's recreation halls—at the Ridge Hall across from the Guest House. In those places toasts were mostly made in Coke and beer. In the area now occupied by Downtown, SED soldiers celebrated at the Detachment Exchange.

Years later I talked with several others who had vivid memories of atom bomb day. Following is some of what I learned.

Hannah Grosvenor, a guest from Washington, D.C., had worked for Charles Vandenbulck during the early years. Vandenbulck, an administrative officer for the Manhattan District, knew all the details of what was going on, as did his staff. They knew about the test at Alamogordo in July 1945 and had spent the following weeks preparing news releases for the dropping of the bomb. Thus for Hannah, the excitement was virtually over the morning the news came out. She recalled Colonel Vandenbulck calling his wife to tell her to listen to the radio. "We sat around in a group listening to the radio for the first official public release—the phone rang and it was Mrs. Vandenbulck, very excited."

Dr. Robert Livingston, retired director of the Electro-Magnetic Division of Oak Ridge National Laboratory, remembers how the tables were turned as wives called the plants to tell the news. "I remember that a few weeks earlier we had been given a deadline to scoop out all the bins and ship out all material. Although we had no details about what this meant, we knew it was highly significant."

Livingston explained that although the work done by his group was understood in its own territory, there was little detail about its larger sense. "I was most impressed by the way the *phenomenal* secret was kept and by the fact that very few even knew what material was being processed." But with even the unusual deadline about the material, the August 6 news came as a complete surprise to him.

"We were too busy to spend a lot of time speculating during those final weeks," he said.

Among the first persons to be interviewed as a "man-on-the-street" by *Oak Ridge Journal* reporters was Charles Kienberger. He said then, "I hope our product will end the war in short

Courtesy James E. Westcott

Young dormitory women celebrate the end of World War II.

Courtesy James E. Westcott

Young and old celebrate V-J Day.

order—the news certainly emphasizes the need to find a way to avoid future wars."

Mrs. Kienberger recalled, "I was terribly homesick, and to me the news meant we could go home to St. Louis. Instead it meant that we were definitely caught up with the pioneering atmosphere of a new era and now years later, I'm very thankful for the privilege of living in such a place. I hope we never have to leave."

Ruth Ramsey Kernohan also remembered the day. She was extremely busy at the time taking care of her month-old twin boys. She heard a boy outside her Orange Lane home shouting about one of those unheard of "extras" up and down the isolated lane. "I thought he was shouting, 'read all about the new automatic bomb,' which shows how much I knew about it. But I did go out and buy a paper. It was all very exciting, of course, but because of the new babies, I didn't do any special celebrating."

Mrs. Webster Gildersleeve was one of those who remembered being rather overwhelmed by some of the more serious and horrible aspects of the bomb. "My husband and I had sons in service, and perhaps being a bit older, this side of it struck us first," she added.

Alice Lyman, known as "Miss Music," was one of the Oak Ridgers who heard the news in another place. It was school vacation and she was visiting her mother in New York when the news broke. The two were headed for a matinee at a theater when she met a friend who asked, "Do you know what you are doing down there in Oak Ridge?" then proceeded to tell them. The Lymans had not heard the news that day, and she commented, "our reaction was simply to gasp." She had a week or so to think about all the implications of the news before returning to Oak Ridge.

Certainly, the recollections of people who were in Oak Ridge on that day could go on almost endlessly. There are many old-timers who remember the emotion-packed time with a deep sense of historical significance and would like to share it with others. Their intention would not be to gloat because they were here, but to relate its impact. It's hard to do.

MISSION TO JAPAN

Jane Warren Larson

A s is well known, Oak Ridgers who worked day and night on the war effort in 1943, 1944, and 1945 helped build an atomic bomb that was exploded over Hiroshima. This new weapon, and the one exploded over Nagasaki, brought about the end of World War II. Official accounts, as well as displays at the Oak Ridge Museum and the Hiroshima museum, give us the facts about this matter. Oak Ridge, however, played another part in this war drama, one that is not seen nor heard about very often. And it is this story that I wish to tell. For this is the story of one man's journey from Oak Ridge to Hiroshima, as excerpted from personal diaries. He was a doctor, commissioned a wartime colonel in the Army Medical Corps of the Manhattan District. He was my father, Stafford L. Warren, who as chief medical officer took a survey team to Hiroshima, arriving there one month almost to the day after the bomb exploded over the city.

My father was professor of radiology at the University of Rochester Medical School before the war and became a civilian advisor to the Manhattan District in April 1943. He was commissioned as a colonel in November of that year, with responsibility for the health and safety of the military construction sites—the towns, laboratories, and industrial plants—of the Manhattan District. The situation was complicated, of course, by the need to handle and control radioactive products and by-products, and my father's expertise in this area made him a natural for the job.

I arrived in Oak Ridge in September 1943, to work as a technical editor and I still remember my thrill in early October upon getting a phone call to meet my father at the Guest House where he had signed in for the night. The area around this newest of buildings was a mess, with floors of dried mud and the paraphernalia of a busy construction site. We sat on a pile of two-by-fours with the lowering sun at our backs and talked, guardedly, about my dormitory accommodation, the new hospital being built, and the difficulties of getting pasteurized milk for the cafeteria. He informed me that he, my mother, and two younger brothers would be moving down in December.

After that events moved quickly for us. By July 1945 my father was preparing for the Trinity shot in Alamogordo, New Mexico, where his group evacuated ranchers and livestock, ruled on sensible protection for observers, and set up experiments basic to an understanding of the medical hazards of the gigantic burst of radioactivity about to be released. This included one unique experiment thought up overnight and designed to determine the effect of radioactivity from a nuclear blast. The medical group ran lines of wire in a fan from the approaches to ground zero into the mountains and placed rats along the wire at measured intervals. It must have been eerie scrambling up and down the ravines in the pitch dark on the night before the test, with those cages of rats.

On August 6, 1945, the bomb made from Oak Ridge's U-235 isotope production was dropped from the *Enola Gay* and exploded at a height of 560 meters above the city of Hiroshima. The Nagasaki bomb was dropped three days later. My father left Oak Ridge for Albuquerque on the seventh, and there received orders from General Groves to "organize a survey party to go to Hiroshima and Nagasaki to make measurements to (1) ensure safety of troops occupying cities, (2) record [the] amount of activity, if any, on ground, and (3) determine [the] amount of blast and other damage. We are to remain only the time necessary to make these records. If Japan does not sue for peace, we are to use our nucleus of men for tactical force but Dr. Friedell and I are to return to District."

And so began my father's mission to Japan. The diaries and letters, handwritten from August 7 to October 15, 1945, were produced primarily for my mother, a writer, to help her understand the terrifying journey from which he might not return. After the war, when both my parents traveled to Japan as tourists, they used the diaries to retrace his route. They found the spot where my father bought two little wooden frogs for fifteen cents and used the occasion to tell his men not to indulge in looting, but to pay for everything without exception. They also found the home of the Japanese scientist who had surrendered his sword to my father and returned it to the deceased man's family.

On August 12 a party of twenty-six men led by Dr. Friedell, joined my father at Hamilton Field, California. "Left Y-12 at 2:00 p.m. in cars with Jones convoying," he wrote in his diary. "Left Albuquerque at 5:00 p.m. for San Francisco. Arrived about 11 p.m. Hamilton Field near San Rafael. Friedell and others to arrive in a.m. and we are to take off about noon." Another entry in his notes mentions an urgent concern: "We are bad off for sensitive instruments." This problem stayed with him all the way to Japan. Manhattan Project production plants and research laboratories were stripped of their portable Geiger counters, ion chamber instruments, calibrating sources, and batteries at this time, and these things were shipped west.

One senses an urgency as they left the United States and landed at Hickam Field, Hawaii at 11:05 p.m., August 13, and left three hours later for Kwajalein, where there was lunch and gas for the plane. They reached Tinian, in the Marianas, the next day on the fifteenth, losing August 14 by crossing the dateline. "Finished getting equipment for party," my father wrote, "everything but arms. General Groves says we are to be Groves Special Atomic Bomb Mission to Hiroshima. Other half under me by Guam and on the *Monitor* to Nagasaki...." Orders were developed as they proceeded on this mission and changed as circumstances required it. On the evening of August 16, the entire group left Tinian on the *Green Hornet* (a 4-motor C54 special Manhattan District plane) for Harmon Field, Guam, and then drove a long twenty mile trip into the port. On August 17, making themselves known finally and having been furnished arms, "Captain Olsen welcomed us on *Monitor*. Com. A. L. Main very cordial. Didn't know we were to be passengers until one hour ago and went to get us immediately and sailed one hour later."

On board the *Monitor*, life slowed a little and the party had time for laundry, target practice, and instrument tests. My father, who had occasional difficulty with an unhealed leg wound acquired before the war, was glad to sleep. Nevertheless, he also took time to get acquainted with the ship and crew, as was his habit. "The crew have heard over radio," he wrote, "that A-bomb left lethal amounts of material on ground. I said I doubted it." On August 20 it was decided to transfer the Warren party to two destroyers headed for Okinawa. To the destroyer *Landsdown* went eight men, and to destroyer *Buchanan* went six men and my father, who thereupon had a bad time. To my mother, who knew of her husband's fear of heights, he wrote: "In a fairly good sea, we transferred by breeches buoy to two destroyers. Thrilling. You would have liked it!" After the war, he told a relative that getting out on the seat of that breeches buoy without crawling was the bravest thing he ever did.

At 3:00 p.m. on August 22 (after a 21-knot, 1000 mile dash), my father went ashore by whale boat into Buchner Bay, Okinawa, to arrange for a landing of his party the next day. After leaving some men ashore, he had another awful scare. He wrote:

> Hoffman and I returned in whale boat, leaving about 5:30 p.m. Almost ran on reef in choppy water twice. Were instructed that our ship had berthed near a flattop. There were four in sight with destroyers around them. It was six miles to the nearest one. It was not ours. It was getting dark and one was apt to get shot at in the dark. A fast LST went across our front laying down a heavy smoke screen. We went ahead hell bent for ten minutes without seeing or hitting anything. The waves were very choppy and the boat had to be bailed occasionally. Two of the crew wished they were home. Three rain squalls hit us with high winds and complete black-out. We kept asking at each ship and finally located ours amid the battleships at the outer part of the harbor. Aboard at 9:00 p.m.

The next day, at noon, the Warren party left the destroyer and "landed at Brown Beach and mudhole." They had entered a world of tents, rain, and utter confusion. Senior officers on the island didn't know what to do with them. "We've been busy trying to get settled," my father entered in his diary, "trying to find out where the rest of our party is and what we do next. Things are

239

spread all about and transportation is hard to get so one accomplishment a day is good going.... There are still a fair number of uncaptured Japs on the island and there is some shooting every night, often near us ..." For eleven days Dad fretted about the orders that didn't come. He was anxious to get going, as he felt the mission might not be successful if too much time elapsed. He and his boys were ready for any dangers, he said later.

Finally, on September 2, a Sunday, the Japanese surrender was signed. The diary notes that on Okinawa "everybody worked just the same. Bed at 10 p.m. Firing all night as usual. No planes out because of typhoon." Nevertheless, it soon became clear that whatever was holding up Dad's travel plans was being cleared away. On September 6, Dad flew to Yokohama, south of Tokyo, noting that the men were to be moved into Nagasaki by boat later. "Arrived in Yokohama at 1800," he wrote. "No conveniences. Thumbed ride with jeep hauling supplies [cheese, etc.] to race track. Wildest ride I ever had, dust, left-handed driving, narrow-rutted road. Arrived at message center and finally got a messenger jeep to take me to Hotel New Grand. Told to go to International House. Found DiSilva, Nolan, Morrison, Col. Wilson, etc. Slept on davenport, burdened with mosquitoes and cold water."

The following day he described more of the setting and the scientific findings:

> Office in customs house, large number of high ranks and extreme formality. All wooden buildings burned out. Stone and concrete only left. Wrecked autos and street cars everywhere ... Col. Harage and Maj. Anderson translated latest Jap. Med. report on Hiroshima. No doubt about gamma ray single lethal dose under detonation. Report summary sent to Groves. Leave tomorrow for Hiroshima by air. Scientists cooperative though dignified, polite yet formal. I do not trust them completely yet. The general opinion is they do not feel that they have surrendered, only defeated for the time being.

On Sunday, September 9, with Dr. Admiral Tsuzuchi and Dr. Major Motohashi, two Japanese medical officers who served throughout the mission as interpreters and escorts to Colonel Warren's party, three senior American army officers and my father landed at Iwakuni Airport about fifteen miles from Hiroshima. Colonel Warren had his first shocking glimpse of the city's devastation by air: "Hiroshima is flat rubble in the center for a radius of about a mile with nothing upright." He recalled after the war:

> We landed on the field in a DC-3 with considerable difficulty because the field was potholed with bomb craters. There was a welcoming party composed of the local mayor and just scads of cases of beer. Apparently the Russians had been there from Tokyo the day before and left just before we landed. They had demanded beer and all kinds of things. The Japanese couldn't understand the fact that we didn't want the beer, that we didn't want any celebrating, but that we wanted to get to our hotel as soon as possible because we had to get our Geiger counters all calibrated so we could get to work the next day.

The party then was introduced to transportation in wartime Japan. "We were taken from the airport in a bus that had a big funnel on the front dashboard, to the right of the driver. There was a five-gallon glass carboy [of gasoline] on the floor ... and in the back a charcoal burner which when everything was going right would run the engine but at greatly reduced power ... Everywhere we went we'd see buses stalled, with the chauffeur out back trying to get the charcoal to glow." The bus finally broke down, and they transferred to an open military truck which took them, in the rain, to a military barracks and then to a ferry station where they went by boat to a hotel on an island about five miles down the harbor from Hiroshima. "Jap hotel, Jap bath, getas, kimono, ceremonial banquet and slept on mat and hard pillow on floor under net," he wrote.

The next day the advance party went by boat and Packard automobile to the city, a rough two-hour trip. His description is bleak. "Police et al., Chief of Staff, ceremony and speech at ruins of castle in rain. Ruin of city is complete, only a few hundred people wandering about. Rode around city. Flies very bad, covered people's faces and backs. No radioactivity anywhere."

They returned to Mirashima after a visit to Uyinia Hospital and had a quiet evening meal of raw fish, shredded fish, etcetera. The next day they went to the hospital again and finished the day at the tuberculosis sanitorium some two and a half hours away. There was a banquet for the visitors that night, featuring the chief of police, women, singing, and much merriment. My father reported that the Japanese "couldn't understand us. They thought we would rape all the gals, rob the stores ... This evening we had their confidence and it was like a natural party of distant friends. Slept with gun handy, just the same."

The third day, September 11, began at Mirashima with a visit to the shrine of the goddess of peace. Colonel Oughterson went through the ceremony, with Dr. Tsuzuchi translating. Colonel Warren made a speech about lasting peace between the nations. "This shrine was where the Jap soldiers, particularly the kamikaze, came to ask for forgiveness of goddess for going to war. More speeches, and then the party rushed to the boat for a two-hour trip to Iwakuni Airport by 1100 to await Farrell who was to pick us up for Nagasaki."

But now the developing monsoon season took over and prevented their plane from landing. The party was forced to repair to a military training school behind the airport to wait it out. My father describes inedible meals from which he became ill, and vicious huge mosquitoes. After four days of waiting for the weather to allow their plane to come in, they finally pulled out by train. During that interlude, however, and thanks partly, I am sure, to my father's gregarious nature, the Americans began to conquer their distrust of the Japanese.

The group began to discuss many things with their two Japanese companions. Dr. Tsuzuki was a professor and chief of surgery at the Tokyo University Medical School and an ex-naval colonel. He belonged to an official military scientific advisory committee and was called in by the military on August 7 and asked (1) was the Hiroshima raid due to an atomic bomb, and (2) could it be neutralized or prevented or protected against. The answers were (1) probably yes, and (2) no one knows. On the day after the Nagasaki's bomb, the emperor himself summoned the scientists and asked the same questions, to which he received the same answers. In addition to Dr. Tsuzuki and Dr. Motohaski, a Japanese English teacher from the Naval Academy, Mr. Yamata, joined the discussions. Subjects such as family life, religion, relations between men and women, and attitudes towards war were apparently discussed and are described in detail in the diaries and letters.

One day the Americans sat on a balcony and watched a B-29 go overhead, southward, in the rain, and waved at school children who waved back. They learned that the children had been brought by their teachers to pull up weeds and sweep up glass and debris. Doctor Motohashi said the public did not know the war was being lost. Neither did the Diet. Only the military and possibly the emperor knew the true situation.

Finally, on September 24, my father wrote:

> Major Motohashi left for Hiroshima to send the telegram announcing our departure, to arrange for the special car, to pick up the K-rations left at the police station and some beer. He got back for supper which was a celebration. We ate K-rations with cheers and drank tea [water amoebae and liver flukes made water unsuitable for drinking unless boiled, noted this doctor], and beer and exchanged songs and signed fans and short snorters and cavorted until 23:00 when we saluted all the excess police and departed in the dark by bus through one mile of bomb craters along and in the road to the railroad station. It took one hour, and how the driver knew the difference between a huge puddle and a bomb crater full of water I could not guess. We took bets on which was which as we wound in and out ... We got our luggage aboard the special car—covered ragged old-style bench seats fixed and facing each other. A high *benjo* [toilet] in the middle of the car smelled to high heaven but we smelled just as bad.

And so the party left Hiroshima for Tokyo, arriving the next night at 9:00 p.m., "looking like coal miners." The next day, Sunday September 16, and the three days afterwards, were spent in Tokyo preparing for the flight to Nagasaki, grounded by bad weather, and visiting hospitals along with Japanese scientists. My father spoke to a former MIT graduate in engineering, a twenty-six-year-old Japanese private (raised as a child in America, but drafted through threats to his family into the Japanese Army four years before), who said that in his army unit they thought until the last week of the war that Japan was winning hands down.

When my father returned from Nagasaki to Tokyo on October 2, he prepared to leave for Hiroshima again as soon as there was a weather break. The trip was going to be difficult because, in the meantime, Hiroshima had been hit by typhoons and flooding that wiped out the Mirashima Island Hotel, many bridges in the city, and both railroad and automobile roads. A

243

landslide wrecked the tuberculosis sanitorium with eighty percent casualities, including a majority of the Japanese doctors making records for the Groves Atomic Bomb Mission. Added to all that disaster was the fact that my father and his party nearly perished trying to get to the city. Their plane was grounded day after day because of faulty equipment, buried wheels, and the ever-present terrible weather. Finally, on October 7, an attempt to fly was ended when they were forced back from Hiroshima because of the storm, becoming lost in the dark over the ocean. They were saved at the last moment when the pilots found the airport beam from Tokyo and brought the plane back to safety.

Two days later, on October 9, while the party waited for good weather ("Typhoon to West petering out. The one in China now headed this way."), my father's party "went to Admiral Tsuzuki's house over in the unburned part of Tokyo. Very foolishly," he wrote, "I didn't tell my security man where I was going ... In Tokyo, the houses are faced by a fence with a little sliding door. You go into an entryway, take off your shoes, leave them there, and then go in the house. Then the sliding door is shut which makes a solid wall along the street. Aside from the fact that our jeep was out there we could have disappeared entirely."

My father reported that Dr. Tsuzuki insisted that he and his aide, Sergeant Brownell (along with Major Motohashi), must come in and have tea. They entered a small sitting room, ten feet by ten feet square, containing a foot-operated Singer sewing machine, a small table and chairs, and some of Dr. Tsuzuki's paintings on the wall. The ceilings were low for my father, with doors at his forehead. He wrote:

> We sat around the table and he brought swords out. Motohashi drew out each one and, being a championship sword expert, explained the great age of the blades (200-350 yrs. old) and the handles. He took practice positions and swings with me sitting two feet away, and I thought how easily my head could have come off. But we went on talking about sword play and the care of the blades and old and new army and navy style when the tea came in. They put the swords in the scabbards and wrapped them up in a silk cloth, while both Brownell and I sighed with relief.

These swords were the kind the Samurais had used to decapitate their victims, and the presentation had been long and suspenseful. Regarding one sword, Major Motohashi had said: "Admiral Tsuzuki's father inherited it from his father. On behalf of Dr. Tsuzuki I have great pleasure in giving you this ... we have such admiration ... etc., etc." With all the weaponry around, my father and Sergeant Brownell grew very anxious, and with a lot of bowing and scraping they made their exit, without even stopping to lace up their boots. My father said later that he had been with these two Japanese officers for almost six weeks, and that they liked each other. Otherwise, it would never have worked.

It was Admiral Tsuzuki's sword that my mother and father took back to Japan after the war. My father and Colonel Friedell left Japan in the *Green Hornet* with their groups on October 12, and reached the United States on October 15, 1945. Because of the unwinding of the military operation and preparations for the Bikini Test, my father's official report of his mission to Japan was brief. Only by referring to his personal papers does one get a more complete story.

Courtesy James E. Westcott

A military ceremony in Oak Ridge on June 17, 1945. On the far left stands chief medical officer for the Manhattan District, Colonel Stafford L. Warren. In front is Colonel K. D. Nichols, district engineer for Oak Ridge.

THE LOST WORLD OF BLACK OAK RIDGE

Thomas W. Thompson

Ever since the *Enola Gay* made its fateful appointment in the skies over Hiroshima, Oak Ridge has been synonymous with the atomic bomb. Like the nucleus of the atom itself, the splitting of which unleashed the awesome power that flattened that Japanese city, the history of Oak Ridge and the mission of the Enola Gay seem one, as if protons and neutrons in a nucleus of common experience. Yet upon close inspection, two very different historical traditions become distinguishable: that of southern Appalachia and that of modern science and technology. Incredible as it may seem, on the spot where huge electromagnetic machines painstakingly separated U-235 from U-238 ore, small farms only a few months before had produced tobacco and other crops; and, on the ridges above, where housing for thousands of itinerant workers stood, oak, poplar, hickory, and several species of pine once grew tall, thick, and undisturbed. It was from the northernmost of these ridges, Black Oak Ridge, that the city of Oak Ridge took its name.

More incredible still was the fact that on those farms and in those woods around Black Oak Ridge flourished a culture that in many ways more closely resembled the America of Abraham Lincoln than the America of Franklin Roosevelt. That scientists from all over the world should journey to this relatively remote section of eastern Tennessee to usher in the atomic age presented an irony too delicious to ignore. A reporter writing for the *New York Times* observed how "the centuries jostle each other," how the people surrounding Oak Ridge had "been projected into the twentieth century." The reporter probably exaggerated the differences; but differences were real, and they attracted notice. In a sense, nineteenth-century and twentieth-century America met at Black Oak Ridge. It would take the crucible of war and the iron will of an army general to fuse the two.

If ever there was an archetypal general, it was Leslie R. Groves. Experience with the military started early; shortly after his birth on August 17, 1898, his father accepted a position as chaplain in the army. Like most military families, the Groveses traveled, moving whenever the father received assignments. Less typical were other features of family life: strict Presbyterianism combined with scholarship. The two apparently helped the future general. After studying engineering at the University of Washington, Seattle, and at the Massachusetts Institute of Technology, he went to West Point Military Academy where he played center on the football team, graduated fourth in his class, and received a commission as second lieutenant in the Corps of Engineers.

Following assignments in the continental United States, Hawaii, and Nicaragua during the 1920s, in 1931 Groves became chief of supply in the Office of Engineers in Washington, D.C. Promotions came, although slowly. By 1941 he wore the rank of colonel and oversaw all military construction in the United States, including the constuction of the Pentagon in Arlington, Virginia. A large and energetic man, Groves had the reputation of getting things done. He could be blunt, and when the occasion warranted, ruthless, but subordinates respected him. In September 1942, the secretary of war selected him to head the Manhattan Project, organized to develop the atomic bomb.

One of the first decisions Groves made was to set up a plant for producing purified uranium near Black Oak Ridge. Isolation, the availability of water and electricity, and a transportation center eighteen miles away in Knoxville made the location ideal. The potential labor pool also appealed to Groves. Perhaps a Calvinistic outlook, which the people of the region shared, reminded him of lessons learned at the knee of his Presbyterian minister father. Whatever the reason, he considered the people an asset. "Above all," he said, "I knew the labor supply of East Tennessee was of a very high order from the standpoint of willingness to work. And, I knew that if we had to use many female operators ... Tennessee girls would be much more easily trained and would do better work than those of some other sections of the country. The principal reason for this was that the women here were not so sophisticated—they hadn't been reared to believe that they 'knew it all.'"

The attitudes Groves detected stemmed from a history u-nique to the region and its people. What were predominately lowland Scotch began arriving in easten Tennessee during the 1740s and 1750s. Since most came to America from Scottish settlements in northern Ireland, the appellation "Scotch-Irish" applied when distinguishing them from other immigrant groups. The Scottish-Irish connection went back to the reign of James I who had encouraged Scottish emigration to Ireland as a means of subduing the native Celtic Irish. Taking their Calvinistic faith with them, these lowland Scots established settlements in and around Ulster, earning in the process a reputation as a pugnacious frontier people. At the same time, the experience of living among a hostile Catholic population further strengthened commitment to a creed which, as the catechism of the Westminster Confession makes clear, was already austere. "All mankind," it simply states, "by the Fall, lost communion with God, are under His wrath and curse, and so made liable to all the pains of this life and to hell forever." Other groups, of course, contributed to the ethnic amalgam of southern Appalachia, but the Scotch-Irish were the most influen-tial, not only in terms of numbers but especially in religious outlook. While it cannot be said that this religious outlook accounts for everything in the southern Appalachian character, it certainly makes it easier to understand.

Combined with the experiences of Ulster and Calvinism was the indomitable factor of geography, which in the setting of east-ern Tennessee, translates into the Appalachian Mountains. The Appalachians are not particularly high, but they are steep and rugged and continue range after range. Before the advent of mod-ern transportation, they posed an almost impenetrable barrier to settlers; and once in them isolation became a way of life, even though it meant, in many cases, only a marginal existence. Even the arrival of industrialization, which began in the 1870s with exploitation of the region's coal and timber resources, subsistence farming remained the primary means of livelihood and isolation the most obvious characteristic of daily life. When General Groves decided to place uranium enrichment plants in the Black Oak Ridge area there passed only one road through it. As one nearby resident remembered in 1946, "All the folk in these parts were farmers. They worked the ground and minded their own business, peaceful folks living a simple life. We didn't pay much attention to the outside world and they didn't bother with us."

Out of these unique historical and geographical circumstances, a distinctive culture had emerged, a culture that differed fundamentally in many respects from the America that had grown up around it. Protected by the physical isolation of mountains, it had existed more or less autonomously for over a hundred years. In a culture wedded to tradition and the land, change could and often did evoke strong reaction. Poverty, along with a religious creed that emphasized individual responsibility for salvation in a hopelessly wicked world, made optimism and belief in progress difficult to accept. Instead, a more somber, melancholy view prevailed, a mood the lyrics and harmony in the Appalachian Mountain ballad has become famous for. In the popular "Mary of the Wild Moor," the attempt to return home, a common theme in many Appalachian ballads, ends typically in tragedy.

It was one cold winter night
      When the Wind blew across the wild moor,
Poor Mary came wandering home with her babe
      till she came to her own Father's door.

Oh, Father, dear Father, she cried,
      come down and open the door,
For the child in my arms it will perish and die
      By the wind blew across the wild moor.

The old man was deaf to her cry,
      Not a sound of her voice reached his ear,
The watch-dog did howl and village bell tone
      And the Wind blew across the wild moor.

Oh, why did I leave this dear spot
      Where once I was happy and free,

But now doomed to roam without friends or home
    And no one to take pity on me?

Oh how must the old man have felt
    When he came to the door in the morn.
Poor Mary was dead but the child was alive
    closely prest in its dead mother's arms.

Half frantic he tore his grey hair
    And tears down his cheeks they did pour.
The cold winter night she was perished and died
    by the wind across the wild moor.

The old man in grief pined away
    and the child to its mother went soon,
And no one they say have lived there to this day
    And the cottage to ruins has gone.

And the villagers point to the spot
    Where the willers dropped over the door,
Saying Their Mary died, once a gay village bride
    by the wind blew across the wild moor. *

Yet despite hardship and isolation, the people of the region clung tenaciously to their traditions. Proud, individualistic, and secure in their beliefs, they preferred to be left alone, to pursue their lives unfettered and as they saw fit.

Beginning in the autumn of 1942, the isolation of the mountains and its people came under fierce assault. The other America, the America of science and technology, had arrived in this valley between the Cumberlands and the Great Smoky Mountains; and it had only one purpose in mind: to vanquish enemies across the seas. This America was the "arsenal of democracy," and nothing was to be dismissed, including science, as a possible way of achieving victory. President Roosevelt created the Office of Scientific Research and Development and placed it under the direction of Dr. Vannevar Bush. It was Bush, along with Dr. James B. Conant, chairman of the National Research Committee, who initiated the Manhattan Project for which General Groves and J. Robert

Oppenheimer ultimately took charge.

Clearing of the land around Black Oak Ridge got underway in September 1942 as thousands of workers began pouring in from all over the country. By July 1943, over 500 trailers sat near the site. Dormitories for 13,000 people, barracks for another 16,000, homes and apartments with 10,000 living units, ten schools, and a hospital shot up. Seventeen restaurants, thirteen supermarkets, and seven theaters appeared almost overnight. During the peak period of construction, a prefab house went up every thirty minutes. Elsewhere huge machines moved earth to make way for construction of four colossal plants, which went by the code names K-25, X-10, Y-12, and S-50. With the exception of X-10, which functioned as a plutonium research laboratory, the others employed various ways of producing uranium 235. All plants operating at once consumed twenty percent more electricity than all of New York City. In addition to the construction, some 300 miles of roads went down and fifty-five miles of railroad track were laid. In a scant thirty-six months, the area around Black Oak Ridge grew to 75,000 people and became Tennessee's fifth largest city.

Change of such magnitude and pace inevitably produced friction. The government forced about 3,700 people off the land, and not all left willingly. Having lived on the land for generations, they were loath to part with it for any price. For some it was the second time the government had made them move, the first being the Tennessee Valley Authority (TVA) project, which had begun several years earlier. Some of the displaced took jobs with the project; others purchased farms elsewhere. One farmer along a remote edge of the project managed to escape notice for a year before an army patrol plane spotted him feeding his chickens. Meanwhile rumors spread about the purpose of the project. One theory held that the Vatican was being built on the site; another that a New Deal social experiment was underway. Tight security made matters worse. Not even burial of the dead in deserted cemeteries within the confines of the project went unchallenged. "They open up every coffin at the gates, they do," one resident remembered, "and they look at the corpse and then stick him with a needle to see if he's sure enough dead."

Frustrations plagued residents on the project site as well.

Courtesy James E. Westcott

Old world and new world meet on Black Oak Ridge. Mr. William Henry Alonzo, age eighty-two, lived by himself in a small house outside the Blair Security Gate. During the lonely evening hours he visited with the guards on duty at the gate to spin yarns of days gone by.

Tending to come from more diverse backgrounds and possessing more education, they often became impatient with the slower, more traditional lifestyles of the locals. Jokes that poked fun at the stereotypical images of the "hillbilly" became popular, and marriages between workers on the project and local residents were termed "mixed." Others commenting on the situation observed that "like the mud, one thing that is always with you is the hillbilly-furriner feud. Hillbillies are good people, but, like the rest of us, provide their share of laughs for those unused to their ways."

Despite these difficulties, the first shipments of enriched uranium left for Los Alamos, New Mexico, the bomb site, in March 1945. On July 15, 1945, General Groves arrived to observe the test. At five-thirty a.m., on July 16, 1945, an explosion lighted the desert sky with an intensity many times brighter than the midday sun. Groves turned to Dr. Bush and the two shook hands. American science and technology stood preeminent.

But with the flush of triumph also came anxiety, a feeling born out of the realization that science and technology had progressed to the point where they now threatened human existence. For some, faith in science and technology became less secure. Oppenheimer sensed it, noting how the huge mushroom cloud brought the passage from the *Bhagavad Gita* "I am become Death, the shatterer of Worlds" to mind. No East Tennessee fundamentalist witnessed the blast, but had one, he might have uttered a similar thought expressed by the Prophet Ezekiel: "Thou hast defiled thy sanctuaries by the multitude of thine iniquities, by the iniquity of thy traffic; therefore will I bring forth a fire from the midst of thee, it shall devour thee, I will bring thee to ashes." Perhaps therein lies the contribution of the Appalachian to the scientific and technological mind: namely, that scientific and technological progress, while many times useful and good, exacts a price; and that, because of the existence of evil and the absence of total free will, the ultimate price always remains hidden. It was a lesson the less optimistic world of Black Oak Ridge never forgot, but one the contemporary world seems reluctant to accept.

---

* "Mary of the Wild Moor" is quoted from *A Song Catcher in Southern Mountains: American Folk Songs of British Ancestry* (New York: Columbia University Press, 1937), 335-336.

OAKRIDGEDNESS

Charles Counts

AUGUST 1985 (remembering *Hiroshima* forty
years ago). Words explode on this page of
memory. I have been
"in solitude" pushing
back my thoughts, aiming at recreating
my space.

Settled now in my old barnlike workshop, not a modern "sealed"
building, rather a primitive handmade undesigned space. During
dark rainy nights bats emerge; I hear rats gnawing into new nests
against future cold, celebrating the animal urge to survive ...
    I remember a hut in childhood. A rambling
structure built from "nothing" but scraps
scavenged from piles of trash. Our naive thievery
had been extensive, but here were materials
discarded in the rush: intrepid spirit and
industriousness rewarded from peers and parents ...

Inside, however, the shelter provided a space for serious "sinning"
in pre-teenage exploration. Parents would not have "spared the
rod," so we were always home for supper.
    "Oakridgedness" has to do with growing up
in this new, new world of technological change
and permissiveness, mediating between double standards
of home and community.

That also must have been culture shock to our own parents who had come to adulthood from poverty, agrarian roots, and the so-called great depression.

Human opportunity did not always
ensure the growth of human potential,
but Oak Ridge did provide doors to
vacant lots of land,
empty space,
vast realms of exploration
in old and new cultures

Oakridgedness has been a steady diet of change. We had come there expecting to go home tomorrow. Now all these years later we are "home."

Rushing to win
pushing to survive
Oak Ridgers are a blend of
the eternal struggle of both
good and bad
but then we were not living by design
we were surviving by chance
big government toying with unwitting fire ...

Being human we tasted
sweet technology
ours, a triumph of existence, (only now are we
paused to ask ultimate questions):
seeing the Cumberland mountains stripped
from highland view, we are now schooled to
demand a balance of science and nature.

Oakridgedness means we have grown old
unwinding webs of persistent mystery
dependent
interdependent, stretching a "meanwhile" morality.

Oak Ridgedness means the sense to abandon "separate but equal" mentality of WWII vision. It means progress in a whole society, demanding excellence, human values, providing cultural leadership in a place patiently accepting (almost) the persistence of change.

The Aftermath

Oakridgedness, we cannot escape you,
creator of life, forecaster of death.
We pause in time of silence
to listen to possibilities of peace,
entwined with technical testings of unknown
substances. And we wonder.

PART II

THE POSTWAR
YEARS

THE TRANSITION
YEARS

WORK BUS, 1945

Robert R. Hentz

Peaple came out of the drugstore on the corner. The proprietor
closed the door behind them. The lights went out except for
the one in back that stays on all night. There was a stir in the
small group that was breaking up. Goodbyes were said. The
townsmen were homeward plodding their weary ways and leaving
the world to darkness and to me. Well, not quite. There were a few
other people on the corner waiting for the work bus that would
take us to work on the night shift at a site of the atomic-bomb
project some thirty miles away. Also, there was the light of a street
lamp and the store's neon light casting irregular patterns of red and
yellowish light on the wet concrete walk and asphalt street. A small
southern town was tucking itself in on a mild, wet November night.

The lights of the work bus appeared over the hill. It bore
down with tires humming on the wet road, stopped, picked up its
new passengers and continued on its way, leaving the sleeping
town behind. In the bus, cigarette smoke hung in the air and curled
from yellow circles glowing in the dark. Some of the passengers
were trying to sleep, some stared out of the windows into the
impenetrable curtain of night, and others chattered the lively and
earthy gossip of the hill country. Suddenly, a passenger started to
sing a hymn and one by one the other passengers chimed in. The
sound of their singing swelled, flooded the bus, and overflowed
into the night. "If I could hear my mother pray again ..." they sang,
and then folk and country songs. They sang in excellent harmony

263

and with such spirit that it made my scalp tingle. A warm feeling of comradeship swept over me. Their singing achieved an effect for which no amount of skill could substitute. I was reminded of Wordsworth's definition of good poetry as the spontaneous overflow of powerful emotions.

These people seemed to lack the inhibitions to which I was accustomed. None had a particularly good voice, but none would hesitate to sing out confidently a first line, and then all the others would join in. I was the only one not singing. Why? In part, it was because of a sense of not belonging. They belonged. Their singing made them one, gave them a feeling of fraternity. I had experienced that feeling in basic training as one in a company of fellow soldiers dragging back to camp after a long march. On approach to the camp, the company would form into order, strike up a song, and proudly march into camp. It was a good feeling. But here I did not belong, and their singing suddenly made me feel lonely. Someone sang out, "In the pines, in the pines, where the sun never shines...."

The people on the bus came from the farms and small towns of mostly backwoods hill country in the southern United States. Their country had just emerged victoriously from a cataclysmic war to which they had unknowingly contributed the monstrous device of denouement. "When the roll is called up yonder..." they sang with a religious feeling that was simple, that expressed fraternity, that filled not a church but a bus taking them to produce the stuff of atomic bombs. Their war was over, but fratricide and the seeds of fratricide remained scattered throughout the world in which they lived. "Cheer up my brothers. Stand in the sunshine. We will understand it all by and by," they sang. Maybe, I hope so.

Lights appeared in the distance. The bus rolled to a stop, and the singing ceased as a military policeman boarded the bus to check passes at an entrance to the site.

Work Bus, 1945

Courtesy James E. Westcott

Off-area buses brought thousands of East Tennesseans to work in Oak Ridge.

POSTWAR FRONTIER TOWN

Mary K. Cox

My role in the Oak Ridge experience has been a trying, exciting, and wonderful adventure and after forty years, I must say that I feel honored to have been a part of it. I should point out, however, that I did not always feel honored. In truth, I came very close to leaving after the first month or two. And I came in the postwar years, when the tension and uncertainty had diminished somewhat.

I arrived in Oak Ridge in January 1946, with my husband and two children—one an infant. My husband Paul, an auditor, had been here briefly in 1943 before being sent to Colorado where the uranium for the plutonium project was mined. We expected to be in Oak Ridge for only a year, not the rest of our lives as it turned out. We lived in an E-2 apartment while waiting for a house. There was no telephone and no hope of getting one. A washing machine was out of the question. I had to wash by hand in what I came to call the "futility room." The bathroom was upstairs (more like up-the-ladder), and I had a twenty-pound baby.

To quote from a 1946 Christmas letter, "We have plenty of new-city gripes: houses that leak all over—it's not unusual to rush in with an armful of pails when it starts raining. We get up in the middle of the night to let the plumber in to fix whatever is stopped up. The maintenance department doesn't know that people sleep mostly at night. We walk for groceries over roughly crushed rock, scuttling for the ditches when the trucks come by, stand in line to get mail. We get up at daybreak to stand in line to get our names on the list to have milk delivered for *sure*, instead of going to the grocery to find it all bought up for the day. We run after the newsboy to beg him to let us subscribe. We watch a huge football field built in a week, sodded, and a game on Saturday." My hands were red from washing every day; the baby buggy mired down in the gravel, so it was of little use. Life was hard.

Worse than the physical discomforts was what seemed to me to be the lack of any personal dignity. I was almost a nonperson. I made what I thought was an appointment to see the doctor, and was told to come at two p.m. I found a whole roomful of other people who had been told the same thing, and had to wait for several hours, holding a fussy baby. The bank would not allow my name on our joint bank account—it had to be Mr. and Mrs. Paul M. Cox. Although Paul gave me a power of attorney to choose the house we would live in, I was not allowed to do so. Only he could attend to this. Even women who were heads of families and held jobs had to get a special permit to rent an apartment or house. Blacks were arbitrarily relegated to the Scarboro area, two miles from town. The Manhattan District and the military were the boss of everything.

The famous Yale sociologist Talcott Parsons delineated two classifications of social roles: (1) Instrumental—getting things done, and (2) Expressive—seeing to the emotional needs of people. Believe me, I felt that the *only* concern in Oak Ridge was instrumental. The mission was to produce refined uranium and let the chips fall where they may.

The army had moved about 1,000 families from the area and built (1) a giant gaseous diffusion plant (K-25), (2) an atomic pile, (3) an electromagnetic plant (Y-12), and (4) a city—streets, sewers, housing, electricity, police-fire-recreation departments, school system, hospital all in an incredibly short time. Such miracles can be accomplished only when the urgency is great, and only by the young. Older people have more sense. From my present perspective, I can see that the "instrumental" behavior was truly necessary, but at one time the slings and arrows really stung. General Groves, never a genial fellow, must have been a thoroughgoing instrumental type; he did get things done.

After a few months, my husband and I were awarded a

C-cemesto at 103 Gorgas Lane, just above Jackson Square. Even though we shared it with another family for a short time, it seemed like a palace after the E-2 apartment. We met some fine neighbors, and I began to experience the sense of mission and specialness of Oak Ridge. A wonderful feeling of cameraderie began to seep into my soul. Getting things done in spite of difficulties started to seem exciting.

I believe it was the Oak Ridge Symphony Orchestra, however, under the leadership of Waldo Cohn, that finally saved me from going home to Illinois in defeat. I read a rehearsal notice one evening in the paper, and said to Paul, "Please keep the children tonight. I want to check out the symphony." He said, "Okay," and right away I had a home in Oak Ridge. I had played violin in orchestras since high school, and I began to feel less isolated, less abused, less bereaved. Soon I had friends among the musicians. To this day, many of them are my good friends, although forty years have passed.

I am sure a similar role was played for other people by the Playhouse, the Art Center, the ballet groups, and a host of clubs and organizations. This was a city of young people, cosmopolitan, well educated, isolated out here in the mud. We had to find ways to make life good, and we did.

In 1948 only nineteen percent of Oak Ridgers were over forty, compared with thirty-five percent for the nation as a whole. These differences would probably be more pronounced had there been a national census taken in 1946.

The city was guided by a corps of young scientists and professionals, engaged in a young science without precedent—the science of fission products. The city had been planned for 8,000 workers during the war, but had burst into a city of 75,000, principally construction and plant production workers from the surrounding area. The scientific people had come mostly from the nuclear-related sciences affiliated with Columbia University, University of California at Berkeley, and the University of Chicago.

In the postwar years, we were caught up in the emergency idea. The graphite reactor was built in eleven months with an AAA priority. (Now it takes ten years, including lawsuits and other controversies.) We were a community of young, energetic strangers out to change the world. The local people who had been dispossessed had an understandably hostile attitude toward us. On the average, Oak Ridgers had more education and more money to spend than their neighbors. Most of us had at least a high school education and many had college degrees. Some figures suggest that there were upwards of 300 Ph.D.'s living in Oak Ridge in 1946. In contrast, the average county resident had attended school for less than seven years. Of course attitudes differed.

Our feeling of isolation and of being misunderstood by folks in the surrounding area, as well as our quite real physical hardships, combined to make us extraordinarily helpful to one another. Many car pools for driving to work were formed, and my husband said, "If you think women are gossips, you should hear the conversation in my all-male car pool." These were times of great uncertainty about the future of Oak Ridge—now that the war was over. Rumors were rife.

The women in our neighborhood had informal "coffee klatches" every morning after the men had gone to work and the children were off to school. We borrowed and lent everything we had; we pooled information on child care, ration coupons, the best method of removing coal soot from painted walls. We all had soft-coal burning furnaces. There were no old families, no status structures, and very few telephones. We happily carried messages from the telephone down to the corner.

A big effort was made to keep us happy while the city's fate hung in the balance. Even for a short time after the war, bus service and movie theatres were free. Our rental agreements stated that no business was to be conducted in the homes. I was teaching piano at home and asked about the legality of it. The official said to me, "I can't give you permission to do this, but for goodness sake, go right ahead. It makes for more satisfaction if people can arrange music lessons for their children. Say nothing about it and we won't either."

There were boardwalks through the woods which provided shortcuts to Jackson Square, Cedar Hill School, and homes of friends on different streets. Our homes had no lot lines and no fences. Children, dogs, and delivery men ran freely through all yards. "It's not your yard," the kids would say. "It belongs to the government." And they were right.

My neighbor on one side was from the Deep South, and on

the other side from New England, while I was from the Midwest. Points of view differed greatly. Very often I was in the position of mediation, like it or not. We all had children of similar age. It was an education just to live on our street; and an even larger education to live in Oak Ridge as we slowly began to turn our youthful energy toward infusing the expressive into the instrumental nature of this postwar frontier town.

Courtesy James E. Westcott

Living in postwar Oak Ridge brought few more comforts to residents than had existed during the war, with the town still dotted by boardwalks and open storm drainage gullies. Yet, in this frontier community, people began to take pride in their homes, growing magnificent flower gardens as seen here in August 1946.

THE MANY FACES
OF SECURITY

Ellison H. Taylor

T he word "security," like all nouns, comes with either a small or a capital "S." Except at the beginning of a sentence it comes with a small "s" when it means what a baby feels in its mother's arms or what you leave at the bank to secure a loan. With a capital "S" it has come to mean a system of regulations, people, and devices to protect some property or enterprise. To most visitors to Oak Ridge, and probably to many residents, Security means those sometimes clever, sometimes stupid, and usually inane billboards on all the roads leading to the installations. But to people who worked a long time on the Manhattan Project, Security has shown many other faces.

In the winter of 1942, I was an instructor in chemical engineering at Cornell. One day I got a telegram from H. C. Urey at Columbia saying my former professor had recommended me for "urgent war research." Could I get a leave for four months? That seemed more exciting and useful than teaching chemical engineering, so I asked permission from the department head. He demurred a bit, citing the importance of keeping engineers coming out, but said that if I really wanted to I could go to Columbia. I accepted Urey's offer by return telegram. "Urgent," the offer had said; I assumed I'd be gone by the end of the week. I wasn't. Nor the next week. Then no word for a long period. I began to get nervous about my state of limbo. Finally, I talked to one of the chemistry professors who, I knew, had some sort of war research contract.

"That's simple," he said. "They're just investigating you. It takes awhile." Eventually, they decided that I was harmless, and I joined the Manhattan Project for four months—later extended to about forty years.

My formal introduction to Security came in stages. For example, on my first day at Columbia, one of Urey's colleagues explained the problem they wanted me to work on, and then told me it was part of a project to make a superbomb from uranium. If that proved unworkable, he said, then at least they could make an airplane that could fly indefinitely without refueling. He finished by telling me that all this was not to be discussed with anyone outside the project, and that there was no time to waste since the Germans were known to be interested in the same thing. I used to wonder, when I stood on my apartment house roof during air raid alerts, how the German project was doing.

So far as I can remember, that first conversation was all I was ever told about Security. The physical aspects of Security (rules, guards, devices) were in evidence even then. The windows and doors of Havemeyer Hall, the old chemistry laboratory at Columbia where we worked, were decorated with metallic tapes which, when disturbed, sent an alarm to the Pinkerton office on 125th Street, about ten blocks away. At night our research notebooks all went into an antique Mosler safe in the office of Urey's secretary, and it too was connected to the Pinkerton office. Any attempt to open it before the preset time would automatically activate the alarm. And further Security included a staff of guards on duty at the doors of the building. One morning Urey's secretary opened the safe before the preset time. Within minutes Pinkerton men, guns drawn, charged out of their car and up the walk, only to be confronted at the door by Columbia's own equally well-armed guards. Fortunately, they parleyed rather than opening fire, and nobody was hurt.

My first realization, however, that there existed a whole full-fledged entity called Security came a little later. We were expanding to other floors in Havemeyer, and partitions were being put in to separate us from those sections still used by the chemistry department. These partitions left us just the back stairs and the elevator for getting from floor to floor. At night, when only a few were working, the back stairs were locked and a guard placed at each elevator door to control access. During the day I always used the stairs to get about, but one day I was confronted by a young man in a trench coat who said I couldn't use them anymore. I said, more or less, "Who says? I work here." He opened his trench coat, pulled out his wallet, and showed me his identification. He was a second lieutenant in the U.S. Army, and he let me know that he was part of Security and that he was in charge of those stairs. Soon he was replaced by a more permanent barrier, and we were limited to our creaky elevator.

One thing I noticed after coming to Oak Ridge in 1945 was the relatively small amount of information we were given at Columbia, compared to the people at Chicago. We knew, in a vague way, that the headquarters of the project was at the University of Chicago, and I guess we knew it was code named the Metallurgical Laboratory; but still it was a vague sort of place where Urey and the other big shots went occasionally. We knew that Site Y was somewhere in the far west, and we knew Site X was near Knoxville and was called Dogpatch; but I never heard of Site W (Hanford) until I came to Oak Ridge. And I don't believe the Chicago people knew details of what we were doing, but they knew enough to make visits to Columbia to learn about such things as fluorine chemistry. The day after Hiroshima, however, the huge extent of the project became known to everyone. It is revealing how successful wartime Security was when I recall how much I learned from the newspapers that morning.

By the time I came to Oak Ridge, I was familiar with most of the outward aspects of Security on the project: badges, guards at the doors, safes and locked filing cabinets for notebooks and reports, and the various grades of secrecy that had to be applied to documents and what we said. A new aspect here, however, was that Security spilled over into everyday life because of the guards at the gates of the reservation, and the requirement of passes for *all* residents and visitors. It was rumored, and probably happened, that sheriff's deputies hung around the gates to see if they could spot illegal liquor when a trunk was opened and searched. An incident that I know personally involved not liquor, but surplus electronic and mechanical gadgets that a girl had bought from Edmund Scientific as a birthday present for her boyfriend. The guards thought it was a secret weapon, which it probably had been before it was surplused. It took a lot of talking to get it all back.

Security was always in evidence during the war, but was never anything we were too concerned about. It served a function and came to our attention mostly through annoying requirements such as having to get the right signatures on requisitions, or having to remember every morning to wear your badge. There must have been cases of injustice or damage done by Security, but these were merely part of the injustice inherent in war, and in any case didn't come to the attention of the scientific staffs.

The postwar years, however, brought a change in the relations between Security and scientists. The principal reason was probably because the nuclear bomb, "The Secret," had been demonstrated to work. Obviously, after Hiroshima, there were still details of great importance still unknown by potential enemies, but they were details that could be discovered by straightforward measurements or intensive empirical investigations. These might cost a lot of money, but anybody contemplating such an investment, and determined enough, knew that there was no real barrier to their intentions. Essentially every scientist on or off the project knew that on August 5, 1945, our monopoly of atomic energy had ended.

Some politicians and part of the public, however, did not understand this, believing instead that if Security were only tight enough, the United States could maintain an enduring advantage over the rest of the world. They blamed communism and disloyal scientists, not Hiroshima and the universal knowledge of science, for allowing other nations to make their own atomic bombs. The implication of communism in several espionage cases (Bruno Pontecorvo, Klaus Fuchs, and the Rosenbergs, for example) was seen by some politicians and segments of the public as compelling reasons for Security taking wholesale action to forestall other acts of espionage. Under pressure from such attitudes and opinions, Security began to move more forcefully into our lives, and in ways less benign and more threatening. Thus there ensued a period, from the end of the war until the early fifties, in which many people, initially cleared by Security during the war, learned that their clearances were in question.

Surprising or not, if the new clearance cases had been based on substantial evidence, they would have been accepted and supported by most scientists. We took seriously the continuing need for secrecy and our agreement to uphold it. I have no statistics on what fraction of the postwar Security cases were based on correct and damaging information, but in all the cases I knew about, the allegations were either demonstrably false or trivial.

One incident involved membership in a political action committee associated with the Congress of Industrial Organization (CIO). In two or three cases the charge was that persons had cosigned a letter to the editor of a scientific news magazine. This letter, which could have been interpreted as partial support for an article in the magazine endorsing international control of atomic energy, was also partly critical of U.S. policy. In addition, there were one or more questionable associates to explain, or vague testimony from former landlords or neighbors. (Questionable associates never seemed to be balanced against upright ones, and favorable accounts were summarized as "no derogatory information.") The people concerned in these cases were cleared after hearings in Oak Ridge, and hopefully suffered no more than the uncertainty of the moment and the affronts to their integrity.

Other cases, however, were more costly to the individuals involved. One case concerning allegations about a man's wife—about her associations—required the husband and wife to attend a hearing in another state. These allegations turned out to be erroneous. The investigators had neglected to check dates and places; the events they described could not possibly have involved the people they claimed. Instead, the investigations chose to go along with the derogatory information, causing considerable financial and great emotional expense to the couple. Though the case was dropped after the discrepancies were noted, the AEC Security could have decided the case in Oak Ridge if they had simply let the defendant know what the supposedly derogatory information was.

The most serious damage done by Security was to a man whose clearance was revoked when he was preparing to return to work after a bout with tuberculosis. The allegations in his case pertained to associations, begun years before, with alleged communists, as well as alleged membership in a communist-dominated organization (a bookstore), and a charge of falsification of a security questionnaire. He was cleared in the end, but only after one hearing in Oak Ridge (where the AEC refused to restore clearance) and a security review hearing in Washington, D.C. The worst feature of the case was the length of time over which it was dragged out: eight months waiting for clearance after a routine application; ten months until he was notified of the denial of clearance after the first hearing; a month or two waiting for the transcript from the Oak Ridge review board hearing; and finally, six months waiting for the favorable decision from Washington. Two years, in other words, for a convalescent to live in uncertainty! Two years without salary and without a clear future!

He wasn't an unknown. He had worked for some years at the National Bureau of Standards; he had participated, early in the war, in development of the proximity fuse; and near the end of the war, he had done scientific liaison work for the Manhattan Project, employed directly by the headquarters of the Manhattan District in Oak Ridge. Little wonder he suffered a relapse and was never able to return to work after his vindication.

One can understand that Security, at times, might have felt surrounded by spies and traitors, and that it felt compelled to do something. This tendency, however, was strengthened in the post-World War II years by public and political reaction to stories of espionage and communism. Although the examples that were known involved indefensible breaches of trust, their practical importance was not nearly as great as the public assumed. The real secret was revealed at Hiroshima; details after that were of little consequence. But politicians such as Senator Joseph McCarthy began to make political capital of the supposed laxness in Security, both on the project and elsewhere, and created enormous pressure on the Security system as a whole, not to mention the country. This helps to explain, but not to justify, the lapses in justice which were so common for several years after the war in clearance investigations by the AEC. Suspicion by association is a sometimes necessary investigative tool in finding criminals, but it should not degenerate into guilt by association as it did during the postwar years.

SECRECY IN THE FIFTIES

Thomas F. Howard

No one has been able to write about Oak Ridge without dwelling on the importance of secrecy during the war years. Usually there is some reference to the opening of the town to the public in 1949, with a suggestion that this marked the passing of an era when secrecy was of great concern. It comes to me, though, that it was really after the war that secrecy in Oak Ridge became most pervasive. The gates and fences were gone, yet secrecy persisted in the everyday life of the 1950s in subtle and powerful ways. There was still a formal apparatus to prevent the development of public knowledge—loyalty oaths, security clearances, lie-detector tests, badges and so forth—but what was most effective was an almost unconscious conspiracy of silence in which secrets were protected by voluntary non-communication. This was a culture of secrecy, which extended even to matters that weren't military or classified. One result that might be surprising to outsiders is that it was possible to grow up in Oak Ridge and not have any idea how important a role the city continued to play in nuclear weapons production.

We were given to think that the military phase of our history was pretty much over—Atoms for Peace was the slogan when I was a kid. When I went off to college and was asked about Oak Ridge and the bomb, I would reply confidently that it was all peacetime applications today; the military stuff was in Los Alamos. I did know there was something secret and presumably military about Y-12, but I didn't have the vaguest idea what it was or how important it might be. Absolutely no one ever talked about weapons in public, with the result that they just floated out there at the edge of consciousness, unthought about and obscure.

At most social gathering, people talk about their jobs and what's going on at work. But I don't remember hearing much shop talk when I was growing up in Oak Ridge. As a result, I had at best a hazy idea of what most adults actually did, despite the Oak Ridge school system's good science courses, innumerable trips to the Museum of Atomic Energy with visiting relatives, and the fact that my father was a scientist at the Oak Ridge National Laboratory (ORNL). Eventually I acquired a fairly clear idea of what my father did, but the jobs of most other adults remained black boxes: people were said to work "at the Lab," or "out at the plants," and that, it seemed, was all there was to be said about *that*.

This kind of thing was predictable for people who made nuclear weapons for a living. But most of the ORNL people like my father were probably doing work that they could talk about, and the funny thing is that they didn't very much. It may be that veterans of the Manhattan Project—and that was a large proportion of the adults whom I knew through my parents—had just gotten so used to not talking about their work that they were never quite able to switch back again.

This professional reticence not only concealed weapons production, but also tended to throw scientific research as well into a kind of murky half-light where no one on the outside could understand it. On the positive side, it produced a high degree of sociability; the habit of confining work-related talk to working hours probably made people good at connecting with each other on other interests. This contributed to the often noted vigor of community institutions like the Oak Ridge Civic Music Association and the Playhouse, as well as a high level of parental concern with the school system.

I finally learned of the extent of weapons work at Oak Ridge fifteen years after I graduated from Oak Ridge High School, when in 1978 the government tried to suppress publication of an article in the *Progressive* magazine on "how the H-bomb works." (The government was never able to develop a convincing case—no laws had been broken—and had to give up its efforts after a few months.) Howard Morland, the author of the article, had arrived at his conclusions using unclassified data and personal interviews. An antinuclear activist and writer, Morland wanted to understand the actual mechanism of the hydrogen bomb in order to make sense of such questions as why the Defense Department wanted to go on with underground bomb testing. He traveled around the country and spoke with workers, famous and obscure, in the nuclear industry, employing all his ingenuity to tease out bits of information that would explain how the bomb actually worked. (He recounted this process in an engaging book, *The Secret That Exploded*, published in 1981.)

The actual "secret of the H-bomb" turned out to be almost a by-product of this voyage of discovery, and not very startling. Morland's principal contribution was to illuminate the daily workings of an occupational subculture in which the production of weapons has become just another complex industrial process, not all that different from the manufacture of computers or airplanes. It could have been about Oak Ridge, and it was.

The *Progressive* censorship case was one of those events that illuminate the spirit of the times in new and unexpected ways. The tenacity with which the government tried to protect the "secrecy" of an idea that the Russians must have had since 1953 and the degree of support for this attempt at censorship even by supposedly more liberal members of the media, made people realize the power of the taboos connected with nuclear weapons. What was most striking to me personally was the fact that I had completely failed to grasp an essential fact about my hometown until well into my adult life: that Y-12 was one of the most important stations along the nuclear weapons assembly line.

Seen from this perspective, the strangeness of life in Oak Ridge during the hyper-security days of the war, which has been the subject of so much discussion, actually seems quite unexceptional. There was a war on; the Germans were thought to be building the bomb; we had to beat them to it; this meant a crash program of thousands of people working night and day surrounded by tight security so the enemy wouldn't find out and redouble his efforts to get there first. That's pretty straightforward. Dramatic and unheard-of for the people involved, no doubt, but not hard to understand: extraordinary measures for extraordinary times, which everyone thought would end when the war ended.

The *really* interesting thing to ponder is the way this emergency mentality was made into a permanent part of everyday life, to support the production of nuclear weapons after the emergency had passed. The routinization of bomb production was accompanied by the routinization of secrecy. Who needs fences and guard towers when people have stopped noticing what's going on anyway? By discouraging discussion of technical details, the system discouraged discussion of the rationale of the entire process. People did their jobs and kept quiet when the question of responsibility came up. People who didn't know never found out because they were diverted from thinking that there was anything to find out. This habit of secrecy was odd, in a way, for there was a lot of encouragement in Oak Ridge—in the schools and in the generally liberal atmosphere of the town—for asking questions and looking for better ways to do things. But this worked only up to a point. Where it could have accomplished the most, this spirit of enlightenment was never really provided. Oak Ridge might have become a forum for vigorous and well-informed public debate in nuclear weapons before the arms race began. But it didn't, and a historic opportunity slipped away.

Courtesy Department of Energy

Oak Ridgers celebrate the opening of the gate in 1949, casting the secrecy of the Atomic City into a new dimension.

GROWING UP IN OAK RIDGE

Courtesy James E. Westcott

GROWING UP IN THE ATOMIC CITY

Carolyn Korsmeyer

T hose first years in school I spent a lot of time under my desk, bunched into an egg shape with the soles of my feet at one end and upside-down hair at the other. You weren't allowed to put your hands over your ears, and the bells pounded at your head. Pulsing blasts, one after another, seemed to go on for so long that this time you knew it must be for real.

Then they would stop, and there would be huge silence and a flood of air. We unfolded, crept out, and shook the cramps from our legs. We didn't have to sit down at once but were allowed to wander to the window to look out and see for ourselves that the outside world was still there.

The warning bell for a civil defense drill was the same as the one used for fire drills, but it was released at rapid intervals, like a hyphenated scream. For the fire drills you left the building and stood in the recess yard well away from the dangers of flames and falling roofs. For protection from the Bomb, ready with its first breath to blow you to kingdom come, you didn't even leave your classroom.

It never looked like a mushroom to me. I thought of it as something inverted, like a waterfall boiling up from its source. It was something that could be pictured only from a great distance blooming over its prey, or else abstractly in a diagram of concentric circles: Center—annihilation; first ring—fire; second ring—melting heat; third ring—radiation.... I forget the details, probably because at the time I tried very hard to ignore them. We were told how far it was from the center to the outer ring, and we were told how much time we had to make the distance. We were not told how to run that fast.

We were at the center. We knew about the Bomb because this was its source. In fact, it was the reason we were here at all. The Bomb was made right here, which made us terribly important. So when we were not crouched underneath our desks or sweating through a nightmare, the Bomb was a source of pride. Little dancing atoms were the town's insignia. They vibrated across civic posters, restaurant menus, club badges, public signs. Possessively, we claimed the Bomb as ours.

We were at the center also because somewhere deep inside Russia there was another Bomb aimed right at us. We were on the list of the top ten cities in the U.S. that the Russians wanted to bomb. For years we kids repeated this conviction: the top ten, maybe even the first of the top ten on the list of cities the Russians wanted to bomb. I imagined a white piece of paper torn from a pad with "1. Oak Ridge, Tennessee" penciled at the top. No one I knew could name the other nine.

Our innocence of the other targets is significant, for in the unreliable memories of that childhood there is an insulated quality, as though we were, without knowing it, contained. Some of that feeling is doubtless the general ignorance of being very young, but surely some of it was special to the place. It was an island we lived on, surrounded by a world utterly different. Driving out of town one could catch glimpses of that other world: thin, sour-looking people who turned their backs when you drove by, who disappeared into rusting pickups, unpainted shacks, tilting trailers—improbable places to live, though they seemed to be at home. Or, on a quiet Sunday morning, up the valley through the woods would drift an uncanny music, more shouting than singing, the faint sound of worship so passionate and strong it echoed on our ridge. I would stand at the edge of the woods and hold my breath to hear the roaring, tidal sound, like a chant, like the ebb and flow of water, like nothing I could put a name to. They were the Holy Rollers (so I heard), and they worshipped God at the top of their lungs. I wondered if I had ever seen them as I peered from the back windows of the car on family drives beyond the town.

288

Many generations lived on the weedy edges of those county roads, but in our town there were only two: parents and children. Grandparents, uncles, aunts, cousins, all lived somewhere else. In the mornings our fathers went to work and in the evenings they came home. In between, our mothers stood at kitchen windows and watched their children play in the yard or in the near-deserted street, or saw them disappear down the hill into the brown woods. We children lived in multitudes. Our friends were invariably close by, next door or up the street. The hilly roads were empty enough for bicycling and roller skating, and we filled the extensive back yards with Red Rover, Simon Says, and Swing the Statue. And the woods were always there, snaked with trails and secret places.

The whole world I grew to know was quite set aside from the business of the town. The plants where atoms were split and bombs made were placed at the far edges of the area, cloaked in security so taken for granted that it forestalled curiosity. Life in the middle, a life of homes and schools and churches and a few stores, went on as if independent, so that there was an old gulf between the life I came to know and the whole reason we were there. In fact, I was in college before it occurred to me how odd it was not to know what your father did at work. (I discount the little girl who lived up the street, who bragged that her father put the screws into the atomic bomb. She was silenced one day by an older boy who announced with authority that the atomic bomb didn't *have* any screws. That showed her.)

The miles of woods that filtered those mysterious Sunday voices started at the very edge of my neighborhood. The trees had grown so close that few of them attained great height, but they were dense enough to hide a person only a short distance away. It was difficult to pass through the growth except by trail, but there were dozens of these, and once you learned the pattern you would not get lost.

We tramped old trails clear again, founded villages of mossy stone, charted maps and built treehouses. There my friends and I peeled back centuries in our games. We were Indians, the ones who had made these trails. It didn't occur to us that anyone might have lived here in the time between us and the Indians. We gave ourselves picturesque and uninventive names like Running Deer and Silver Moon and Wildflower; and we imagined that we walked in

289

the densest forest without disturbing a leaf, glided through under-brush like a breeze, whistled like all the birds, made friends with the fox, the deer, and the mountain lion.

The woods became a second neighborhood. I knew the paths there better than the streets of town. In summer green leaves swam above our heads, thickening the air with color and permitting only glimpses of the sky beyond. Striding down the hill and then gazing up was like diving in deep water and seeing the mottled surface of the waves above. We roamed through the woods day after day, hardly like breezes, blundered into cobwebs, collected ticks and poison ivy, and came home enchanted.

In winter the woods became a vast landscape of sticks and frost, a bleak mesh of brown and grey against an oyster-colored sky. It was then that one could more clearly see the network of paths, some wide and trodden thoroughfares, others viney and obscure. The uneven hills prevented clear sight down a path for any distance, but if one were able to scale a very tall tree, it would be evident that the widest and longest paths eventually met a dirt road that snaked along the border of the valley.

This was G Road. It marked the edge of a small, old commun-ity, one we Oak Ridge kids occasionally invaded at the end of long hikes. There ancient people sat on stoops, bony girls carried babies and spoke in shrill voices, boys at gas stations smoked, spat, and showed gaps instead of teeth.

G Road was a place of hiding between a stream and a forest, and from time to time (it was said) escaped convicts from Petros made their way there. From time to time, therefore, we were supposed to stay home.

And G Road was an evacuation route. One of those roads marked in red on civil defense maps, paths on the way from danger should the bells ring and the plant whistles begin to wail in earnest. It annoyed me that G Road, our gateway to the past, our landmark for adventure, the boundary between the imaginary world in the woods and the strange, real one beyond—that G Road should also be an evacuation route. This lent the place a vague menace, less likely but more disturbing than a stray convict.

In time, I outgrew play in the woods, though for years I would wander down in a yearly pilgrimage, watch the trails become overgrown and gradually disappear, and wonder loftily what

Courtesy James E. Westcott

The youth of Oak Ridge bear the emblem of their town's legacy.

younger kids did with themselves if they didn't play in the woods. As for my friends and me, as our imaginations became less and less sufficient for our adventuresome yearnings, we climbed higher and higher trees, picked our way over barbed wire fences to scale the water tower at the bottom of the hill, or exercised our new driver's licenses by driving further and further into the country in search of the unfamiliar. I think what I looked for most was age, evidence of long habitation. A crumbling brick structure, said to be a Civil War powder mill, sagging barns, pocked tombstones—all such things manifested both a decay and a permanence that one would not find at home.

Looking back, two aspects of Oak Ridge stand out in my memory—its displaced quality, and the nature around. We were in the South, but not southern; in Appalachia, but a scientific and professional community; in a place newly formed, without tradition. Yet at the same time, the stability of surrounding nature dominated the way we lived. Today, my own city-bred children recoil from a June bug like they've met Godzilla, look upwards at night and exclaim, "Hey, stars!" and I realize how much my own childhood passed in ease with natural beauty—stars, sunsets, lakes, woods, hills, and ticks, poison ivy, and all.

"OUT!" CHILDREN AT PLAY (1945-1950)

Marilou Awiakta (Bonham Thompson)

an you come out? A tree's down in the woods! A big one! The storm last night must've done it." Wayne jiggled from one bare foot to the other on the porch steps of our B-house, which were griddle hot in the July sun. "It's the biggest tree you've ever seen. Goes from one side of the hollow to the other! Let's walk the log."

"I have to ask Mama."

Since she was nearby in the kitchen, Mama asked first, "Have you finished your chores, Marilou ... made your bed, run the vacuum, dusted?"

"Yes, ma'am. All but the dusting."

"Hm ..." It sounded like "no," but she was smiling, probably thinking of times she'd told me about when she was ten years old and played in trees. "I guess the dusting can wait," she said. "Go on out."

Out! Out! Out! The place to be. Children in the neighborhood of South Tampa Lane (and there were dozens of us) played out as much as possible and wherever the whim took us—tree-studded yards, unpaved streets, deep woods. Mama said we sometimes looked like schools of fish swimming around.

As I bolted through the back door, she called, "Remember, dares go first." The words tied onto me like ribbons on my long, black braids, bumping gently against the back of my mind as Wayne and I ran through my yard, then by the Smiddies' house. Our feet were summer-tough, so we hardly faltered as we crossed the gravel-packed dirt of Tabor Road and made our way down the rough path where the woods began, to the boardwalk, just below the lip of the hollow. A different world here—shadowed, cool, alive with rustle, twitter, hum and the succulent odor of moist loam and growing leaves. From the direction of the tree we heard shouts and laughter.

"Wayne, do you think anybody's walked the log yet?"

"Bet not. Too high."

The boardwalk carried the sound of our running feet ahead of us, and a girl's voice rang out, "Hey, y'all. Somebody's comin'!"

We arrived. And stopped short.

The tree was awesome. Its trunk, immense and straight, reached across the "V" of the hollow—perhaps twenty feet high over the deepest part. On the far side, the wide, heavy limbs had taken smaller trees with them as they crashed down. Here and there a branch shook where some of our friends were exploring the damage. On the near side, where we stood, was a crater, smelling of deep earth—the biggest hole I'd ever seen. Upended at its edge was the tree's vast wheel of jagged roots. The great taproot—which had held longest and snapped off clean—stuck straight out for about four feet, showing its might. Yet the wind, which we had never seen, had been stronger. And the tree, though felled, was still alive and would be weeks in dying. The mystery of it all was irresistible.

Down in the crater, Janice and her cousin, Linda, stopped rummaging long enough to shout hello. And Freddie, who had ventured a little way out on the trunk, jumped down and said to me, "I dare you to walk it!"

I gauged the danger of the tree. Slowly pulling the end of my braid through my hand, I weighed the advantages of being the first to walk it.

I looked back at Freddie and said, "Dares go first."

Freddie shook his head.

But Wayne jumped onto the trunk, near the base. The most wiry and agile of us all, he could have climbed the tree even if it

295

Courtesy Department of Energy

"The boardwalk, just below the lip of the hollow. A different world here—shadowed, cool, alive with rustle, twitter, hum and succulent odor of moist loam and growing leaves."

had been upright. He moved around, getting "the feel" of the log. Freddie yelled, "Wayne's gonna walk it!"

Heads popped up through the fallen branches; two boys and a girl began climbing down. Out of sight, someone wading in the creek called, "Wait for me." From farther up the hollow came the snap of twigs as other kids rushed toward the log. When about fifteen of us had ranged ourselves below it to watch, Wayne gripped the bark with his feet, took his mark on the fallen branches, lifted his arms for balance, and slowly began to walk.

We held our breaths, thinking with him: *Steady as you go ... Steady ... Keep your eyes on the mark ... The highest part now— don't look down ... Steady ... Don't hurry ... Almost safe ... Keep going ..."*

"He made it!" We hollered and cheered. Above us Wayne beat his chest and gave a Tarzan yell.

Then Linda said she'd try. And Freddie said, "Me next."

We whiled away most of the afternoon with the tree. On the way home, three of us stopped by Mary Jean's house to play on her rope swing. It was the best one in the neighborhood because it hung from a high limb, had a sturdy knot on the end of it and a wide clearing around it. You could get a good running start and swing in a soaring arc without risk of braining yourself on another tree.

The rest of the day went as usual. Since most of our fathers worked at the plants (doing what they weren't allowed to say) and left work at the same time, everyone had supper between five-thirty and six-thirty, then drifted out again, most often to South Tampa Lane, which was a dead end and flat. During twilight we played "Red Rover," "Crack-the-Whip," or "Hopscotch." (When the street was finally paved, we also rode bicycles and roller-skated).

"Hide-and-Seek" and "Kick-the-Can" were our favorite games after dark, when the woods seemed to draw closer to the small houses, bringing the scent of honeysuckle, and street lights cast soft, white circles on the road. "Hide-and-Seek" was fun but the problem was that those who were "caught" were likely to tell on those trying to make "home-free." In "Kick-the-Can," the "caughts" were helpful because the clatter of tin set everyone free.

We learned the wisdom of mutual advantage and also of

knowing your adversary. Having played together so much, we knew the ways of anyone designated "It"—who ranged far, who tricked you by pretending to be out of sight, who "hugged the base." Each of us created a strategy accordingly. Scattering wide during the count—when "It's" eyes were closed—we maneuvered back to the base, creeping along the edge of the woods or around the houses, darting from bush to tree. Strategy plus speed, silence and surprise were the keys to success. In France, in the mid-1960s, when I was an interpreter for the U.S. Air Force during the NATO withdrawal, I would adapt the skills I'd learned in these games to power politics, which are "Hide-and-Seek" and "Kick-the-Can" on a grand scale—except the stakes are higher.

An important element of our summer was going barefooted. "School's out, shoes off!" was our motto around home. From the first of May, the persistent question to our parents was, "Can I go barefooted?" Some said "yes" right away. Others like mine, who were Appalachians "of the old school," insisted, "Wait 'til the ground warms up. It's hot on top but cold underneath. It's not good for your bones. It'll make you have rheumatism later in life."

Now I appreciate my parents' wisdom, but at the time I said, "Other kids are doing it." And the next day I asked again, "Can I go barefooted?"

We didn't need books to tell us "the earth is a living organism." We knew it through our feet and we wanted that connection as soon as possible. Also, because we lived on the atomic frontier, where change and flux swirled around us, we intuitively reached toward Mother Earth to help us feel rooted, grounded, centered. Mama suggested an even deeper meaning of going barefooted, which she said I would some day understand:

Mother's Advice While Bandaging My Stubbed Toe

If you go barefoot in the world
you have to take bad stubs in stride—
or hide in shoes. "Be plucky, like an Indian,"
that's what my papa said to me.
And always test the "seems" of things—
briars may lurk in dew-drenched grass
and jagged glass in heaps of leaves.
The toughest sole can't bear these
without a wound.

298

Bare feet can't tease nature. So
choose our path with wary eyes
and do likewise with humans too.
Be wary, but run on ...
Go barefoot and feel the joy
and when pain comes, bind up your toe
and go your way again.
"Be plucky, like an Indian."[1]

Good advice. As children, however, we weren't often thinking of deeper meanings. We were concerned with ourselves and what to do next.

Our choices were governed not so much by seasons as by weather and availability of playmates. In fair weather, we played out. In foul weather, we stayed in the house or on the porch, reading, listening to the radio or amusing ourselves with checkers, Parchesi, or jacks. Most friends came from the neighborhood, which followed the contour of the hilltop—North and South Tampa Lanes and the upper portions of Taylor and Tabor Roads. Except for two flattops, the houses were cemestos—A's, B's or D's—and in every house were two or three children. (Oak Ridge had a young and very prolific population.)

Gender in playmates didn't matter much. Age did. "Little kids" (age 8 down) rarely played with "big kids" (9-13). (My sister Adele was in the first group, I in the second). But the groups often played close to each other—"school-of-fish style"—and the main cause of fussing was when someone tried to butt in where he/she didn't belong.

Although our mothers usually were at home, they answered most of our pleas for peacemaking by saying, "Go straighten yourselves out." Except, of course, in near-tragedies like the Joan of Arc play, which the little kids staged down in the woods.

Lee Ann, who always whined, had begged for a leading role. "You always make me be a dog or a cat," she said. "This time I want to be *somebody*." The directors, Cleo and Joyce, who were sisters, said, "Okay, Lee Ann, you can be Joan of Arc." They made a pyre of branches at the foot of a tree, stood Lee Ann on top of it and lashed her to the trunk. Then Joyce held a match to the pyre. At the first curl of smoke, someone ran to get the nearest mother. Tragedy was averted but everyone involved had to "stay in" for the rest of the day, except "Joan of Arc."

Imaginary stories were popular with all of us. Plots began with an idea: "Let's pretend that you're Tarzan, he's Boy and I'm Cheetah" (my favorite role) or, "Let's play house" or, "Let's play war" (World War II had just ended). From there we improvised the script, sometimes with odd results, such as when Cleo and Joyce suggested, "Let's play 'the Crucifixion.'"

Joyce said, "Cleo, you be the Virgin Mary, I'll be Jesus, and Lee Ann you be the Roman soldier who gives me a drink of vinegar." An oak sapling in our yard was selected for the cross, with a stepladder propped against it. Joyce climbed to the top, held out her arms and dropped her head. The "Virgin Mary" knelt at the bottom. For want of a long-handled sop, the "Roman soldier" was given a bucket of water.

When Joyce cried piteously, "I thirst! I thirst!" Lee Ann doused her with the whole bucketful.

"God damn you, Lee Ann!" Joyce charged down from the cross and beat her up before anyone could prevent it.

Aside from the atom, Oak Ridge had two things that made our childhood different from that of most children from other places. One was the fence. It encircled the whole area, about ninety-four square miles. When I tell non-Ridgers about it—the barbed wire, watchtowers and armed guards—they look worried and say, "Didn't you children feel *oppressed*?"

I laugh when I remember how free and safe we felt to roam at will. "Where are the children?" "Out and gone," was a frequent exchange among our mothers. Of course, we had to tell them our general direction—"the woods" or "Jackson Square to the movie" or "around home." But other than that, nobody worried. Everyone knew that to molest a child on government property was a federal crime. The FBI would be after him—fast. Whether or not this was *legally* accurate, it was commonly believed to be, so it had the same effect.

Which brings to mind the second difference in our Oak Ridge environment—FBI men. We spotted them easily—by their dark suits, white shirts, and neat ties, usually blue—and they were very polite. I made a jingle of our attitude toward them:

HONEY, RUN ANSWER THE DOOR
Is it Fuller Brush, Jewel-T
or the cleaner passing by?
Oh, no ma'am, it's none of them,
it's just the FBI.

If there was nothing else to do, Adele and I sat in the living room with Mama while the FBI man asked her questions about the neighbors. (A family could be moved out overnight for breaking security). Mama was always polite but noncommittal. Once, when Adele was about four years old, she was cuddled on Mama's lap sucking her thumb while the FBI man was asking the usual, "Do Mr. and Mrs. C. talk a lot?" (meaning "Do they mention his work?"). "Are they loud?"

Adele took her thumb out of her mouth and said indignantly, "She yells at her children!"

In her mind this was grounds for arrest.

At Elm Grove Grammar School, which was at the bottom of the hill, we students had a favorite guessing game: "Who is the secret agent?" We'd heard that the FBI had them in unlikely places, and we decided that the one at our school was the custodian, who ambled around the halls pushing his broom, listening. I wonder if he knew we thought he was a secret agent. Or if he *was*...

At recess the playground offered a creek, a few swings and seesaws, and a field. One end of the field was used for softball and the other for the ever-popular "Boys-Chase-the-Girls," followed by "Girls-Chase-the-Boys." The name was the game, literally. Mary Jean (of the rope swing) was my best friend and we were the two fastest runners in the school. She was a bit faster than I and had the longest hair—thin, honey-brown braids that came to her hips (mine were thick and shoulder length). Usually Mary Jane won "Girls-Chase-the-Boys" and she would have won "Boys-Chase-the-Girls" too if she hadn't loved the way her braids flowed out behind her as she ran. A boy always grabbed one of them. I tied mine under my chin.

On the surface, the playground—like our childhood—seemed open, unsophisticated, carefree. But hidden from the casual observer, between the edge of the field and the sheared-off side of a pine-topped hill, was The Ditch—deep, rocky, and menacing.

We were living in the Cold War era. Since Oak Ridge was considered a prime target, scientists had warned us of what could happen in an atomic attack—about the death-light, fireball, and fallout. School disaster drills were frequent. At the blast of the horn—more startling than the fire drill bell—we lined up in the halls, then hurried through the double doors and ran to The Ditch.

Huddled there, with our hands and bare knees pressed against sharp rocks, we waited for the "all clear" to sound. Little kids giggled and punched each other. But many of us big kids were silent, forced back into the terrible ditch at the edge of our minds that we tried to keep out of our sight: World War II. Memories of it jabbed us: *Pearl Harbor ... War ... Will Daddy Have To Go? ... Air Raid Drills ... Convoys ... Dreaded Telegrams—"We Regret to Inform You" ... Images from Radio and Newsreels: Guns, Bombers, Tanks ... Men Dying, Children Crying in Rubble, Dachau Survivors Looking Like Skeletons ... and always, always, the fear that the enemy was nearby, just over the next hill. Then Hiroshima, and the end of war forever. Or was it? What if...?*

"All clear!" The siren brought us scrambling out of The Ditch, out of bad memories. Out! Out! Out! "Free to wander hill and glen/ and be safe as if our own kin patrolled the fence." We recovered joy quickly, regrouped, flowed away. Sometimes loners drifted off—slightly disoriented, as if seeking direction—then drifted back again. We were children at play. We were also children who, like the "earthquake goldfish" of Japan, responded to the first harmonic tremors of an upheaval we felt but could not name—the Atomic Age. We were going to need all the lessons of our childhood, especially, "Keep your eyes on the mark ... don't look down ... steady as you go ..."

I did walk the log, in the fullness of my own time. Weeks after the great tree fell and I'd become well-acquainted with it, I gripped the bark with my feet, took my mark, lifted my arms, and walked the log ... alone.

As my life turned toward my fourteenth year—and puberty—I spent hours by myself, roaming the woods, listening. By that time the branches of the tree had moldered, the crater silted in, the trunk settled lower in the hollow. Washed clean, dried and tough, the roots were my favorite part of the tree, the comforting part. I felt the wind of change rising, in my own body and in Oak Ridge. It was 1950. The fence was down. Long-time neighbors were moving away, some to different towns, some to different parts of town;

new families were moving in. Technology was gaining power. The era of the atomic frontier and of my childhood were drawing to a close. Although the change seemed good, somewhere deep in my mind I was anxious, sensing perhaps that one day the wind would reach gale force and threaten to topple me by loosening my roots. One thing would save me. The great taproot of my Cherokee/Appalachian heritage would hold fast.

[1] *Abiding Appalachia: Where Mountain and Atom Meet*, by Marilow Awiakta, St. Luke's Press, Memphis, 1978.

COLD HANDS, WARM HEART

Sandra Whitten Plant

My family arrived in Oak Ridge in January of 1951 on one of the coldest days of the year. The temperature went down to three degrees, a frigid welcome to nine-year-old Sandra and my brother Jim, age eight. We didn't consider the climate inhospitable—we had a wonderful time sliding on the frozen puddles around our new home, an E-2 apartment on Viking Road near the center of Oak Ridge.

An E-2 was the two-bedroom two-story center section of a four-unit apartment building once very common around Vermont Avenue and West Tennessee Avenue. Many have been torn down or moved, but our old house is still standing.

Jim recalls that the heater was broken on our parents' 1950 Chevrolet that brought us to Oak Ridge. "Don't you remember how the palms of our hands stuck to the car windows?" he asked.

His remark was not intended to gain sympathy for two little waifs from Birmingham who had been moved by their parents to the frozen wilderness in Tennessee. On the contrary, we loved everything about our new hometown, icicles and all.

We lived our few first years in Oak Ridge in that apartment on Viking Road. Our days were spent at Pine Valley School on

New York Avenue, now the School Administration Building. We waited for the red and white school buses at the intersection on Vermont Avenue and Viking Road.

Most of our Saturdays were devoted to spending our thirty-five cents allowance at the record store or drug store at the Municipal Market across the Turnpike from the present location of Union Planters National Bank. That familiar old gray market building was located on the site now occupied by Lockwood Greene Engineering in a building that for years housed Ark Bowling Lanes.

Sometimes Jim and I and friends went to the Center Theater in Jackson Square on Saturdays. Most Oak Ridgers think of the place as the Oak Ridge Playhouse. To us, it will always be the Center Theater with its double feature every Saturday, a cartoon, and a serial like "The Shadow," or "Superman."

Those were truly the good old days in the economic sense. Admission was nine cents. I always bought a package of grape Charms candies for a nickel and a box of popcorn for a dime. My Saturday entertainment splurge left me with eleven cents for the rest of the week.

Our family moved to the Woodland section of town just as I entered junior high school. At that time, the only junior high was Jefferson, and it was located on the hill above Jackson Square. My seventh grade class met in a wooden annex that stood in the general vicinity of the reserved seating at Blankenship Field.

The bus stop was a wooden covered shed located across from the Jackson Square Post Office. I remember without affection the long, daily trudge from the top of that hill, down the long concrete stairway, and across Jackson Square to the bus stop.

Sometimes if I had a dime, I made a detour to the Kay's Ice Cream store that was located in a narrow wedge that has now been taken up by the present Jackson Square Pharmacy and Samuel's. I always got a double scoop of lime sherbet. I had to eat quickly for it did not travel well on the crowded bus to Woodland.

Woodland was a wonderful place for growing up. I have ridden a bicycle on every street and lane in the neighborhood. A friend and I used to go on bicycle adventures. At each intersection we would flip a coin to decide which turn to take. Our route was sometimes circuitous and strange. We liked it that way, but we

Courtesy Sandra Whitten Plant

Sandra, her brother Jim, and her parents.

always "arranged" for the flip of the coin to get us back to the Woodland Drug Store that was operated by a friendly pharmacist, Mr. Roach. What wonderful cherry cokes they made at the soda fountain, a treat that cost us each a dime.

Our woodframe house at the top of South Purdue Avenue was designated by the government as a number nineteen dwelling. The exteriors of the homes in our neighborhood were painted either red, gray, or yellow. Like all the others, our house had a coal chute facing the street for the convenience of the crews from Roane-Anderson Company who delivered coal for the furnace.

Ours was a stable neighborhood. Some of the same families who lived there in the 1950s still live there—the Kellys, the Howards, the Kingsleys, and the Harlans.

The Carmichael family lived behind us on Potomac Circle. My brother and I both babysat for the Carmichaels' young son, Freddy, who was born after their other three children were grown. Leonore Carmichael was a librarian with a lively interest in many things. Norman, her husband, "worked at the plants," as they said—but his real love was photography.

I will never forget the tremendous influence the Carmichaels had on my life, especially in introducing me to art and classical music. They always rented paintings from the Art Center's rental collection and they owned a Kermit Ewing oil painting which hung in their living room. I had never seen real paintings nor known how to look at them until Leonore Carmichael told me that "every brush stroke and every color was there for a purpose."

The first classical music I ever heard was at Oak Ridge Civic Music Association concerts with the Carmichaels. I heard the young pianist Philippe Entremont on the stage at Oak Ridge High School in the 1950s, several years before he became famous.

The most momentous occasion of my cultural expansion was the night that Bidu Sayao, the Brazilian soprano, gave a concert on our hometown stage. I remember that she sang an aria from *La Traviata*, from *Manon*, and a piece by the Brazilian composer Hector Villa Lobos. I never recovered from the beauty of her voice or from the power of the music.

The Carmichaels took me backstage after the concert to get her autograph. It was a stormy night in Oak Ridge and thunder was booming as I waited in line for the diva, who was a tiny, dark woman with huge brown eyes. A giant square cut topaz dangled from each ear lobe. I don't know who persuaded her to sing in Oak Ridge—maybe she needed the money. I'm just glad she brought opera to my life—with a little help from the Carmichaels.

After opera came the dancing, and I am sure no one who grew up in Oak Ridge in the 1950s escaped the influence of Ethel Howell's ballroom dancing classes. The late Mrs. Howell conducted dance classes after school in the cafeteria at Oak Ridge High School. It was a regular school activity called "the social dance club." The boys lined up on one side of the room and the girls on the other. With her back to the boys, Mrs. Howell demonstrated their steps to the jitterbug, the rhumba, the waltz, and the cha-cha-cha.

Next, the girls watched intently as she taught us our steps. The horrible part came when she made us take a partner of the opposite sex and put the steps together. She was very strict about decorum, and she never allowed unorthodox dance postures such as arms around the neck or wandering hands.

Although I thought it would be agony, my mother persuaded me to take additional ballroom dancing lessons taught by Mrs. Howell at the Oak Terrace Ballroom, now a furniture store in

Grove Center. I did this when I was a junior and senior in high school and I found I enjoyed it. Karl Rapp was in my class, and once he and I were the host and hostess for the monthly formal dances she had for her students. The girls wore formal dresses with mandatory white gloves. The boys wore suits and ties, and nobody dared chew gum.

Dancing brings me to another highlight of growing up in Oak Ridge in the 1950s. The Y-Teen Dances provided something to do besides drive around town on summer Friday evenings. When I first started going they were held in the Green Room of the Ridge Recreation Center. That was the building adjacent to the Jackson Square tennis courts that was torn down to make way for the Executive Seminar Center. The music was 45 rpm records and the dance was the "bop," a 1950s variation of the jitterbug from the 1940s.

Later the dances were held in a large room at the Oak Ridge Nursery School in Grove Center. Great crowds of Oak Ridge teens gathered at these dances. The favorite records were "Searching" by the Coasters, anything by Jerry Lee Lewis or Buddy Holley, and some memorable numbers like "Short Fat Fanny" and "Boney Maroney."

My parents made all these adventures possible by bringing our family to Oak Ridge. My dad was a machinist when he came, and he later became a foreman in the special projects shop at Y-12. I had no idea what we did at Y-12 and he didn't discuss it, but he got lots of phone calls at night when there seemed to be a problem in his shop.

I finally figured out what he was working on after several occasions when he invited visitors from California to our Wood-land home for dinner. The visitors were all from Lockheed Mis-siles and Space in Sunnyvale, California. I decided that he must be working with them on some kind of parts for rockets and missiles. I was pleased with myself for solving the mystery, and I was proud of him for working on something so important to our country's defense and to its technological advancement.

After finishing high school in 1959, I went off to study journalism at the University of Georgia, married a lanky young man from Rockmart, Georgia, and lived for a number of years in Marietta. Oak Ridge was far from my thoughts except when we visited my parents.

But my old hometown was jolted into my thoughts one day in 1970 when my husband called me and asked how I'd like to live in Oak Ridge. He had been offered a position with an Oak Ridge bank that he would like to take. The idea of returning home was not very exciting to me, but we did it.

The circumstances were just the opposite of my first arrival in Oak Ridge. We came in the blazing heat of August in 1970. Our temporary home was in the garden apartments where almost everybody lives at some time or other. Our children loved the spacious lawns around the garden apartments. An old friend from high school and her children called and came by. I returned to school. We went to an ORCMA concert...

I was captivated once again by Oak Ridge. The adventure was beginning again.

POLITICS

Courtesy James E. Westcott

311

A TOWN'S INCORPORATION

Sue Ellen Hudson

T he incorporation of Oak Ridge was something like the old "that's bad news, no that's good news" story. The first attempt in 1953 to turn this government-run town into a "normal city" was a resounding failure, pitting 1,120 yes votes against 4,584 no votes. Although many people thought self-government was a good idea, they voted against incorporation because they feared high taxes and the loss of benefits in a town where everything from water use to garbage disposal was provided by Uncle Sam.

While the uncertainty of incorporation stopped the citizens short of turning Oak Ridge into a "private" town, it did nothing to dampen their dreams of someday owning the flattops, cemestos, singles, duplexes, and other housing units they then rented from the government.

On August 5, 1955, President Dwight Eisenhower responded to the need of Oak Ridgers for permanent housing by signing into law the historic Oak Ridge Disposal Bill. Shortly afterward, the home-buying priority regulations were published. In a capsule, those living in a house were given first opportunity to buy it; those in a duplex according to how long they had lived there. As early Oak Ridger Joan Wallace puts it,

> The prices were incredibly low, but the houses needed work. For example, when they were built, people didn't have all the modern appliances that we had by the mid-1950s. There were

313

usually only two electrical outlets in a room, so most structures had to be modernized. But they were still good buys, and
after the people of Oak Ridge became homeowners, their
thoughts turned more seriously toward incorporation.

By 1959 some of the old uncertainty about incorporation had
waned. When the issue was again proposed on May 5 of that year,
Oak Ridgers turned out at the polls to vote 5,552 in favor and only
395 against.

The road leading to this memorable day, however, had not
been paved with silver. Robert McNees, one of the members of the
original advisory town council, as well as city councilman from
1959 to 1975 and mayor of Oak Ridge from 1961-65, remembers:
"There were many conflicting motivations for incorporation. The
home ownership made a lot of difference, and the desire to govern
ourselves was very strong. But there was also a bunch of local
politicians who wanted to get their hands into the act and develop
a power base of their own as contrasted to the county." He feels
that although the part they took was for negative motives, nevertheless these power-inspired individuals made a real contribution
in pushing the city towards incorporation.

At the time of the first referendum in 1953, there were only
two ways for a town to incorporate under the laws of Tennessee.
The first was the council/alderman form of government; the
second, the manager/council form.

As an early advocate of incorporation, Mr. McNees recalls
that "neither form was very good;" thus those working on the new
movement for incorporation tried to put together a better law, one
that was "both efficient and, hopefully, totally free of undue
adverse, corruption-type influences."

Looking back at that time, Mr. McNees remembers "lots of
postmidnight sessions, many arguments, and plenty of hassles
about who, what, how and where." Eventually a plan that called
for the election of seven council members-at-large was drawn up
and taken to the state legislature. It didn't pass. Instead it was
amended to provide for a new plan, called the modified council/
manager form of government, which provided for precinct-type
elections. This explains why Oak Ridge has twelve council
members today. Moreover, today this plan is a Tennessee statute
under which any city can choose to incorporate.[1]

Courtesy Department of Energy

Oak Ridge Advisory Town Council in 1958, one year before incorporation.

At the beginning of incorporation, there was also the task of implementing a smooth transition of governmental authority from the Atomic Energy Commission (AEC) to the city itself. According to Mr. McNees, the success of that was almost entirely due to "the good will and good intentions" of the people at the commission.

"They had kept everything in an exceptionally high condition," he says. "The roads were well taken care of and everything was operational. They did an excellent job of presenting to Oak Ridge a viable, well-maintained municipality that was capable of taking care of itself without going head over heels in debt during its first year of existence."

Mr. McNees adds, "The AEC was farsighted in many of its actions and very generous with our city." He gives the example of how the AEC was faced with the decision of whether to sell the utility system to the city or to give it to them. They donated it.

Upon incorporation in 1959, Oak Ridge moved one step closer to becoming a normal town.

Also the AEC deeded $35 million worth of municipal property and set up an assistance plan in lieu of paying taxes. "You see," Joan Wallace explains, "although the federal government (AEC) would be using Oak Ridge facilities such as our fire department, we couldn't officially tax them. So this assistance plan was initiated." It was agreed that one cash payment would be made annually to run for ten years, the amount to be decided on each year. Later, this plan was revised to a continuing annual contribution tied to the property tax.[2]

At first, however, the commission's generosity was not without its problems when budget time rolled around. "You have to remember the AEC was government, and in government there are always old bureaucrats who are wanting to hold on to their jobs," Robert McNees recalls. He tells the story of how after the city had figured one of the early budgets, some of the councilmen took it over to the AEC offices so the commission could decide what their contribution would be. In the room where the city officials and AEC officials gathered, there was a blackboard with the shade pulled over it. As the meeting began, the commission people walked over to the blackboard, pulled up the shade, and proceeded to tell the city what they thought the city's budget should be. "This meant the commission felt they were still running the town even after Oak Ridge had incorporated."

Following that, though, a compromise agreement was struck, effectively ending any interference by the commission in future budgets of the city. It was decided that a specified number of dollars worth of AEC property would be considered "taxable." If Oak Ridgers increased taxes on themselves, the commission would increase their amount of payment. On the other hand, if the city decreased taxes, the commission would decrease their payment.

When incorporation was finally realized in 1959, Oak Ridge immediately plunged into its first campaign for a city council election. Four weeks of intensive personal-contact campaigning by the candidates followed. On June 2 twelve council members were elected.

The first act of this newly elected body, which met on an average of four to five times a week, was to put a planning commission into business, giving the city the protection of a zoning ordinance and a set of regulations for residential subdivisions. In the months that followed, scores of other ordinances were drafted and discussed.

This transition from government-run town to incorporated city had been for the most part a smooth one with no disruptions in services. Most of the people who worked for the government simply moved over and worked for the city, but a score of new jobs were available to Oak Ridgers both at the labor and management levels.

A help-wanted ad appeared in the newspaper several months after incorporation. "Clerks/Clerk-Typists/Clerk-Stenographers: The city of Oak Ridge plans to open shop April 1, 1960. All persons interested in working for a new and progressive organization should contact the Personnel Office to obtain an application form."

The city had suffered few birth pangs in the switchover. The economy was good. Business downtown was booming. "The Great

317

Oak Ridge Desert" (a bare area of town once dotted with army barracks during the secret years) was now a well-planned, modern shopping center with Loveman's of Chattanooga opening a new store shortly after incorporation. The cash registers were ringing, but nowhere were the good times felt more abundantly than in the school system.

Mr. McNees recalls that years before incorporation, the AEC had a basic concept for maintaining a school system that would attract and keep bright, young people with children in the community to accomplish the projects they had underway. One of the main reasons he and his first wife, Mary, came to Oak Ridge in 1952, rather than taking an intended job in Tonawanda, New York, was the excellent school system.

He remembers how in 1957 the old advisory town council of Oak Ridge "made the request that there be a public election for an advisory school board of five members;" this was adopted. When the city incorporated in 1959, these five members were re-elected. "They had two years of the job experience," he says, "before they actually had to take charge of things, and I think the city is a lot better off because they did."

"Our top priority in city council," he emphasizes, "was to continue what we felt was one of the best school systems in the South."

On the issue of segregation in Oak Ridge during the 1950s, Mr. McNees sadly shakes his head. He thinks back to the days before the 1955 directive from AEC headquarters in Washington, which mandated that Oak Ridge schools become the first public school system in Tennessee to integrate its students. He tells how the advisory town council in 1953, under the leadership of Waldo Cohn, passed a resolution requesting that the Atomic Energy Commission end school segregation at once, in view of President Eisenhower's recent stance on segregation in federally operated areas. "Immediately the ill will and bigotry one finds in almost any community surfaced," he says, "and there was an effort made to recall Cohn as chairman of the council. That's how Mary and I first became involved in local politics. We helped organize opposition to that recall election."

He remembers the vote was sixty percent to remove Cohn and forty percent to keep him. The rule was that you had to have two-thirds of the vote, so we won although we lost the vote."

Mr. Cohn resigned as chairman anyway. "This cost Oak Ridge a great deal of benefit in the form of leadership from Waldo Cohn," Mr. McNees says. "He would have been a positive, constructive influence on city affairs thereafter. Instead, he chose never to become involved again."

In talking about the 1955 directive to desegregate the public schools, Mr. McNees says:

> It's to everybody's credit that the integration of Oak Ridge schools went so smoothly and peacefully as contrasted with the horrible experience our neighbors in Clinton were subjected to. This shows a great deal of wisdom and foresight on the part of the advisory town council and the Atomic Energy Commission. Other people were suggesting we go slow, let's wait until Tennessee does it, but they were willing to bite the bullet and go forward. Oak Ridge was the beneficiary.

There were other desegregation problems in Oak Ridge, however, in restaurants, cafeterias, laundromats, and barbershops. "We created an advisory board on human relations with Jim Spicer as chairman," Mr. McNees recalls. "They did everything they could to help move the community toward a desegregated status. Restaurants were a big hang up."

He tells the story of the time he and Mr. Spicer went to Atlanta to talk with Stanley Davis of Davis Brothers Cafeterias:

> For the first time, we saw the other side of the desegregation question. Stanley Davis was a man of high moral principles, but he was tormented by the decision he would have to make about Davis Brothers Cafeterias and what it meant to his people here and to his other cafeterias around the South.

> It was a moving experience. And we weren't sure if Davis would go along with us or not. Neither Jim nor I spoke for twenty minutes after leaving his office and starting home. Finally Jim said, 'Well, Bob, did we win or lose?' Being a gambler and always betting on the underdog, I answered, 'I think we won.' That night Stanley Davis called and said he would integrate his chain of cafeterias the next day.

The following day Mr. McNees put the new policy to the test. He and a black man from Oak Ridge went to the local Davis

319

Brothers Cafeteria and had lunch together. It was a tense scene at first. "We got a dozen angry, baleful, death-to-you-type looks from people going down the cafeteria line," says Mr. McNees, "as he and I sat there having our first integrated lunch in the city. We weren't stupid, though," he adds. "There were three plainclothes policemen out there."

Barbershops soon fell into step along with the laundromats, housing, and other places. Finally the city council passed the Public Accommodations Act, which provided equal access for people of all races to all public buildings and businesses, as well as to housing in Oak Ridge.

Another concern of the early leaders of the city was to establish a government free of corrupt influences. These leaders, mainly "imports" from outside the region, were sophisticated men and women who, for the most part, were blessed with fine minds, recalls McNees. They were committed to the idea of establishing a political system that worked for the betterment of everyone and not just a few. And since Oak Ridge was a new town, free of the old traditional restraints of the surrounding communities, it managed to avoid many of the abuses committed by political machines. There was no old political machine as found in other places.

Illegal (bootleg) liquor with its companion gambling was one of the "corrupt influences" that the council fought head-on. In recalling this struggle, Mr. McNees chuckles, "I received my share of discourteous treatment from waitresses in the old establishments where gambling had been going on in the back room. They gave me the cold shoulder because once liquor was legalized, the gambling that had gone along with the old activity of bootlegging went also. My stand had cut into their tips."

In those early years when the wet/dry vote was brought before the people, Oak Ridge and Anderson County always split the vote. The city would inevitably go wet, the county dry. This sometimes led to bizarre happenings. Mr. McNees tells the story of how one night before a vote, the county officials found the Edgemoor Bridge to be unsafe for travel so they closed it down. People who lived on the other side of the river couldn't get to the polls the next day to cast their votes. Election night, however, the bridge was supposedly repaired and the following day it was once again found safe for travel. "It was all just fine that following morning," he says, laughing.

In a more serious tone, Mr. McNees gives full credit to the many people who were involved in the efforts to clean up the corruption in Anderson County. One of the most important moves was to do away with the old justice-of-the-peace system for dispensing justice. A trial justice court was established in its place and full legal procedures implemented.

"I've never regretted coming to Oak Ridge rather than going to my original destination of Tonawanda, New York," Mr. McNees remarks. "But I, like the other people here, felt frustrations when the bureaucratic system ran the town. We didn't want some faceless person in Washington making our decisions for us."

He concludes: "Oak Ridge was started on the large part by bright and farsighted people. It was from these people that the impetus came to incorporate. They, along with others in the city, knew the time was coming for the government to pull away. It was a mutual feeling between the government and the people that Oak Ridge should be on its own."

[1] In August 1986, Oak Ridge voters approved a seven-member council, voted at-large.

[2] In the latter part of 1985, what was known as the Department of Energy buy-out bill became law, providing Oak Ridge a lump sum of $21.1 million and terminating the annual assistance payments.

A COMMUNITY'S DISPOSAL

June M. Boone

Sell Oak Ridge ... the entire town? Could such a monumental real estate job really be accomplished when there wasn't a single home owner among its 36,000 residents?

In 1946, 40,000 people had left the community. Those remaining believed in Oak Ridge's future and wanted to be a part of it. But they needed that sense of permanency that comes with home ownership and self-government. Many had sold their homes before coming to Oak Ridge and yearned to feel again that the houses they lived in were their own. Others who had only rented previously soon caught the "home owner fever."

Could it happen? Oak Ridgers believed it could. And for many years the prime questions asked of friends and neighbors were, "Do you want to buy your house?" "Are you planning to remodel?"

When did it happen? How did it all begin? How did Oak Ridgers get from being pampered home-renters with gratuitous unlimited water use, coal delivery, garbage disposal, lawns seeded and fertilized, drains unstopped, and houses kept painted, to being happy home owners paying their own way?

It began in 1949 when David Lilienthal, head of the newly formed Atomic Energy Commission, announced the eventual plans for home sale and self-government for Oak Ridge. Or perhaps it began in 1948 when in a transcribed speech for the opening of the new radio station, WATO, Mr. Lilienthal promised "a general program to convert Oak Ridge from a war-built city to a permanent community." Or perhaps the hope may have been stirred as early as 1947 when Mr. Lilienthal told Oak Ridgers that their city would remain a major segment in the long-range AEC program, and announced the proposal for the first permanent housing: 450 garden apartments on the Turnpike in West Village.

Permanency: Oak Ridgers *pounced* on the word. Permanency meant home ownership. But it wasn't until 1950 and the birth of the Scurry Panel that Oak Ridgers really dared to begin to dream. Headed by Dallas attorney Richard Scurry, the panel's purpose was to study the feasibility of disposing of the land and homes in Oak Ridge and of turning the municipal government over to its residents.

When Roane-Anderson, manager of community facilities, renewed its three-year contract with AEC that year, provisions were included for the change to self-government should it materialize. Meanwhile, Roane-Anderson had announced that 823 families living in 432 flattops in East and West Villages and other demountable housing, including hutments and victory cottages, would be vacated and the structures removed from the city. Over 3,400 trailers had already been transferred to college campuses around the country to relieve the housing shortage precipitated by returning servicemen using the GI bill. As undesirable housing disappeared, new homes sprang up to replace it. A new area in Woodland was completed, and construction began on row houses, apartments, and additional cemestos.

In 1952 U.S. Senator Kenneth D. McKellar of Tennessee introduced a bill for home sale, giving the present occupant first choice at purchase. In that same year, AEC made a Valentine's Day announcement of home prices in *The Oak Ridger*. An estimate of highs and lows, with pictures depicting house types, ran as follows: Cemestos for $2,665-$8,910, Woodland-Gamble Valley singles for $5,220-$8,145, Woodland-Gamble duplexes (both units) for $5,445-$9,180, TDU's and T's and M's for $4,590-$7,425, flattops for $1,170-$3,825, L's (both units) for $7,740-$8,730, and new homes for $8,010-$11,340.

Twenty sample vacant lots were also included. The highest price for a lot was on East Drive near Englewood Lane—$1,350. The lowest, $225, was for an Alger Road lot near the East Drive intersection.

The newspaper ran detailed tables giving all figures involved. These were estimates based on a sampling of 185 houses and lots. Thirty-six different types of single and duplex dwellings were appraised, and the tables listed average prices and comparisons of the probable monthly payments with the present rent. The figures revealed that the majority of monthly payments would be lower than current rents.

The future of home ownership now rested with the residents and their response to the questions: "Would you be willing to buy on the basis of estimates published by the AEC?" In May the results of a U.S. Census survey showed that nearly sixty percent of the people favored property purchase, and by September eager-to-own residents were circulating petitions for immediate home sales.

New houses were in the near future also, with the okay from the Federal Housing Administration (FHA) for 550 Title 9 houses in West Village and 500 Title 8 houses in East Village—all to be built on land vacated by flattops. At the same time, Management Services, Inc., successor to Roane-Anderson as manager of community facilities, announced the sales of 238 flattops to be removed from the city. Some of these structures would eventually be seen near Oliver Springs, on Oak Ridge Highway, and as far away as Fontana Dam in North Carolina.

The remaining flattops, located on West Outer Drive, Wadsworth Circle, and off Jefferson Avenue, were to be remodeled. The most significant modification would be the addition of siding and gabled roofs. Repairs and other improvements would be made where needed.

Housing changes of every kind were taking place as Oak Ridgers, who simply couldn't wait, began remodeling the homes they hoped to buy. The first person to build an addition to a cemesto before owning it was Glen Harter on East Passmore Lane. At the same time St. Mary's Church expanded its D house convent to a nine-bedroom structure. *The Oak Ridger* published a series of articles on these activities, entitled "Superior Interiors."

On September 10, 1953, the C. E. Colleys were the first family to begin construction on a privately built house in Oak Ridge. Having lived in a flattop on Irving Lane for "nine crowded years," they called their new venture on Ditman Lane, "From a matchbox to a mansion." And on December 11, 1953, Clergia L. Terry and his family moved from a garden apartment into a Title 9 house at 200 Butler Road, making local history by being the first Oak Ridgers to move into a privately owned house.

Dreams of home ownership were finally becoming a reality. The Title 9 houses on leased lots in West Village were easy to buy, and more Ridgers were building on leased land. In March 1954, the John J. Keyes, Jr. family moved into the first privately built home on leased land, on East Drive. That summer R. R. Brookshire and Richard Overman also moved their families into privately built homes on leased lots on Ditman Lane.

In 1955 the number of old homes with new looks increased surprisingly. Houses had once been assigned according to the number of individuals in the family. But the houses seemed to have shrunk in size over the years as the number of family members increased, or small children who shared rooms were now old enough to need separate ones. Shrinking walls were expanding. Carports were closed in, cramped eat-in living rooms and kitchens spread out into spacious dining areas. Even basements were being dug. Sally Latham's "Superior Interiors" series in *The Oak Ridger* gave way to another twenty-part series called, "Bulging Walls," with pictures and discussions of ways in which various styles of "shrunken" homes were enlarged and altered.

In August Ed Spitzer, owner of the newly opened Dairy Queen in East Village, was the first person not connected with any government project to be given local housing. On July 9, 1957, the Dairy Queen lot became the first commercial property to be sold.

Impatience was the Oak Ridge word as residents awaited formal organization of the committee in Washington that would struggle to get the Disposal Bill through the drafting stages and onto the floor of Congress.

Finally, August brought the long-awaited news: the Oak Ridge Disposal Bill had passed! On August 5, 1955, President Dwight Eisenhower signed the bill into law, saying, "I consider this one of the major achievements of the Congress." Oak Ridgers shared his sentiment. The signing generated an excitement in the city that hadn't been felt since the end of the war. The arrival of FHA appraisers and the publishing of home-buying-priority regulations added to the excitement.

In announcing the regulations, AEC allowed thirty days for comments before making the regulations final. An article in *The Oak Ridger* on December 8, 1955, read: "Two weeks now remain for residents to make their views known of the priority regulations announced tentatively by AEC for the community disposal program. So far, few comments have been made in writing."

The priority set-up on single family houses gave the current occupants first choice, followed by any Oak Ridge resident, then any person connected with AEC in Oak Ridge, which meant any person who worked in Oak Ridge who was head of a family. First priority in a duplex would go to the occupant living in the house the longest. The "junior" occupant would have second choice. If neither occupant wanted to buy the duplex, the "junior" occupant of another duplex house would be a qualified buyer.

On the day a given house was offered for sale, the occupant had thirty days to make up his mind about buying, then sixty days to complete the deal. Those not wishing to purchase their house could continue renting for a period of at least one year.

The key year for home and land sales was 1956, beginning with a historic ceremony to transfer land deeds to two families who became Oak Ridge's first local landowners. The two were the Dana Nances of 106 Orchard Circle and the W. K. Ergens of 103 Orkney Road. In February, with a community population of 30,000, there were now forty-six privately owned homes still on leased land.

President Eisenhower named the Housing and Home Finance Agency (HHFA) as sales agent for the property disposal, and the agency promised to "work out the selling problems with a minimum of red tape."

Under banner headlines *The Oak Ridger* published the average prices of the twenty-eight types of houses. In July Albert Cole, head of HHFA in Washington, signed the letter formally declaring the feasibility of a property sale in Oak Ridge, and on May 22 the newspaper devoted four full pages of fine print to list all 4,900 homes and their sale prices.

In July, with home ownership so close, a new surge of remodeling began and *The Oak Ridger* decided to resume the "Bulging Walls" series of the previous year.

On September 7, a day well remembered in Oak Ridge history, 433 houses went on sale and on September 11, six families became a part of that history by being the first to buy their homes. Participating in this "first" were Mr. and Mrs. Otis Arnold, 125 Euclid Circle; Mr. and Mrs. Luther Brannon, 151 Turnpike; Mr. and Mrs. L. C. Brock, 111 Atlanta Road; Mr. and Mrs. Reuben Hickman, 175 California Avenue; Mr. and Mrs. N. N. Landay, 122 Euclid Circle; and Mr. and Mrs. Charles Williams, 314 Delaware Avenue. Of the six, all were cemestos except the Brannon house which was here before Oak Ridge. St. Stephen's Episcopal Church purchased the first cemesto house to be used for a parsonage—an F-house at 102 Dixie Lane.

By the end of 1956, 2,394 houses had been offered for sale, with 723 houses and eighty-two vacant lots sold. The Anderson County Registrar of Deeds' office in Clinton was so swamped with Oak Ridgers that AEC was asked to provide local office space and personnel to accommodate home buyers.

In the "Twenty-fifth Anniversary" edition of *The Oak Ridger*, Dorothy Senn called 1957 "the year of the house." The major part of the sales of original government housing was accomplished that year. Lots were sold to those wishing to build, as was much of the commercial property.

March brought a high point in sales when the two-thousandth home, a rehabilitated flattop at 115 East Wadsworth Circle, was purchased by Mr. and Mrs. Carl Morris. Preliminary discussions were also underway concerning the sale of the East Village Title 8 homes to present occupants.

As pride in ownership fanned the remodeling flame into a citywide explosion, Sally Latham's "Bulging Walls" series became the new homeowner's bible. They pored over pictures and ideas that had been used successfully on other houses of the same type as theirs. The series continued throughout the year and into 1958. Eventually, "open houses" gave interested and curious remodelers a firsthand look at some of the ingenious ways in which homes had become more attractive, spacious, and practical.

Houses were also being resold. By the end of March, 200 houses purchased under the disposal program had been resold, with most sales netting at least $1,000-$2,000 profit. Mid-July brought another milestone when James S. Wininger bought the house at 108 Malvern Road. His was the four-thousandth home sold.

In January 1958, Oak Ridgers saw the last of the "boomtown jerry-built housing," the unrehabilitated flattops, leave the city. Then in November the 500 Title 8 East Village homes were sold to Shelby Construction Company of New Orleans. And in July, the largest offering of multiple dwelling units, the four-family E's, K's and TDU's, were ready for sale. In early 1959 brick-row houses, N apartments on Hillside Avenue and efficiency apartments in Jackson Square were assessed and put up for sale. And in mid-February, Joseph Porath bought all of the four-unit E and K apartments, a total of 760 units.

By July, on the third anniversary of the disposal sales, the city of Oak Ridge was eighty-five percent sold. Remaining were fewer than 700 individual lots, three commercial properties, the Oak Ridge Mental Health Center, seven duplexes in Scarboro Village, three dorms, garden apartments, brick apartments, and 140 acres in twelve parcels.

In three years, $32,000,000 worth of property had gone from public to private ownership. Nine thousand acres of land, thousands of houses, dorms and commercial buildings had exchanged ownership.

The year 1960 brought an end to the disposal program. The last seven dwellings in Scarboro Village went to the highest bidder and with the garden and brick apartments going to private owners, the community disposition program had completed its job.

Many years passed between the days of renting and the reality of home owning. Much of the time was spent in anticipation and then frustration because things weren't moving fast enough toward the ultimate goal, the chance to own a house. But once begun, the massive disposal program was completed in just four years. Once-pampered renters were now happy, tax-paying, home owning Oak Ridgers, and nearly half the homes were unrecognizable as original government housing.

Joe Brown, head of Oak Ridge and Richland, Washington disposal programs said, "It has been the biggest real estate job ever tackled in the history of the country, and there'll probably never be a bigger one." And before that "biggest real estate job" was completed, it had already changed Oak Ridge from the U.S. city with the lowest percentage of home owners to that with the highest percentage.

THE HOSPITAL REFERENDUM

Joan Wallace

I n the 1950s, when the federal government began thinking about disposing of some of its Oak Ridge properties, the hospital was among the first on the list. It was necessary, of course, that the ownership and management of this facility, along with that of the homes and land, be settled before the town could begin to incorporate as an independent government. Moreover, it was at that time, in 1957, that President Eisenhower had approved the construction of a new, 175-bed hospital which the federal government planned to donate to the town—leaving behind the old building that had served Oak Ridge during the war years.

But the burning issue of 1958 became: Who would operate the new hospital? Who would assume the role that the government had played until now? The federal government naturally wanted to transfer ownership of the Oak Ridge Hospital to a group that could operate independently—not only without government control, but without subsidy. And the issue was left to a referendum. Thus, through this process, Oak Ridgers were drawn into one of the most heated political issues in the young city's history.

The ballot read, "The purpose of this referendum is to determine the wishes of the eligible voters of the community of Oak Ridge, concerning the entity to which the Atomic Energy Commission will transfer the title to the Oak Ridge Hospital which is now under construction." AEC could have simply transferred the hospital to whatever group it chose and avoided the referendum, but it decided instead to leave the decision to the community. Some observers have noted, however, that such a decision took the heat off AEC—removing its officials, in a way, from the turmoil of making such a decision.

The first group to make a move for ownership was the newly formed Oak Ridge Hospital Association (ORHA), which for the most part represented the status quo—those who were operating the hospital.

Soon a number of groups expressed an interest. The Oil, Chemical, and Atomic Workers, Local 9288 entered the competition. The Catholic church stepped forward as well. The Oak Ridge Ministerial Association indicated that Anderson County might be an appropriate choice, although the Anderson County Court (the county's governing body) stated it had no desire to operate the hospital. Then the city of Oak Ridge was mentioned. A group called Citizens for City Ownership was even formed to promote the idea of a city-owned hospital.

In February 1958, however, the Methodist church began to make a stronger stand. The Reverend J. A. Bays, pastor of First Methodist Church, the Reverend Fynes Jackson, Trinity Methodist Church, and thirty Methodist laymen invited a representative of the Methodist Committee on Hospitals and Homes of the Holston Conference to meet in Oak Ridge. While the Reverend Carroll Long of Johnson City, chairman of that committee, said that they were "merely coming to see if we can be helpful, not to get control of anything," in March an announcement was made that the Methodist church was considering an attempt to become owners of the hospital. A date of May 20 had been set for the referendum, and the Methodists requested that this date be postponed. Thus the referendum was reset for August 7, which was the date for the regular county election.

By the time of the referendum, only three interested groups were placed on the ballot: Oak Ridge Hospital Association, Holston Conference of the Methodist Church, and the city of Oak Ridge. (The Catholic church and the OCAW had withdrawn.) Moreover, incorporation was in the works by then, and the Advisory Town Council was busy with a referendum of its own to determine the manner of electing future council members.

As for official loyalties on this issue, they were generally divided two ways. Town Council, for example, was divided between those who favored the Hospital Association, and those who favored city ownership. Public Administrations Services, a private consulting firm hired by AEC, and *The Oak Ridger*, the city newspaper, both favored a city-owned facility.

The vote on August 7 was 2,766 for the Methodists, 2,599 for the Hospital Association, and 2,487 for the city. It had been decided that there would have to be a majority vote, so a run-off election was set for November 4 between the Methodist Church and the Hospital Association.

Soon the campaign between the two groups got underway. Residents were choosing sides and arguments were heated. Charges went back and forth between the various sides. The Hospital Association met September 4 at Ridge Recreation Hall to discuss plans, while the steering committee of the Methodist Church met to make its plans as well.

The Hospital Association lowered its dues from $10 to $5 a year to encourage more people to join. Arthur Sands, a chemical engineer at the Y-12 Plant, was named to chair a committee to present the association to the community, encouraging residents to join. "This will enable them to participate in the affairs of Oak Ridge Hospital Association," Sands said.

Moreover, the bylaws of ORHA were changed to guarantee that the hospital would be operated by the citizens. Another change involved requiring a minimum of twenty-five ORHA members to be present for any hospital business to be handled. These measures were taken because the organization had been perceived by some Oak Ridgers as "the doctors' group."

News of hospital referendum campaigning and other activities had to compete for news space in *The Oak Ridger* with integration moves taking place in Little Rock, Arkansas, as well as incorporation of the city, both of which were top news stories of the day.

The Methodists announced that they would hold an "invitational banquet" September 29 at First Methodist Church to kick off the campaign. The Reverend Bolton Boone, administrator of Dallas Methodist Hospital in Texas, was to be the principal speaker. The Reverend Carroll Long, chairman of the Holston Conference Committee on Hospitals and Homes, Johnson City, was to speak as well. Meanwhile, construction of the new hospital was proceeding on schedule.

On the night of the banquet, with Chris Keim as moderator, it was announced that the Methodists had been endorsed by the Committee on Political Education of the Central Labor Union, which represented 3,500 workers. Reverend Boone spoke first, telling them that the Methodists were "facing the challenging opportunity of owning and managing a large hospital. The opportunity," he said, "of accepting in fee simple a large hospital, fully equipped, with a sizeable operating fund and with the guarantee of assistance funds for a two-year period makes the average hospital trustee and administrator feel he has passed to better worlds beyond."

He also traced the Methodists' background in operating hospitals. Reverend Long then got up and spoke as well, saying that "contagious Christian characteristics of understanding and concern give a psychological lift to the patient and help set the tone of the administration and staff." He also spoke of the experts in the Methodist National Board of Hospitals and Homes as well as other Methodist Hospitals who could be called on.

A few days later, Arthur Sands said that the Hospital Association would reply to comments made at the dinner. He referred specifically to the comment made by Reverend Long, who had said that the Association was not experienced enough to operate a hospital, but added that detailed responses were not ready yet. Three days after this statement, on October 5, the high school in Clinton was bombed, apparently by anti-integrationists. Thus other news delayed the Hospital Association statement getting into the newspaper.

On October 14, Sands' statement on behalf of the Hospital Association reported that the present hospital administration had greatly reduced the hospital deficit. And he insisted that "The Hospital Association would provide greater local control than six local delegates to the Holston Conference." He added that "Oak Ridgers are intelligent enough to see the irony of three outsiders— two from Johnson City and one from Dallas—telling local people in Oak Ridge how outsiders can do a better job of local operation than a local consulting group can."

Sands also cited the Hospital Association as dedicated

whether they were Christians or of another faith. "You do not have to belong to one particular denomination in order to be Christian, or even to one particular faith in order to be dedicated to humanitarian concerns," he said. "Non-sectarian does not mean non-Christian or non-religious."

Mr. Long wrote a long letter commenting on points made by Sands. In addition, local residents were writing letters to the editor supporting one side or another in the coming referendum. On the day before the election, one full page and part of another were devoted to letters to the editor in the local newspaper. And a full-page advertisement promoted the Methodist cause.

There was one more major event before the election—a radio forum with three persons representing the Methodist church—Chris Keim, the Reverend Paul Brown, and Sarah Ketron; and three representing the Hospital Association—William Pollard, Dr. Ray Johnson, and Carl Martin, vice president of the hospital board. Questions were sought before the program was broadcast, and Joan Ellen Zucker, news director, WATO, and Mrs. Fran Tench, president of the League of Women Voters, screened the questions.

Pollard, who had earlier supported the idea of a city-owned hospital, was asked why he now supported the Hospital Association. "The hospital," he said, "is being built by the people of the United States as a gift to the people of Oak Ridge. It is not appropriate that public property and community facilities be transferred to any group." He also spoke of the "outstanding management job" done by the present hospital group and the "fine spirit" in the hospital.

Keim, on the other hand, stressed the long experience the Methodist church had in operating hospitals. "I believe that the Methodist ownership is the best for Oak Ridge—not just now but ten or fifteen years from now," he said. In response to a question, Keim said that only hospital trustees could make bylaws.

Martin, responding to a question on ORHA policy, said that trustee meetings would not be open to the public.

And when asked why the Hospital Association was opposed to religious services, Pollard, who was also an Episcopal priest, said, "I have held baptisms at the hospital and celebrated Holy Communion. I am confident that the hospital is not opposed to religion." He added that Bibles were at each nurse's station. Both sides indicated their interest in a nursing school and medical arts building.

Election day finally arrived and a heavy turnout of voters went to the polls. They chose the Methodist church to own and operate the hospital by a margin of 1,259. The vote was 4,209 for the Methodists, and 2,950 for the Hospital Association. All city precincts had majority votes for the Methodists except for Cedar Hill and Scarboro. Many churchgoers (not only Methodists) apparently felt more comfortable with the idea of a church-run facility.

Courtesy Department of Energy T. R. Cook Photo

Chris Keim speaks on the day of the new Oak Ridge Hospital dedication.

By the end of the year, the hospital's first board had been chosen, with twelve of the sixteen board members Methodists. Paul Bjork was appointed in 1959 as the hospital's first director, and finally, on February 15, 1960, formal dedication and opening ceremonies took place at the new hospital. Principal speakers were the Reverend W. F. Blackard, superintendent of the Clinton District, Holston Conference of the Methodist Church; and Charles Shilling, deputy director, AEC Division of Biology and Medicine, Washington, D.C.

Some 15,000 people toured the facility during the weekend of the opening celebrations. And a week later, on February 22, 125 patients were moved from the old army-built hospital into the new building. Mothers in the maternity wing were moved first, then those from gynecology and surgery, followed by other patients. When the move started, sixty beds were ready in the new hospital. As soon as a patient was moved from the old building, his bed was taken to the new building and prepared for the next patient.

After years of effort to get approval for a new hospital, plans being accepted, bids let, sometimes bitter controversy over who would operate it, and two elections to choose the owner, the move from the old building to the new took just four hours and ten minutes.

MARGARET MEAD
COMES TO TOWN

Courtesy *The Oak Ridger*

A TEENAGE REMEMBRANCE OF "MONUMENTAL MAGGIE"

Bonnie Lee Dings

"You can't get rid of the Bomb."

"You may get rid of bombs, but you'll never destroy the Bomb."

And because of the Bomb, Margaret Mead continued, the second generation of Oak Ridge, the "Atomic City," had an obligation to "organize the world." The globally famous anthropologist was speaking on May 18, 1964, some twenty-two years ago, to an assembly of students at Oak Ridge High School (ORHS).

She thundered, "What are you doing today? What are you spending your energies on now?"

"What's happened to the Y.C.A.C.?"

Her inquiry received only blank expressions from her teenage audience. Indeed, none of the students in that room had ever heard about the Youth Council for Atomic Crisis.

Mr. Tom Dunigan, the high school principal at the time, explained to Ms. Mead that the Y.C.A.C. organization "finished work in 1947. The people who were enthusiastic about it moved on. No one picked it up."

Ms. Mead seemed distressed. She recalled the early days of the high school newspaper, the *Oak Leaf*, when the front page of every issue carried a logo with the picture of the "mushroom cloud." She noted, "It was good to see a high school taking some responsibility for what was happening in the world."

Nothing, absolutely nothing, in all our months of preparing

341

for Ms. Mead's visit—reading and rereading her books, discussing them in Ira Green's sociology/anthropology class, debating her treatises in Sunday school and social groups—had readied us for her pronouncements. At this point in our young lives, a year before the first major fireworks of Vietnam and the roar of student demonstrations around the world, we were perplexed by her allegations. Were we as conceited and inconsiderate as she'd pegged us? Were we blasé about our city's role in the history of mankind? Were we uncaring about the "folk" of the Tennessee hills, the native population of the clandestine terrain that brought the Manhattan Project here in the first place?

In post-Chernobyl 1986, the "city fathers" debate the wisdom of calling attention to Oak Ridge's nuclear past, in terms of marketing strategy. But in 1964 these concerns were far from our thoughts. I was editor of the *Oak Leaf* at the time, and I noted that our recently updated page one logo carried the atom symbol. (The very next year, in fact, the class of 1965 purchased a large metal atom symbol for the brick front of the school exterior facing the Civic Center. In that same era, checks from the Bank of Oak Ridge no longer featured the "mushroom cloud" either, but they did bear the atom symbol.)

Following the school assembly, Ms. Mead asked to have a more intimate discussion with a smaller group of young people before her departure. Fifteen sons and daughters of scientists and the ORHS English/journalism teacher Dale Woodiel gathered in Virginia White's Outer Drive living room that Saturday afternoon. The guest of honor was over an hour late. When she did arrive she plopped into one chair, propped her feet on another, and began puffing on a cigarette. She snarled, "Why should you kids respect your parents? All that they've done for you is to bear you. All that proves is that they're fertile." The only reason to respect them, she said, is because "when you're crossing the street, they know more about automobiles than you do."

So much for our parents. On to us. "You young aristocrats! You wish to erect a barrier between yourselves and 'lesser beings.' You should be mixing with them instead," she declared. We should "blend" for the betterment of the population as a whole. Oak Ridge's main problem, she insisted, was that pretentious northerners who had grown up in a mobile class system refused to adjust to a southern caste system. (She explained her own daughter's education at a prestigious private school as a convenience rather than as a lack of obligation.) She said she knew quite a lot about our "privileged" lives here and our Ivy League intentions after high school.

"Worrying about getting into college is pure rot," she stormed. "There are more colleges to get into now than ever before. In the post-World War II era, we have formed a national pyramid with Harvard at the top, and people have become obsessed with trying to beat the national averages to get into those colleges which are the most difficult to get into.

"Before the war, college made sense. I don't recall anybody's being broken-hearted over the issue of college entrance. We have made a piece of unmitigated rubbish by worrying so much about college. This concern could spread until everyone in the United States has a nervous breakdown."

She quipped, "Children are refusing to learn how to read. Why? It's the most reliable way of not going to Harvard!"

Ms. Mead advised, "College will be just like high school— you won't have time to think about the world if you're so busy staying on top. It would be a lot better for you to pick out a college where you'll have time to read and think and do something for the world while you're doing it. Do *something* to get away from the rat race!... The best thing to do is figure out where to go that's a good place to go. It's ridiculous for good people to worry all through high school about getting into college. Students are pressured too hard to make up their minds. They're making decisions long before they know what they're making," she said.

At a time when tuitions at major colleges elsewhere and university standards within Tennessee itself were both relatively low, none of us in the room had plans to go to an in-state school.

"Why," she wondered, "do you have to be so obsessed with winning ... with being on top? Going to the best colleges in the country without a thought of returning to this area to contribute anything you've learned.

"Do you feel no responsibility at all to take those science projects of yours out to some of the schools in the surrounding counties and teach your fellow students there what you've learned? Have you considered doing a project with someone who might never have the chance for college?"

● ● ●

I have thought about the visit of the late Margaret Mead quite a lot recently. Had she been here to participate, would she still feel that the teenagers are pampered, self-involved, and without regional consciousness? Moreover, did she peg us for what we really were in the sixties? How accurate were her perceptions?

I was unaware of the "hillbilly" stereotype I applied to my county neighbors until I felt it applied to me personally. On the first day of my association with my freshman roommate at the University of Chicago, I noticed her paying a lot of attention to my unpacking. She admitted to being flabbergasted that I had shoes—many pairs of them, in fact. In her Central Park West upbringing, she had assumed that all Tennesseans went barefooted most of the time. (Imagine the shock her family had when they heard their daughter's roommate was from "the hills.") My husband had a similar sting in the service when another sailor noticed him receiving a correspondence course from the University of Tennessee while at sea. The sailor was astounded that Tennessee even *had* a state university.

Once out of college, married, and away from many of the Oak Ridgers I'd grown up with, I realized how much I'd missed by not knowing my contemporaries in neighboring communities. For the first time I met people from Norris, Powell, Clinton, and Cleveland, Tennessee, many of whom have remained close friends for two decades now. I admitted my elitist attitude toward their secondary school education compared to mine, and they admitted to being intimidated by a graduate of Oak Ridge High. Many have run circles around me academically and intellectually.

My children already are getting an appreciation for the energy, artistry, and scholarship of their East Tennessee neighbors. They participate in county- and regionwide academic and athletic contests. Field trips to historic settlements take their classes to places I never knew existed. They have enjoyed seeing their regional heritage venerated at the Museum of Appalachia in Norris and at the Children's Museum of Oak Ridge, and their scientific heritage honored at the Museum of Science and Energy in Oak Ridge. After attending courses, plays, concerts, and athletic events at the University of Tennessee, that is where they

344

would *choose* to go, all other things being equal. The heritage of East Tennessee no longer escapes me, or my family. And the awareness I have gained in the past two decades started when Margaret Mead paid a visit to Oak Ridge High School over twenty years ago.

WOMAN WITH A BIG STICK

June Adamson

Three times within a decade, anthropologist Margaret Mead came to East Tennessee carrying her big stick. Although she didn't physically hit anything, she did verbally strike out at many things. Her visit to Oak Ridge in May 1964 was a memorable one. The shock waves were intensely felt as she struck out at the town's sacred cows, including science itself. Most Oak Ridgers didn't know then that this was her mode of operation wherever she went. She struck out at fatherhood, traditional marriages, Little League, and similar things wherever she went; but in Oak Ridge, where anything concerning science was not to be sneered at, she struck many nerves. She also struck many nerves when she accused Oak Ridgers of making unto themselves an enclave of learning, of prosperity, and failing to share with surrounding communities. Never has Oak Ridge had such a cantankerous speaker. In recent years Oak Ridge, science, and scientists have been given an incisive going over by many, notably the popular press. Margaret Mead, however, did it first.

Although she returned to East Tennessee twice more—for a science conference in Gatlinburg in November 1966, and for an "Environment 2000" Workshop at the University of Tennessee in February 1971—she never returned to Oak Ridge.

I remember Margaret Mead with both pain and pleasure. As a young woman, I had read many of her books and admired her from a distance, as did many. Her book, *Male and Female*, was the

346

first I read to make sense about the problem of being a woman. I did not recognize then her mastery of the non sequitur and other fallacies, and I later found more helpful books on the subject of being a "person" and not just an extension of someone else.

Mead had seemed to me the voice of sweet reasonableness and I didn't even catch on to her techniques at the airport where I met her as a journalist covering the story. I played right into her hands as she asked the questions. As I wrote in a page one news story the next morning, her main questions concerned what had happened to Oak Ridge's children over a twenty-one year period. She was particularly interested in where they went to college following high school; whether they left Tennessee for advanced study, which many did.

She asked about the children of the black community. She expressed interest in the isolation of those children, even though the junior high schools and high school had been desegregated for nine years. She specifically wanted to know whether the black community was within the city limits, and of course, it always has been, however isolated. Good questions, and I was concerned about them too, although I'm sure she didn't recognize that. Then she wanted to know, "Does the African Violet Club still exist?" I recognized then that she had a source of information about Oak Ridge, and I tried to find out who it was. She admitted she had, but wouldn't tell me who. Soon after she left town I learned that it was Thelma Present, who had lived in Oak Ridge for a short time before moving to Knoxville with her physicist husband.

I should have had a clue to the nature of her lecture that night when she told me, "Oak Ridge is the first place where the 'servant problem' turned up in America—you people blamed it on the war." This was the kind of fallacy of reason that she sometimes fell into, since only a very few Oak Ridge families had "housekeeping;" some had a once-a-week cleaning woman, but the majority who did not work outside the home did their own housework.

Driving into Oak Ridge, she commented that she felt Oak Ridge was "first" in many ways in its adjustment to a new kind of community life, but she didn't necessarily mean it as a compliment. The grandmotherly-looking, gray-haired lady peered intently through her glasses at everything around her. She seemed quite delighted to see her name on the welcoming marquee of the motel

347

along with Representative Charles Halleck's. "I get mixed up with the oddest people on these trips," she commented. She also observed that having her name on a marquee in Oak Ridge was a first-time experience, and said, "You know, I think this shouting of names in Oak Ridge must be a hangover from wartime security when you couldn't even print names." Maybe it was.

She was up early the next morning, at it again, asking questions—me following her. There was breakfast with Alexander Hollaender, then director of the Oak Ridge National Laboratory Biology Division, and Claire Nader, sociologist and sister of Ralph. Later that day, the late Marge Weinberg was hostess at a luncheon, and the guests included representatives from Oak Ridge High School, the long ago defunct Community Relations Council, and the Oak Ridge Mental Health Association. Again, most of her questions were about the children.

That evening came her now-famous attack. She picked on men of science, saying that Oak Ridge was an enclave of these men who were weak fathers and did nothing for the surrounding communities. Her announced topic was "Children in a Scientific Community."

She raised sharp questions: "Is this a good place to bring up children?" "What is the child in the privileged home learning?" She said she feared a vast gap between the intellectual scientist who has come here for research and the uneducated "native" who works here or lives nearby. She pointed out that there were physicists, chemists, biologists in abundance, but too few sociologists, historians, and philosophers. "These humanities are represented in Oak Ridge only by wives and preachers. Scientists don't marry scientists, fortunately, and that makes for a mixture that saves the day," she commented. (What may have been "generally" true then, is no longer true. Sociologists and economists have come to do research in Oak Ridge too, and she would be surprised at how much "philosophy" many scientists know and share. She obviously did not meet such couples as Liane and William Russell, both scientists of international reputation, who have contributed much to the preservation of the state's total environment.)

Although there were some who matched sharp questions to some of her remarks, including William G. Pollard, Alvin Weinberg, William Arnold, and Waldo Cohn, I left that crowded

348

auditorium thinking I was the only one there who disagreed with much of what she had said. I felt hurt and angry when *The Oak Ridger* newspaper came in for its share of Mead's criticism. She said she had changed her mind several times about her topic after reading what the local press had announced as her lecture. And she implied that this newspaper was in the same class as a notoriously bad one in another city.

When the audience laughed at her remarks concerning the press, I wanted to sink into the floor. I thought they were laughing at me, too. It was only during the following weeks that I came to understand that sometimes people laugh because they are uncomfortable. But no one spoke to me as I left the auditorium, so it was a bad night, not only for Oak Ridge, but for me. I tossed and turned all night, wondering how I could keep any journalistic objectivity. I was so frustrated by what I perceived as an unfair evaluation, I wept, and announced I had no intention of covering her appearance at a Ministerial Association breakfast the next morning—a Sunday. It was an "If you feel like it" assignment anyway, since I had spent many extra hours on the Mead visit already.

After all the tossing and turning, I awoke early, adrenaline surging. It was fifteen minutes before time for the breakfast. I threw on some clothes, drove as fast as I could to the meeting place. My stomach was churning and I couldn't face eating, but I had to know what she would say that morning.

I was distressed to find only one seat left in the packed dining room—right next to her, this powerhouse of a woman with the razor-sharp tongue. I had come only to listen. I didn't want to talk to her, but we nodded. Then she said something to the effect that she knew I was angry with her because of her remarks the night before. I told her I thought she was only playing the great American parlor game of picking on its local press. When she stood up, she said, "Since the press is here, I am going to use it to get some points across, even though she (me) is still mad at me for some of the things I said last night." That might have been the closest Margaret Mead ever came to an apology.

That morning her attacks continued. She accused those present (not just me) of not being able to stand criticism. T. H. Dunigan, then principal of Oak Ridge High School, cited the work of the Tennessee Valley Authority in laying groundwork for interaction between newcomers and Appalachian natives, noting that the former had improved the technology of the area. She didn't appear to listen. She was critical of the community because a Ku Klux Klan meeting had recently been held in the city. When it was pointed out that the Klan meeting had been held in reaction to a positive thrust to make Oak Ridge an integrated community, she replied, "A positive thrust is often ignorant." To every comment made, she had a similar quick, negative comeback, her fiery tongue flicking in and out, only waiting so she could reply. Asked whether a city ordinance should have stopped the meeting, she replied, "The Klan meeting should have been stopped by a climate of opinion that wouldn't allow it."

Did her visit change anything that wouldn't have changed anyway? Probably not, though she did give Oak Ridgers a challenge. Perhaps it was the beginning of defensiveness that has developed over the years since. And that has not been good for Oak Ridge.

She spoke of the role of the father in modern society. She said Oak Ridge fathers used science fairs as "something to win with." She said students should stop competing, that science fairs are intended for the lonely gifted child who is much brighter than his/her teacher. Too bad she didn't speak with some of the fathers who tried to talk their sons out of such competition. Again, however, her remarks were food for thought.

My contact with the controversial anthropologist two years later in Gatlinburg was pleasant, although I did not expect it to be. I took the newspaper assignment with some trepidation. She said she remembered me when we met that first evening of registration, although I had a strong feeling that if she had been taller than I, she would have looked down her nose at me. It was another accidental meeting that seated me next to her at breakfast again. But this time I could eat.

Our conversation covered a variety of topics—the proposed college of Oak Ridge, the problem of too many cars in America and what to do about it in big cities, and finally, the drafting of young men to go to Vietnam. She agreed, "Oak Ridge should have a college. There are so many talented people there who could teach, so many, in fact, they wouldn't have to teach very much of the time." Too bad it didn't happen. This was one statement with which I totally agreed.

At the seminar itself, she confined herself to briefing reporters on her scientific subject, anthropology, and it was a delight to eavesdrop on her conversation with Ralph Birdlwhistle as he was explaining his new theory of communication by body language. Somewhat off the subject of science, she was highly critical of busing, terming it an attempt "that does nothing but put some children in worse schools."

She reflected on her 1964 charges that Oak Ridge had not made its influence sufficiently felt in Appalachia, and said she felt there was a reaction in Oak Ridge to the adjustment of property ownership and self-government. She observed that Ridgers would probably remain preoccupied with both these major changes for a while, and that this was perhaps the reason for Oak Ridge's indifference to surrounding areas. She remained convinced of this indifference, at least in this conversation.

To a question about whether she would make a return visit to Oak Ridge, she said, "In about ten years." Why so long? "Because I would like to see what happens in the meantime," she replied.

She did make a third visit to Tennessee, if not to Oak Ridge. It was to the University of Tennessee in 1971, and the content of what she said then might have been the most pertinent of all to present-day Oak Ridge. For the unspoken but ever-present question at that meeting was: Will there be any kind of environment for mankind in the year 2000 if the present rate of pollution continues?

In her formal talk, "Forget Maximization," in action groups concerning the quality of life, and in an interview with members of the press, she stressed two major points. First, something can be done to preserve life on this planet, and done in time if everyone works at it. And second, that Americans are too prone to create a "climate of opinion" about a topic such as pollution so that "No one can possibly be for it, then consider the problem solved, take their marbles and go home."

As for the Appalachian mountaineer, she replied to a remark that cities don't want them with, "Fiddlesticks! The North wants them to come so they can be exploited more."

She had a good word to say for television, this time in answer to a critical black student. "Without television we wouldn't be where we are with Civil Rights. It's given people a voice all through the system. I've been in favor of 'black power,' but I'm not sure that's the way to solve the Appalachian problem." To a question on white power, she was emphatic, "Nonsense! What we're talking about here is minority groups. There's white power in South Africa because they're in the minority, and they're going to get massacred." In this statement, she may have demonstrated remarkable foresight.

In another of her famous remarks, she challenged American middle-aged women to work to improve the environment. "Most of them just sit around and polish the brass left to them by their dead husbands. I doubt that we'll get through this crisis if we don't start making use of this resource." Asked later about the popular idea of educating women after their children are grown, she became sarcastic: "Of course this is being pushed by the system. Women after middle age are the last bit of cheap, uneducated labor available."

Today I still remember the anger I felt over some of her first words in Oak Ridge. Some of her barbs I took in a too-personal way. But as a later editorial in *The Oak Ridger* noted, local reaction to Mead mellowed. How could she know of Oak Ridgers' involvement in Anderson County politics—in Roane County politics—in Campbell County politics—in state politics? How could she know of the outreach programs of Oak Ridge's many churches? Of individuals interested in furthering community action throughout the area? Apparently, no one told her how many from Appalachia were and still are served by the Methodist Medical Center of Oak Ridge, then the Oak Ridge Hospital of the Methodist Church, the Planned Parenthood Association, nor of the many Appalachian children helped by the Daniel Arthur Rehabilitation Center. Then there was the Oak Ridge Mental Health Center, now renamed for the regional purpose it always served. And the list goes on.

As Joanne Gailar wrote so eloquently in a column published in *The Oak Ridger* newspaper December 30, 1980, "I can't help but wonder whether Margaret Mead might have been a little less caustic [and more helpful] and viewed us 'outsiders' in a more charitable light ... had she had a different correspondent."

Courtesy June Adamson

Dr. Margaret Mead (L) and June Adamson (R) at the Gatlinburg Science Seminar in the fall of 1966.

RESEARCH AND PROGRESS

Courtesy Department of Energy   Westcott Photo

POSTWAR RESEARCH AND DEVELOPMENT

Alvin M. Weinberg

We were young, all of us, when we came to Oak Ridge during the Second World War. We knew even then that what we were up to would change the world forever. Our enthusiasm and our energy were boundless. After all, how many souls can participate in the discovery and development of a new source of energy: one whose military power would permanently alter the relations between great nations, and whose peaceful applications would make real H. G. Wells' dream of *A World Set Free* based on cheap and limitless atomic energy?

That the wartime potential has been realized, none can doubt. And of course Oak Ridge played a crucial role in this. The Hiroshima bomb was fashioned from U-235 separated mainly at the Y-12 electromagnetic and the K-25 gaseous diffusion plants. The X-10 graphite reactor was the very first nuclear reactor to generate substantial amounts of heat (about 1,000 kilowatts), and to produce gross amounts of the new element, plutonium. Indeed, the original Clinton Laboratories was built to test the chemical processes for separating plutonium used at the huge Hanford plutonium factories; and Oak Ridge has always maintained this war-born tradition of chemical technology.

As for peacetime applications, much has been accomplished. Nuclear power has, worldwide, replaced about five million barrels of oil each day. In the United States, some sixteen percent of our electricity is generated from nuclear reactors. That nuclear power has not yet fulfilled all of its promise must cloud the extraordinary accomplishment of nuclear power—a new source of energy which in the remarkably short time of forty years accounts worldwide for five percent of man's primary energy! Oak Ridge has played a prominent, and in some instances, a central role in this development.

Beyond all these developments, Oak Ridge has contributed greatly to the scientific and technological development of the South. These accomplishments were thoroughly surveyed by Dr. William G. Pollard in his *Atomic Energy and Southern Science*, published in 1966. Dr. Pollard reviewed many of the most important scientific developments at Oak Ridge during the twenty years following the end of the war. He emphasized the special role of Oak Ridge as a catalyst in the scientific flowering of the South. Much of my review draws on Dr. Pollard's excellent book.

Oak Ridge and Nuclear Power

The Oak Ridge National Laboratory (ORNL) played a central role in the development of nuclear power in two ways. First, and perhaps most important, was the Oak Ridge School of Reactor Technology. By the end of the war, there were hardly two dozen individuals in the United States who understood the technology of nuclear reactors well enough to guide the development of commercial nuclear power; and since the wartime nuclear reactors were aimed at producing plutonium, not power, what knowledge there was, was not entirely relevant to the design of nuclear electricity-generating plants. Eugene Wigner, the first research director of ORNL, recognized that the reactor design techniques that he and his group had developed at Chicago had to be disseminated—and this was the origin and purpose of the Oak Ridge School of Reactor Technology (ORSORT). Frederick Seitz, later to become president of the National Academy of Sciences, spent the year of 1946 as director of ORSORT. The faculty consisted of scientists and engineers who had worked, mainly with Wigner, in designing the Hanford reactors. The students were experienced technical people from U.S. industry and government. Many of the ORSORT alumni have since become prominent in American nuclear energy affairs.

The most famous student was Vice-Admiral (at that time, Captain) Hyman Rickover. His mission was to develop a nuclear-powered submarine, the first true submarine, since its power plant would require neither oxygen nor recharging of batteries. Captain Rickover wisely understood the importance of ORSORT. He not only sent many of his enthusiastic lieutenants to its classes, but he also threw the navy's support to the school.

What kind of reactor was best suited for powering a submarine? The Oak Ridge reactor experts insisted that for this purpose, only two characteristics were truly relevant: compactness (since submarines are small) and reliability. These could be achieved with a reactor that used separated U-235 as fuel, and that used water under pressure as both moderator and coolant. Indeed, even before Captain Rickover appeared on the scene, during 1944, a group at Oak Ridge had conducted experiments on reactors moderated by water. Thus Oak Ridge scientists were to offer the captain a practically ready-made solution to his quest for a submarine propulsion reactor: pressurize the water-moderated reactors which had been the subject of wartime experiments at Clinton Laboratories.

The engineering of the first pressurized water reactor was done by H. Etherington at Oak Ridge and was carried to completion by him at Argonne National Laboratory. Karl Cohen, who had spent a few months in Oak Ridge, first realized that naval pressurized water reactors could become the basis of a whole nuclear power industry. It was he who insisted that *slightly* enriched uranium from the diffusion plant at K-25 could serve as an economic fuel for a commercial power plant. ORNL also discovered that hafnium-free zirconium could be used to clad the fuel in a pressurized water plant. Thus one can claim that commercial nuclear power had its origin at ORNL with the conception of the pressurized water naval reactor, the development of hafnium-free zirconium, and Karl Cohen's insight into the economic practicality of slightly enriched uranium.

Oak Ridge has been involved in many other power reactor developments since Captain Rickover's *Naulilus*—the Nuclear

Aircraft, the Power Package, the Molten Salt Breeder, the aqueous Homogeneous Breeder, the Gas Cooled reactors, the Nuclear Ship *Savannah*—but none has had the far-reaching influence of the original work on the pressurized water reactor for naval propulsion and, eventually, for civilian power. Nevertheless, we must remember that the forty years since 1945 are but a moment in technological history. I would hope that the brilliant work of H. G. MacPherson and his associates on molten salt breeders and of Paul Kasten and his team on gas-cooled reactors will eventually give birth to commercially important nuclear power systems based on these ideas.

These different reactor projects have motivated far-reaching developments in metallurgy, in solid state physics, and in chemical technology at ORNL; for example, Hastelloy-N, a nickel-based alloy developed for the molten salt reactor has become a commercially important high-temperature alloy. Much of our knowledge of the effects of radiation on solid materials has come from pioneering work of the Solid State Division at ORNL. And the processes based on solvent extraction to separate plutonium from irradiated nuclear fuel, or to win uranium from low-grade ores, were developed in the ORNL Chemical Technology Division.

Basic Research and Its Support
Though ORNL has made innumerable discoveries in almost all of the physical and biological sciences, I would venture that its influence on science and technology has been most profound and far-reaching through its development of powerful new tools for research, tools now used universally. Most important is the large-scale production of isotopes, both radioactive and stable. Though radioisotopes had been used in science and in medicine since the discovery of artificial radioactivity in the mid-1930s, their widespread use had to await large-scale production at the X-10 reactor in Oak Ridge. Paul Aebersold and Waldo Cohn were responsible for organizing the production and distribution of these tools of science, medicine, and industry. Had ORNL done nothing else in its forty-three-year history, the large-scale use of radioisotopes made possible by ORNL would assure the Laboratory an honored place in science.

The other important tool of Big Science developed at ORNL

was the water-moderated, thin-plate research reactor. Beginning with the Materials Testing Reactor (MTR) in 1952, ORNL has built the Low Intensity Test Reactor (LITR), Oak Ridge Research Reactor (ORR), Tower Shielding Facility (TSF), Bulk Shielding Reactor (BSR), High Flux Isotope Reactor (HFIR)—variants of this basic reactor design. Many dozens of research reactors, all based on this simple principle pioneered at ORNL, are now in use throughout the world; and the United States fleet of nuclear submarines is powered by pressurized versions of the original MTR.

Other research tools carrying the ORNL trademark include the original A-1 amplifier of P. R. Bell and W. H. Jordan; a series of isochronous cyclotrons developed by R. Livingston and his group; the Moak ion-source; ingenious ion exchange methods now widely used in biochemistry; solid state counters, which have been commercialized at Oak Ridge Technical Enterprises Corporation (ORTEC); transuranium elements from the HFIR, to mention a few.

Of particular significance was Oak Ridge's role in the computer revolution of the early 1950s. Under the guidance of A. S. Householder, ORNL cooperated with the Argonne National Laboratory in the construction of one of the first programmable Von Neumann-type computers. The machine was dubbed Oak Ridge Automatic Computer and Logical Engine, or ORACLE. When it was completed in 1953, it was the world's most advanced computer. Though ORACLE held this distinction for only a few months, it was an important landmark in the computer revolution.

Nor has Oak Ridge neglected its unique research facilities in pursuing its own investigations. Neutron diffraction, which requires a reactor, first became a systematic method for analyzing crystal structure through the early work of E. D. Wollan, C. Shull, and Wallace C. Koehler, and of Levy, Peterson, and Brown. It is now a standard method that supplements the more usual x-ray diffraction methods for studying details of crystal structure. Much of the chemistry of the strange new nuclear species resulting from fission was elucidated at ORNL, even to the discovery of the new chemical element 61, promethium, by C. Coryell, J. A. Marinsky, and L. E. Glendenin.

ORNL has always been one of the world's leading centers for

research in classical nuclear physics and chemistry. These researches are based on an ever more sophisticated family of accelerators—Van de Graaffs, Isochronous Cyclotrons, Linacs—culminating in the Holifield Heavy Ion Facility, which is a mecca for the study of nuclear reactions involving heavy ions. Indeed, Oak Ridge scientists were among the first to study the behavior of heavy nuclei. It all began in 1950 when the hydrogen bomb was being developed. Edward Teller had raised the possibility that at the extreme temperatures of a hydrogen bomb explosion, the nitrogen nuclei in the atmosphere might ignite in one awful and final conflagration. Though Hans Bethe had shown this to be impossible on theoretical grounds, Alex Zucker at ORNL built the sixty-three-inch cyclotron to measure the likelihood of such reactions. Needless to say, Zucker's measurements eliminated the possibility of the atmosphere exploding; and in the process he established Oak Ridge as a center of heavy ion nuclear science.

Courtesy James E. Westcott

In 1958 Senator John F. Kennedy and Mrs. Kennedy visited Oak Ridge National Laboratory. Here they are shown around by the Laboratory Director Alvin Weinberg and Senator Albert Gore. "ORNL has always been one of the world's leading centers for research in classical nuclear physics and chemistry."

Biology

The biological effects of radiation were studied at Oak Ridge from the beginning, but only after the establishment of the Biology Division under the leadership of Alexander Hollaender did biological research at ORNL acquire world prominence.

Biology at Oak Ridge was aimed at elucidating the effects of ionizing radiation on living things. The approach was two-pronged: on the one hand were the large-scale mouse experiments in which both genetic and somatic effects of radiation were measured; on the other hand these large and very expensive applied researches were supported by a myriad of basic researches in biochemistry, microbiology, cytogenetics, and embryology. Thus Oak Ridge became both the originator of what we would call Big Biology and a highly productive center for research into the basic mechanism underlying the interaction of radiation and living matter.

The combination has been remarkably successful. The mouse genetics experiments of W. Russell and L. Russell have been used to establish genetically "safe" levels of exposure to ionizing radiation, and the studies by Upton on radiation carcinogenesis are still regarded as classic. Hardly a field of modern radiation biology is untouched by the outpouring of discoveries of the Oak Ridge group: Astrakhan and Volkin's discovery of messenger RNA; Cohn and Carter's introduction of ion exchange and paper chromatography methods for isolation of nucleic acids; Howard I. Adler's mini-cells and, much more recently, his discovery of a simple way to culture anaerobes; W. Arnold and B. Strehler's discovery of delayed light emission in photosynthesis. No wonder that the Biology Division has acquired a worldwide reputation, with almost two dozen of its members and alumni being elected to the National Academy of Sciences.

The original mission of the Biology Division was to investigate the interaction of a physical agent—radiation—on life. This had enabled the division rather easily to turn to studies of the biological effects of other physical and chemical agents as well. This of course fits in well with the current national concern over the effects of many environmental agents on living matter.

Medical Science

Though ORNL's work in biology, by and large, was somewhat removed from medical practice, at least three developments have had important impacts in medicine. First, bone marrow transplants were investigated at ORNL in the 1950s as a means of combating overexposure to radiation. These constituted some of the very first transplants of organs, other than blood, between animals. The accompanying studies of immune rejection have been at the very foundation of successful transplants of kidneys, hearts, and other organs. Second, P. R. Bell and the group at Oak Ridge Associated Universities (ORAU), were among the pioneers in medical isotope scanning. Many of the techniques they developed are now routinely used. Finally, there is the extraordinary development of zonal centrifugation by N. Anderson and collaborators at K-25. This by-product of the centrifuge developed for separating uranium isotopes has given rise to a whole family of important medical techniques, such as the General Medical Sciences and Atomic Energy Commission (GeMSAEC) clinical analysis system, and the centrifuge method of removing foreign proteins from human vaccines.

Courtesy Department of Energy
Westcott Photo

The first shipment of a radioisotope for medical use was made on August 2, 1946, in Oak Ridge, from the then Clinton Laboratories. The shipment consisted of one millicurie of Carbon-14 for the Barnard Free Skin and Cancer Hospital in St. Louis, Missouri. This ceremony, marking the first shipment of a radioisotope for peaceful purposes, was held in front of the loading face of the Oak Ridge Graphite Reactor, the world's first full-scale reactor.

Ecology and Waste Disposal

Oak Ridge was the first place where radioactivity was handled on an enormous scale. This required the development of techniques for disposal of radioactive wastes, and investigation of the ecological effects of radioactivity in the natural environment. A very large team of ecologists, perhaps the world's largest, was gathered under S. Auerbach, to study the paths followed by radionuclides through different natural habitats, the effects of ionizing radiation on trees and animals, and the accumulation of radioactivity in the various trophic levels. Supporting these experiments and observations was a very active group of "systems ecologists" who developed mathematical techniques for tracing the movements of radioactivity in nature. Though the Oak Ridge ecologists were primarily interested in radioactivity, the techniques they developed have been widely applied to many other environmental questions: for example, the effect of hot effluents from power plants on bodies of water; the CO_2-greenhouse effect; and more recently, the problem of acid rain. Thus Oak Ridge continues to play an important role in the scientific investigation of some of our most important environmental questions.

Because Oak Ridge was the first to be confronted with the enormous amounts of radioactivity generated in nuclear reactors and their associated chemical plants, many techniques for dealing with these wastes were pioneered at Oak Ridge. Among these are the use of monitored landfills for low-level wastes, tanks for temporary storage of high-level wastes, and solidification and sequestration in bedded salt for permanent disposal. The latter is one of the techniques now being developed as part of our country's program for permanent disposal of high-level radiowastes.

One of the most promising techniques developed at ORNL is hydrofracture and grout injection. In this method, intermediate levels of radioactivity are mixed with grout and injected 1,000 feet below the surface into horizontal crevices formed by high pressure "hydrofracture." The radioactive grout sets up permanently and is thereby sequestered. More than a million curies of radioactivity have been sequestered in the Oak Ridge hydrofracture plant. Although a few curies of activity have escaped, apparently because of a faulty procedure in an injection, the hydrofracture method may yet be vindicated and used widely for intermediate and possibly eventually, high-level wastes.

Reactor Safety

The Three Mile Island accident in 1979 has cast a pall on nuclear energy in the United States. Concern over reactor safety shares with waste disposal the distinction of causing about fifty percent of the American public to turn away from nuclear energy. For nuclear energy to flourish, both these issues must be resolved to the satisfaction of the public. I have already pointed to the important role ORNL has played in research in waste disposal. Equally important, ORNL has been a leader in research on reactor safety. For more then twenty years, ORNL has conducted experimental and theoretical investigations aimed at improving the safety of reactors. These researches constitute a massive contribution to reactor safety in many areas: release of fission products from melted fuel, brittle fracture of pressure vessels, sophisticated analysis of control systems, thermohydraulics of reactor accidents, and techniques for designing reactor shielding, to name but a few. ORNL also is the site of the Nuclear Safety Information Center (NSIC), which has collected and disseminated information on nuclear safety since the 1950s. Its most important product is the journal *Nuclear Safety* which is distributed throughout the world.

NSIC is but one example of some half-dozen or more information centers that have operated at ORNL for many years. With science having become so complex, information centers that disseminate and organize knowledge in various specialties have become important elements of the scientific enterprise. ORNL among the big laboratories has been aggressively active in these efforts.

Thermonuclear and Other Energy Sources

Though ORNL began as a pilot plant for demonstrating fission processes, even by the 1950s it had branched into other energy sources—most notably, thermonuclear fusion. Today this is the largest single scientific enterprise at Oak Ridge. And although the goal of inexhaustible energy from fusion has yet to be gained, ORNL plays a key role in its quest.

Similarly, ORNL contributes to our understanding and development of other energy sources—conservation, solar, ocean thermal, and even coal and synthetic fuels. Though most of these developments come after 1970, their roots are to be found in

ORNL's earlier involvement in environmental questions.

During its forty-three years, ORNL has become one of the world's leading centers for research in energy and environment, as well as basic science. I hope this short review will help the reader understand better the roots of ORNL's strength, the better to appreciate its potential for continued contributions to science of high social purpose.

THE COMING OF AGE OF SOUTHERN UNIVERSITIES IN SCIENCE

William G. Pollard

Before the Second World War, the South's economy was still largely rural and had a minimum of industry compared with the North and the West Coast. Economic conditions were precarious for many of the region's people, and the long hot summers made industrial development an almost insurmountable barrier. Moreover, the universities of the region shared in this impoverishment, especially in science. They reflected the general economic problems of the region. At meetings of national university associations, for example, such as those of Land Grant Colleges, Graduate School Deans, and the American Physical Society, members from the South had little to say. They were forced to assume the secondary role of mere observers among members from universities of the North or West who could contribute to the "important" problems. So they formed the *Southern* Association of Land Grant Colleges, the Conference of Deans of *Southern* Graduate Schools, and the *Southeastern* Section of the American Physical Society in which they could play dominant roles.

I won a graduate fellowship in physics from Rice University in 1932. The year before, Sir James Chadwick had discovered the neutron; and when I arrived at Rice there was already an active research program under way on proton recoils from neutron collisions. My four years at Rice were a highly exciting time in physics. The discovery of what later turned out to be annihilation radiation by Gray and Tarrant was the first. This was quickly followed by the discovery of the positron in cosmic radiation by Carl David Anderson, artificial radioactivity and the production of electron-positron pairs from gamma-ray photons by the Curies in France, and the realization that a neutral neutrino always accompanied the electron in beta-ray types of radioactive decays. Fermi advanced a theory of beta radioactivity based on electron-neutrino pairs, and I chose it for my Ph.D. thesis in 1935. In this same period, Cockroft and Walton in England produced the first artificial nuclear transformation with protons, Lawrence and Livingston developed the cyclotron at Berkeley, and Van de Graaff the high voltage electrostatic accelerator.

In the summer of 1936, I joined the faculty of the University of Tennessee as assistant professor of physics, full of ambitions and dreams of continuing this heady course of development. The eight years which followed were quite productive for me personally, but the isolation of the university from the centers of activity in the North and West was depressing. I attended meetings of both the American Physical Society and its southeastern sections, but there was a sharp contrast between the programs. The section meetings were almost exclusively devoted to teaching, while the national meetings had all the excitement of research and discovery. My colleague, Alvin Nielsen, managed to scrape together a little grant money that enabled him to build an infrared spectrometer of good resolution. With this instrument there was some experimental research in the physics department of the university, but not enough to attract graduate students. The exciting community of research which I had known at Rice seemed an impossibility in view of the severely limited resources available at Tennessee.

In spite of all this, my eight years of teaching at the University of Tennessee were a happy and personally fulfilling period of my life. The southern universities in general couldn't contribute very much to the discoveries of science, but they could and did make a major contribution to the education of the next generation of scientists. This was the situation in which I found myself, and I threw myself into it with enthusiasm.

In 1939 World War II broke out in Europe, and in 1942 the university took responsibility for a large contingent of Air Corps trainees for which I was assigned the responsibility of scheduling for meals, classes, drills, and flight training. Then in 1944 I was granted a leave of absence for Manhattan District work on gaseous diffusion separation of uranium isotopes at Columbia University. I returned to a full professorship in September 1945 with visions of an ivory tower existence and a resumption of my work in physics. This combination was very soon ended by my role in organizing the southern universities to take advantage of the outstanding research staff and facilities at the Oak Ridge National Laboratory. In October 1946 the Oak Ridge Institute of Nuclear Studies was incorporated, and the remainder of my career, until my retirement in 1976, was taken up in guiding that corporation, now known as Oak Ridge Associated Universities (ORAU), in its amazing development over the years. In 1980 I published an account of these developments in a book entitled *ORAU From The Beginning*.

The key to the flowering of research and graduate education in science in the southern universities certainly lies with the Oak Ridge National Laboratory (ORNL). When the wilds of East Tennessee were chosen by the Manhattan District for the location of its major facilities, the result was to create in the region a major nuclear research facility with an outstanding international staff of physicists. The physicists who were assigned here thought of it as the boondocks, while scientists from the rest of the country who knew of Oak Ridge called it Dogpatch. But ORNL in the postwar period played a profound role in the development of southern universities. Participation programs for faculty and students, and the training in radioisotope techniques were all developed by ORAU.

At least two other events were almost equally important for the improvement of southern universities. One of these was the emergence in this same period of the extensive grant programs of the Atomic Energy Commission and the National Science Foundation for research support of individual scientists and the fellowship programs of both which supported graduate students in science. (ORAU assumed the nationwide administration of the AEC Fellowships.) The other event was the widespread installation of air-conditioning which was responsible for the explosive industrial development of the South, with the increased tax income going largely to the universities. Quite apart from Oak Ridge and

ORNL and the programs of ORAU, these two developments would have, on their own, promoted great changes in graduate education in science in southern universities.

Clinton Laboratories, which soon became Oak Ridge National Laboratory, supported a great variety of research in all the sciences. Its major emphasis was of course the design and development of nuclear reactors for research and electric power generation. But this entailed extensive research in all aspects of physics and chemistry. Neutron diffraction and radioisotope production were extensive developments. The programs in engineering and material science at ORNL were outstanding. The biological research developed under the leadership of Alexander Hollaender was for a time the best in the world. The research in medicine, carried out by ORAU rather than ORNL, under the leadership of Marshall Brucer, made significant contributions in scanning teletherapy and instrument development for medical applications.

ORAU set for itself the goal of bringing the rich and varied research in Oak Ridge to bear on southern universities. Programs were developed to make it possible for faculty and students from the universities to actively participate in research in Oak Ridge for extensive periods and to take back to their institutions the knowledge, enthusiasm, and abilities they had gained. A reciprocal program supported staff members of ORNL and ORAU in making visits to the universities. Medical college physicians participated actively in teletherapy, thyroid uptake, scanning, and other programs of the ORAU Medical Division. More recently the *Unisor* project of ORAU at the Hollifield Heavy Ion facilities at ORNL resulted in the active participation of faculty from its sponsoring universities. At its peak these programs brought more than a hund·ed faculty and students to Oak Ridge each year for periods of three months or longer.

Another program of ORAU which made a major contribution to the rapid adoption of radioactive tracer techniques in all the sciences, particularly in biology and medicine, was the radioisotope techniques courses initiated in the summer of 1948. This training, accomplished in only four weeks, made it possible for researchers in all fields to safely handle radioactive materials and incorporate this powerful new technique in their investigations.

Courtesy James E. Westcott

In 1955 Eleanor Roosevelt visited the Oak Ridge Associated Universities Cancer Research Hospital. Accompanying her are William Pollard and Dr. Norman Anderson.

The final impact on science, from those who got their basic training in Oak Ridge, is inestimable. Coupled with this training was the radioisotope production service at ORNL which made a great variety of radioactive isotopes widely and easily available. Because of their nearness to Oak Ridge, researchers from southern universities benefitted especially from these courses.

In 1966, in celebration of the twentieth anniversary of the founding of ORAU, I made a study of the research contributions of its member universities and ORNL in the twenty-year period. It was published by ORAU and entitled *Atomic Energy and Southern Science*. This report showed the remarkable progress made in twenty years of research and graduate education in all the sciences by southern universities. ORNL still stands out, but in physics, chemistry, and engineering, campus after campus is beginning to flourish in the South. And in medicine at Virginia, Duke, Vanderbilt, Birmingham, Houston, and elsewhere the beginnings of what will grow into great medical centers in another ten years are evident.

In October of 1986, ORAU will celebrate the fortieth anniversary of its formation in 1946, and it has struck me that the report that I wrote twenty years ago is uncalled for today. The southern universities are now fully on a par with the prestigious universities in other parts of the country. It no longer makes sense to single out the South for special treatment. The accident of the war which placed ORNL in East Tennessee can be seen in retrospect to have been a major factor in this transformation. ORAU, because of its early formation soon after the war, was able to secure a large place for southern universities in ORNL and maximize its impact on higher education in the region. As one whose professional career spans both the pre- and postwar periods, covering a full half century, and who was in a position to seize the opportunities as they arose, I take great personal satisfaction from the role I was privileged to play in this achievement.

MY! HOW ORAU HAS GROWN

Thomas F.X. McCarthy

You know how it is when you meet someone whom you recognize but remember only as a child? You gaze at this strapping youth or lovely young lady, and your first reaction is, "My! How you've grown!" Well, that's what has happened to Oak Ridge Associated Universities (ORAU)—it has grown!

It happened like this: in September 1945, a party was held by Dr. Robert M. Boarts, professor of chemical engineering at the University of Tennessee (UT) for Dr. Katherine "Kay" Way, a former faculty member of the UT Physics Department, so that she could visit with some of her old colleagues. The time was just a month after the revelation to the public that Oak Ridge was one of the major "secret cities" that had brought the world into what was then referred to as the Atomic Age.

As could only be expected, the main topic of conversation was nuclear energy and the part Oak Ridge might play in the oncoming atomic age. During the animated discussion, the guest of honor, Katherine Way, suggested that it would be a wonderful thing if university science faculties in the South could use the great facilities in Oak Ridge as an educational tool in the university programs and at the same time aid the nation's peacetime nuclear research and development programs.

The upshot was that Dr. William G. Pollard, a member of the UT Physics Department, took Way's wishful thinking to heart. The next day he discussed the idea with Dr. Kenneth L. Hertel, the head of the Physics Department, and the two then conferred with Dr. Fred C. Smith, dean of the university. The result was "A Proposal for the University of Tennessee Sponsorship of Basic Research," and another proposal, "Basis for Collaboration between Monsanto Chemical Company and the University of Tennessee in a Research Institute." (At the time Monsanto operated Clinton Laboratories, the forerunner of today's Oak Ridge National Laboratory.) Both proposals were submitted to UT President James D. Hoskins, who acted by naming Pollard, Hertel, and Boarts as a committee to carry on with the project.

Coincidentally, Clinton Laboratories representatives had discussed with UT faculty members the possibility of Laboratories staff members carrying out a program of graduate courses at the Laboratories. The university approved the idea, and, with several UT staff members getting involved, the first courses under the program began, later developing into the Oak Ridge Resident Graduate Program.

Meanwhile, the new committee met with congressmen, top officials of the army and navy (including General Leslie R. Groves, wartime head of the Manhattan Engineer District), southern university executives, and David Lilienthal, chairman of the Tennessee Valley Authority.

It wasn't all sweetness and light, however. Commenting later on this period, Pollard said, in part:

> Looking back on this Washington trip, I recall it as a very gloomy affair. We did luck into seeing Senator McKellar (senior senator from Tennessee).... However, it was quite impossible to keep the conversation with him on our subject, and the whole meeting was spent partly in listening to his adverse remarks about Mr. Atlee, who had addressed both houses of Congress ... on the subject of atomic energy controls, and partly in listening to reminiscences of various unrelated events and escapades of ... his youth. A good part of the time we spent in pacing the streets of Washington with a feeling of frustration and distaste for the whole project.

375

Two conferences in December 1945 involving all the groups—Clinton Laboratories, the K-25 gaseous diffusion plant, and the Y-12 electromagnetic separation plant, and an expanded group of universities—led to the formation of an executive committee, headed by Pollard, to study various phases of the proposed program. The new organization was titled the Oak Ridge Institute of Nuclear Studies (ORINS), later to be changed to Oak Ridge Associated Universities (ORAU).

The committee set up two major programs: the Research Participation Program, which permitted graduate science students and university faculty members to come to Oak Ridge to carry out research programs, and the Oak Ridge Resident Graduate Program, under which young scientists employed in Oak Ridge could work towards graduate degrees without leaving their positions to return to school. Both programs went into effect before the actual chartering of ORINS.

The formal incorporation took place on October 16, 1946, with fourteen universities as charter members. The founding members were Alabama Polytechnic Institute (now Auburn University), Catholic University of America, Duke University, Emory University, Georgia School of Technology (now Georgia Institute of Technology), Louisiana State University, Tulane University of Louisiana, University of Alabama, University of Kentucky, University of North Carolina consolidated, University of Tennessee, University of Texas, University of Virginia, and Vanderbilt University.

There followed a hectic period for ORINS, as the government dissolved the Manhattan Engineer District, with ORINS forced to enter into a new contract with the civilian agency, the Atomic Energy Commission (AEC). Fortunately, the process wasn't as difficult as it might have been and soon the Oak Ridge Institute of Nuclear Studies was in business.

The new corporation was operated by a council, consisting of one representative from every sponsoring university, and a board of directors, elected by the council, that directed the operation of ORINS for the council but subject to the council's approval. The first president of ORINS and chairman of the council was Dr. Frank P. Graham, University of North Carolina. During the first meeting of the ORINS Board of Directors, held February 14-15,

1947, Pollard was appointed as acting executive director. In October 1947, Pollard was appointed to a five-year term as executive director, and the work of organizing a staff began.

Then Monsanto Chemical Company announced its withdrawal as operating contractor of Clinton Laboratories. Undaunted, ORINS proposed to operate the facility, but the AEC announced that the University of Chicago would undertake the Laboratories' management. When the University of Chicago withdrew, however, Carbide and Carbon Chemicals Company (now Union Carbide Corporation)—which already operated the electromagnetic-separation and gaseous-diffusion plants in Oak Ridge—assumed operation of Clinton Laboratories, and the name was changed to Oak Ridge National Laboratory (ORNL). A working arrangement between ORINS and ORNL began and has continued ever since. On the one hand, the AEC would suggest programs that ORINS was ideally fitted to handle, such as the AEC fellowship programs; and on the other, ORINS would suggest programs that it thought would be of benefit to the nation that the AEC could sponsor, such as the basic radioisotope techniques courses that ORINS wished to offer.

In the early years, Paul M. Gross, second president of ORINS, received a letter addressed to him as president of the "Oak Ridge Institute of Unclear Studies." Gross often told the story and said, "At the time, we weren't sure that the misspelling was a typographical error!"

The organizational setup of ORINS into four main divisions—plus executive, administrative, and service departments—was one that remained in effect for more than fifteen years.

The Special Training Division operated the basic and specialized courses in radioisotope techniques. The courses were at first limited to United States citizens, but foreign participants were admitted as early as 1949. Then, as an outgrowth of President Eisenhower's "Atoms for Peace" program, a course was presented especially for participants from foreign countries, and a quota of foreign students in basic courses was maintained until the courses were discontinued in 1977.

In this first foreign-student course, a bus trip of Oak Ridge and its environs was provided for the newcomers. At one point outside Oak Ridge, the bus entered the nearby town of Wartburg.

377

When the sign *Wartburg* came into view, the German contingent chorused "Vahrtboorg!" in a joyous Wagnerian shout. They were right at home.

Another story involves a Georgia Tech-Tennessee football game in Knoxville. Dixon Johnson, ORAU's first information department director, and his wife Betty had invited a Belgian participant and his wife to go with them. The visitors were absolutely amazed at the performance, and when it was over they told the Johnsons that they hadn't seen anything like it since the liberation of Brussels.

The Medical Division was established in 1949 at the suggestion of the AEC that ORINS undertake to study the uses of radioactive materials in the diagnosis and treatment of cancer and other diseases. In conjunction with this research, the Medical Division operated a thirty-two-bed hospital where patients were treated without charge. This hospital was closed down in October 1974 when the cost of patient care exceeded the funds needed for research purposes. Outpatient diagnostic care is now being provided to hospitals in the Oak Ridge-Knoxville area, on the referral of a physician.

The University Relations Division administered ORINS's original programs: the Research Participation Program and the Resident Graduate Program. It later took on a series of other programs, such as the AEC Fellowships, scientific and educational conferences and seminars, and many others.

The fourth of the original ORINS division also came into being in 1949 as a result of the AEC's decision to remove the fences around the residential area of the city and open it up to the general public. The AEC, however, realized that there was nothing "atomic" for visitors to see in the Atomic City. Accordingly, when Dixon Johnson proposed that ORINS set up and operate the American Museum of Atomic Energy that would explain the nation's nuclear research programs in nonscientific terms, AEC agreed and the Museum Division was added to the ORINS contract.

In the short span of five weeks, an abandoned government cafeteria building on Jefferson Circle was remodeled, exhibit materials and artifacts were borrowed and constructed, and when on March 19, 1949, the AEC admitted the public to the Atomic City so did the American Museum of Atomic Energy.

Courtesy James E. Westcott

The opening of the gates to the city and the opening of the new American Museum of Atomic Energy in March 1949 brought hundreds of people to Oak Ridge including these Hollywood stars. The mechanical hands are lighting a cigarette for Marie "The Body" Macdonald while Gloria Grahame and Rod Cameron look on.

Courtesy Oak Ridge Associated Universities

From his seat on the backhoe, ORINS Executive Director William G. Pollard officiated at the ground breaking for the new Central Administration Building for ORINS in 1959. Standing, from left to right, are Wayne Range and H. M. Roth of the Atomic Energy Commission's Oak Ridge Operations Office and Paul M. Elza, J. Walter Mumford, and Lawrence K. Akers of ORINS (now ORAU).

Inside, the visitors were treated to an atomic education in easy-to-understand terms. An introductory short film explained atomic structure and the process of fission. Cartoon characters like Dagwood and Mandrake the Magician brought the lessons down to the youngsters' level (though many adults benefited, too). A scale model of the first reactor at Oak Ridge National Laboratory (the second nuclear reactor in mankind's history) and many other exhibits and illustrations emphasized the many uses of radioactive materials in chemistry, biology, and industry. At the conclusion of their guided tours, visitors could bring away a real atomic souvenir—a dime whose silver atoms were bombarded with a neutron source and made hot enough to activate an adjacent Geiger counter. (The duration of the dime's radioactivity was such as to render the souvenir inert by the time its owner reached the museum's parking lot, but the metal-and-plastic case for the dime certified that it had been irradiated at the American Museum of Atomic Energy, Oak Ridge, Tennessee.) Years later, when the government began coining the largely copper "sandwich" dime, with no silver in its makeup, the neutron irradiator was retired, and other souvenirs replaced the dimes.

During the first ten years of its existence, ORINS's expanding staff and facilities were lodged in buildings and offices provided by the AEC, scattered throughout the residential and adjoining areas. The administration building was on Illinois Avenue; the Special Training Division and ORINS Library were housed on Laboratory Road; the Medical Division was on Vance Road, with an annex at the University of Tennessee-AEC Agricultural Research Laboratory miles away near Solway Bridge; the Museum Division was housed in the American Museum of Atomic Energy at the west end of the city; and the maintenance shops and other offices were located in a wing of the AEC printing plant near the Elza Gate entrance at the east end of the city. It was estimated that a person in a car would have to travel more than eleven miles to visit each ORINS division and office by the shortest route. And every building and its equipment was AEC property. Pollard would gleefully point out that the only piece of corporate-owned property could be (and occasionally was) carried about in one of his coat pockets: the ORINS corporate seal.

But, finally, on the occasion of the tenth anniversary of the founding, ORINS purchased some thirty-eight acres of land off Raccoon Road and Badger Avenue in the center of Oak Ridge on which it subsequently built its present Central Administration Building, the Energy Building, the Marmoset Research Facility, and the William G. Pollard Auditorium.

A decade later it became increasingly clear that the term "nuclear studies" in the corporate name was a restriction that didn't describe the growing range of the organization's activities. For example, there was the establishment of a data processing center in the Medical Division to collect, store, and process information on whole-body radiation; the center's facilities were later extended to provide services to other research activities of ORINS. Since ORINS was clearly exceeding its semantic limits, the name was changed to Oak Ridge Associated Universities (ORAU). It became official on January 1, 1966, and ORINS's sponsoring institutions now numbered forty.

In its nearly forty years of operation ORAU has derived most of its operating funds through its status as a contractor to the Atomic Energy Commission, the Energy Research and Development Administration, and now the Department of Energy. ORAU is the oldest government contractor in the community, and has established through the years a productive relationship between government, industry, and the academic community. ORAU also has done work for other government agencies, its member institutions, other colleges and universities, and the private sector.

Much can be said of the success of an organization that started out as the Oak Ridge Institute of Nuclear Studies with fourteen sponsoring institutions, one employee, and one contract, and which is now Oak Ridge Associated Universities with forty-nine member colleges and universities and some 450 employees. In the words of William E. Felling, ORAU's executive director, "When the Oak Ridge Institute of Nuclear Studies started, its budget for the first year's operation was about $54,000. Our fiscal year 1986 budget for operation of Oak Ridge Associated Universities is nearly $28 million. Clearly, Oak Ridge Associated Universities has come a long way, and I have every reason to believe that its future will be even brighter."

EDUCATION

Courtesy Department of Energy   Westcott Photo

INTEGRATION OF OAK RIDGE HIGH SCHOOL

Sandra Whitten Plant

O ak Ridge became the first community in the state to comply with the 1954 U.S. Supreme Court decision outlawing segregation in our nation's schools. This dramatic step took place in the school year of 1955-56, the year I entered Oak Ridge High School as a freshman.

How well I remember that September day when I put on my circular skirt, tightened up my waistcincher belt and headed off for my first day at Oak Ridge High School. The questions on my mind that morning were not racial ones, as I recall. I had the usual apprehensions about beginning a new school year. Would I fit in? Would I make new friends? Could I do well in the college prep courses I had chosen?

I was a little concerned about the threat of picketing by a parents' group calling itself Oak Ridgers for Segregation. This group had met throughout the summer and distributed a flier prior to the opening of school asking that children be kept home from school.

Some of their theme was expressed by this quote: "This is going farther and faster than the Supreme Court recommended."

The flier also stated, "If you are opposed to interchanging of the races, make known your opposition. Keep your child or children out of school for at least nine days." One of my friends, a gregarious blond from Mississippi, was kept home for the first week of school because her parents did fear trouble.

If my parents paid any attention to this group, I never knew it. Several friends told of being driven to school by their parents because of the fear of trouble. But when the school bus stopped that September morning at the corner of South Purdue and Princeton Avenue, my neighbors and I climbed aboard.

The same kind of red and white buses that picked me up in my Woodland neighborhood also had made a route through the Scarboro community in the black section of town picking up many of the black students who would be starting their first day at the two schools integrated that year, the high school and Robertsville Junior High. The briefly existent all-black Scarboro High School had graduated its last class of fifteen students on June 2, 1955.

As those buses squealed to a stop at the circular drive behind Oak Ridge High School, the bus-riding students clambered off and crossed the covered bridge leading to the cafeteria entrance. Racial slurs that had been smeared on the walkway the previous night had been removed by the time we arrived.

A photographer from *Life* magazine in New York was on the scene snapping pictures of the smoothness that marked opening day. "Calmness" was the word used by *The Oak Ridger* describing the entire integration process of 1955. Perhaps the most volatile scene that took place that day was a white student who objected to being photographed by the national news. A few days later in my Journalism I class, the teacher, Reef Waldrep, asked a few of us in the class to go through the *Life* photos and point out any shots of the offended student so they would not be used.

After all the attention paid to integrating the schools, I was a little disappointed to discover that there was only one black student in just one of my classes. He was a neat, quiet young man named Jimmy Lewis. The teacher in that General Science class was the late Mary McNees, a woman who, along with her husband, Town Councilman Robert McNees, had taken a firm stand for integration in the community. My four other classes were just as white as they had been before. In later years I had black students in my high school classes, but only a few as I recall.

One of the most popular students in the senior class that year was Archie Lee, a black student who was awarded a General Motors scholarship. In my class, a young black student named C. H. Shannon made quite a name for himself as a singer, and everyone loved to hear him do solos when the school chorus performed for assembly programs. Three black girls in the class were such close friends and such characters that everyone knew them and called them "The Three Musketeers."

In my four years at Oak Ridge High, I personally knew of only one incident that might be described as racial. One of the black students in our junior class bleached a streak across the top of her head and pulled her hair up in the popular ponytail style. One of my friends told the black student that her hair style looked like a skunk. The black student chased my friend all the way to our American History class and threatened to knife her. That is the only negative occurrence I remember.

What helped to make the integration of Oak Ridge High a peaceful reality? At the time, back in 1955, I really didn't know the answer. It may have been the small number of blacks in the schools, but I doubt that was the reason. School records show that at the end of the first month of school in 1955, there were 1,642 students at Oak Ridge High School. Of these, forty-two were black.

I was, of course, aware of incidents of objection to social change in our community. Parents complained and some even wrote letters debating the issue in the letters column of *The Oak Ridger*. A shot was fired into a dormitory room that had been rented to a black man. Until this time all blacks had been housed in facilities in Scarboro. The man was not in the room at the time the shot was fired. The incident was investigated, but no one was charged.

Perhaps a certain amount of credit should go to Oak Ridge High School Principal Thomas H. Dunigan. He greeted the newly integrated student body at the opening assembly acknowledging the newness of the situation. Dunigan's remarks were quoted in *The Oak Ridger*, September 6, 1955. "I shall strive to see all individuals first as human beings and respond to their personalities before responding to their races, color or religion. Note, I did not say we should ignore race. It is a reality to be considered, but it should not come before all other considerations."

In the same edition telling of the peaceful and historic integration at Robertsville and Oak Ridge High, there was an ominous headline giving a clue to the tragedy that was to strike in Clinton the following year: "County has 20 Days To Answer Integration Suit." The accompanying story told of a federal court lawsuit involving integration of Anderson County Schools.

Some credit for the smooth transition in Oak Ridge must go to the school administration. Bertis Capehart, who had been acting superintendent of Oak Ridge Schools, was officially named superintendent on January 6, 1955. The announcement came from the office of Fred W. Ford, who was director of community affairs for the Atomic Energy Commission.

Capehart had been in the local school system since 1945. He rose through the ranks, becoming its fifth superintendent. Scarcely a week after his appointment an announcement was splashed across the front page of *The Oak Ridger* for January 12, 1955, in a banner headline: *"Local Schools Integrate in Fall."*

The story outlined the directive that had come from AEC headquarters in Washington saying that Oak Ridge Schools were to be the first public school system in Tennessee to integrate white and Negro students.

The Oak Ridge Schools had at the time the services of a skilled communicator, Reef Waldrep, who was my journalism teacher and advisor to the high school paper. Waldrep also wrote all the public information articles for the school system and a column for *The Oak Ridger* called "School Corner."

The period of time after that announcement on January 12 was a very emotional one. For many persons, the idea of black and white attending the same school was against everything they believed. But Capehart kept the lines of communication open. And Waldrep and *The Oak Ridger* made all details of the situation available to the public.

The day following the January 12 announcement was a day that filled my eighth grade classroom with stunned disbelief. I was then a student at Robertsville Junior High the first year it was opened. Until then, all junior high students went to the original Jefferson Junior High located in Jackson Square at the site of the old high school.

From a personal point of view, I recall that the earlier Supreme Court decision had caused some amount of comment from me and my classmates. But none gave it serious consideration because we assumed this directive would move just as slowly as the other wheels in Washington.

After the announcement of January 12 we knew that our first year at Oak Ridge High would be a trailblazing year for us and the school system. Many of the white youngsters who lived in Oak Ridge had come here from Alabama, Georgia, and other southern states. Going to school with blacks was something we had never even considered.

My own family had come to Oak Ridge from Birmingham, Alabama, when I was nine years old. My parents never made racial remarks nor taught me any ideas of racial superiority. But we were a working class family, and we never questioned the separation of the races. Many times I had been to department stores in Birmingham and seen the two sets of water fountains, one for whites and one for "colored." Having to provide two sets of bathrooms, for race and for gender, must have been terribly expensive for department stores and public buildings, but that's the way things were.

I had ridden on street cars many times when the conductor moved the green board that divided the seating. Behind each seat was a chrome bar with two holes on the top. If the car had a load of mostly whites, the conductor took the green sign and moved it closer to the "colored" section in the back of the car. The sign had prongs that fit in the holes on the chrome bar. From the front of the car, the lettering on the sign said, "White." From the back of the car, the lettering said, "Colored." At the time, I never questioned this system nor did I wonder where blacks could buy a meal or obtain medical treatment.

I wonder now what the black students over at Scarboro School were feeling after the announcement that we would be together the following year. Most of them were from southern states as well, and I wonder if they were feeling the same apprehensions that we had in that eighth grade classroom over at Robertsville. Until the integration of the schools, there were few avenues for blacks and whites to get acquainted in Oak Ridge. And the schools were only a first step because housing and public facilities were not opened until years later.

What happened next changed my entire way of thinking. Our teacher at Robertsville, Charles Davis, sensing the anxiety among his students, decided to do something about it. All other classroom projects came to a halt, and we studied the integration situation in detail.

What Davis did was unorthodox, but very effective. How did he make the decision to face the situation head-on with classroom study? From an easy chair at his home on Outer Drive, Davis reminisced with me some thirty-one years after that memorable study. He took an early retirement from the Oak Ridge Schools in 1973 after a career that included completing a doctorate and working as a guidance counselor.

Davis recalls that he felt strongly that "equality before the law is the only way. My own feelings ever since I was a kid in Montgomery, Alabama, were that there ought to be some kind of social justice."

"I felt that integration was the right thing to do," he said. "I knew there would be problems, but it was the right thing to do," he emphasized.

"From listening to students in my class, I knew they and their families were feeling a lot of tension. I felt that students needed something more than your emotions to go on, so I thought it would help if we really got it out in the open and talked about it," Davis recalled.

This particular class was an "unusual group of people," he said. "A lot of kids in that class were very open. I never got the feeling that there was an adversary relationship between teacher and students, so I knew we could communicate.

"The thing that really decided me was a remark I overheard when a group of the boys were talking. One of them said. 'I'm gonna kill the first nigger that gets in my class.' Then I knew that I had to do something," Davis said.

"I remember talking with these boys, trying to get them to think. There were two boys—Evans Webber and Mike Brady—who were very helpful in talking with the other boys. They were natural leaders and the others would listen to them," he said.

"I felt that if you students had some kind of knowledge—that you might not like integrated schools, but you could tolerate it," he said.

So the study began.

Davis started with the historical precedent for the 1954 Supreme Court decision, covering all court actions and results from the mid-1800s to that landmark decision known as Brown vs. the Board of Education. We studied all minorities. One of my friends, Mary Beal Davis, now Mary Fell, librarian at Woodland School, became very involved in a study of racial discrimination against the American Indians.

How did Charles Davis develop the lesson plan? "Probably most of that came out of my head," he remembered. "I had hit on a method of working from an outline to make a lesson plan. I asked myself the question, 'What is it the kids ought to know about this subject? And what kind of conclusions do I want them to draw?'

"I hoped the kids would take the outline and fill it in. I'm sure that's what I did with integration."

I do not recall Davis ever giving an opinion during the entire study. He stuck with the facts and gave us assignments in which we had to dig out more information and share it with the class. This provoked many lively discussions.

On one of those days, the interchange became very emotional. One student asked the now familiar question, "Would you want your sister to marry a black man?" Another said, "I don't want anybody to make me be friends with blacks."

Our teacher patiently explained that we had the freedom to choose our friends now and we could continue to choose our friends when the schools were integrated.

We studied the real meaning of the word "prejudice." I remember going home and telling my parents that it didn't mean, as I had presumed, that "you hated blacks. It meant that you were prejudging someone or something before you had the facts."

Until this study I had thought the word "integrated" was spelled with an "r" before the "g" as in intergrate. My attitude on integration, as well as my spelling of it, were completely changed by my teacher's leadership. I can't remember when the change took place. I just know that when the announcement was made on January 12, 1955, I was upset. When I entered high school in September, I felt that every person deserved the same opportunity at education as I had.

I asked my former teacher if he had to get permission from the school authorities before he began our study of integration. The question made him smile. "No, I didn't ask anybody. I just did it.

"As I recall, teaching in Oak Ridge in those days was a nice experience. You had a lot of freedom to do things, so I didn't have to get permission," Davis explained.

Did he get any complaints from parents? "No," he said. "Most of them seemed glad that I was doing something. I didn't get any flack from parents until later when I got the responsibility for directing sex education."

What was going on with the other teachers? "I'm sure a lot of others did something in class. But some of the teachers were dead set against it and didn't want it to happen."

But integration did come to the Oak Ridge Schools that school year of 1955-56, when the schoolhouse doors were opened to all.

OAK RIDGE'S FIRST PRIVATE SCHOOL

Kathryn Sonnen

As the community of Oak Ridge grew and developed in an environment of secrecy, there were among its workers many Catholics—4,000 by the close of World War II. By that time, the parish of St. Mary's had been serving the Catholics for two years. The resident pastor had been Reverend Joseph Siener, who was succeeded in 1946 by Reverend Francis A. McRedmond.

After the war Reverend McRedmond saw a need for a parish elementary school. This East Tennessee parish had served, after all, members formerly from parishes throughout the United States, especially from the western, northern, and eastern sections where it was then customary for a Catholic parish to have a grade school. Once here, these parishioners produced a generous building fund amounting to $90,000. Under the leadership of Father McRedmond and with the help of a parish building committee, it was deemed feasible for St. Mary's to build a ten–classroom elementary school, with a cafeteria, kitchen, offices, teachers' lounge, and gymnasium. The gymnasium briefly served as the parish church, seating about 500 persons. The site was purchased from the federal government in the spring of 1949. It was located on twelve acres in the central section of the community between the Oak Ridge Turnpike and Vermont Avenue. The construction cost was $220,877. St. Mary's elementary school became the community's first private school, and the only elementary school, public or private, to draw its attendance citywide.

At the beginning, Father McRedmond cautioned the parishioners that there could be no school unless he could get the consent of a teaching order of nuns to direct the school. That consent was at least equal in importance to the permission by the bishop of Tennessee for the school to begin. Father McRedmond did succeed in getting agreement from the Dominican Order of Nashville for nuns to provide teaching and direction of St. Mary's School; but he also won consent of the bishop, confident of the permanence of Oak Ridge. The Dominican sisters were familiar with St. Mary's Parish, since some of them had spent short summers there giving religious instruction to the Catholic children. That contact acquainted both the children and their parents with the white-robed nuns.

Catholic parish schools have a twofold purpose: (1) the elementary religious instruction of Catholic children and (2) the secular academic instruction. "The school provided a Catholic, homey, Christian atmosphere," one nun remarked, "that tried to bring out the 'whole child'—spiritually, physically, emotionally, and intellectually." Such goals were and are customary throughout the United States. A parish school opening in 1950 in Oak Ridge was part, then, of the "normalcy" the community was expected to achieve once the federal government removed the wartime gates and sold the land.

Not an unusual practice in Catholic schools is the admission of non-Catholic students when enrollment permits. When St. Mary's School began, there were a few non-Catholic families whose children were enrolled. Among them were daughters of Dr. and Mrs. Lewis F. Preston and a daughter and son of a Claxton family named Kimbrell. In neither case were the children eligible—due to a residence requirement at that time—to attend the Oak Ridge public schools. Since then, several Oak Ridge non-Catholic families have chosen to send their children to St. Mary's.

Much credit goes to some people who helped get the school open on September 10, 1950. Among them are Bishop Adrian and Father McRedmond and the all-important Dominican sisters, six in number, including Sister Mary Francis, the first principal and teacher in the seventh grade. For the 1950-51 school year there were only grades one through seven. Eighth grade was added the following year, and in May 1952 a first class of nineteen girls and boys was graduated.

Prior to the school's opening in 1950, St. Mary's Home and School Association was formed with Mr. John Burr as president. Among its immediate concerns were meal preparation, playground equipment, and enlisting volunteers for playground monitors and health-check assistants. Soon, however, the topic of discussion was whether to admit Negroes. When questioned on this, Father McRedmond replied that they would indeed be admitted, provided they were members of the parish. At this writing the school is desegregated for both pupils and faculty.

In September 1956, when the enrollment had increased from the original 200 to 300, Sister Mary Francis was succeeded by Sister Jane Dominic as principal. By the late 1950s and early 1960s, St. Mary's enrollment rose to 500. In 1983-84, during the pastorship of Reverend Richard Buchignani, a kindergarten class became part of the school. That school year, enrollment stood at 198, with twenty in the kindergarten. In 1985-86, during the pastorship of Reverend William Gahagan, a preschool with fourteen children was added.

Since the opening year, St. Mary's has had from one to seven lay teachers on the staff. The largest number of sisters in any one year has been six, and over the years there have been eight different Dominican principals.

St. Mary's School is accredited by the state of Tennessee educational office and is a member of the National Catholic Education Association.

In 1950-51 St. Mary's Catholic School drew children away from the already crowded Oak Ridge public schools. It was another educational product launched in an apparently saturated market, and it has continued to serve the purposes for which it was originally established.

Courtesy James E. Westcott

The 1953-54 St. Mary's third grade. Mrs. Marshall on the far left was a lay teacher.

PIONEERING IN SPECIAL SCHOOL SERVICES

Sarah Ketron

Today, in the Oak Ridge schools, the pupil personnel department is under the supervision of a director and consists of
seven central office personnel, thirteen counselors, and
thirty-five special education teachers in the various schools, all
providing services ranging from traditional counseling and record
keeping to the innovative diagnostic center and classes for the
handicapped, homebound, and gifted. This large staff, and these
many services, might have been hard to imagine for the first
superintendent, Dr. A. H. Blankenship, who started the school
system in 1943 and who brought in the first director of guidance.
His philosophy, though, and his recognition of the need for a
guidance program set the scene for this latter-day development. A
graduate of Columbia University, Blankenship had come from
one of the leading institutions in the field of guidance, led by such
pioneers as Esther-Lloyd Jones, Sarah Sturdevant, and Ruth
Strang.

Grounded in the teachings of these people, Blankenship
brought to Oak Ridge a belief in the uniqueness and importance of
each child. It was, he believed, the opportunity and overriding
responsibility of the school to take the child "where he is" and help
him develop to his maximum ability. Such expressions as "the
whole child comes to school" reflected his recognition of the
relationship between home, school, and the child's emotional
health. Although staff recruitment was difficult during the war

years, Blankenship attempted to recruit those who held these basic beliefs—easy to state, but difficult to put into practice.

In those hectic years, Blankenship set up an administrative plan that he hoped would make this application possible. The plan included: (1) an administrative staff, composed of a central office, principals, and counselors, (2) an administrative council made up of a representative teacher from each school, and (3) a parents advisory council with a representative from each school. The last was a forerunner of a board of education. Each of these groups met monthly with the superintendent and the central office staff to give opportunity for evaluating and planning school affairs.

By the fall of 1944, school enrollment had jumped from 637 in three schools (one high school and two elementary schools) to 8,043. This required great increases in staff and all facilities. Thus in the elementary schools, the guidance staff was given a coordinator, a part-time psychologist, and three visiting teachers. In the high school, two counselors were added. And all the schools were assigned a public health nurse and a doctor from the city health department who was on call. Clearly, with the great influx of students and teachers, with the confusion of construction, and with the beginning of a new, warborn community, such a support staff was essential.

If the staff was to serve each of the 8,043 adequately, in accordance with the principles of Dr. Blankenship, guidance personnel faced an uphill battle. For at the time, even the basic "tools" for guidance—tests, records, counseling, consultation, and placement in proper curriculum—had not been developed. Counselors wondered when they would find time to work individually with pupils and teachers, and when they could assess each pupil's needs and abilities. Soon, however, a system of standardized testing was established, and counselors interpreted results to teachers who recorded these results in each pupil's cumulative folder. Shortly, a method of reporting pupil progress to parents was also developed.

Beyond that, though, the whole staff became engaged in curriculum design. The mechanism through which this work was done was the workshop, another Blankenship innovation, a vehicle through which teachers could meet, exchange ideas, and develop overall concepts for teaching. Since teachers were employed for ten months and pupils attended only nine, Blankenship determined that the extra time could best be used in this way. Thus joint meetings of all school faculties were held in systemwide, monthly workshops. For example, all teachers from kindergarten through the eighth grade met in their grade sections, while all English, social studies, math, and science teachers on the secondary level met in "subject matter" groups. After the first year or two, the systemwide workshop began to meet half a day on Saturday. These meetings gave cohesion to the schools and seemed to be enjoyed by most staff members.

Under the leadership of the superintendent and the central office, the counselors and principals held the administrative staff workshops one week before teachers arrived and one week after school ended. It was here that time was given for guidance personnel and principals to meet separately on matters especially pertinent to their work.

Once school began, counselors were responsible for placing pupils in homerooms and scheduling them in required and elected classes. The homeroom was the unit through which guidance work was done, and the teacher of that homeroom played a key role in the program. Requirements followed standards set by the state of Tennessee, though Oak Ridge schools were not part of that system.

In those early years, a retired army sergeant was assigned to the schools to see that all school-age children enrolled and attended. Absenteeism was a problem. All counselors and visiting teachers worked with absentees, believing it was important to find and treat the cause of absence. It was viewed as a symptom of home conditions, personal problems, or failure of the school program to meet the needs of the student. In a few years an attendance counselor, not a "truant officer," was added to the guidance department.

With the increased number of guidance services offered in the schools, the need for coordination became evident. During the administration of Superintendent Ostrander (1946-1951), one of the high school counselors, Bertis Capehart, was appointed director of guidance. Under his leadership, a class of visually handicapped was established at Cedar Hill School. A class for mentally handicapped was offered in 1952 at Highland View, and speech and hearing clinicians were added to serve all schools. Thus, so-called special education became a guidance responsibility. This was a natural development as guidance personnel discovered pupils whose needs could not be met in the larger classrooms where teachers had so many other responsibilities.

With counseling, attendance, research, health, psychology, and special education now a part of guidance, the guidance department became a typical pupil personnel services department. A manual describing the services was published under that title. It was prepared in a workshop group under the leadership of Mr. Capehart and has since undergone several revisions reflecting changes in programs. The latest revision was issued in 1970.

In 1954 Oak Ridge suffered a major budget cut, resulting in the reduction of teachers for art, physical education, and music—as well as visiting teachers in the elementary schools. This made meeting the needs of individuals much more difficult in subsequent years. Fortunately, the rest of the guidance staff remained intact.

Despite evidence that preventive strategies applied early resulted in fewer problems and made teaching easier, counselors in elementary schools have been rare. With a pilot program at Linden in 1967, Oak Ridge was one of the first systems in the South to provide elementary counseling. Since that time counseling has been provided in all elementary schools. Now there is a full-time counselor in each school. This is still uncommon in Tennessee and the South, but national growth is shown by the records of the American Elementary Counselors' Association.

Not all school personnel and parents wholeheartedly endorsed or supported the school system's overall goals. Some objected to parts of the curriculum. Others thought too little or too much emphasis was placed on the three R's. Some thought too much attention was given to personal and social growth, while others held the opposite view. Counselors were frustrated by having too little time to give to all pupils because college-bound students (usually over ninety percent) took up so much time consulting about college choice and scholarships. Parents of both high and low achievers complained that their children received too little counseling. Counselors agreed and pleaded for help. Administrators urged better and quicker guidance and psychological services, along with more help in testing and keeping records. Some found the workshop programs burdensome. And all personnel found building a school system of the Oak Ridge type challenging, but hard, agonizing work.

A short-lived citizens group organized in the late fifties to seek changes in the schools. They called themselves Citizens for Better Schools (CBS), and brought about much discussion and debate. With this, the administration sought outside assistance. Calling in a consultant to evaluate the situation, the school staff learned it had failed to inform citizens adequately about both programs and pupil progress. As a result, the *Staff Bulletin* was enlarged and sent to all homes. Even today, regular school reports continue to be published in the local newspaper.

Oak Ridge faced another problem, however—one quite unique when compared to the average American town. Because Oak Ridge schools attracted such first-rate superintendents, usually from outside the town, it became its fate to suffer frequent changes in leadership. Between 1943 and 1972, for example, nine superintendents served in the Oak Ridge schools, with an average tenure of less than three years. Naturally, this presented some problems of continuity and consistency. Fortunately, during this time, the pupil personnel staff had remained constant and was able to provide some of the continuity lacking because of transitions in leadership.

But this was not the only time the role of counselor and administrator intersected. In the realm of discipline, they again were dealing with similar problems. Usually, it is the duty of counselors to assist in finding the cause of misbehavior, while helping the pupil's parents and school personnel understand it. It is the responsibility of administration to enforce rules. But after the turbulent sixties, the pupil personnel department was asked to prepare a booklet for yearly distribution to each family, outlining the responsibility of pupils, parents, and school personnel in maintaining a school situation conducive to learning.

It was during this decade, too, that the pupil personnel department assumed yet another responsibility: sex education. It started with a pilot program instituted at an elementary school in 1968, which brought about a lively community debate. Strong differences emerged, with some arguing vociferously that sex education did not belong in the schools. In 1973, however, the state department approved an Oak Ridge curriculum outline which had been developed by a committee of parents, teachers, principals, and counselors under the leadership of the pupil personnel director. The director had become involved in this curriculum matter earlier when an elementary principal had a frightening experience with a girl unprepared for puberty. His call was for "help" for girls and their parents. The director responded and thus inherited another responsibility for the department.

Two problems that had been with the pupil personnel department from the beginning, though, were reporting and records. And perhaps no problem has taken more time and effort on the part of the teachers, guidance personnel, administrators, and participating parents than designing a suitable reporting system at the elementary level. Some teachers and parents were accustomed to letter grades. Others thought these inaccurate and argued that they did not reflect concern for ability, effort, and personal and social growth.

The original report card was a long checklist. It contained, like all those following the five-point scale: Excellent, Good, Satisfactory, Poor, Unsatisfactory. It provided space for comments.

Revisions took place in 1945, 1946 (when junior high was established), the mid-1950s, 1970, and 1984. The 1970 revision introduced the comparison of actual achievement to expected achievement as indicated by a summary of standardized tests. It introduced release time for teachers so they could provide parent conferences. The 1984 revision provided forms for kindergarten, grades one through three, and four through six. The four through six form used letter grades. These forms provided space for comments, and the parent conference remained an important part of the reporting system. High school reports have always followed requirements for letter grades. Reports were issued quarterly until recently the state required six per year. Dates for issuing reports are published in the local newspaper so parents may know when to expect them.

Maintenance and storage of adequate records has also been a problem. In the early days, little thought was given to the notion that pupils had a right to their school records many years later. In the sixties, microfilming was considered but found impractical. Not until the 1970 revision of the cumulative record was a practical method of long-time storage developed. Accurate records of pupil attendance and progress are a necessary but burdensome process for the staff. Automation has helped.

In a real sense, Oak Ridge schools did pioneer in the field of pupil personnel services in this section of the county. When the University of Tennessee established the Tennessee State Testing and Guidance Program in 1953, the Oak Ridge program had been in progress for ten years. A 1953 survey reported that there was "a widespread lack of understanding and acceptance of guidance in the technical sense of the word." Not until the National Defense Act of 1958 was any significant impetus given to the program, with the University of Tennessee serving as the focal point in its development. Oak Ridge's proximity to that school has been of great help. The most important factor, however, has been the support of the staff and community. Their continuous growth and progress constitute the real worth of pupil personnel services in Oak Ridge.

COMMUNITY LIFE

Courtesy James E. Westcott

COMMUNITY LIFE

MA BELL REACHES OUT

June M. Boone

Imagine, if you can, enough flattops, cemestos, victory cottages, hutments, and dorms to house 75,000 people, and fewer than 9,000 telephones!

How could you cope without a telephone—either in your own home, that of your neighbors, or at least in some house on your street? Besides all the other inconveniences, such as not being able to chat with a friend, make dates, call repairmen or pharmacies or shop, what about emergencies? What if your house caught fire, or you were being burglarized, or someone in the family needed medical attention *stat*?

Strangely enough, early Oak Ridgers, many of whom were accustomed to having a phone, took it in stride. Though they knew VIPs had them, the lack of their own phones was merely another of the many inconveniences that came with the territory, such as living in a newly built, fast-growing wartime town. It was no worse than not having a choice about where you lived or the size of your house, being compelled to ride buses, having to shop in Knoxville, or standing in line for many of your much-needed items.

In emergencies Oak Ridgers "utilized the utility pole." Installed on poles at about 500-foot intervals throughout the city and marked with a wide red stripe, these red phones, easily located by a small red light at night, were a direct line to the police department. From there, emergency vehicles, cabs, and doctors were dispatched to residences or wherever needed.

There were pay phones in Townsite, East Village, and West Village. The remainder of the time Oak Ridgers did without, until early 1946 when pay phones were also installed in the recreation halls, bus terminals, cafeterias and drug stores, and other public places. I recall having to make plans with classmates either at school or on the bus to and from school. I walked to friends' houses in the evening and on weekends to discuss going to movies or roller-skating, and let my mother know ahead of time when I planned to stop at the Wildcat Den after school.

The dormitory residents fared better, with desk and pay phones. But according to many who resided there during the early years, the pay phones were in constant use and the desk phones were not for resident use except in a dire emergency. June Young, who was a nurse at the hospital and lived in Columbia Hall, remembers the way it was. "With the dorm overflowing with women of a variety of occupations working all kinds of shifts, the pay phone was always in use."

While Southern Bell Telephone Company provided service to the army in Oak Ridge, it was really the army—through the Signal Corps—who operated the system.

Clyde Hatten, who came to Oak Ridge for Southern Bell in January 1943, remembers the first telephone switchboard. It was installed in a vacated building on the hill behind the present Classic Chevrolet location on the Turnpike in the east end of town.

"The building had been a beer joint called the 'Blue Moon,'" Clyde said. "And from there the trunk lines went to Clinton. All Oak Ridge calls were routed through the Clinton office at that time."

Operation of the telephone system by the army also included handling such transactions as reading and collecting bills. According to Colonel P. F. Kromer, Jr., chief of Central Facility and Services Division of USED (United States Engineering Detachment), in Oak Ridge during the war, "military necessity dictated this course of action—it being essential that the army should exercise full control over all operations at the 'project.'"

The first telephone directory, published in September 1944, at a time when the city was nearing its peak population of 75,000, was very small. Besides the need for secrecy about important scientists in town, there simply weren't many phones to be had. A few VIPs were listed in the book, but many of the most important ones were not.

VIP Colonel K. D. Nichols, District Engineer with the army, was one of those listed. And some names still well known in Oak Ridge also appeared in that first directory. For security reasons they weren't listed by addresses, but as follows: A. A. Addison, USED; A. K. Bissell, TEC (Tennessee Eastman Company); G. E. Boyd, CL (Clinton Lab), etc.

Cafeterias included in that first book were: Barracks, Colored, East and West Village, Engineering Works, Warehouse and White Hutment, all operated by Roane-Anderson. Grocery stores were also listed, as were beauty shops and the city's six drug stores, and of course the dorms.

I was nearing graduation from Oak Ridge High School in 1946, and like many of my classmates simply had not decided in which direction I wanted my life to go. And when the *Oak Ridge Journal* carried the announcement in May that phones were to go under civilian control, I had no idea that this information would be of importance to me, other than the fact that having a phone in our home again was a possibility.

The items in the newspaper read: "Southern Bell Telephone company, which up to now has furnished telephone service to Oak Ridge through the army, has been requested to assume full charge of the telephone operations at Oak Ridge.

"The army will discontinue its operation and support of the system at a date to be announced later, after definite plans have been formulated by the telephone company."

The switchover to Southern Bell was to be a part of an overall shift from army to civilian control when the Atomic Energy Commission (AEC) would eventually take over Oak Ridge.

According to Colonel Kromer, reasons for the takeover were: "The army's desire to have Oak Ridge function in the manner of a normal community, and to relieve the government of certain subsidies attendant to present telephone service, which can no longer be met in the program of more economical operations at Oak Ridge." One advantage of the changeover would be eventual expansion of service to more Oak Ridge residences, but it was emphasized that the expansion would depend upon Southern Bell obtaining necessary material, of which there was an acute shortage

411

in the country. At the close of the announcement, Colonel Kromer reiterated his earlier statement: "Now that restrictions are no longer necessary, Southern Bell has been asked to come in and operate the telephone system as it does throughout the Southeast. This is in keeping with the army's desire that Oak Ridge assume function of a normal city as quickly as is practical."

Commenting on the army's announcement, W. E. Duncan, Tennessee Manager for Southern Bell, said:

> There are many problems incident to the transfer which must first be worked out before telephone operations can be taken over. Plans must be submitted to the Tennessee Railroad and Utility Commission, and although material has been fully adequate to serve essential needs of the army and key personnel, there is not sufficient plant and equipment presently installed to provide residential telephone service at once to all who may want it.

At the same time, Major Paul Ramsey, chief of Community Service, announced that plans included the establishment of business offices. And that new directories would be mailed by September 1.

It would be some time before all Oak Ridgers desiring phones would have them. As they became available, many priority jobs such as telephone company employees and hospital workers were given phones. But by August 24, 1950, an item in *The Oak Ridger* reported: "There are now 13,818 telephones in service in Oak Ridge, compared to 8,234 in November 1946. There are also eighty-nine long-distance circuits now serving the city." The entire area surrounding the Southern Bell communication network was bustling with activity at the time of the takeover in the fall of 1946.

Buses, still the main mode of transportation, lumbered noisily in and out of the sprawling Central Bus Terminal in a steady stream. The Peacock Restaurant, located directly across from the bus terminal, fed a constant flow of hungry shift-workers. Dorms along the Turnpike were filled to overflowing, and the busy police department building was located at the corner of the Turnpike and Bus Terminal Road. To the right of the police department was a short street called Milan Way which connected Bus Terminal Road to Administration Road. And on this street the heart of Ma

Bell's communication system functioned. The switchboard was housed in a small yellow brick building. Next to it was the tall red brick switching plant. Behind these two buildings, in the former Tennessee Eastman Medical Building, were the business offices.

The Southern Bell takeover meant that new personnel was needed to replace the women of the army who had vacated their jobs. It was then, in the fall of 1946 amid the hustle and bustle of the town, that I was about to embark on a career as one of the new voices of "Ma Bell."

Some of the former USED girls continued on as "official operators" for AEC, while others became supervisors to the new Southern Bell operators. For a time, "official operators" occupied the last two positions on the long switchboard and handled all official calls. Later they were moved to the administration building.

Several experienced operators were brought to Oak Ridge from the Knoxville office to train the new girls. No one seems to recall the exact count of new operators hired, but I, who was among the first ones, remember that for weeks I would arrive at work on Monday morning and discover new faces ready to begin their intense one-week training course. I shared their anticipation and anxiety when they donned a cumbersome headset, climbed up on a stool in front of an intimidating switchboard, and used the first phrase they had learned, "Number, please?"

Doris Ward Householder remembers that "It was great, being able to talk to telephone operators all over the country."

Doris was hired a week after her sister, Berniece Ward Baer. Like me and many of the new operators, Berniece and Doris came to Oak Ridge with their family. Berniece remembers how lucky she felt in being hired as an operator: "I filled out an application and was interviewed by Mrs. Lyndal Russell and was told to report for training the next day. And that was only two days after I was laid off at Y-12!"

The official transfer from army operation and supervision to operation by Southern Bell took place Tuesday, November 1, 1946, at midnight. With the establishment of a civilian communication system in a heretofore army-controlled town, and the outlook for more phones and quality service in the offing, 1946 brought early Oak Ridgers their first taste of normalcy. Southern

Community Life

Telephone operators in 1946. It was in that year that Southern Bell Telephone Company assumed full charge of the telephone services from the army.

In addition to the telephone services, the whole of the Oak Ridge community was transferred from military to civilian control in 1946. In this photograph, Major General Leslie Groves, commanding officer of the Manhattan District meets in Oak Ridge on October 1, 1946 with TVA Chairman David E. Lilienthal. Lilienthal had already been mentioned to be chairman of the newly formed Atomic Energy Commission. His appointment was not announced by President Harry S. Truman until October 29, 1946.

Bell's switchboard operations in Oak Ridge lasted fifteen years.

Though the red brick switching structure still stands, the telephone plant building with its equipment is now located at the top of the hill on East Division Road. The small yellow brick building is gone now. A new phase of my young life began inside its walls and even after forty years, it's a little sad to turn onto that now quiet street and see the empty lot where the building once stood.

Oak Ridge has come a long way in forty years, from only a few phones controlled by the army, to one phone (often two) in nearly every home. Some residents still waited years for phones after Southern Bell assumed operation, but it was necessary that Ridgers begin learning about the "waiting game." Ma Bell's arrival in town was the realization of merely the first of many dreams and hopes of Oak Ridgers that would manifest themselves only after long periods of waiting.

The quality of telephone service continues to improve with each new breakthrough in communication technology ... in ways we never dreamed possible when Southern Bell reached out to touch the community of Oak Ridge. Yet even in this day of "do it all yourself," there are times when rather than get out the directory, look up an area code and phone number, I'd like to just pick up the phone, sit back, and wait to hear the voice of one of Ma Bell's operators ask, "Number, please?"

1950 THE CONTRACT

Maisie Tunnell

T he city of Oak Ridge was barely seven years old. But this precocious child, mothered by necessity and fathered by the mighty scion of science, industry, and government, was facing the prospect of going out into the world on his own. His every need has been anticipated and generously provided by the anxious parents in order that he might be free to develop his potential. This child had fulfilled every expectation on that August day in 1945. His future was secure. Now he could take it easy and enjoy the fruits of his intellect and industry. No way. He was increasingly annoyed by parental admonitions concerning his adult responsibilities. He found himself dangling in a most undignified posture, tenaciously clinging to an ever-stretching apron string as the newly formed Atomic Energy Commission sought to free itself of the care and expense of the unnatural child.

The stretch began in February 1948 when the AEC proclaimed that "each resident should make every effort to save the government's money as if it were his own." But when Oak Ridgers at a town council meeting voted ten to one against opening the security gates that protected their identity and privacy, and rejected every plan for self-government and incorporation, the Enforcer was sent in. The AEC established an Office of Community Affairs. On September 19, Fred Ford became its acting director and city manager. It was said that the Roane-Anderson Company, caretaker and landlord for the 35,000 residential units and their occupants, was "the best whipping boy the Army ever had." Fred Ford took the punishment for the AEC. His capable and sensitive handling was a great help in easing the exceptional city into the mainstream of normal community behavior.

In May 1949 residents of the many dormitories were given notice that their services would be cut and rents raised. Government subsidies in this area had been withdrawn. Outraged dorm-dwellers called for Congressional investigation. There were charges of mismanagement and bribery by AEC. Few Ridgers missed the evening news on WATO as Fulton Lewis, Jr., took up the cause of the irate renters. In October the Congressional joint committee final report cleared the AEC of all charges.

In July 1949 and January 1950, the AEC "evicted" a total of 1,255 families by decree, removing them from their temporary housing—flattops and demountables. Permanent housing would be made available without restrictions based on size of family and income as had been the case with original housing assignment. The offerings found little favor with the dispossessed tenants. They looked longingly to the hills where the well-designed and artfully positioned semipermanent cemestos nestled in the beautiful wooded Oak Ridge landscape. Woodland homes? Not large enough for normal size human beings. Boring. No view. Garden apartments? Not suitable for families. Too expensive. The aristocracy of cemesto dwellers was reinforced.

Until. In April 1949 the Office of Community Affairs posted a new rent schedule for housing. The increased rents were more controversial by reason of classification into zones with greater increase for more desirable locations and natural features.

And furthermore. Cost of electricity and water would no longer be included in the rent—meters would be installed.

Moreover. The government would fog no more. Residents would have to control their own flies.

And on top of that. In October 1949 Roane-Anderson moved to evict six couples who refused to sign and return the new rental contracts.

And there were rumors of uneasiness among cemesto dwellers whose bedrooms outnumbered the number of occupants. It seemed that everyone knew someone who had invented dependents in order to move ahead in the alphabetically sized ABCDEF cemestos.

In March 1950 the apron string, stretched to the limit, snapped when fees were cut in half for Roane-Anderson's housekeeping.

And so it was that many Oak Ridgers were flung kicking and howling into adulthood. Some escaped into the boondocks fearing eventual high taxes and civic responsibility. The majority, realizing their unique opportunity to pioneer the creation of a hometown, entered eagerly into its planning and operation.

Soon they were laughing and reminiscing, writing and singing about the good old days. Much of this good humor found its way into the Oak Ridge Lions Club minstrel shows which played for three consecutive nights annually to standing-room-only audiences from 1947 to 1956. The minstrel style, the entire cast blackfaced with the exception of the pompous interlocutor who was straight man for the punch lines delivered by the end men, was a perfect vehicle for good natured lampooning of local personalities and events.

Looking back on the rapidly developing issues of civil rights, from the far-reaching recommendations of the Supreme Court in 1948 to the violence accompanying desegregation of schools in our neighboring Clinton from 1956 to 1958, it seems incredible that the minstrel could have survived in Oak Ridge until 1956. It was a strange anomaly—prominent Oak Ridgers as blackfaced Po'k Chops, Flip-Flop, and Hambone, singing darky songs while racial tensions in Clinton were building to a state of emergency. The performers and those who attended and applauded should not be indicted as bigots or racists. They were innocent of any intent to ridicule or disparage. The minstrel show was a conventional frame on which the jokes were hung.

The use of the minstrel form, however, at that time attested to the insularity of the community of Oak Ridge and the immaturity, biological and political, of its homogeneous population. They were still enjoying the role of sheltered prodigy, not quite ready to exchange it for that of average citizen. There was no great concern about national issues other than those affecting the local situation.

One of the local issues of 1950 that affected almost everyone was housing. The Lions Club minstrel of that year, drawing on the events of 1949-50 documented in this writing, threw the spotlight on this problem in an olio (between–acts number) entitled *The Contract* or *The Gripes of Wrath*. This skit, introduced as a combination of "the best features of the classic hillbilly and Greek drama, Thornton Wilder's *Our Town*, and the early mellerdrammer," also fixes a moment in time in the life of young Oak Ridge.

Curtain

On stage left is a Chic Sale in which is Grandpa, whose lines are spoken from a window in the left side wall. In front of the structure are Ma, Pa, and the Boys seated on logs adjacent to the chopping block and wood pile. On stage right a room is suggested by a table, floor lamp, two chairs, and a single wall with a door placed so that the audience can see on both sides of the wall. Near the top of the wall is a grating or vent through which occasional puffs of black smoke are blown.

Pa rises to speak.

Pa: Now we-uns air the chorus fer this here drammer—bein' sort of spirits familiar in these parts.

(Each character speaks his name in following) I'm Pa. I'm Ma. And I be Grandpa. And them critters is our younguns. (To audience) and you know who you be.

Ma: Bless yore hearts. T'explain th' actin' of the actor is the reason fer the chorus, and t'make appropriate comments on the same. This play's what's called a tragedy; hit shore is.

Pa: Hit's powerful sad.

Grandpa: Hit stinks, I tell ye!
Ma: Hit's a shame. And now we'll interduce ye to our cast of characters. (Enter Nell) Here's Nell, the true-blue heroeen. (Grandpa holds out a sign *Whistle*) (Enter Villain) And the villainous overseer. (*Boos* as above) (Enter Cuthbert) And the hero, brave and true. (Applause as above).
(Each character remains on stage until others appear, then leave, Nell and Cuthbert together, Villain behind.)

419

Community Life

The Lions Club minstrel show was standard fare in Oak Ridge until 1956, at which time the rapidly developing civil rights issues led to its termination.

Pa: The scene's a livin' room—the walls are shaky and they need a coat o' paint—in a house with mornin' glories round the door and so on. Hit could be—well just any town.

Grandpa: But hit ain't!

Pa: But now the play's the thing! The show must go on!

(Nell enters through door R with 5 gallon can labelled *Climax Wall Cleaner* and begins to clean wall. Villain sneaks to door, twirls mustache and cape, and knocks. Nell goes to door.)

Nell: (Curtsies and gives him her hand) Enter, kind sir. Our humble home is honored by the presence of our Overseer. (Struggles to retrieve her hand and finally succeeds) Will you sit?

Villain: No, it pains me, Madam—

Nell: Oh? Where does it hurt?

Villian: It pains me, Madam, to be the bearer of bad news. Heh, Heh, heh.

Nell: (Hands to heart) Then the rumors—?

Villian: (Bowing head) Are true.

Nell: You mean—

Villain: Yes. My henchmen will be around tomorrow—to install the meters! Benevolence is at an end. Good day, Madam.

(Villain leaves. Nell sinks down in chair and bows head on arms—jumps up to turn out light and returns to position sobbing loudly as Cuthbert enters with lunch box.)

Cuthbert: (Haltingly as if reading lines. He speaks all lines in this way.) Why sit you here weeping in the dark, sweet wife?

Nell: (Runs to him and sobs over his shoulder loudly) That

	awful overseer was here today.
Cuthbert:	We are undone. They have found out that our two extra bedrooms are not occupied. Did you not tell them of your old mother, my old father, and our old maiden aunt who are away just for the present?
Nell:	Oh, it isn't that. (Crying loudly) The overseer says we're going to have to pay for our electricity!!
Cuth:	He is a dastardly villain. I will tell him so. I will use strong language.
Nell:	But that won't pay the bills. Cuthbert, we will have to sacrifice something. You must give up your membership in Kiwanis.
Cuth:	Never! I will starve first. That is it. We will starve a little. That will save electricity, too.
Nell:	Alas! Alas! What will become of us?

(Lights out. Voices of chorus come from darkness.)

| Ma: | Now folks, this blackout indicates a little time has passed—while our hero tries to find a way to make some extry money. The blackout also indicated fair Nell has saved a dime which means that they kin eat not one but two slices of baloney. |
| Grandpa: | Turn on them dad-blamed lights. I can't see the pitchers in the catylogue. |

(Lights on. Again Nell is Climaxing wall. Climax is very sooty. Villain sneaks in without knocking and places hands over Nell's eyes)

Villain:	Guess who?
Nell:	(Struggling to free herself, she blacks villain's face with Climax and turns on him.) How dare you enter my home without knocking?
Villain:	After today, me proud beauty, I would not dare.
Nell:	What mean you, sir?—After today?
Villain:	After today, Madam, you will be living in the High

Rent Zone 1, which will entitle you to the privilege of having your door knocked on before my entry. Of course, there is a slight fee for going first class. (Rubbing hands) Shall we say—uh—$12.50.

Nell: Have pity on us, sir. (Kneeling) We cannot afford such privilege. My husband is only a poor phyzlling struggicist—I mean struggling physicist. Oh, tell me why—why is our humble home to be placed in Zone 1? (During this speech Nell manages to black her face with Climax)

Villain: You have—a tree, Madam!

Nell: You dog! Out of my house. (She throws Climax at him as he walks away leisurely, laughing villainously. Nell stands dejectedly as lights go out.)

Pa: And so is piled cruel blow on cruel blow. But fate with Nell and Cuthbert is not through, sir, for even now it's safe to bet your dough thar's still a Ford (Ma: yells "That's Freddy!") in Nell and Cuthbert's future.

Ma: (Lights on. Nell and Cuthbert are seated at table eating an old shoe. Nell is carving while Cuthbert eats the strings spaghettiwise. Villain creeps to door, places contract in front of door, knocks and runs away. Cuthbert goes to door, picks up papers, and reads silently. Nell comes to read over his shoulder. Both gasping, fall to floor in faints, tossing contract aside.)

Ma: Mer-ci-ful Jaybird!

Pa: Reckon air they daid?

Grandpa: (Who has been watching action) Don't jest stand thar, ye danged idjuts. See what the writin's about.

Pa: (Picks up paper and reads enough that audience recognizes it as The Rental Contract.)

Ma: Whut do hit mean, Pa?

Grandpa: Hit means war, Womern! Fetch me my shootin' arn. I'm a-standin' pat!

423

Ma:	Now, Grandpa, you jest set still.
Pa:	Naw, this hain't our fight, Grandpa. We'uns live in the United States.
Ma:	Look—they're a-comin' to. (Nell and Cuthbert rise, place contract on table, and sit down on either side of table. Villain creeps to door and eavesdrops.)
Nell:	This is it, Cuthbert. We will sign the contract and together, my beloved, we'll await—the end.
Cuth:	Affix my signature to such a document! Never, I say (carefully stomping foot) never, never, never.
Villain:	(Enters boldly. Places fountain pen near Cuthbert's hand and waits, arms folded)
Cuth:	You will never get away with this. I will get a lawyer. I will sue you. Yes, I will.
Villain:	Heh-heh.
Cuth:	Then I will report you to the Town Council.
Villain:	Heh, heh, heh.
Cuth:	You are a cad, sir. I will not sign.
Villain:	(Pushing pen and contract at Cuthbert) Sign the Contract.
Cuth:	(Stomping foot) I won't—won't—won't. (Nell comes to stand beside him, hand on shoulder.)
Villain:	(Louder) Sign the Contract!
Cuth:	No, no, no, a thousand times no!
Villain:	(Shouting) I said sign here!
Cuth:	Never, Never. Never. (Jumping up and down)
Grandpa:	Stubborn little cuss, ain't he?
Villain:	I go, but I shall return. You cannot escape me. Heh, heh. (He leaves)
Nell:	We are trapped, Cuthbert. Trapped, I tell you! Like

rats in a trap! Is there no one to save us?

(Noise of pounding hooves outside)

Cuth: Hark! I hear footsteps—approaching on horseback.

(Outside sounds of "whoa" and dismounting. Enter riders dressed to suggest cowboy and Indian. Indian carries big shovel.)

Nell: Who are you, sir, and what means this intrusion?

Lewis: I'm Lewis Fulton, Senior, Ma'am, and this is my faithful companion, Pluto.

Pluto: Ugh.

Lewis: I heard about your troubles. I come to offer my services.

Cuth: But what can you do, sir?

Lewis: Well you see it's like this. We dig up the dirt (Pluto shows how) and I spread it around—all over the nation—and out of it grows public opinion. Mighty powerful weapon—public opinion.

Nell: Oh, how can we ever thank you, Mr. Fulton?

Lewis: Don't thank me, ma'am, thank my sponsors—Pfluegelpheffer's Fetid Fertilizer. Come, Pluto. (They leave. Noise of hoofbeats receding. Cry of Hi-yo Silver Away!)

Cuth: Perhaps there is yet hope. Did he say Pfluegel-pheffer's Fetid Fertilizer, dear?

Nell: (As she and Cuthbert, arms entwined, go out door and off stage). No. Pfluegelpheffer's Fetid Fertilizer.

Ma: So Fearless Fulton took up the cause of Cuthbert and our Nell
And all throughout the nation people rallied. What happened after that it's hard to tell. In words. We're gonna sing it fer ye in a ballad.

Grandpa: Sing it, younguns!

Chorus: Mule Train—Git up! Git up!
Mule Train—Clippety-cloppin over hill and plain
Seems as though they never stop.
Clippity-clop, clippity clop, clippity, clippity,
clippity-clopping along.

(Verses are sung by individuals, a line to each)

Verse: Thar's a note of invitation fer Congreshnul
Investigation
Thar's a big refrigerator—boy, is that a hot pertater!
Here's a bunch of headache pills fer the fellers on the
hill
Git along, Mule, git along.

Verse: Hyar are letters by the score to the paper's editor
And this thousand here, I figger, are subscriptions to
the Ridger.
This looks like a bomb to me, and it's addressed A I T,
Git along, Mule, git along.

Verse: Here are herrings wrapped in tissues fer confusin' of
the issues
This is red tape over here fer use when matters start to
clear,
And straight jackets, I'll be derned, labelled "Whom
it may concern."
Git along, Mule, git along.

Chorus: (During singing of which lights go out while Nell and
Cuthbert return to room.)

(Nell and Cuthbert are walking the floor when noise
of overtired horses is heard offstage. Enter Lewis and
Pluto in sad shape. Pluto's shovel handle is broken,
and the shovel is decreased in size.)

Nell: Tell me, quickly, what news?

Lewis: We are lost, ma'am.

Nell: Oh, why—

Lewis: They had the biggest shovels, ma'am, covered it up

426

faster than we could uncover it. That is all. Good-
night. (Lewis and Pluto go out. Lewis returns to stick
head inside.) Don't ferget Pfluegelpheffer's Fetid Fertilizer, ma'am. (He goes offstage, and noise of hoofbeats sound as Villain sneaks to door to eavesdrop.)

Nell: Our last hope! Gone! Gone with the wind!

Cuth: Let us not stoop to calling names. Mr. Fulton made a
noble effort.

Nell: I will fetch the contract. Let us make an end to this.
There is naught left for us but to sign.

Cuth: I will never sign that contract. That which is dearer to
me than life itself—my honor—is at stake. We have
had no steak for weeks. Never will there be steak for
us here. We must pull up stakes and flee.

Nell: Oh, whither can we flee?

Cuth: Whither? Across the border. Yes, we must go over the
border.

Nell: You mean we must go to—

Cuth: Yes, to Clinton.

Nell: Ask of me anything but that, Cuthbert. My duty lies
here. As Chairman of the Committee on Finding
Ways to Finance Projects Without Money, I cannot
leave.

Cuth: Then I must needs go alone. I leave you with these
words for your memory book, "'Tis better to have
loved and lost—much better." Farewell. (Nell falls to
her knees, begging him not to leave and clutching at
his knees, but he shakes her off and goes out, stepping
over the Villain, who goes inside at once.)

Villain: Ah, hah, my proud beauty, now I have you in my
power. (Nell and Villain go one to each side of table
and begin to play cat and mouse around the table.
This is interrupted by a knock at the door where stand
two children dressed as midgets. They carry suitcases.

427

Nell goes to door.)

Midget: Pardon, ma'am, but could you direct us to the new permanent housing development for midgets?

Nell: Gladly. Go to the intersection of the Turnpike and Scarboro Road and turn left. A sign says *Woodland*. You can't miss it.

Midget: Thank you.

Nell: But you may as well get rid of your suitcases. You won't have room for them. Goodbye and good luck. (Nell and Villain resume their game at the table and after some time—)

Nell: Let's quit beating about the bush. What are your intentions, sir?.

Villain: My intentions, sweet Nell, are and ever have been only to take you away from all this. Your little hands are too fair for endless scrubbing of this old cemesto. Your comfort and happiness alone have motivated me throughout these trying weeks. Come, Nell, fly with me to a Garden Apartment and we will grow old together sitting in the sun.

Nell: (Mae West-wise) Well, why didn't you say so in the first place, Big Boy? Let's go. (They go)

Pa: To wind things up we've got to find a moral in our play
But if to hunt fer it you folks ain't willin'
I'll tell ye. Things bein as they air today
Sometimes it's purty hard to tell the heroes from the villains.

(Grandpa holds out sign—THE END)

OAK RIDGE CEMETERIES

Connie J. Green

I t was a favorite place on a moonlit night when our Girl Scout troop leaders were asleep. We'd creep from our bedrolls, slip away from the cluster of cots, then tiptoe across the lawn. Not until we were on the dirt road did we dare turn on our flashlights. Huddled together, we'd move slowly toward the fenced area a few yards up the road.

In the moonlight the tombstones glowed whitely as ghosts. An occasional car passing on the Turnpike or the hoot of an owl on the ridge were the only sounds we heard. The car tires had a lonesome ring to them, but they were nothing in eeriness compared to the owl's call. We knew there were likely to be ghosts in the cemetery; the owl seemed to know it too.

With our flashlights we picked out names and dates on the old tombstones. Through the years we became well acquainted with the families who slept beneath the soil in cemetery Number 21, the East Fork Missionary Baptist Cemetery. I always located the tombstone of the Rev. J. Seiber, April 28, 1816 - May 25, 1891. "Aged 75 years and 27 days," the engraving proudly proclaimed. His was a long life—much longer than the lives recorded on many other gravestones. Next to him, beneath a sturdy hedge that had been trimmed, lay Alvina Seiber who survived him by four years. And nearby was the tombstone of Elizabeth Seiber, February 23, 1853 - October 23, 1923. "She did what she could." And my imagination was off and running with those words. What did

Elizabeth do? Was she the only child of the Seibers? If not, where were the others buried? Where had they all lived? And how? There were times when I wished one of the ghosts, that I felt must be around, would make himself known and answer some of my questions.

The old Crowe cemetery, as Number 21 was commonly known, was a favorite place for Girl Scouts to explore when they visited the Scout camp next door. But it was by no means the only old cemetery in Oak Ridge. The city was, and still is, dotted with them, each with its unique history and its silent voices speaking from the past to those who take the time to walk slowly and make out the fading inscriptions.

When the United States government decided to build the Manhattan Project in the hills of East Tennessee, the disruption affected more than the living. At the time farms and communities were scattered across the landscape. Each community had its church, and each church had its cemetery. In addition, many farms had small family cemeteries. All in all, sixty-nine cemeteries were listed by government officials in the area where the city and the plants would be built.

The living were ordered to move. For the most part, the dead were allowed to stay. Two cemeteries were removed before plant construction began—Number 13, Josiah and Phoebe Mounger Cemetery in the X-10 area, and Number 31, A. G. and Effie Ivey Cemetery in the Y-12 area. Cox Funeral Home of Lake City moved the graves in both cemeteries.

Since that time, other cemeteries have been removed from residential construction areas: Number 28, Snodderly Cemetery; Number 50, Hamblen Cemetery; Number 64, Tunnell-Hudson Cemetery.

But numerous cemeteries remained in the middle of residential areas. Children growing up in Oak Ridge became accustomed to passing the cemeteries on dark nights as they returned from the movies or walked to a friend's house. Those who lived in houses next to the cemeteries agreed that the cemetery occupants made ideal neighbors—quiet and noncomplaining.

One such cemetery is Number 39, Woods Chapel Cemetery, which sits at the corner of Michigan Avenue and Outer Drive. The lone identified occupant of Number 39 is Elijah Wood, Co. K, I

Community Life

With the construction of Oak Ridge in the 1940s, "the living [in the area] were ordered to move. For the most part, the dead were allowed to stay." According to government records at that time, there were sixty-four cemeteries in the area where the city and the plants were built.

U.S.C.H.A. In the 1880 census Elijah Wood is listed as a mulatto who was born about 1834. In spite of his being the only grave with an inscribed stone, he is not alone in the cemetery. Approximately ten other graves are there, marked only with fieldstones.

Not all cemeteries tuck neatly into corners. Some major Oak Ridge roads weave around the old cemeteries. For example, Georgia Avenue intersects the Turnpike at a ninety-degree angle, only to make a large arc around Number 42, Walters Cemetery, before heading up the hill to intersect Outer Drive. Walters Cemetery contains three graves with inscriptions and three graves with fieldstones. It is attributed to Ira DeBord et ux.

Many of the cemeteries are found along what were, before 1943, the primary roads through the area—Bethel Valley (the X-10 road), Bear Creek Valley (the Y-12 road), and East Fork Valley (now the Turnpike). But a trip up the side roads that intersect these main valley roads leads to more cemeteries. Wherever the land provided a living, it provided a place for the living to bury their dead.

The cemetery names echo the history of this area: its people— Hendrix and Hendricks, Gallaher, Gamble, Scarbrough; its churches—New Zion Baptist, New Bethel Baptist, East Fork Baptist, Mount Vernon Methodist, Robertsville Baptist, New Hope Baptist.

The Clinch Bend Chapter of the Daughters of the American Revolution has performed a major service for history buffs and for those interested in genealogical research by copying inscriptions from gravestones in all the area cemeteries. The study was begun in 1940 and renewed in 1968. D.A.R. members were unable to locate eight of the sixty-nine cemeteries listed on government records. Not found were Number 44, Gorman; Number 47, Hackworth; Number 52, Walters; Number 53, Kelly; Number 55, Gray; Number 65, Scarbrough (Pine Ridge); Number 66, Grills; and Number 68, Shelton. Searchers, however, found three additional cemeteries that were not listed by the Atomic Energy Commission. In her book, *Inscriptions from Old Cemeteries on the Oak Ridge (Manhattan Project) Area*, Marjorie P. Parsly lists seventy-two cemeteries. She, with help from her family and from other D.A.R. members, has copied all inscriptions from all gravestones located during the search. Her book, available in the reference section of

433

the Oak Ridge Public Library, is an invaluable aid to historical and genealogical research on the area. Approximately 1,700 names are indexed in Parsly's book.

The following are among the inscriptions Mrs. Parsly copied. In Number 42, Scarbrough Cemetery:

123. *Juncy Keith*, born
10th July? 1792 and died—
July 1839
"She was killed by lightning."

138. *Hutsell Peters*
March 16, 1890 - March 20, 1920
"Just in the morning of his day, in youth and love he died."

In Number 21, East Fork Baptist Church Cemetery, the cemetery visited by a whole generation of Oak Ridge Girl Scouts and located near the Roane County line, north of the Oak Ridge Turnpike and on the north side of Newcastle Lane:

Candis Agnes, wife of
William H. Teffetellar
Dec. 14, 1856 - Oct. 5, 1928
"She faltered by the wayside and the angels took her home."

The oldest tombstone found by Mrs. Parsly is that of Polly Rankin, buried in 1811 in Number 19, Scott Cemetery. The inscription reads:

Polly Rankin
Depd 16 Nov. 1811, ag'd 23 yrs.

Number 40, the Hendrix (Raby) Cemetery, located on the north side of Hendrix Drive in Hendrix Creek subdivision, is of interest to Oak Ridge historians. Within a small fenced plot lies one marked grave:

John Hendrix
died June 2, 1915.

Hendrix is known as the "Prophet of Oak Ridge." The original small stone which marked his grave was stolen. The present marker was erected by a Jefferson Junior High School ninth-grade civics class with money raised by students and teachers at Jefferson and at Robertsville Junior High School.

Some cemeteries are still in use today; among them are Number 16, New Bethel Baptist Church Cemetery near the ORNL enclosure; Number 4, George Jones Memorial Baptist Church Cemetery on old Wheat Road; Number 21, East Fork Baptist Church Cemetery on the north side of Newcastle Lane; Number 7, Crawford Cumberland Presbyterian Church Cemetery half a mile east of K-25; Number 30, Robertsville Baptist Church Cemetery on the west side of Iroquois Road; and Number 32, New Hope Baptist Church Cemetery about one hundred feet east of the East Portal of Y-12.

The Department of Energy maintains most of the cemeteries, while the city of Oak Ridge maintains about a half-dozen more.

Oak Ridge cemeteries provide important information about a culture that preceded the Atomic Age. Even more vital to those of us who grew up here, they are a tactile link to that past we could only wonder about on moonlit evenings.

HISTORY OF THE OAK RIDGER

Don McKay

W hen the Atomic Energy Commission (AEC) assumed control of Oak Ridge following the war, they decided that the business of newspapers was an item best turned over to private enterprise. Thus they arranged with the *Oak Ridge Journal's* printers, Chandler Waters Company in Knoxville, to produce a newspaper which was dubbed the *Oak Ridge Times*.

With a lot of hoopla and fanfare, the *Times* commenced publication, pledging a seven-day operation with an abundance of newspeople and one lonely advertising salesman. On the seventeenth day the banner line proclaimed, *"We Quit!"*

In a nutshell, they found out in a hurry that it would take more than news to create a success. So did the AEC, which realized at this point that it would require someone with a sufficient knowledge of the business and with a bankroll large enough to withstand some hefty losses before a profit could be turned.

Following the *Times'* failure, the AEC advertised throughout the industry and consulted with numerous persons. Jim Brown, publisher of the trade magazine *Editor and Publisher*, and Roy Roberts, editor of the *Kansas City Star*, came up with the name of Alfred G. Hill, at that time the publisher of the *Chester Times*, (Chester, Pennsylvania). Hill was known as a newspaper doctor, having taken over several ailing newspapers throughout the Midwest and turned them into money makers.

Hill proved to be interested, as was another gentleman from

436

Lawton, Oklahoma. Apparently Hill's credentials were more attractive, since he was given the permission to start publication. He did not bid on the basis of a percentage of gross business, as was the government's usual way of doing business; he merely offered a flat rent on the east end of No. 1 laundry building on Tyrone Road.

It is interesting to note that Hill, an ardent Kansas Republican, was positive that Thomas Dewey would be elected to the presidency that fall, hence he made the proposal to enter Oak Ridge with a new business. On the other hand, Silliman Evans, publisher of the Nashville *Tennessean*, a devout Democrat who had surveyed the community with an eye for the same venture, was convinced that Harry Truman could not possibly return as president. Thus he declined to make an offer.

When the deal was made, things began to happen fast. The first order of business was to name me, at that time the advertising manager of the *Chester Times*, to the position of publisher of the upcoming newspaper. Hill had readily realized that the main problem was securing enough advertising to make the paper profitable. Thus he needed a publisher with experience in that field.

The second appointment came out of the *Times* newsroom. Dick Smyser was appointed managing editor. Smyser was relatively new to the staff, but had been around long enough to impress the management with his rare news-gathering and writing ability.

Things became hectic as a myriad of problems had to be faced. Since our original investment was to be small, we began to scour the countryside for used equipment; many dealers were contacted, advertisements were scanned, and several trips were made to Oak Ridge. Plans were also drawn up for remodeling the building we would occupy, and a contractor was hired to make alterations. Also, a mechanical superintendent was hired to participate in many of the equipment decisions.

At this point, other prospective employees were interviewed. (It was expected that some of the former *Oak Ridge Times* employees would be interested, but they avoided the new publication like the plague). Several *Clinton Courier-News* employees applied, but apparently they were only using the promised new enterprise to procure raises from their Clinton boss, because none of them joined.

One month prior to the date set for publication, I came to Oak Ridge and took up residence in an efficiency apartment on Tennessee Avenue. The printing press arrived the same day, totally disassembled in a boxcar. It was one of the original units manufactured for *PM*, a short-lived daily in New York City. A press erector followed a few days later. Soon, all kinds of printing machinery arrived, including four Linotypes equipped with Teletypesetters, which were brand new labor-saving devices.

Teletypesetters represented about the first stage of a revolution in the newspaper business, leading to a complete change in the method by which publications are printed. It is interesting to note that Teletypesetters have gone the way of Linotypes in the industry, there being none anywhere in Tennessee or probably the country at this writing.

Rentenbach Engineering (Tom Rentenbach was one of many who thought we were crazy) made the necessary changes in the east end of the laundry building, with machinery being erected and other items being placed. Barger Transfer was also involved with unloading and transporting equipment. At the time, it was said that this company was facing grave financial problems, but that their work for us saved them.

During this time, I interviewed prospective employees, called on prospective advertisers, purchased office furniture, and supervised the placement of equipment. One week before publication, Smyser joined the staff and pitched in, particularly in interviewing applicants and setting up news sources. An unforeseen boon came from a recently established newspaper in Morristown which was in trouble. We had several applicants from there, four of whom wound up on our staff. Somehow or other, wind of our venture reached all the way to Spencer, Iowa, and our advertising manager and circulation manager, as well as a couple of others, joined us from there. When our original mechanical superintendent left, shortly after our start, one of the Spencerians put us on to a talented printer from Miles City, Montana, who joined us and proved to be an essential cog in our operation over the years. Eventually, we wound up with four newspeople, four advertising salesmen, six printers, two pressmen (one from Chester), front office staff, the aforementioned circulation manager and a little army of carrier-salesmen.

The operating contractor for the city, Roane-Anderson Company, loaned us desks and chairs from an abundance of items stored in a warehouse. That boon quickly evaporated, however, when they were soon ordered to take it all back. We were then forced to scurry around for replacement items, and we again turned to the used market for typewriters, adding machines, and the like. (This article is being written on one of the old typewriters, purchased some thirty-five years ago. At this stage, it is approaching antiquity).

Advertisements were another problem. In one of my early visits to Oak Ridge I dined at one of the two restaurants operating at the time, the Oak Terrace. I made friends with its two managers, Bob Phillips and Roscoe Stephens. They pledged to purchase the first full-page advertisement in our publication. Beyond that the advertising prospects were dim. There were only two automobile dealers in town, and the so-called department store, Taylor's in Jackson Square, was nothing but several concessionaires. The problem with the businesses was that when space became available, it was opened to bids. The bidder who offered the highest percentage of his gross sales (regardless of what that eventual gross might be) was given the space. As a result, most of the business tenants had overbid and therefore had little margin left with which to herald their wares. This worked fairly well during the war years, when the biggest problem was procuring goods for sale, but not so well in postwar days when competition raised its head.

One advertisement prospect, who owned a supermarket, greeted me with: "...see no reason why I should support you." We assured him that we weren't interested in his support, that if he couldn't make money on the use of our columns, we weren't interested in his business. Two weeks after our start, he purchased a three-quarter page and continued on that basis for the next several years.

As January 20, 1949 neared—the date set for operation—we began to sweat. We still faced what seemed insurmountable problems. The press had not even been completely assembled. Work was feverish, with people scurrying everywhere trying to get the first issue ready. Finally, though, the last bolt was put on the press on the nineteenth and the first trial run made. The next day Mrs. Hill pulled the lever to start the press run, and *The Oak Ridger,*

A Newspaper Is Born

Dick Smyser, Alfred Hill, Don McKay, and Joe Hill put out the first issue of *The Oak Ridger* on January 20, 1949. It was the same day as President Truman's inauguration.

The Oak Terrace recreation room in the 1940s. It was the main social area in Grove Center. The Oak Terrace restaurant was where Don McKay dined during the first weeks after his arrival in Oak Ridge in 1949.

with the Oak Terrace advertisement in it, appeared for the first time. It was the day of President Truman's inauguration, which was our lead story. The local news, however, occupied half of the front page, a policy decreed by Mr. Hill.

Although the first issue did not print very clearly, Oak Ridgers still greeted the new daily with enthusiasm. It could have been because we gave away the first two weeks' editions free, charging fifteen cents a week thereafter. Initial subscribers were given certificates worded to that effect.

During this period, several Chester executives came to Oak Ridge to provide assistance. Mr. Hill himself authored many news stories. Mrs. Hill set up a chain of correspondents for us, generally from local school districts and from Clinton, Kingston, and Oliver Springs.

About this time, we began to encounter, from outside the town, a certain antipathy towards things having to do with Oak Ridge. This feeling, no doubt, arose through the perception that scarce commodities had been made available to Oak Ridge during the war. We soon realized that perhaps we should not have adopted the same name that *Time* magazine had bestowed upon us. Rather, we should have titled it something like the *Anderson County Herald*, or some other innocuous name. At any rate, here we were in business, occupied with the daily excitement of gathering news and peddling space to make the enterprise work. In perhaps a week, all of the *Times* executives who had been lending a hand departed, and we were on our own.

Another big problem, in these early days, was the lack of a legitimate department store. Taylor's, after all, was only good for a few hundred dollars a month, and it usually took sixty or more days to collect that. We, of course, griped about the situation to Roane-Anderson. Finally, they cancelled Taylor's lease and went about the business of finding a more suitable tenant. In due time they made a deal with Loveman's of Chattanooga to take over the space in Jackson Square. This resulted in an investigation by Congress, but in the end the matter was approved and Loveman's moved in and commenced operations. Their first month's outlay for advertising amounted to about five times that of Taylor's in its most prolific month.

Beyond these problems, our new enterprise met some pleasant surprises, too. Almost from the beginning there was a gradually increasing use of our classified columns. Since numerous citizens had grown used to using classified advertising in the *Oak Ridge Journal*, they looked to us to continue this policy. Another early boon was the purchase of Norris by a Philadelphia firm, headed by Henry David Epstein. They had the task of selling property in that TVA-created community and seized on *The Oak Ridger* as a chance to fulfill their mission. Soon after we started they bought a series of full-page advertisements. Ridgers were prime prospects, since there was no way at this point that they could buy homes inside Oak Ridge.

In the beginning, many Oak Ridgers suspected that the newspaper was held under wraps by the AEC, despite the fact that we had been given an absolute free hand to publish anything and everything of news value. This feeling dissipated in a hurry, however, once we launched a series on dismal living conditions for blacks in a group of hovels termed "hutments." After we took the government apart on that issue, "letters to the editor" started to pour into the paper. The *Ridger* has always been fortunate on that score, since Oak Ridge is a town replete with many articulate readers.

One of our first big news events was the gate opening, when the city was opened to outsiders and the plant area was closed. This took place on March 21, 1949. *The Oak Ridger* covered it to the fullest extent, also using the occasion to sell special advertisements touting the affair. For me, though, that date marked the arrival of my family on a permanent basis.

After a few months, the time finally came to turn a profit. But it was then that we were suddenly hit by a printer's strike. The aforementioned Teletypesetters were the reason. The Knoxville local could see them taking some of their jobs unless they had jurisdiction. But while it took six years of apprenticeship to become eligible for full status in the union, a person with moderate typing ability could punch tape with relatively little experience. Yet the printers demanded that they be paid the same scale, which would represent no savings at all. Consequently, we stood fast and they walked a picket line for thirteen months. Luckily, we had one printer who gave up his membership and kept us operating. We were fortunate that most readers and advertisers stuck with us, despite many efforts by the union to convince them otherwise. At one point during the strike, a union representative came to us, offered to pull the picket line and to give our present printers cards in the union if we would grant jurisdiction over the Teletypesetters.

Near the end of this period, the newspaper started showing a small profit. It was about time, too, since Alfred Hill had started us off with a mere $5,000 and provided us with only enough news-print for a year. He asked us if we needed more money, but we were stubborn on that point, going out week after week to collect money from accounts in order to meet the payroll.

BUILDING THE OAK RIDGE ART CENTER

Jane Warren Larson

The Oak Ridge Community Art Center was created in 1951 by a small band of visual artists who met in an empty grocery store at Ogden Lane and Outer Drive for the purpose of getting acquainted and providing teaching and exhibit opportunities for the community. When I joined them late in 1962, the night seemed extremely dark; in the room where we sat, the soft old wooden floor and dingy walls absorbed all the light shed from isle-oriented ceiling bulbs. It was, I thought, an inhospitable retreat for artists. Nevertheless, the center offered classes for beginning, intermediate and advanced art students, exhibits of out-of-town and traveling shows, sidewalk shows, special lectures, membership galas. There was a rental program for original paintings and prints, a printing press for use by members and fonts of type, a set of lithographic stones, an arrangement for showing foreign films, and a quarterly newsletter.

Along with everyone else in the group, I soon wondered how we could better pursue our artistic goals. Oak Ridge was poised for new growth, having painfully readjusted from a population peak of 75,000 during the war to 23,000 by 1962, and though the city had a postwar master plan calling for a community cultural center, nothing had come of it. Membership stood at around ninety-five persons. Ready for a new day to dawn, we artists were clearly languishing in the dark.

Quite suddenly, our floor space was rented to a grocery chain in December of that year and we faced eviction. As the man said who faced hanging, it tended to concentrate the mind. We decided to declare our anticipations for the future and build our own art center. The question then became *how*? I was elected president of the Art Center in January 1963. Today, I look back at the speed and élan with which we moved into the new year, matching our herculean efforts to the task. We did build our Art Center, with the help of what must have been nearly one hundred percent of the town's citizens, and without an NEA grant, without matching funds from the state of Tennessee, and without any outsized help from the business community. This is how it happened.

Although finance and construction of a building suitable to our needs seemed nearly impossible, Art Center members approached key segments of the community for a little help above and beyond the call of duty. The president of Union Carbide Corporation Nuclear Division, the major contractor in Oak Ridge, devised a unique plan of attack based on a self-liquidating, cost-payment arrangement fitted to the art community money pool. The Oak Ridge Town Council and city management offered to lease us one and one-half acres of city land, and in addition provided imaginative but minimum-burden plans for a building. Finally, a well-known and very generous local contractor offered to build for us at cost. Thus the groundwork was laid with offers of cooperation that did not entail an undue drain on any one segment of the community, but did address our need. It was finally time to raise money.

After some discussion, a carefully written brochure was chosen as an instrument. There is nothing so reassuring as an accurate document on hand when one is thinking about supporting a cause. A depiction of the new building decorated the front of the brochure. We then described plans for some 3,800 square feet under roof, which would give us room for classes, work space, and a gallery. We also provided a scaled floor plan. Next, our proposal for financing the effort was described. We asked for a $20,000 mortgage and $5,000 in cash donations in order to build the bare bones of our dream. In 1963 these cost figures were in line with other modest construction sites in Tennessee. And finally we described the cost-payment approach—a practical way to finance the dream.

445

"The Art Center plans to pay for this building by retiring a mortgage with monthly payments similar to the rent we have paid in the past," the brochure read. It continued:

We plan to borrow $20,000, and have been able to obtain the loan on very favorable terms, so that payments will be about $158 a month—not much more than we have been paying in rent (about $100).

This loan will be made provided we obtain at least 150 signatures of heads of families to co-sign the note. This is where we need your help.

In addition, we must raise $5,000 in a building fund before we break ground, and more would be better. The Art Center has set aside $1,000 from its budget for this purpose. If 400 people contribute $10 each, we will have $5,000 without strain ...

In order to properly thank those who help us on this project, the Art Center plans to mount a permanent plaque at the entrance of the new building on which will be listed the names of all who donate $50 or more to the building fund. In addition, a second plaque will be mounted listing all those who co-sign our loan, guaranteeing $200 or more on the note.

Co-signing is not a donation or even a pledge of money. It is simply a method of guaranteeing that the Art Center will eventually pay back each $200 (or whatever was designated) of the loan. This is a common type of financing, used for non-profit, community organizations such as churches where the membership is willing to co-sign the note. We all have faith in the permanence of our Art Center, and there is every reason to expect that no one would ever be called upon to pay any part of the sum they guarantee by co-signing. However, let us take an example of the worst that could happen to us. Suppose the Art Center should build its building, and then in five years be unable to meet its monthly payments and close its doors.

In five years the Art Center will have paid off some $5,000 of the $20,000 loan, so that the bank is still owed $15,000. The Center has the leased land and a $30,000 building, which will then have to be sold. In a forced sale, this building might bring $12,000. In this case $3,000 is still owed to the bank. Even assuming that a third of the co-signers has moved away, the remaining co-signers would each then have to pay a portion of this $3,000—or something like $30 a piece. This is not going to break anyone. On the other hand, it can work the other way also. If the building sold for $18,000, there would be $3,000 left over, which would be split among the co-signers, giving each one a profit of some $30.

Thus, we appeal to our membership and other interested citizens of Oak Ridge to come forward....

The response to this down-to-earth brochure, and to my brief dinner speech opening the drive, was nothing less than spectacular. In two weeks the loan was co-signed by one and one-half times the number of families needed—185 families in all, guaranteeing a loan of $35,000. Cash donations were oversubscribed by about $3,000. In spite of much skepticism, we aimed for a November starting date—after all, our students were waiting!—and on November 4, 1963, we broke ground.

It didn't take long to get the center built, either. As *The Oak Ridger* rather tartly observed on March 13, 1964, "On the first Sunday of February, the building—within sight of so many other construction projects that have been delayed, and delayed and delayed—was occupied."

Classes started up alongside volunteers who rushed to put in partitions and hang lights, paint woodwork, and clean sinks. Every member put in hours of work. Gifts started pouring in—a handsome, hand-formed glass chandelier for the lobby, an executive desk and chair for the same area, folding doors and banquet drapes, redwood benches, a forsythia bush and a dogwood, mammoth flagstones for the path to the door, and free gravel for the drive. Large black letters saying *Art Center* were mounted on the building facade. Eventually, too, a sign appeared at the beginning of Badger Avenue—"To the Art Center."

Gradually, Art Center volunteers developed long-term projects. One rule had to be learned—that simple was beautiful. Fancy open cement blocks enclosing the small garden beside the front entrance had to be removed in favor of more tailored ones. Although our building was elegant, we thought, with its butterfly roof and strong eaves, it was still simple and had to be nurtured without frills. Artists understood all about that! And again, extravagant gardening plans went for nought in front of the building when a steep bank shed grass and flowers with every rain.

447

Courtesy Jane Warren Larson   Westcott Photo

The Oak Ridge Art Center in 1964.

Periwinkle finally took hold.

Efforts to beautify the outside of the new center took tender, loving care. A magnificient espaliered magnolia tree settled in, as well as a pyracantha, a hedge of nandina, and a willow. Railroad ties made steps. Eventually, a four-by-eleven tile panel, made by a ceramics class, was mounted over the only problem in the building—an unwatchable door exiting from the gallery into the garden. An enthusiastic crew spent a week covering the plywood walls of the gallery with burlap.

During all the activities, an additional program developed— a class for teaching ceramics. Mr. E. Wilson appeared one day to lead this effort. An early pioneer in ceramics, he introduced ceramic technology to East Tennessee by way of Norris Laboratory during the Depression years and once sent Eleanor Roosevelt a small tea set made of Tennessee's own white, translucent porcelain. Electric potter's wheels were purchased for this program, and a small kiln room was added to the building to house first an old gas kiln bought from a country potter, and later an electric kiln. Soon a craft-oriented gift shop opened on the strength of volunteer sales help. It became a magnet for shoppers and a stimulus to craft creativity.

During the next several years, many developments occurred to establish the Oak Ridge Community Art Center as a dynamic force. Programs were designed that reached out into surrounding communities, a Saturday gallery talk was programmed and school children brought in by bus, and art scholarships were awarded for young people wanting to attend classes. And the board of the Art Center finally found enough steady income to allow the hiring of a managing executive, so that the building could be open for business every day. It was a tremendous milestone in the center's history. In subsequent years this accomplishment might falter, just as budget balances would sometimes turn red, but the organization did not return to the spartan volunteerism of those original ninety-five people who left that dark old grocery store to fight for their dream.

BILL POLLOCK ... MUSIC MAN

June M. Boone

"I guess early Oak Ridgers remember me best for furnishing the music for their dances." Bill Pollock is probably right, since he is known to most of the old timers here as "Music Man" or "Mister Music." His winsome smile is also well known. It's the first thing one notices about Bill.

Today Pollock Sound System furnishes music, special sounds and sound equipment for every conceivable function. But in the forties, with an amplifier, a turntable and records, Bill gave Oak Ridgers their music to dance to. A man with many Oak Ridge "firsts" to his credit, Bill has kept meticulous records of his introduction into the many aspects of the lives of Oak Ridgers.

He is a true Oak Ridge pioneer, having arrived here from Knoxville in October 1943. He was an instructor in electrical training for Tennessee Eastman Company. He was located outside restricted areas in a small building behind the old administration building. The trainees were waiting for clearances that would allow them into the plants for their new jobs.

Later Pollock went around to the different plants and did "on the job training," by advising electricians of new findings and procedures that would improve their work efficiency.

Pollock's records show that he furnished music for his first dance on April 22, 1944, at the old Central Recreation Hall in Townsite. The first "tennis court" dance followed two months later at the Townsite tennis courts below Ridge Hall, and was spon-

Courtesy James E. Westcott

Bill Pollock ... Music man of Oak Ridge.

sored by the Tennessee Eastman Girls' Club. With wooden benches around the court, someone selling Cokes, and Bill's records, the dance was a tremendous success.

There were thousands of single women and men in Oak Ridge in the forties, and the dances gave them a place to meet, get acquainted, and even fall in love. Many Oak Ridgers, including my husband and me, met at a forties dance.

After the success of the first tennis court dance, Pollock and a friend got permission from the Recreation and Welfare Department to stage one of their own, this time at the Jefferson courts in West Village. "Our only cost was the $3 cleanup fee," Pollock said. He and his friend put signs up all over the area, but when the music began that night they didn't know if anybody would show up.

"They did, though," Pollock said enthusiastically. "Four hundred of them! They came pouring out of the dorms, the cafeterias, and the Army Post Exchange up the Turnpike. Unfortunately," he added, laughing, "there was a Recreation and Welfare Department spy among them. Our success was reported to the department and they decided that from then on, they would sponsor the dances and collect the thirty cents per person we had charged."

This was the beginning of one dance a week at each of the two tennis courts, with Pollock furnishing the music. The number of individuals dancing on concrete under the stars in the damp summer air averaged between 500 and 700 each night.

According to Pollock, the largest dance ever took place on the day Japan surrendered. "They were on the Townsite tennis courts long before dark," he said, "and with at least a thousand people there, I had to bring in more horns so the music could be heard." After a full summer of successful tennis court dances, Pollock wondered what the dancers would do when cold weather arrived. "I began studying the possibility of piping music to the recreation halls, which had ample dance-floor space."

His first simultaneous "piping" took place during the Sunday afternoon open house at Ridge Hall. He set up his equipment and sent music into the West and East Lounges and the Fountain Room, all at the same time.

On November 19, 1944, Pollock piped the first music over telephone lines from Ridge Hall to the new Grove Hall for a

Oak Ridge youth dancing at the Wildcat Den in 1947.

The Music Box in the early days. As co-owner, Bill Pollock provided Oak Ridgers with their first opportunity to purchase records in the city.

Tennessee Eastman training-department party. In December he added Jefferson, Central, and Middletown Halls, followed by the Army Post Exchange and Gamble Valley in March 1945.

All dance music to the recreation halls originated from a small booth that Pollock built and moved his equipment into, in Ridge Hall. Another phone line in the booth enabled dancers at the other halls to call in requests for their favorite dance tunes. "We tried to play them all," he said. "But I had one hard and fast rule. I never played two fast numbers together. It was always two slow tunes and one fast. That way," he said, smiling, "the jitter-buggers had plenty of time to rest before the next fast tune."

For a time Pollock was joined in the booth by Burl Henry, who relieved him occasionally and often sang along with the records. Henry was followed by Carl Williams, now associated with WBIR Channel 10 television and WEZK radio stations in Knoxville.

Since there was no radio station in Oak Ridge until 1948, Pollock also piped music, important speeches, and news items of interest to the community, to recreation halls, dorms, cafeterias, restaurants, schools, and the Guest House (now the Alexander Inn).

He furnished dance music for the high school crowd—at proms, at the series of Wildcat Dens, wherever young people gathered. At the Fabulous Forties reunions, which include Oak Ridge High School grads from all the forties years, they still dance to Pollock's music. The same songs they danced to in the 1940s, they still ask for over and over again! Even when the "big bands" like Tommy Dorsey, Guy Lombardo, and Les Brown came to Grove Hall's Starlight Ballroom, which had the largest dancing area of all the halls, it was Pollock's sound equipment they used.

Pollock's amplifiers were, and still are, installed in every conceivable location in the city where amplified sound might be needed. And as an electrical engineer, Pollock built every amplifier he has ever used. "The earlier ones used tubes and were cheaper to build than buy," he said. "Today they're much more complex and not that much of a saving."

The only failure of equipment that he experienced did not derive from his own equipment at all, though it was still an embarrassment. An army and navy E-Award ceremony was scheduled for Blankenship Field. Someone involved in the preparations who didn't know Bill handled the sound equipment in Oak Ridge, brought in a sound system from Knoxville for the event. Pollock still laughs at what took place that evening, even though he was blamed. "The stadium was overflowing with dignitaries and spectators," Pollock said. "The ceremony began ... and there was no sound! Everybody in Oak Ridge knew I always took care of it and assumed it was my equipment—and my fault!"

In 1950 Pollock began furnishing music to the community in another way—as co-owner of The Music Box. This, too, served a great need for Oak Ridge citizens. It was a place to purchase the kinds of records they wanted and couldn't get anywhere else. The Music Box stocked, along with popular music, an extensive inventory of classical records, and at one time RCA informed Bill that his store sold more classical records than any other shop in the area.

"The Knoxville Stores," Pollock explained, "seemed to get by with stocking mostly popular and country music but the many different types of people here called for a greater variety. Classical music was high on their list."

Pollock's services are still very much in demand today. "It's what happens when you retire," he said.

Besides his various commitments connected with his business, Pollock also records the Oak Ridge Community Chorus, Band and Symphony Orchestra, and high school chorus and band, so that records are available to those who wish to purchase them. His own collections of records is extensive. I had 4,000 records in 1950," he says, "all of them 78s." Fifteen hundred of these are stored in shelves across the hall from his office. His office contains several items of sound equipment. He pointed out the amplifier which furnished the music for all the dances. "It's had a coat of paint, but it's the same one," he said.

As part of Oak Ridge's festivities during the statewide Homecoming '86 celebration, the famed tennis court dance was revived for one night. "We used everything authentic," Pollock said. "That amplifier, the same turntable, the same records and horns." For the hundreds of early Oak Ridgers who attended that dance, perhaps the most authentic of all was Bill Pollock ... "Music Man."

BIRTH OF A TRAIL AND AN ORGANIZATION

Liane B. Russell

There is probably no other city in the United States that has within its boundaries a continuous, secluded woodland trail so long that all of the city's inhabitants could stand Indian-file along its length. Not just a trail, but a designated National and State Recreation Trail.

The story of Oak Ridge's eight and a half-mile North Ridge Trail is a story of citizens working to preserve natural areas. When the city was carved out of a large federal reservation, a considerable amount of woodland came with it, and when homes and lots were sold by the government to individuals, much of this woodland remained in public ownership. Some of it is in pockets, surrounded by private lots (though a public access corridor was carefully preserved for each pocket), but the great bulk consists of a continuous strip along the northern edge of the city, running roughly between the crest of the ridge down toward the valley in the northwest—all the way down to the bottom in one area.

Oak Ridgers counted these greenbelts among their blessings, and took for granted that they would always remain there. In the mid-sixties they learned otherwise. Residents of Tabor Road and North Tampa Lane observed surveyors tramping up their streets and through their backyards, and learned that the city was planning to construct a huge power line which, after passing by their homes, would run the whole length of the northern greenbelt before returning to the Turnpike at what was then the western end

456

of town. Following the surveyors' stakes that marked the course of a sixty-foot wide swath soon to be cleared through the lovely forest, my husband Bill and I ventured into the northern greenbelt farther than we had ever gone before and became aware of the variety of its vegetation, its creeks, its interesting geological features, and, above all, the seclusion it offered. We now had much more reason (beyond fear of losing all trees in our own home environment on Tabor Road) to fight the power-line plans, and we became self-taught in the ways of public advocacy. You must dig out facts and be very sure of them, and—with the dedication of an evangelist—you must be able to arouse people to the urgency of an issue. We managed to win the fight in city council. But that's another story.

If it had been possible to avert what seemed like inevitable doom by an ad hoc mobilization of concerned citizens, how much better could this type of thing be done with the strength of an organization? The following year, we were among a small group of people (mostly Oak Ridgers) who founded Tennessee Citizens for Wilderness Planning (TCWP)—with the objective of fighting two proposed developments: the carving up of the Smokies by a major road, and the damming of the Obed River gorge in the Cumberlands. It was not long after TCWP was founded, and efforts toward its two original objectives were organized, that the Oak Ridge greenbelt was discussed as an issue worthy of the group's attention.

During the course of the power-line struggle, it had become apparent to us that there was no real statutory protection for the greenbelt. Even though one battle had been won, might not some other proposed developments be just around the corner? It seemed to us that the best protection for the greenbelt was to build a strong constituency for its preservation, and then try to get some protective ordinances passed. And the best way to build a strong constituency was to provide an opportunity for as many citizens as possible to find out what a treasure they had in this land which they all owned in common. Thus the idea of a trail was born. In April 1969, city council gave unanimous approval to its development by TCWP.

The first part of the trail was a direct offspring of the power-line struggle, for in following the surveyors' stakes into the greenbelt from the top of Delaware Avenue, Bill and I had got to know this part best. We laid out the course of a circular trail (later named Delaware Trail) that started behind the pumping station on the north side of Outer Drive, went out to the city line, dropped down into a creek valley and followed this back to the start. Even within this two-mile loop, an incredible variety of terrain and vegetation types was traversed. On its way out, the Delaware Trail winds through nearly mature deciduous forest with little undergrowth, around the side of a gulch that abounds with pink lady's-slippers and other flowers in the spring, to a point giving a view of the Cumberlands when the leaves are down. Turning back, the trail drops down to what had once been an old homestead, as indicated by the fruit and nut trees planted in a former clearing now over-grown with honeysuckle. Then comes a short segment of an old evacuation road, below huge old beech trees, but the trail soon leaves this to cross a patch of wild iris and follow a spring-fed creek up a narrow valley crowded with mountain laurel and ferns. Watercress grows in the cold spring water. After passing some interesting rock ledges and a sinkhole, the trail returns to its origin. Only at the beginning and end of the trail are any houses visible.

This Delaware Trail segment was officially dedicated on an early October Sunday in 1969, when city councilman Roy Curtiss and city planner Lucien Faust joined a group of fifty-three people walking it. Our daughter Evie and her friend Dellie Kohl had lugged four gallons of cold lemonade out to the overlook, and while the hikers quenched their thirst, Bill told them about the vulnerability of the greenbelt, about the rationale for having built a trail, and about plans for its extension. Future trail portions, like the recently completed one, would for the most part be made just wide enough to walk single-file, or "Indian-file," to cause least disturbance and to give the walker a feeling of being close to nature. "Man doesn't need much more than a deer trail for com-fortable hiking," he said.

A hard-working TCWP committee, under the active chair-manship of Lily Rose Claiborn, soon went on to lay out and clear the rest of the North Ridge Trail. Among the leaders of this project, which involved many members of all ages, were Bob Lefler, an English teacher, and Dodie and Charles Goodman, research scientists at the Oak Ridge National Laboratory. Eventu-

Courtesy William Russell

The Delaware Trail section of the North Ridge Trail in Oak Ridge.

Courtesy *Knoxville News-Sentinel*

Lee and Bill Russell on the greenbelt Delaware Trail, part of the North Ridge National Recreation Trail in Oak Ridge.

ally, the trail extended east to Endicott Lane and west to Mississippi Avenue, passing large outcroppings, crossing creek-carved valleys, offering views where it traverses a power-line clearing, or just winding peacefully through the mixed deciduous forest of East Tennessee.

The committee devised a system of color blazes for designating different portions of the trail. The main portion that runs the length of the northern greenbelt is blazed in white; access trails coming in from several points on Outer Drive or other streets are marked blue; and the circular Delaware Trail is red, with the outer portion of its loop (which is in common with the main trail) being red and white. A trail map is available at the public library or through TCWP.

In line with its objective of building a constituency for greenbelt preservation, TCWP did not keep the trail to itself. It publicized it through the media, had an exhibit on it at the 1970 Earth Day Fair, and offered to lead hikes on it. Soon, several other groups were using the trail—the League of Women Voters, the YWCA, scouts, and hiking clubs. For some of these, North Ridge Trail hikes have become regularly scheduled events.

At the request of TCWP, city council applied for national trail status. The National Trails System, created through an act of Congress, encompasses two kinds of trails ... long "scenic trails" (like the Appalachian Trail), designated by legislation, and generally shorter "recreation trails" (usually located near urban areas), designated by the secretary of the interior or agriculture. The city council request triggered a study by the Department of Interior's Bureau of Outdoor Recreation (BOR) to determine whether required criteria were met: a trail had to be close to urban populations, provide access to significant features of the area, and be ready for use—backed by a guarantee that it would remain open to the public for at least ten years. Not only did the North Ridge Trail fulfill these requirements (TCWP had promised continuing maintenance), but BOR inspectors returned from a field visit full of enthusiasm. They went off to other cities encouraging them to follow the Oak Ridge example. Early in 1973, Secretary of the Interior Morton proclaimed the trail as the North Ridge National Recreation Trail, and the trail was featured in the Department of Interior yearbook *In Touch with People*. Not long thereafter the

Tennessee commissioner of conservation followed suit, designating the trail as a State Recreation Trail. Signs along the trail proclaim this dual status. At the access points, the city has provided signs showing a little green walking person with a pack on his back.

When TCWP crews make their periodic maintenance hikes, they find remarkably little trash along the way (except at trail heads accessible by car). Trail users also do not damage vegetation or dig up wild flowers. Once, Bill saw a little old lady on her knees, digging. It turned out she was planting her favorite wild flower of the region which she had so far failed to find along the trail. The only depredation comes from occasional motorcycles that use the area illegally (National and State Trail status forbids motorized vehicles).

And has the trail built a constituency for greenbelts? Indeed it has. Early in 1976 a real-estate group that wanted to develop a subdivision below the ridge, just outside city limits, tried to convince the planning commission and city council to grant permission to build a road through the northern greenbelt. It would have torn up the laurel-filled valley and the watercress springs along the Delaware Trail. Citizens rose in wrath. In no time at all, 1,976 signatures were obtained on petitions and more could easily have been gathered, but we decided that 1,976, the number corresponding to the bicentennial year, was a good attention-getter for media coverage. The developers' request for the road was turned down. More recently, a request by a private individual to buy a big part of the northen greenbelt was not even officially heard by city council after councillors were reminded by mail how vigorously the earlier road proposal had been defeated. City council had some time before also passed an ordinance requiring a public hearing for any action affecting the greenbelt.

TCWP is now twenty years old and has many major achievements to its credit. Although it was founded primarily by Oak Ridgers, and even now has about one-third of its members living in Oak Ridge, TCWP's sphere of activities extended to other parts of Tennessee where natural areas were in need of protection and local people did not have the resources to work for their preservation. Most of TCWP's achievements have grown from the philosophy that it is not enough to defeat a threat; some positive protection must follow. The Obed River dam was stopped, and TCWP went on to get the gorge designated as a National Wild and Scenic River. The Devil's Jumps Dam proposal on the Big South Fork was also beaten back, and our efforts led to the establishment of the 125,000-acre Big South Fork National River and Recreation Area. The organization worked for laws establishing state scenic rivers, natural areas, and trail systems; and it helped mightily in the passage of state and federal legislation to regulate strip-mining.

But closest to home is the protection of the Oak Ridge greenbelt. The North Ridge Trail has helped greatly toward that end, and in doing so has certainly raised the quality of life for Oak Ridgers. TCWP had made a gift to its city of origin.

PERCEPTIONS OF INDUSTRIAL RISK

Amy K. Wolfe

Many accounts have been written about Oak Ridge, but one of the least discussed dimensions of the city's history has been perceptions of potential public health effects arising from the community's industrial and scientific facilities. Some epidemiological studies of Oak Ridgers and workers at the three Department of Energy (DOE) facilities have been undertaken. However, rarely has this attention been translated into public health concerns among residents themselves. Focusing on Oak Ridgers' apparent unconcern for possible industrially related risks highlights one area in which society and technology merge.

Only in recent years has the topic of risk in Oak Ridge been brought to public attention. In part, this is because Oak Ridge is a city in which industrial and scientific enterprises have been shrouded in secrecy, beginning with the Manhattan Project. Just after the war, though there was much curiosity about what went on in the city, most of the work carried out at the three large facilities in Oak Ridge remained secret. The mystery persists today, although occasionally there have been glimpses into the nature of the activities at the three facilities. Most revelations have pertained to past activities, which the Department of Energy considered safe to reveal once the pressure to protect national defense subsided. In the early 1980s, news reports described not only past practices, but also focused on resulting industrial pollutants such as mercury, uranium, and radioactive isotopes. Through the news media and in public forums, potentially detrimental effects of these pollutants on surface- and groundwater, soils, the food chain, and human health have been discussed publicly.

Revelations about pollution, along with some news accounts characterizing the city as a hazardous place in which to live, prompt several questions. Why, for example, have residents of Oak Ridge continued to live near potentially harmful facilities? Within the community this question likely would appear relevant only to those residents who think that operations at the three DOE plants could pose hazards to their health. For those Oak Ridgers who believe that there has been no risk, one wonders how they respond to allegations about potential hazards in their city.

The phrase "perceptions of risk" refers not only to fear, but also to confidence and doubt associated with industrial activities. Perceptions are influenced by many factors, ranging from individuals' personalities to community dynamics to national trends. Examples of national trends that have helped shape Oak Ridgers' perceptions of risk are the following: political and economic trends in the nuclear industry, including opinions about and the financial viability of nuclear reactors and weapon systems; state and national awareness of environmental pollution; scientific debates over human health effects of industrial activities; and congressional politics and funding. Along with these important elements, however, social and historical factors within the city have affected perceptions. My information is drawn primarily from interviews with residents of Oak Ridge and newspaper accounts.

In general, residents of Oak Ridge apparently do not think that activities at its three DOE facilities present hazards to community members' health. (Some interviewees believe that the facilities place them at a greater risk with regard to possible enemy attack, since Oak Ridge might be an early target.) The reasons underlying this belief, however, vary among different sectors of the community. The most notable differences are found between: long- and shorter-term residents; scientists, technicians, and laborers; and people who work at one of the three facilities and other members of the community.

During World War II the Oak Ridge operations had a clearly defined mission and virtually unlimited monetary support. After the war, when the Atomic Energy Commission (AEC) took control, the single-mission orientation was lost. However, work in the facilities continued to be focused on nuclear projects. Interviewees attribute this to strong leadership in the AEC and national support for nuclear objectives. Toward the end of the AEC's existence, national nuclear objectives became less distinct and funding became more difficult to obtain. These trends have continued to the present, first with the Energy Research and Development Administration and now with the Department of Energy.

One result of these changes is that the orientations of Y-12 and especially Oak Ridge National Laboratory (ORNL) have shifted over time. ORNL moved away from an exclusive focus on nuclear research, to broader energy-related research, and now to environmental research. Consequently, the backgrounds of scientific and technical personnel also changed, particularly since the 1970s. No longer were researchers necessarily nuclear scientists or technicians. Indeed, they need not have supported nuclear technology.

This transition also affected community life. Oak Ridge pioneers saw the place they helped to create inhabited by newcomers who neither shared their wartime experiences nor necessarily had the same vision of, or pride in, the city. It is not surprising, then, that early Oak Ridgers view DOE activities differently from more recent residents. Some of these differences are subtle, matters of degree. For instance, old-timers express a greater confidence in the safety of the city's industrial facilities and a deeper trust of DOE than newer residents. Four factors help to explain long-time Oak Ridgers' confidence in DOE operations and to differentiate their views from those of relative newcomers. First, long-time Oak Ridgers' have a sense of security in the community. Second, they have a personal, professional, and economic stake in the nuclear industry and their community. Third, they exhibit different levels of trust—in DOE, in the nuclear enterprise, in their capabilities, and in the abilities of other Oak Ridgers. Fourth, they see an absence of convincing empirical evidence that residents' health has been harmed by DOE activities.

The first factor contributing to their confidence has its roots in the city's early days when the army ran the community. Because of a variety of restrictive measures taken in wartime Oak Ridge, people who lived in the town during the 1940s felt safe and secure. They were protected by the U.S. Army. Although some of these feelings waned slightly as the city opened to outsiders, remnants of this sense of security influence the group's perception of safety within Oak Ridge.

The second factor which seems to affect early Oak Ridgers' perceptions is their personal, professional, and economic stake in the nuclear industry and in the community of Oak Ridge. These long-time residents contributed to the development of the atomic bomb, the nuclear industry, and the creation of the city of Oak Ridge. Pride in their contributions is evident even today. Their decisions to remain in Oak Ridge after the war and to buy homes deepened commitments to the nuclear industry and Oak Ridge. These older residents seem a bit defensive when responding to questions about risk (though they are even more defensive and weary of questions concerning the correctness of the decision to build and drop the bombs). This attitude is in contrast to that expressed by newer residents, who seem to regard questions about risk as a more legitimate field of inquiry.

Two themes are prevalent among long-time Oak Ridgers who also are scientists. First, they have a personal/professional familiarity with radioactive and other hazardous substances. Virtually all of the scientists I interviewed expressed confidence in their own work, in the safety precautions they have taken, and in the safety procedures they observed. Second, scientists trust the technical competence of other scientists in Oak Ridge. Here the reasoning is that the experience of, and safety precautions taken by, other scientists is like theirs: excellent; thus occupational risks and risks to the community are minimal.

Those scientists I spoke with who moved to Oak Ridge more recently, like the older scientists, are self-confident professionally and trust the technical competence of other scientists. They have an informal network of communication with colleagues and friends who are scientists. Through personal contacts information can be obtained about particular issues of concern, e.g., the effects of mercury contamination. Where these relative newcomers may differ from their older colleagues is with regard to an absolute

467

acceptance of the safety of the nuclear enterprise; newcomers more often express some doubts.

Long-term residents and scientists, however, recognize that work-related accidents due to human error in the nuclear industry cannot be avoided. They think that undue public attention is paid to these accidents, particularly in contrast to problems evident in other, non-nuclear industries. They also recognize that past practices that once were acceptable to them, like certain waste disposal techniques, may be deemed unacceptable by later researchers. Once scientists have heard the opinions of people they trust and/or reviewed the evidence about these sorts of problems, they tend to view them as research problems rather than health hazards.

Long-term Oak Ridgers who are technicians and operators, like early scientists, express the theme of trust when speaking of potential risks. For these people, confidence is placed in safety regulations and in scientists. Trust in scientists, however, is rooted in personal acquaintances and interactions rather than in scientists at large. Typically these interviewees stated that certain scientists they know, or know of, do not think that there are industrially related risks, and that these eminent or brilliant individuals know what they're talking about. Older technicians and operators, therefore, believe that activities at the three facilities do not pose hazards to their health. Like scientists, these individuals scoff at outsiders who think that Oak Ridge is a dangerous place to live.

This point of view also prevailed among long-time residents who did not work at the plants. A notable characteristic about the older housewives with whom I spoke is that they immersed themselves in their children's activities during their child-raising years. They paid little attention to many other aspects of community life. The government facilities and possible health hazards were far from their realm of concern.

A long-time Oak Ridger and member of the Oil, Chemical, and Atomic Workers (OCAW) Union at the Oak Ridge Gaseous Diffusion Plant expressed a different point of view regarding trust. He distrusts scientists, saying that he knows they do not act wisely merely because they are scientists. Scientists, he says, do not know all of the answers, though they often act as if they do. This man trusted his control over his working environment and believed that he determined the degree of his safety. Yet he stated that occupational hazards exist for union workers. For example, when they are rushed to finish a job, safety may become secondary. Although the OCAW took the stance that workers should receive hazard pay, this man believes that the proper course of action is to eliminate the hazard.

Like other long-time residents, this union worker does not think that residents have been harmed by industrial activities because he has seen no evidence to the contrary. For instance, the East Fork Poplar Creek flows near his home. He says that the scarcity of aquatic life clearly indicates an environmental insult. His children and other neighborhood children played in the creek and ate fish or turtles from it when they were young. Still, no ill-effects appeared when the children were young or in later years. While this man acknowledges that industrial operation affected the Oak Ridge environment adversely, he is convinced that residents are safe.

Most other interviewees, both long-time and shorter-term residents, also cited the lack of evidence that people are harmed by DOE operations. Two groups of people, however, sometimes question whether they truly are affected adversely: individuals who know of past or present Oak Ridgers who died from cancer or leukemia, and newer residents who are not convinced that appropriate epidemiological studies have been conducted. These groups of people are open to the possibility that their health may be harmed by their proximity to the DOE facilities.

Contributing to this feeling of uncertainty is a deterioration in the credibility of the Department of Energy since 1983, when mercury contamination of the Oak Ridge reservation became public knowledge. Most of the newer residents I spoke with think the DOE covered up the mercury issue. A few members of this group were perturbed especially because they think the DOE allowed contaminated soil to be used as fill dirt and topsoil throughout Oak Ridge. While most of these people do not think that the mercury will affect the health of Oak Ridgers, their faith in the DOE is shaken. The primary issue here seems to be the availability of credible information from the DOE rather than health per se. Statements by the DOE about pollution and subsequent health effects may no longer be taken at face value by newer residents.

Community Life

One member of the business community expressed a different opinion. He said that it was not his faith in the DOE that was shaken, but his faith in local scientists. Heretofore he thought that the scientists would safeguard the health and safety of the community because many of them live in Oak Ridge, have families in Oak Ridge, and a vested interest in Oak Ridge. But now he is not sure.

The relative newcomers who have some doubts about the safety of DOE's activities are quick to place their views in context. They stress the advantages of life in Oak Ridge, such as a diverse and generally well-educated population; good schools; and the physical beauty of eastern Tennessee. In addition, they say that many other locations probably are more hazardous than Oak Ridge—for example, those that surround chemical production or waste disposal facilities. A few of these people said that they would prefer to live in Oak Ridge than near a smokestack industry where pollution is visible and known. Oak Ridge, by contrast, is clean and relatively safe. No one I interviewed personally has been tempted to move from Oak Ridge because of potential health effects. Nor have they known of Oak Ridgers who have been agitated to the point of relocating. Still, many community residents wonder what effects the negative publicity will have on individuals who might consider moving to Oak Ridge. Apparently Oak Ridgers worry less about public health effects of their industries than they do about outsiders' perceptions of the city as a dangerous place to live and work. *

RELIGIONS PIONEERED HERE TOO

June Adamson

Picking out hymns the piano had notes for. Picking up beer bottles so the services could be held. These were but two of the pitfalls when early Oak Ridgers began to look for a place to worship, a place to fill their spiritual needs.

The Oak Ridge churches date back to the summer of 1943. Their progress, along with the progress of all the churches founded since, has been an important part of the city's history. The nondenominational United Church held its first service July 18, 1943 in the west wing of the Central Cafeteria, one of the first buildings the army constructed. It was conducted by Paul Watson, a young electrician from the Y-12 plant. By October 1943, United Church members moved into the Chapel-on-the-Hill, the only church building in town for a long time. It alternated services with the Catholic Church and with many others as they formed.

But there was more than one nondenominational United Church. The original congregation grew so large that various "United" congregations met all over town during the war. There were groups at the old Jefferson Theatre, at Highland View School, and at Glenwood School. When the war ended and the great exodus from Oak Ridge took place, these congregations began to combine. For example, the groups from Jefferson Theatre and Highland View School combined to meet at Willow Brook School and eventually at the Chapel-on-the-Hill. The decline in numbers resulted not only because people were leaving Oak Ridge, but also because some began joining various denominations organized after the war. The United Church purchased the Chapel-on-the-Hill in May 1955.

St. Mary's Catholic Church was the second church to organize, celebrating its first mass on August 22, 1943. Like the United Church, it too met in the Central Recreation Center in Jackson Square, then called Townsite. Because of dances and parties held regularly on Friday and Saturday nights, the place had to be cleared of beer bottles and other items in time for services. Since the Catholics met earlier than the United Church group, it befell them to do it. Though the place had been cleaned, United Church members recalled the difficulties presented by a tinny piano. "We had to pick out hymns that were possible to play on it. Some of the keys either didn't sound at all or were hopelessly out of tune," an early member recalled.

From the beginning, St. Mary's parish set out to build both a church and a school. One of the first announcements made by Father Joseph Seiner concerned these buildings. The school became a reality by 1950, and was formally dedicated on January 14, 1951. Construction of the church followed a decade later, beginning in 1961.

By the fall of 1943, churches were organizing right and left. A check of the first mimeographed newspaper, the *Oak Ridge Journal*, showed meetings for only two; by the first week in October, Episcopal services had been added, along with services for the Baptists. By November the first Lutheran congregation held services, alternating with the others.

Oak Ridge's third church, St. Stephen's Episcopal, was founded October 3, 1943. As the schedule at the Chapel grew ever tighter, services were moved to the first high school. The church started in a Knoxville hospital room, where Gertrude Gunn, one of the first Episcopalians in Oak Ridge, was a patient. The Reverend Eugene Hopper, Rector of St. James Church and Dean of the Knoxville Convocation, had come to pay Gertrude Gunn a visit. Their talk spurred Reverend Hopper and others to come to Oak Ridge. After surmounting red tape, including passes for visiting ministers, the group arranged for the weekly Vesper Services. Prayer books and hymnals were donated by St. James. There was no choir at the beginning and it was often less painful to read the hymns than to sing them. The first pianist was a twelve-year-old boy who was fond of playing all seven verses of the hymns even when just one had been announced. The first year the church had a membership of twenty-five, and a petition was sent to the diocese. St. Stephen's was admitted as an organized mission at the Diocesan Convention in January 1945.

One of their big problems, however, was the size of the congregation. "You had to have a certain number of people attending services for several consecutive Sundays before housing could be arranged for them." By spring of 1945, the prerequisite for a house was an attendance of two hundred or more at services for eight consecutive Sundays. By a combination of hard "rounding up" work and lovely spring weather, the mission qualified for a small house on Newkirk Lane as a rectory. Later, according to church records, a larger house on Dixie Lane was used. By May 1951, the church building was completed and the congregation moved to its present quarters on Tulane Avenue.

St. Stephen's had a unique way of raising money—by sponsoring local performances of Virginia's Barter Theatre. In the late 1940s, and early 1950s, Barter brought in plays ranging from Shakespeare to Shaw, and some even more contemporary. Despite the fact that some thought it sacrilegious, T. S. Eliot's *Murder in the Cathedral* was performed in the church sanctuary with the Reverend Moultrie McIntosh playing the martyred Thomas Beckett, the English Archbishop of Canterbury in the twelfth century. Sponsored by the church, it was performed on several successive evenings. The most dramatic moment, of course, was Beckett's death at the church door, which the audience had to turn to see. In later years, *John Brown's Body* was performed, creating some notoriety. But St. Stephen's early involvement in racial understanding was further demonstrated in another play, *Green Pastures*. Robert Officer—whose wife, Arizona, was principal of Scarboro school—helped recruit the all black cast, and played "God." The play was presented to large audiences for several performances at the old Oak Ridge High School. Marshall Lockhart, still an Oak Ridger, was director.

The Jewish Congregation grew from a small group in 1943, founded by Major William C. Bernstein, a doctor who was second in command at the army-run Oak Ridge Hospital. "We met at the

Chapel-on-the-Hill on Friday evenings," one member recalled, "so it wasn't too tight a schedule, but sometimes wedding ceremonies from churches had to wait for us."

Early services were coordinated by Major Bernstein and led by lay leaders to make up a "Minyan," the ten men necessary to conduct a service. Sometimes a visiting rabbi was there. Another old timer told of the first Passover service held at the Oak Terrace, then part of Grove Recreation Center. "We were asked by security officials not to mention how many people were there when we wrote home about it. They figured someone would realize from the ratio of Jewish population how many people were here," she said.

The congregation was among the first to obtain land and establish a building fund. According to synagogue records, it may be the only Jewish congregation in the nation to have built its edifice personally. It was built block by block under the construction management of Morris Bailis, a member. Beth El Center, as it was named, was a basic building completed with available funds. The congregation moved to its Temple in 1952, and a rabbi was hired as its official leader in residence in 1953.

Baptists held their first meetings, too, at the Chapel-on-the-Hill. The first pastor was the Reverend Stuart Rule, who conducted his first service in March 1944. Mr. Rule became widely known in the community for his strong stand against legalizing liquor. "Yes, he was positively dry," one member recalled. It was under his leadership that a building fund for First Baptist was started, with fifty percent of all designated offerings going to that purpose. Tom Harvey, one of the charter members, recalled that the church began a building fund early because "we had confidence in ourselves and in the future of the community." There were some problems, such as the continued shortage of steel and the fact that the first bid "was higher than we intended to pay."

As First Baptist grew, mission churches were formed. One was founded in Gamble Valley when it was an area of white construction workers. This group, under the direction of Dr. J. R. Black, later moved to Highland View neighborhood, becoming Central Baptist Church on Providence Road, now one of the largest churches in the city. The first mission church growing out of First Baptist was Robertsville Baptist, named for the street it is on, and organized first in July 1944. By October 1944, another

Chapel-on-the-Hill. Various religious congregations worshipped there during the early years.

Parishioners receive communion in the Chapel-on-the-Hill in 1944.

mission had been formed. It later became Glenwood Baptist. All three of the original missions have thrived and are members of the Southern Baptist Convention. In addition to these churches, others have sprung up bringing the number of Baptist churches in Oak Ridge to an even dozen.

The second pastor at the First Baptist Church was Dr. Madison Scott, a colorful, rather outspoken leader, under whom the drama group produced *Cry, The Beloved Country*. The Alan Paton play indicated the interest of many for better race relations. The drama group also produced *The Other Wise Man* and *The Carpenter*. When Dr. Scott left in 1956, the Reverend Scott Patterson served as interim pastor for a year, then Dr. Edward Gallaway came in May 1957 to serve until his death in 1970—the longest tenure. It was under Dr. Gallaway's tenure that the church adopted the symbol of the atom and the cross, which has continued to be used. It was also under Dr. Gallaway that a Christian Life Group was formed to attend the Tennessee Baptist Conventions each year to move that all Baptist schools and hospitals be integrated. At first "We were not really welcomed," remembered Mrs. Whitson.

The present Church of Christ groups sprang from a gathering in October 1943 at Grove Center. That group became the New York Avenue Church of Christ, which first met at Pine Valley School, then Cedar Hill, and reached a peak of 500 members in 1945, before splitting into several groups. The Highland View Church was first led by Mr. F. S. Timmerman, who left for mission work in Belgium. Later the East Village Church of Christ was formed, then Oak Ridge Church of Christ and finally, the Scarboro Church of Christ.

The first Lutheran services were held in November 1943, and the original group has branched into two separate churches, Faith Lutheran and Grace Lutheran. They stem from different synods, Faith from Missouri Synod and Grace from the United Lutheran Church of America. But originally, Lutherans from all over met together in the East Village Chapel, another traditional structure built by the army. Known together as the East Village Lutheran Church, Faith was organized in April 1948. Grace Church was organized in December 1946, and by 1950 the congregation was ready to dedicate its church in the Woodland area of the city.

The Methodists first gathered in December 1943, and by May 1944, the First Methodist Church was organized, holding its first meetings in the Ridge Theatre. Building plans were made early. In December 1953, ten years almost to the date from the first meeting, the church at the corner of Tulane Avenue on the Oak Ridge Turnpike was completed. Further expansion has made this church one of the largest in the city, with approximately 2,000 members and a sanctuary that seats more than 500.

Methodist members who came early remember that to make the Oak Ridge Theatre seem more like a church, several "right good size" palm trees were purchased. The potted palms were carted to the church each Sunday and carried to a member's home in between meetings. Popcorn had to be swept out on Sunday mornings before services at the theatre.

Out of the first Methodist group came three other churches, two of which have grown, expanded, and completed buildings of their own. Trinity was first, then Kern, the latter partially financed by First Methodist funds until 1948. Both Kern and Trinity own impressive buildings and each has an added educational wing. The third group organized on its own was Gamble Valley Methodist Church, discontinued when the trailer residents it served moved away after the "war years" construction was over.

In January 1944, Oak Ridge Presbyterians first met formally. An early Presbyterian group petitioned the Knoxville Presbytery of the Presbyterian Church in the U.S.A. (Southern) to form a church in Oak Ridge. This petition was denied because a member of that Presbytery, the Reverend B. M. Larsen, was already pastor of the United Chapel-on-the-Hill. The group then turned to Union Presbytery of the Presbyterian Church, U. S. A. (Northern), and this group sent a worker to survey possibilities for a church here. Thus a Presbyterian Fellowship was formally organized by June 1944. The group met in the East Village Chapel on Sunday afternoons, and later that year moved to the Chapel-on-the-Hill as one of the rotating churches there. "Ours was a short shift," a member recalled.

On June 1, 1946, the Reverend Robert L. Thomas became pastor of the First Presbyterian Church, and services moved to Pine Valley School. Members recalled that it was somewhat disconcerting to see the basketball goal of the gymnasium above the

Courtesy James E. Westcott

Parishioners of the First Methodist Church enter the Center Theater in 1950 for church services.

preacher's head like a halo.

The late Louise Cavett became the first full-time church secretary, and because of her hospital visits and other activities became known throughout town for her pithy wit spoken in a deep Southern accent. She referred to any conflict in the church as a "church quake." And she often told friends, "I used to worry about becoming mentally ill, but I don't anymore. I get a shock treatment every Sunday." Many still call her the "matron saint" of the Church.

Building plans in hand, the Presbyterians' first thought in 1945 was to build at the corner of Broadway and Georgia Avenue. Other tentative lots were suggested, but finally, in 1949, the first church building was constructed. The second building served the community with an active Boy Scout program, as well as a wide number of activities, such as the Coffee House, serving young people who needed a place to gather, in cooperation with St. Stephen's Church and St. Mary's Catholic Church. Because of the building austere appearance, members sometimes referred to it as "First Calvin" after John Calvin, the Presbyterian Church's Scottish founder.

During Dr. Samuel E. Howie's tenure, the church began to be called the First United Presbyterian Church. After the union of this church in the U. S. A. and the United Presbyterian Church of North America in 1958 the church dropped the word "United" from its title. The church has long been known for its social concerns, with conferences on such issues as child abuse, and for its strong anti-segregation stand, which meant the loss of some membership.

Two more Presbyterian churches have sprung up since the early years—Cumberland and Covenant.

Although the first Christian Science Church building was not constructed until the early 1960s, the first meeting of Christian Scientists was held in 1944, in the no longer existing Ridge Recreation Center. Later meetings were held at Pine Valley School and then in the East Village Chapel, also long gone. The mother church of Boston formally recognized the church a year after its founding, and the local group established a Christian Science Reading Room in 1945. Today's members recalled that there was a larger membership then, many of whom left after the war years. The first services in the present building were held on the Sunday following Easter in 1962.

One of the most contemporary structures in Oak Ridge is the one completed by the Latter-Day Saints (Mormon) Church. The Mormons, too, had their first meeting during the war years, since a contingency of workers assigned to the Y-12 plant were from Utah. They met for worship, youth activities, and other functions at Elm Grove School prior to the construction of the church. Building plans began early.

The Unitarian Church was among those that began after the war, founded in December 1950. Meetings were first held in individual homes, then at the Chapel-on-the-Hill, Ridge Hall, and even at the old Wildcat Den. Its building on the corner of Oak Ridge Turnpike and Robertsville Road was completed in September 1956, and by 1962 an educational wing added more than double the space.

Other churches, other denominations abound, forty-nine in all, ranging from the most fundamental to the more liberal. Most of them, like the ones whose history is given in greater detail, stem from groups of dedicated worshippers who gathered in Oak Ridge during the war years.

THE B-HOUSE ON OLNEY LANE

Ellison H. Taylor

A story? Don't you read for yourself, now? Oh, about Oak Ridge? Well, I could try. What kind of story? No, there aren't any haunted houses in Oak Ridge. They're all too new. And most of them, too small. Would you settle for a real Oak Ridge house? Even if it's not haunted? Okay, just let me get something from the study.

Now, the name of the story is "The B-House on Olney Lane." And this is a picture of it. That's the porch and just a piece of one of the trees behind it. Olney runs along the ridge off Outer Drive, and that tree is on the edge of the woods. They go down off the ridge to G-Road at the bottom. It's too small for you to tell, but that's your grandmother sitting on the left and your Uncle Bob playing on the floor. And the other woman, waving the cigarette, is Fleta Coe. She was short, a little plump, and wore long hair coiled up somehow. Lively, but restful to be with. Yes, that was her house, hers and Jerry's. Jerry Coe was her husband. She called him Robbie, but his full name was James Robert Coe. No, Jerry isn't a nickname for either James or Robert. But, if you say "J.R. Coe" fast it sounds like "Jericho" which turns into "Jerry Coe."

I didn't look up the exact date, but the picture was taken sometime in the spring of 1947. Yes, a long time ago. Your father was about a year old, probably taking a nap, which is why he isn't in the picture. Why isn't Jerry? I'm not sure, but I'd guess he's down at his dirt mine in the woods filling a wheelbarrow with topsoil for Fleta's garden. She was very fond of gardening. I don't remember him gardening at all, but he did move a lot of dirt. Those cemestos looked pretty bare sticking up out of the clay, and Fleta was trying to get things growing around the foundation. That took lots of trips with the wheelbarrow.

What did he look like? Well, on a hot weekend like that he'd be wearing khaki shorts, a plain T-shirt, and maybe some sort of hat to keep the sun off. He was a little above average height, fairly thin but muscular, and slightly stooped. Here, I have a picture of him at the airport. Yes, I guess you could say he was real cool. That's a good description. That's a Brooks Brothers seersucker suit he's wearing. Yes, I know your father has a Brooks Brothers suit, but it doesn't mean as much now.

Courtesy Ellison H. Taylor

Jerry Coe at the airport.

When does the story start? It already has. I have to introduce the characters, don't I? No, no! I didn't mean to sound cross. I do spend too much time on details, but I get carried away. Just let me tell you one more thing. If Jerry's last load of dirt had exhausted that part of his mine, he'd probably have his machete with him to clear out the brush from a new spot. He was proud of that machete. I think someone had brought it back from the South Pacific. Anyway, he cleaned and oiled it religiously each time he used it, and kept it sharp as a razor. He had a thing about keeping tools oiled. Oh yes, he had a shiny, nickel-plated revolver, too. Sometimes he'd bring that out and oil it while company was there. It annoyed Fleta, and I think it frightened her a little. Why did he have a gun? He used to carry secret papers between Washington and Oak Ridge. Yes, during the war. No, he never had to use it, but I'm sure he could have.

I first met Jerry late in 1945. I came to Clinton Labs just after the war to work in the Chemistry Division. That's what they called it at first. It became Oak Ridge National Laboratory a few years later. I've taken you out there. Remember? Anyway, the man who'd run the division during the war was still there and I was just getting used to him and all the rest of the people when, just like that, there's a new division director. No, the old one wasn't fired. He just went back to being a professor at Chicago. Some people may have heard about the change, but a lot were like me and hadn't. Doing it like that didn't make the new one very popular either, although it wasn't his fault. But there he was, like it or not.

That new director was Jerry Coe. Oh, you guessed that? I don't remember much about the first few weeks he was there. And I don't remember just when and how it came about, but after maybe three months we wouldn't have traded him for anybody we could imagine. It was as if he'd been born to be director. Explain it? I don't know if I can. Yes, he was smart, all right, and he knew plenty of chemistry, but so did lots of people. Yes, he was nice, although he had a pretty sharp tongue when he got annoyed. Yes, he could get annoyed. I remember one day he got a memo about something that struck him as pretty stupid. He got so mad you could hear him way down the hall. "Why don't they do these things in three colors while they're at it?" Yeah, pretty mad. There was a funny side to it, though. His new secretary had overheard him—

she'd have had to be deaf not to. A few minutes later she stuck her head in the door: "Dr. Coe, the Service Division says it'll take another week if they have to do it in color." No, she never did learn to tell when he was serious and when he wasn't.

Where was I? Oh yes, what made him such a great director? Well, what makes a great teacher? Or a good parent. A lot of the same things. What he said was always what he meant. He always stood up for us—and for the Laboratory. And we trusted his judgment. No, he wasn't always right about everything. But about the important things, he usually was. I said he knew chemistry, but he also understood people, which is a rarer gift. You did have to learn to understand how he talked. No, he didn't have an accent, or anything like that. Well, down here in the South, I guess he did, coming from Connecticut and MIT and Washington, but that wasn't the problem. He was used to talking with people who knew all the things and people he knew, so he'd leave out pieces of what he wanted to tell you, thinking you'd know what he meant just by a word or two.

What about Connecticut? Well, Jerry came from somewhere around Waterbury. His father was chief engineer for one of the factories up there. I guess a chief engineer might have enough money to buy his suits at Brooks Brothers. No, they weren't terribly expensive, just expensive. But somehow a Brooks Brothers label meant you knew what good clothes were.

He went to MIT and stayed for a Ph.D. in chemistry. Then he got a job at NES. The National Bureau of Standards, in Washington. He'd been there several years when the war started, and was still on leave when he came to Oak Ridge. No, he wasn't anything like a director. I think his title was associate chemist. No, it doesn't sound like much. You could live on the salary, even with a wife, but not much more. That was why the Brooks Brothers suits surprised me at first.

Oh, the story. Well, the next couple of years were probably the most exciting any of us had ever been through. Yes, "working on the bomb" as you call it was exciting enough, but somebody else was making all the big decisions: "Stop this! Start that!" Everything was temporary. Now we were making decisions, trying to make a permanent laboratory out of the pieces left behind. A whole new kind of adventure. We were even making a difference in

485

things besides chemistry and physics. We all thought atomic energy should be under civilian control after the war, and we worked so hard for it in Washington and throughout the country that we got it. And that was just in our spare time.

Yes, those were two exciting years, and I think Jerry was happy in what he was doing, even if he was tired all the time. We all looked forward to great things under the Atomic Energy Commission. The University of Chicago was going to be the operator, and we were going to show the world what we could do. But for some reason, they couldn't find a laboratory director and just before Christmas, 1947, the Atomic Energy Commission sent down a decision that changed everything. The University of Chicago was out. We would be operated by Union Carbide. And we would have to give up our plans for a major laboratory. Then, within just a few weeks, Jerry went to a doctor for some reason and was discovered to have tuberculosis.

That really shook us. At first the doctors were hopeful: it didn't seem to have progressed very far; maybe a couple of months of rest would fix it—that sort of thing. So experts were consulted, he went to a specialist in Knoxville and he rested in the hospital. He had a room in what was the new west wing (it's where Roane State is now), and I can remember standing outside his window on a warm afternoon in the spring with your father and your uncle. No, you don't take children in to see patients with TB. We spent a good deal of time with Fleta at the house on Olney, too. I remember she had gotten a little kitten to keep her company, and I took some pictures of it one Sunday afternoon. "Miss Cat," she called it.

All the testing and all the rest and whatever medicines were around then didn't seem to make Jerry any better, and sometime in the summer it was decided he should go to Trudeau, the old TB sanatorium in the Adirondacks, on Saranac Lake. So in a hectic few days in the summer they packed up, put their furniture and other stuff into storage down on Warehouse Road and moved north.

Things seemed to go pretty well up there. Jerry had just two spots showing on his X rays and they started to get smaller. We all wrote letters to the Coes, and they had lots of visitors once winter was over in the Adirondacks. Yes, we stopped to see them on our trip to Maine the next summer. With all their troubles they wrote the most wonderful letters. Always cheerful. Except once, Jerry wrote that Fleta cried when she saw the pictures I had sent them of Miss Cat.

The first year didn't complete the cure and Jerry's leave of absence had run out, so that we were worried about their finances. We got about forty people to chip in a certain amount each month to a treasurer who sent them a single check, so they didn't know who was doing it. No, it was pretty easy. We didn't pressure anybody. Only two people knew who was being asked, and only the treasurer knew who was contributing. Yes, we thought it was a pretty neat plan.

Yes, things were looking up for them. Jerry was getting better even if it was a little slow, and they could stop worrying about money. Did they still have a house to come back to? Yes, it was still rented to some girls from biology. You'd like to see the house? I guess there's time to walk over before dinner. Come on.

Yes, this is Outer Drive. That's Cedar Hill School in back of us. No, not very far. That's Georgia Avenue coming up from Jackson Square. We'll cross Outer in a minute. That's Olney on the other side between Georgia and Florida. Here we go! Watch out for cars! Where's the house? Just a little farther up the hill, just to that turn. There. Now look across the street. No, straight across. That's right, nothing but an empty lot! The house was torn down when they sold the houses. I don't know why.

Yes, it is sad. It was a nice little house. But it wouldn't have been the same without the Coes. No, they never came back, at least to stay. Shall I tell you the rest of the story while we walk home?

Okay, Jerry'd just finished his second year at Trudeau. Almost well, but not quite enough to come back to work. We renewed our salary plan for another year, intending to stop as soon as he was working. But then, another kind of trouble. He needed security clearance to work here. Oh yes, he'd been cleared before, but they always started over if you were away as long as he was. There seemed to be some hitch to it, but it took until he was well enough to leave Saranac for the AEC to let anybody know what worried them. Almost a year later. In the meantime they moved to Princeton to be nearer Oak Ridge and Washington, and because they had friends there. Finally, the AEC set a date for an interview in Oak Ridge. Jerry came down and I went with him to the interview. What was the trouble? Oh, some people he'd known years before. No, they didn't seem interested in what kind of people his present friends were. That's how things were for a while back then.

What next? Almost another year before the AEC made up its mind. Then they denied his clearance and gave him a month to request a review if he wanted it. He hired a lawyer in Washington, he and others got letters from everybody they could think of, and in the summer of 1952 the hearing took place. Then a wait for the transcript, to be sure the review board had got everything straight.

Late October 1952. Finally, the transcript. But Jerry was too sick to read it. He had gotten suddenly much worse, had a lung or part of it removed, and was again in a sanatorium. This one was forty miles from Princeton.

By spring Jerry was improving enough to write. Still waiting for a decision on the review. Fleta was now having back trouble. Thought to be something about a disk—rest and proper exercise were recommended. Things will still turn out. And, at last, they did. About six months after the review, word from the AEC that Jerry was cleared.

But Fleta's back trouble was cancer and they never saw each other again. Just letters from separate hospitals. Jerry was still confined to bed when Fleta died. He was discharged eventually, but it took awhile longer before he was well enough to try to work. Later, he married a friend of his and Fleta's from Trudeau, and they moved about for a while, partly looking for somewhere he could work. But he'd been away too long and gone through too much to go job hunting very effectively. The only thing we could find at the Lab wasn't the right kind of job for him. Sometime in 1958 he called me about it from Colorado. Then one last letter to be sure his call hadn't made me think he blamed me for things not working out for him at the Lab. He said they were going to Tucson for a while. I guess that's where he died. No, we only heard about it later. Just his wife and one of our friends were there when he was buried on a rainy day, back in Waterbury.

Well, here we are. Just in time for dinner. Yes, I guess the house might have been haunted, even if it was only a B-house.

CONCLUSION

Courtesy Department of Energy.   Westcott Photo

491

THE "SEEDS OF TIME" THAT GREW: OAK RIDGE TODAY

Joanne S. Gailar

As Macbeth discovered, only witches with soothsaying powers "can look into the seeds of time and say which grains will grow." Yet it requires no supernatural power to look back at the Oak Ridge of 1945 from the perspective of today and identify those seeds back then that did grow to produce the Oak Ridge of today.

In 1945 I thought of Oak Ridge as a community of dislocated strangers, people from all over the United States who were brought together in the hills of Tennessee to work on a single, common project, the success of which could determine the future of our country. Few of us thought that we would stay in Oak Ridge once our mission was accomplished. No one in those days would have considered me strange for not sending home for my wedding presents until I had been in Oak Ridge for five years.

Today Oak Ridge is not only a town of people who share a sense of civic pride and intense feeling of community, but also, in the eyes of some outsiders, a community that is rather closed in, snobbish, exclusive. I first discovered this less-than-favorable view of Oak Ridge in 1965 when an out-of-state student at the University of Tennessee, a close friend of mine who is a good twenty years younger than I, told me that her classmates who grew up in Oak Ridge felt themselves superior to other people, gave themselves "airs." Much more recently, in 1985, in fact, I was dismayed when a personable and outgoing couple told me that after living three years in Oak Ridge, they had received their first dinner invitation to an Oak Ridge home. What particularly distressed me was that this couple appeared to fit right into the Oak Ridge mold. The man worked at the Oak Ridge National Laboratory and devoted much of his time at the Holiday Bureau to repair toys as Christmas presents for children of the poor. The woman, a person of considerable charm, held a full-time job at the Department of Energy. While I would like to think of these incidents as anomalies, I am forced to admit that they may not be all that exceptional, especially when my own husband, a professor at the University of Tennessee, an "outsider," has confessed that he feels a little left out whenever Oak Ridgers get together and "begin the begats"—his way of describing conversations that old-time Oak Ridgers fall into about what's going on with other Oak Ridgers.

Yet despite these flaws I still find that I love Oak Ridge— wholeheartedly and unashamedly—and will never think of any other community as "home." It is only fair to point out that much of my perspective on Oak Ridge is shaped by its contrast to my native town, New Orleans, where the terrain is flat, the distinction between seasons barely perceptible, and the distinction among social classes well defined.

What comes to mind when I think of Oak Ridge today? Geographically, Oak Ridge is an especially pleasant place to live. It is a town surrounded by mountains—not high, formidable mountains like the Rockies, barren in places, but gently sloping, tree-covered, protective hills. Whenever I read the 121st Psalm, "I will lift up mine eyes unto the mountains from whence shall my help come," I think of Oak Ridge, as I do when I hear the song, "The Hills of Home." Then, while Oak Ridge has a temperate climate with no real extremes, it still offers four seasons with white-dogwood springs, scarlet and golden autumns, and at least two or three big snowfalls each winter, none of which occur in New Orleans. Most of all, in contrast to New Orleans, Oak Ridge is a place where a person is valued for what he or she is, not by money or family connections. Few people here today have five generations of local ancestors behind them who determine their niche in society as mine did. Oak Ridgers can take whatever part they wish in the life of their community.

One of my friends, who was the president of an organization

in New Orleans back in the sixties, told me that she didn't want her group to have that "low-heeled-club woman" image. When she said that I almost got up and took a bow, because "low-heeled-club woman" was one of my many roles then, and has continued to be a perfectly acceptable though certainly not an exclusive one for women to play. The women I know in Oak Ridge today encompass a broad spectrum of roles and participate in many diverse activities. These include holding full-time, responsible jobs (as physicist or professor or manager), staying home and playing golf or tennis or bridge, painting in oils or watercolors, "throwing" pots on the wheel, playing violin with the Oak Ridge Symphony Orchestra, acting in plays or writing poetry or going to exercise class.

I also have a number of friends who, though highly regarded in Oak Ridge, would be frowned on or deemed eccentric in the circle in which I grew up in New Orleans. These friends, all former colleagues or other scientists at Oak Ridge National Laboratory, include a kindly, brilliant yet superstitious Nobel laureate who would touch wood when hearing about a friend's good recovery from a serious illness, and would rush out to spend a dollar on the discovery that his wallet contained thirteen of them. My former office mate, a Rhodes scholar, inventor, and a recipient of the Distinguished Service Medal, did such unusual things as take his two-year-old daughter prospecting for six weeks in the desert and, as I overheard him tell an acquaintance, enjoyed performing "harmless little experiments" on his children. Knowing that indeed these experiments were harmless, I couldn't help chuckling to myself as I imagined the reaction of the listener.

Still another friend, a former university professor and one of the foremost authorities in his field at one time, was apparently allowed by the ORNL director to function essentially as a "presence" around the Laboratory. If he had any other role, I never found out what it was, because the main role I knew him in was that of a wanderer and storyteller of fascinating, little-known tales about such world-renowned scientists as Einstein, Niels Bohr, and Szilard, all of whom he knew personally. He would often browse through my books—as well as everybody else's—help himself to an armful of them and shuffle down the hall to his own office. Usually, when my boss became aware of his presence, he hastily summoned me to his office until my distractor went away. I soon

495

learned that it would be a long time before I would see those borrowed books again, not because my visitor was a thief, but because he was the absentminded professor par excellence. This was true not only with regard to carrying off books and not returning them, but also to finding his way to the University of Tennessee, sometimes getting lost en route as well as in thought.

All three of these scientists, who were well accepted and highly valued in Oak Ridge, would not have flourished in New Orleans, at least not among my acquaintances, who would have regarded their eccentricities as unacceptably outré.

I can't say that Oak Ridge is devoid of phonies and intellectual snobs, but I think that what counts in Oak Ridge is being genuine. It's certainly not how wealthy you are as it is in some circles in New Orleans, where, as my father says, money doesn't just talk, it screams.

Apart from a small number of pretentious people, Oak Ridge has many who are intellectually distinguished, like the ones cited. Equally important are those who put themselves out for others—taking care of their neighbors' children, or shopping for "shut-ins," or sitting with acquaintances who are dying in the hospital.

When I found myself suddenly widowed in 1965 with three children still in school, the youngest only twelve, I found that my neighbors and friends would help me stay here. On returning with my children from burying my husband in New Orleans, we found that the dead trees had been removed from our grounds, new grass seed sown, the wrought iron posts in front of the house painted white, and the refrigerator stocked with enough food for a week. And there were flowers on the table.

One neighbor, whom I didn't even know all that well, told me that if I ever got stuck in my automobile anywhere, at any time, to give him a call and he would come and get me. I never had to ask him to do this, but he did stay home from church and fix my heat pump which broke down one frigid Sunday morning. One of my doctors telephoned me and offered his assistance if I ever needed it, and another wrote to me and made the same offer; and friend after friend offered to help in any way he or she could. Three years later, when my older son had brain surgery, and I divided the long days between my job at ORNL and the hospital, a different neighbor brought dinner for me and my other two children every night during the first two weeks. During those years I discovered first-hand that Oak Ridge was a place where a person could make it with one wing down.

Looking back from today, how did Oak Ridge become the way it is now? Which of the seeds of time became the grains that grew? Wordsworth in his poem "The Rainbow" wrote, "The child is father of the man." What characteristics in the "child" that was the young Oak Ridge became the adult Oak Ridge of 1986?

For one thing, Oak Ridge was a town of strangers. The first question people asked one another on being introduced was, "Where are you from?" Hospitality to strangers comes from having been a stranger. Also, since most of us had no relatives here, our friends and neighbors became our relatives. We borrowed from one another during those early days of shortages and depended on one another in time of need. Those of us with cars took those without cars to meet relatives at the airport or to the grocery store or to the doctor's office. Later we formed baby-sitting groups and nursery school groups. For another thing, Oak Ridge was essentially a town of young people. Most of us were in our twenties and early thirties when we came here. We had not yet drawn in our horns, and we related to one another openly in easy friendship.

To attract educated people—scientists and engineers—to the area, the founding fathers had the foresight to provide good schools and community services, and these have been maintained by the people they attracted. They care about good schools and good city government and serve willingly on city councils and the school boards. The diversity of clubs, athletic facilities, and cultural opportunities today reflects back to the broad interests, the heterogeneity of those who came.

Perhaps one of the factors that figured most prominently in shaping the Oak Ridge of today was natural selection. As early as 1946 the first mass exodus from Oak Ridge began. Many of our GI friends from the Special Engineer Detachment left as soon as they mustered out of the army to return to their former hometowns. Those who are proud to be from Oak Ridge, who think of it as "home" today are the ones who stayed, grew flowers and shrubs and put down human roots as well.

In 1955 there seemed to be another mass exodus—at least for

me. In that year I lost four of my very dearest friends. People who left over the years included urbanites who liked big-city life—the shows, the art museums, the hustle and bustle. They included people who liked anonymity. I had one friend who didn't like to see people she knew everywhere she went—the grocery store, the doctor's office, the Playhouse. She felt she lived in a goldfish bowl. I had another friend with a sense of self-awareness who could satirize herself as a "provincial New Yorker." She liked large diamond rings and fur coats and high fashion, for which Oak Ridge didn't furnish much of a setting. In 1967 a young couple I knew characterized Oak Ridge as a "suburb without an 'urb," and not long ago we said goodbye to a single man in his early thirties who yearned for good wine stores and a chance to hear more concerts than are available in this area.

Only a few left without some reluctance. There were some who hated to leave but had such good offers elsewhere that they felt unable to turn them down. These included my next-door neighbors on East Pasadena Road. The man, who taught violin at Oak Ridge High, got an offer to teach at City College of New York and felt that he must take it. Some who were ambivalent about leaving seemed to have to justify their departure by looking down condescendingly on Oak Ridge. One of these was a good friend who left in 1955. I wrote a poem titled "The Visit" about the evening that he and his wife returned for a weekend:

Suspending food upon your fork
At dinner you were full of talk
About the shows, the restaurants
The art museums, your latest haunts.
You'd "found" New York.
And our Town? It's ridiculous—
We can't afford a city bus;
Our theatre group is mere child's play
While you—old scout—explore Broadway.
You've outgrown us.
The way your conversation ranged
I saw we had become estranged.
You had to knock my town to prove
That you were right to make a move.
Dear friend, you've changed.

So from 1945 until the present there has been an outflow of people for whom Oak Ridge is not the kind of place they want to live in.

The people who stayed were in most respects a heterogenous lot and did not all stay for any single reason. Some couples remained in Oak Ridge because the husband was dedicated to his research. Others stayed because the husband was satisfied enough with his job and the wife really wanted to stay. Other reasons included the temperate climate, the proximity of the Smoky Mountains or the excellent school system or perhaps the undefinable ambiance of the town.

If there is any one characteristic shared by many of the people who stayed, I think it is a willingness to maintain and improve the quality of life here, be it through participating in the Playhouse or town council, Children's Museum, Oak Ridge Civic Music Association (ORCMA), the Arts Council—to be an actor rather than a spectator, in a word to be "involved." The other side of the coin is the feeling of pressure, if not downright guilt, some people feel in wanting more time for themselves and therefore declining to serve on the ORCMA Board or to help collect money for the Art Center or to bake a casserole for the church dinner, especially when it's a cause they believe in and the person who asks them to help is even busier than they are.

What then, is the special quality of Oak Ridge? Ernest Hemingway described it in a short story, "A Clean Well-Lighted Place." In the story an old man sits in a cafe night after night until the wee hours of the morning. The younger of the two waiters, who has a wife at home, wishes the old man would leave so that they could close up. But the older waiter, who has no one at home waiting for him, understands how the old man feels. The old man likes the cafe because it provides some order and clarity to his life. It's what a good cafe is supposed to be—a clean and well-lighted place.

The story, of course, is metaphorical. For Hemingway, finding form and order through the act of writing provided a clean, well-lighted place. And Oak Ridge—with its mountains and temperate climate, its well-kept lawns, dogwoods, and flowers, its Playhouse, symphony orchestra, and Art Center, its Children's Museum and newspaper, and especially its people, who care about one another and provide an atmosphere in which the human spirit can flower—is a clean, well-lighted place.

PATERNALISM IN OAK RIDGE

Amy K. Wolfe

Many East Tennessee communities can trace their origins to specific corporations. Some of these towns, like Ducktown, were founded for several industrial companies, while others, such as Alcoa and Rockwood, became company towns. Alcoa, for instance, was founded by the Aluminum Company of America while Rockwood became the home of the Roane Iron Company. Still other East Tennessee communities, though company towns, were founded not by private industry, but by the federal government. Examples of this type of community are Norris, linked to the Tennessee Valley Authority, and Oak Ridge, established by the army.

Categorizing Oak Ridge as a company town contradicts the local tendency to describe the community simply as a unique place, founded under unique circumstances, populated by a unique group of individuals, with a history unusual and precedent-setting. Oak Ridge is not entirely unique. Like other company towns, Oak Ridge was founded for industrial purposes, and it developed because of, and with, its industry. In this sense the process of community development was similar to other company towns, though the particular components of the community differed. Comparing Oak Ridge with another local company town, in this case Rockwood, throws into relief those characteristics of Oak Ridge's development that are more truly unique.

In its early history Rockwood, like Oak Ridge, was a company town. The community of Rockwood, located approximately thirty miles southwest of Oak Ridge, was formed in 1868 to be a support community for the Roane Iron Company's operations. The Roane Iron Company built and owned most of the houses, helped establish schools and churches, operated a company store, and paid employees company scrip. Any company-supported construction or amenities apparently were viewed as necessary for the overall success of the company. Examples of the company's paternalistic tendencies were the evacuation of employees from Rockwood during an epidemic in 1872 and the assistance given to its out-of-work miners in gaining employment in Georgia in 1874.

There were and continue to be significant contrasts between Oak Ridge and Rockwood. Among these contrasts are differences in community size, population, composition, types of industry, and time periods in which the communities originated and developed. Also, Oak Ridge was created by the federal government to fulfill a wartime mission. At the outset, Oak Ridge was intended to be a temporary city with temporary industrial facilities. Unlike Oak Ridge, the origins of industry in Rockwood were in private capital. No short-term, mission orientation was evident amongst founders of the company or in the city of Rockwood.

In Rockwood the scale of industrial and community development paled by comparison with Oak Ridge. Initial capital investments in Oak Ridge and Rockwood illustrate dramatic differences in the scale of each venture. During the war years the federal government spent over $1 billion for Oak Ridge community and industrial development. Construction of the town of Oak Ridge alone cost about $96 million. Moreover, it should be remembered that activities in Oak Ridge constituted only one part of the enormous Manhattan Project. By contrast, the Roane Iron Company's capital stock at the time of incorporation was $100,000.

Some sense of the magnitude of the project in Oak Ridge also can be obtained by realizing that the city grew from a population of zero to approximately 75,000 in three years. By 1950 the population declined dramatically to about 30,200. Since then, Oak Ridge's population has fluctuated to some extent, dropping to a low of almost 27,200 in 1960. In 1980 the population size was nearly 27,700.

By comparison the population of Rockwood grew slowly but

steadily, except during the Great Depression years. In part, increases in Rockwood's population can be attributed to annexations of areas surrounding the city. Nearly 700 people lived around the blast furnaces in 1870. That figure grew to approximately 2,300 in 1890; 3,700 in 1910; 3,900 in 1930; 4,300 in 1950; and 5,300 in 1970. Rockwood's population now approaches 5,800.

Both Oak Ridge and Rockwood, like other newly created towns, were frontiers. Pioneers first inhabited the towns under uncomfortable and difficult conditions. In Oak Ridge, stories of mud and dust, of neighborhoods being created virtually overnight, and of endless lines have become part of the city's lore. However, unlike most frontier communities, including Rockwood, Oak Ridge was surrounded by a fence and patrolled by armed guards. Restricted access, along with a shared and secret mission, conferred special status on individuals living in the community. These characteristics also separate Oak Ridge from frontier towns like Rockwood.

The population composition of the frontier communities of Rockwood and Oak Ridge also differed. Early residents of Rockwood, for instance, worked primarily for the Roane Iron Company either in or around blast furnaces or in mines. Residents can be classified into four groups: emancipated blacks, whites native to East Tennessee, whites from other states, and white immigrants from Europe who may have worked previously in other states, such as Ohio or Pennsylvania. These groups comprised three major job classifications: managers, miners, and laborers. The Roane Iron Company usually brought managers and the superintendent to Rockwood from other locations. Although these people lived in the best houses in Rockwood at that time, the homes still were situated within walking distance to the furnace.

Miners had somewhat higher status than laborers, because theirs was a skilled profession. A number of miners were of Welsh ancestry, coming to Rockwood either directly from Europe or indirectly from other places in the United States. For a while a number of miners lived in an area called "Welsh Row" on early maps. This area, immediately adjacent to the Roane Iron Company's furnace and mines, eventually was buried by slag from the furnace. Miners tended to move from Rockwood in the late 1920s after local ores were exhausted and after the mines were shut down following a series of mining disasters.

Laborers, whose status was the lowest, lived in the smallest company houses. These houses were similar for both white and black laborers, but residential areas for the two groups of laborers were segregated. Black men worked mostly at the blast furnaces and coke ovens, the particularly hot jobs.

The situation in Oak Ridge was quite different. The spatial configuration of social class apparent in Rockwood generally was not in evidence in Oak Ridge. One reason for this was the planned isolation of Oak Ridge's three major industrial installations. Distance from the facilities thus had no relation to social class. Another reason was the scarce and quickly constructed housing in wartime Oak Ridge. In some respects Oak Ridgers took whatever local housing they could get. Nevertheless, early Oak Ridge can be described as a four-class society. Scientists, top military personnel, and individuals who were especially critical to the success of the project occupied the top rung. The three other tiers of social hierarchy in early Oak Ridge were military men in the Special Engineering Detachment (SED), construction workers, and black people.

The army tried to entice scientists and other critical personnel to stay in Oak Ridge for the duration of the project. Thus, for example, these people generally were given priority with regard to housing. Such favoritism, however, was tempered by factors like marital status, family size, and age and gender of children. By contrast, because the men in the SED had no choice with regard to being in Oak Ridge, the army was not concerned with offering inducements (e.g., good housing and relatively high wages) to stay. This was the case even though many members of the SED were physicists, chemists, and engineers who often participated in the same activities as civilians.

Although the jobs that construction workers performed were critical to the success of the project, the army apparently did not view individual construction workers as indispensable. Thus construction personnel who lived within an eighty-mile radius of Oak Ridge were unable to acquire on-site housing. People whose homes were outside of that area were allowed to live on the reservation in temporary construction camps, in dwellings such as trailers and hutments.

Conclusion

The lowest rung on the social hierarchy in Oak Ridge was inhabited by blacks. Oak Ridge, like many southern communities at the time (including Rockwood), was segregated. In Oak Ridge, black people lived almost literally on the other side of the tracks in Scarboro, in what was designated the "colored hutment area." Job options were limited to construction, janitorial, maid, cafeteria, or possibly laundry work. Living quarters consisted of hutments. Unlike white people, black residents were segregated by sex even if they were married. Originally, there was no place for black children in Oak Ridge; they had to be left back home with relatives.

Over time, the communities of Rockwood and Oak Ridge changed along with their industries. These changes did not occur in isolation; they resulted from the interaction of events and forces both internal and external to the communities. For instance, the first major developmental transition in Rockwood, beginning in the 1890s, was economic diversification. Citizens of Rockwood made a concerted effort to enlarge the economic base of the community for two reasons. First, the iron industry was unstable, affecting both the Roane Iron Company and other iron manufacturing operations in the South. Rockwood's heavy reliance on a single industry could be disastrous should that industry fail. Second, events in Cardiff, approximately four miles northwest of Rockwood, affected diversification. Cardiff was one of many towns which developed in the late 1880s and early 1890s as a result of land speculation surrounding the growth of mining towns along actual or anticipated railroad routes. However, the Cardiff Coal and Iron Company went into receivership in 1891, followed by the Panic of 1893, causing the demise of the town of Cardiff. Because of the extensive economic links between Cardiff and Rockwood, these events inspired Rockwood businessmen to diversify.

Many of the new businesses that flourished in Rockwood at the turn of the century were started by men formerly associated with the Roane Iron Company. Some of these men became involved in the community's political life. So, although the Roane Iron Company was no longer the sole economic and political force in Rockwood, the power and influence of the company remained strong during this time.

The next major transition in Rockwood's development resulted from two concurrent events: bankruptcy of the Roane

Iron Company and the Great Depression. This period marked the end of corporate paternalism in Rockwood; it was a bleak time for the town.

Three events made recovery possible. First, in the 1930s the Tennessee Valley Authority (TVA) built Watts Bar Dam approximately ten miles downstream from Rockwood, providing new job opportunities for residents and encouraging people to move into town. Second, the old Roane Iron Company blast furnace was restarted by the Defense Plant Corporation because of production needs for the Second World War. Third, with the development of Oak Ridge, a number of Rockwood's citizens found employment. Despite these factors, Rockwood's economic base has fluctuated since the 1940s.

Although industries and businesses have operated in Rockwood through its history, no one enterprise has exhibited the control of the Roane Iron Company. Certainly other businesses have influenced the town economically and socially. But corporate paternalism never reappeared.

Social and corporate development in Oak Ridge followed a somewhat different course. The first major transition in the development of Oak Ridge came with the shift from wartime to postwar peace. The wartime mission had been fulfilled. After the war a mission orientation remained, though the mission was different. The transition from war to peace was captured in the following statement made by one employee: "In the old days they used to have a poster around here that said *'You Can Lick Japan!'* Now they've got one that says, 'You Hold The Key To World Peace.' And we're working the same way with the new poster as we did with the old one.... It's a business now, and I'm in it...."[1]

At the same time, the nature of corporate paternalism was changing in Oak Ridge. Corporate paternalism always took a different form in Oak Ridge compared with other company towns. Since the army basically ran the town's industrial and community life during the war, corporate paternalism reached its peak in this era. The army exhibited a generally benevolent paternalism, however, rather than the often negative paternalism expressed by the companies in typical mining towns. In Oak Ridge the army tended to protect residents and make an admittedly difficult life easier than it might have been. Missing in Oak Ridge were both an

505

indifference towards citizens as well as a tendency to trap workers into indebtedness generally associated with company towns. Though still authoritarian, a more positive type of paternalism was exhibited in Oak Ridge than in those company towns like Rockwood where moderate forms of paternalism were apparent.

After the war the government tried to determine how to withdraw from its role as overseer and operator of Oak Ridge. The army's "benevolent dictatorship" began to dissolve in 1947 when the status of Oak Ridge changed from that of a temporary government/military installation to one of a civilian town. Although the Manhattan Project officially ended, work continued under the newly created Atomic Energy Commission (AEC). The AEC thus became the corporate entity ultimately in charge of Oak Ridge. Under the AEC's guidance, the city and the AEC facilities gradually were opened to the public. An early step in the process of normalization was the opening of the gates to the city in 1949. However, fences remained around the plant areas. Apparently, the decision to open the gates was unpopular among Oak Ridgers, who had grown accustomed to the security and isolation that the gates ensured.

The nature of corporate paternalism in Oak Ridge changed once again in 1955 when legislation was enacted to allow home and land ownership. When the government demonstrated its willingness to let the people of Oak Ridge establish this sort of economic stake in the community, residents demonstrated their willingness to become somewhat independent from the government. Whereas residents voted against incorporation in 1954, they were overwhelmingly in favor of incorporation in 1959 (by a margin of fourteen to one). That the impetus for normalization and community independence came largely from the government rather than citizens distinguishes Oak Ridge from company towns like Rockwood.

Normalization and incorporation of Oak Ridge were early signs of continuing tension between the federal government and the city. It seems that the government and the city wanted both dependence and independence from one another. For example, the federal government largely has controlled the economic life of Oak Ridge by funding scientific or production projects and by owning and controlling most of the land in the city (which is therefore nontaxable). At the same time, the government has tried to cut its ties to Oak Ridge. Most recently, this withdrawal was demonstrated by the federal government's decision to make a one-time payment to county and city governments rather than annual payments in lieu of taxes for federally owned land.

On the other hand, the city of Oak Ridge also has sent mixed signals to the federal government. Because of obvious and strong economic dependence on the government, Oak Ridge has tended to support or accept federal decisions regardless of how these decisions have affected the city. Active opposition to a federal decision or action has been rare in Oak Ridge. At the same time, Oak Ridgers have tried to wean themselves from virtually total economic dependence on the federal government by diversifying their economic base. However, most new industries in Oak Ridge to date are spin-offs from the three Department of Energy facilities. Therefore, they too are dependent on national objectives and congressional decisions for their economic success. Although Oak Ridge has become more independent from the federal government in post-World War II years, total independence has not been and may never be attained. *

1 Daniel Lang, "Career at Y-12," *New Yorker* (February 2, 1946): 54.

HONOR TO THE FOUNDING ELDERS

Marilou Awiakta (Bonham Thompson)

"I spend a lot of time with the Elders. They've lived long enough to move beyond the ego to the calm. I need their counsel."

> — Wilma Mankiller, Principal Chief
> Cherokee Nation of Oklahoma
> Descendent of "Mankiller of Great Tellico" (Tennessee)

Chief Mankiller's words make me think of you—the Founding Elders, my parents and their contemporaries. Because of you there's an Oak Ridge to come home to. Thank you for home*making*—and for what you continue to do, home*keeping*.

I remember you in the frontier days when we all came to Oak Ridge—in the 1940s and early 50s, the time of my childhood and youth. Most of you were in your thirties then. Although atomic energy was the keystone of our community, even the word "atom" was new to the public mind. Looking at Oak Ridge from the outside, many people considered it a dangerous, futuristic place, as remote and alien as a space colony floating in the blue-hazed billows of the mountains. To us it was home. While we children played, you worked. Worked hard, creating the root system for dwelling, school, and church, for laboratory, society, and city government. And all of it "from scratch."

I don't see how you did it, especially now that I'm doing the same kind of work. But I didn't have to start from scratch. When I married and moved to Memphis in 1957, the city was flourishing like the green bay tree, its "rooting" six generations in the past. However, in researching my second book, *Rising Fawn and the Fire Mystery*, I went back to 1833, when Memphis was a pioneer town, a gateway to the West—to the future—as Oak Ridge was a gateway to the Atomic Age. I discovered that whether it has a population of 1,000 or 75,000, a frontier in any century is a raw place—a hurly-burly, physically primitive, dangerous, invigorating, lonely, freewheeling, "do-for-yourself-or-do-without" place. For a family to survive, the parents and other elders must have courage, stamina, shrewdness, faith—and an earthy sense of humor. When I tell you what I saw in Memphis, you'll know why I often smiled and thought of you and our days together:

There were:
—Dirt streets—mud if it rained—and holes in them big enough to drown an ox (or swamp a car).
—Small, look-alike houses, mostly of logs.
—A few stores, a hotel: rough-hewn, square or shoe-box shaped, strictly utilitarian. Overall, Memphis was a drab-looking place, except for close-drawn woods and the Mississippi River.

We had woods and the Great Smokies, but structurally Oak Ridge was drab too, with its ash-gray houses and barrack-style public buildings, that were painted such a boring color that you made fun of them.

Federal ownership. A big difference from privately owned Memphis. Humor in both places, but in Oak Ridge, government bureaucracy was a major target. You made jokes like these:

"How many men does it take to pick up the garbage?"
"Ten. Two to take the top off the can. Two to carry the can to the truck. Two to dump it. Two to carry it back. Two to put the top back on!"

or

"How long did they take to paint the inside of our house?"

"Long enough to raise a litter of pups. First the 'ceiling crew' came. Two weeks later the 'wall crew' came with flat paint. Two weeks after that the 'spotters' came to touch up the walls—with *enamel*!"

"Wait a minute. That's only four weeks. Takes six for pups."

"Well, it took me two weeks to get used to the shiny spots!"

or

"The red tape around here is so bad that if you want to make a baby, you have to fill out a form—*in triplicate*!"

"Humor is the saving grace," Mark Twain said. And you had it in abundance. In the midst of hardships, you created fun (as your Memphis counterparts did) with laughter, dancing, plays, picnics, parties, music, clubs, and visiting with relatives and friends. By example, you taught us children not only the value of work, but also of the "saving grace" so necessary for perspective—for survival.

You were good horsetraders, too. And Tennesseans have always admired the ability to cut a shrewd, fair deal. The government needed you for the Manhattan Project and you laid the terms on the line—among them, the best teachers for your children. And we got the best. Never mind that the buildings were rough in the beginning, the education going on inside was second to none. And you supported the work as parents, teachers, counselors or interested citizens. Also, federal ownership was an advantage for education—money poured in; whereas in Memphis, the pioneers had to begin with a privately funded class (for boys only) in a house, and build from there. On that frontier I would have grown up illiterate.

Pioneer churches were freewheeling, building-wise; people had to use available structures, which led to some funny situations. For example, Memphis Methodists, whose favorite axiom was "Whiskey leads to dancing," had to meet for a while in the Blue Ruin Saloon, so-named because its gin gave regular customers a blue tinge to their skin. In Oak Ridge, after an ecumenical period of taking turns using the Chapel-on-the-Hill, religious groups found other quarters. We Methodists went to Sunday school in the high school above Jackson Square, then hurried down the hill to the Ridge Theatre for church, where it was dim, cool, and seats

510

were soft. This state of affairs shocked some "hard-pew" advocates, one of whom I quoted to my father:

"It's a sin and a shame,"
said Miss Mabel Trevain,
"these children are churched in a movie.
With those billboards they'll sink
and grow up to think
that God looks like Clark Gable!"

Daddy laughed when he heard,
"Why the woman's absurd ...
You can think better than that.
How much worse it would be
if you grew up to see
that God looks like Miss Mabel!"

As you did elsewhere, you Elders "Kept your eye on the mark ... steady as you go." From watching you we learned to walk in balance, which included the ability to cope with the swarm of different people.

Memphis had "the swarm" on a small scale—less than 1,000 residents, but a constant flux of people with different origins: Native American, European, or African American. They came to trade, unload cargo, settle, or head West. (Some also came to "raise Cain.") Since material resources were few, inner resources had to be many.

Oak Ridge had a *big* swarm—people from all over the United States came to settle among Appalachian families, like mine, that had lived in the area for generations. Oak Ridgers had a common purpose—to work on nuclear energy. And fortunately, government security kept many of the worst "Cainraisers" at bay. But the fission of the atom in the laboratories was mirrored in the community. There was high energy and high confusion. Life had to be sorted into an orderly pattern. It was up to the Elders to create the pattern.

One of the best parts of it was that everyone had a similar lifestyle, regardless of occupation. Our neighborhood on South Tampa Lane was typical: families were involved in science, construction, city government, cafeteria management, the ministry, teaching, accounting. A business entrepreneur lived in a D-house

511

next to a grocer who had converted a school bus into a "rolling store." When it wasn't en route, the bus was parked in front of the family's flattop house. Needless to say, the rolling-store kids were the most popular on the block.

Neighbors/families worked and played together—kept each other company. In hot weather everyone was outside a lot, for we depended on "mountain air-conditioning." In cold weather, tending the fire was a constant family chore, just as it had been for Memphis pioneers. While their major heat came from a fireplace, ours came from a coal furnace. Remember how the coal was dumped in a closed bin near the furnace, just inside the house's back door—which faced the street (always confusing to non-Ridgers). Almost everyone came in through the back door and tracked coal dust through the kitchen into the living room. Fire was a *presence.* It had to be fed regularly in daytime, banked at night, stirred up in the morning. Parents taught children its ways and every family member old enough to be responsible took a turn firing the furnace, as we took turns with other chores.

Our pioneer life was a "hands on," communal experience that included the joy of just being alive. After years of fear and horror, World War II was over. The dark clouds had rolled back, the breeze was tonic-fresh, the sun full on our faces. For a season we rejoiced and were glad.

Then the wind changed. As it seems to do on every generation's frontier.

In Memphis, the change came in the late 1830s, when the federal government shoved the natives (Chickasaw Indians) out West to make way for Big Power, Big Money—the cotton industry. The city grew past its sapling stage and branched into "good" (wealthy) and "bad" (low income) neighborhoods, into divisions of class and race, into the "we's," who had power and money, and the "they's," who didn't. Some Elders thrust to one side or the other. But as Memphis leaned in the wind, the wisest Elders found their counterparts among the newcomers and began shoring up the roots of the community in every sector. Only a few Elders, however, recognized and warned against the deadly borer making its way toward the city's heart—slavery. It caused damage that Memphis leaders of today are still working to heal.

Although Oak Ridge had segregation to contend with, we did

not have the extreme of slavery. What we did have was a season of high and bitter crosswind, when the city swayed with change. It corresponded approximately to my youth, 1950-60. When the fence came down in 1949 and real estate gradually transferred to private hands, the city began to take on color—literally, in paint and construction, and figuratively in business and political patterns. Slowly, the population stratified; neighborhoods changed. Private wealth was not the catalyst. Science was. Federally, and therefore locally, the push was for scientific research, education, and development. As one high school student put it, "Science is 'It' in Oak Ridge." The change in the wind was good in many ways, but there were drawbacks.

Some Elders noted the change away from an egalitarian climate by saying, "It was more fun in the old days when we were all in the same boat." Children younger than I complained that they had lost their "roaming grounds." Property lines often extended into the woods; some people put up fences. It was becoming difficult to play in the hollows and hills without trespassing.

As a teenager I felt a bitter edge to the crosswind, a bitterness that through strands of family, education, business, and politics webbed out from Oak Ridge to the surrounding area. One wind came from the direction of "outsiders" (mostly scientists) and the other from "natives" (mostly non-scientists). They sounded like this:

Outsiders: "We've done everything for these people and they're still backward."

"They're so uneducated they don't even know what the word 'science' means."

"They don't articulate properly."

"They don't have any 'culture.' Just listen to that Grand Ole Opry stuff they call music."

"As for the University of Tennessee, who ever heard of it?"

"Bunch of fundamentalists."

Natives: "They're looking down on us, but we're not looking up to them—and it gets their goat."

"You have to have three degrees to get them to sit down, much less listen."

"They're all book learning and no sense. Show them a rock

slide coming down the mountain, and they'll show you a map that says there's no rock there."

"They come in telling us who we are and what to do like the world began with them. But I'm here to say different."

"They talk about our University like it was nothing."

"Bunch of atheists."

Extremes from both sides. Not from every one, certainly, but from enough to create the kind of root-loosening crosswind that no tree, no community and no individual can long withstand without severe damage. Someone had to shore up the roots while the wind blew its course.

The wisest of you Founding Elders did just that. You had already begun a network of cooperation between outsiders and natives, between the laboratories and the University of Tennessee and between neighbors. You strengthened those times by years of patient work—by home*keeping*. You explained to the young that not all people in any group are alike, or as one native put it, "One braying jackass don't make the herd." You said that in time the season could change for the better. And today in Oak Ridge, who could deny that you were right. On the surface, many institutions reflect mutual cooperation and understanding, among them the Museum of Science and Energy, the Children's Museum and its Regional Appalachian Center, Oak Ridge Associated Universities and various service groups. I have no way of knowing, however, about that vast labyrinth beneath the surface, where politics, history, religion, and human relations intertwine and where traumas from seasons past reverberate for generations.

I only know that for me the damage took twenty years to heal. In the "time of bitter crosswind," I was a sapling. Unlike the Elders, I didn't have the girth and tough bark, the far-flung roots and spreading branches to hold me to balance. All I had was my long, tenacious taproot of highlander heritage that my parents kept packed tight in the earth of my homeland.

My shorter roots were tearing loose. I swayed one way, deeply angry at the disdain poured on my people and our culture. Then I swayed to the other, defensive of friends and Elders—so called "outsiders"—who were not as some natives described them. Adding to the degree of sway was the fact that I was born in Knoxville and living in Oak Ridge, a child of the mountain growing up with the atom. Could such opposites ever meet in peace?

Exacerbating the conflict of loyalties was a conflict of world view and communication. Appalachians and Cherokees—my relatives—are symbolic peoples. We view the world in cosmic connection, where the tangible is a reflection of the intangible, of the spirit. We speak of this connection in images. Science, on the other hand, is based on facts that can be demonstrated and proven. It tends to create an objective mindset, which speaks literally and views imagistic thought as subjective, primitive, unreal—and at worst, "occult." What I was experiencing was the basic conflict between the intuitive and the analytical mind, but at the age of sixteen I had neither the knowledge nor the power to define it as such. I only knew it was painful—a stone blocking my way, for the path I had chosen was poetry.

I asked advice from Papa, my maternal grandfather. A Methodist minister with a live-and-let-live philosophy, he was six-feet tall and square-handed. Earlier in his life he had mined coal, then taught Greek and Roman history at Hiwassee College to pay for his education there. He listened sympathetically as I described the bitter crosswind. "The government and some outsiders make the natives feel shoved out," I said. "And they *literally* shoved out the old pioneer families in Wheat, Scarboro, Robertsville, and Elza to make room for Oak Ridge. Some of the tombstones in the Wheat cemetery go back to the 1790s."

"And back then," Papa said, "the settlers were the 'outsiders.' This was Cherokee country ... had been for hundreds of years. Their capital was over near Tellico. The settlers called the Indians 'uncivilized' and 'heathen.' The government made them walk the Trail of Tears to Oklahoma. But the Cherokee knew a secret. The settlers had to learn it. And these new folks in Oak Ridge will too, if they want to last. *The mountains have been here a long time.*"

I took his meaning. "People come and go ... seasons come and go. Mother Earth abides and heals. Hold on ... work patiently ... wait ..."

But I wanted action. I wanted the stone out of my way. "In that case," Papa said, "you'd better be like water. Flow around it. Or vapor yourself and rain down in another place."

Which place? The French teacher at Oak Ridge High School, Margaret Zimmerman, suggested the answer, for she gave me a vision of the land of Pascal, where "the heart has its reasons that the reason knows not of." A land linked to Appalachia through Huguenot immigrants who intermarried with the Scotch-Irish and Cherokee. Historically, the French, Scots, and native Americans have been drawn to each other by their similarities: a cosmic connection to the world, imagistic language, fierce independence—and a humorous pragmatism based on the "long view" of events. A fusion of these genes runs high in my blood, and when Margaret Zimmerman said, "the heart has its reasons ..." every cell in my body demanded, "Go to France!"

From that moment I was outward bound, driven by the need to find an equilibrium between heart and mind, mountain and atom, art and science—and a language to express the balance. Eleven years later, in May 1964, I stopped in Oak Ridge to take my final bearings for France. Dr. Margaret Mead, the distinguished anthropologist, was also in town to give her critique of the community. I heard her describe the need for balance in Oak Ridge in much the same terms as I defined my own.

But what I felt as a "bitter crosswind," she called "'a vast gap' between intellectual scientist and uneducated native ... eggheads and fundamentalists ... those highly educated for the modern world and those culturally deprived." She said, "You (scientists) are 'missionaries to the natives.'" Never once did she suggest that natives might have valuable knowledge to exchange, although with her on the stage was one of our wisest Elders, Dr. William G. Pollard—physicist, Episcopal priest, director of the Oak Ridge Institute of Nuclear Studies—a man reared in Knoxville. Beside him, representing the wisdom of non-natives, was Alvin M. Weinberg, humanitarian, director of the Oak Ridge National Laboratory. Dr. Pollard's face was calm, unperturbed. Maybe he would tell her, "Margaret, the mountains have been here a long time."

I couldn't. I had to pack. I was traveling with our two daughters who were under five years old. My husband, Paul, had gone ahead to his duty station at Laon Air Force Base, which was in the middle of sugar beet fields ninety miles northeast of Paris—a region the French call "the flea fields" because it has been invaded eighty-seven times since the days of Julius Caesar. The only housing available for us there was a small government trailer with a lean-to built on it. And I would be flying the Atlantic alone with the children, not in a luxury jet but on a government transport. It all sounded like another "frontier" to me. But now I was responsible for the homemaking and homekeeping. It was heartening to find my parents and other Elders spinning the web of life as you always have—with courage, stamina, shrewdness, faith and humor. Unchanged also were the mountains, the Ancients who, from generation to generation, teach the art of survival to those who will listen.

I carried my strand of the web to France, where thanks to you Elders and the knowledge coded in my genes, I remembered how to spin my part of the pattern. I discovered that stone and water are one of Nature's most beautiful combinations. By its weight and mass, the stone alters the course of the water. And water, with its patient flow, changes the shape of the stone. Together, they sing magnificiently. Like Science and Art. I also experienced being the "outsider" and came to bless the "bitter crosswind" for all it had taught me about human relations. Most importantly, I finally understood and could say to myself, "I am a Cherokee/Appalachian poet. To find the 'eye of my work'—the center— I have to come home."

You Elders were there to meet me, in the summer of 1977, sharing your wise counsel and support as I began to write *Abiding Appalachia*. Because you had been honest with me as a child— telling me exactly what the atom can do to help or to harm and what our responsibility is for its use—I found the point where mountain and atom meet. I also found a way of expressing it, for as Neils Bohr said, "When it comes to atoms, language can be used only as in poetry. The poet, too, is not nearly so concerned with describing facts as with creating images and mental connections."

Now it is 1986. I've just returned from the Cherokee National Holiday in Tahlequah, Oklahoma, where the mountains are so much like ours in East Tennessee. Seven generations after the Trail of Tears, as Elders at that time foretold, the Cherokee are strong again—65,000 in the West and 8,000 in the East. Two years ago the respective tribal councils reunited at Red Clay, Tennessee, where they last met in 1837. Twenty-two thousand relatives and friends came to Tahlequah for the Holiday, which had the theme, "Honoring the Cherokee Family."

At the powwow, held on the athletic field of Sequoyah High

Conclusion

School, Chief Wilma Mankiller called for a dance to honor a distinguished Elder of the nation, saying, "Without his counsel through the years I would never have become chief." Paul and I joined the throng of people circling the slow, steady beat of the drum in rhythm with an ancient song. Children mingled with Elders, matching their steps to the pattern. I thought how mysterious the web of life is, how real the strands that connect us all. No matter how wide the web spins, circling round and round are children and Elders of the present, of pioneer times, of centuries when none but native people lived on the land. I danced in honor of them all.

But especially, I danced for you.

THE HUMANITIES IN
OAK RIDGE

Jim Wayne Miller

Asked to comment on the humanities in the Oak Ridge school system and in the community at large, an early Oak Ridger, Jacinta Howard, expressed a widely held view: Since the school system was fashioned for the most part by scientists, there was always more emphasis on science than on the humanities. This was especially so after Sputnik went up. Moreover, "I don't remember anybody coming to Oak Ridge talking about the humanities," Mrs. Howard says. Even after the fence went down in 1949 and things opened up, she recalls that there were no writers coming to read or speak. Margaret Mead was the first person connected with the humanities to come to Oak Ridge. Mead scolded scientists for not taking an interest in broad education. A lot of people took offense, Mrs. Howard remembers.

Given the very special purpose of Oak Ridge, and the unique concentration of individuals dedicated to the town's purpose, it is not surprising that the sciences should have received great emphasis in the local school system. Nor is it surprising that among the scientists gathered at Oak Ridge, there would have been those who saw it as their appropriate role to devote themselves exclusively to their research and not to the concerns of how science relates to other areas of education or to public affairs. As Alice Kimball Smith points out in *A Peril and a Hope: The Scientists' Movement in America, 1945-1947*, scientists have not always thought of themselves or been thought by others as apolitical, or their work incompatible with public affairs. Isaac Newton directed the Mint; Benjamin Franklin served as U.S. Ambassador to France. But there did later develop, because of increasing specialization in the sciences, a general assumption that "one of the marks of a first-class scientist was exclusive preoccupation with research. Private indulgence in music, travel, or mountain climbing was acceptable, but public display of interest in things other than science required special justification." Such an assumption could lead to strict compartmentalization of thought, so that a research scientist might maintain that the splitting of the atom had nothing to do with the dropping of the atomic bomb; that science and technology were altogether separate and distinct areas; that the utilization of research was solely the responsibility of government and industry. This point of view was surely represented among the scientists at Oak Ridge.

But it was not the only point of view. As J. H. Rush points out in his memoir, "Prometheus in Tennessee," there were others who were painfully aware of the implications of their work. Rush, a physicist who worked on the Oak Ridge atomic bomb project from 1944 to 1946, recalls his concerns and those of his colleagues in the Clinton Laboratories after armistice: "We knew as did few others that the bomb represented not merely a weapon but a radical new technology, and we felt strongly that atomic energy and the problems it would create needed to be dealt with through open, democratic processes." Rush and his colleagues knew that "People would need to be informed, educated to the potentialities of this new frontier.... We must watch the immediate reactions of Congressmen and other people in government, be alert to any hasty, ill-informed developments of policy."

As time passed Rush and some of his colleagues began to realize more fully the implications of a "new order of power over [mankind] and the environment ... henceforth the consequences of man's acts must be weighed with utmost caution." Rush was sobered by the thought that "a handful of specialists working in secret [had] weighed the arguments and decided to hazard the planet" to the possibility of a worldwide chain reaction when the bomb was tested.

As a result of these concerns, which transcended his strictly professional responsibilities, J. H. Rush helped organize the Federation of American Scientists. And as Alice Kimball Smith's book about the scientists' movement in America documents, Rush and others at Oak Ridge were involved in the public implications of their work. They did not see themselves as specialists only. They were in tacit agreement with Ralph Waldo Emerson who, in his historic Phi Beta Kappa address at Harvard in 1837 titled "The American Scholar," declared: "Man is not a farmer, or a professor, or an engineer, but he is all ..." Rush and his associates knew that in addition to being scientists they were also citizens, and this knowledge and concern, despite their professional specialties, involved them in the humanities.

There is much confusion about just what the humanities are. Few people are able to distinguish between the words "humane," "humanist," and "humanitarian" with any precision. And Americans with a more informed understanding tend to think of the humanities as only academic subjects or disciplines. We are not altogether wrong to associate the humanities with music, art, literature, history, philosophy, and other related fields and activities. But the humanities are something beyond or in addition to the subjects and disciplines of inquiry we associate with them.

We can understand the humanities in contrast to the sciences by considering that, as a scientist, we may ask: "Will it work? If so, how?" But as a person employing the perspective of the humanities we might ask: "Do we need it? If so, why?" As scientist we are concerned with *how* to do a thing, as humanist with *what* to do and *why*. (And to varying degrees we are all both scientist and humanist, as Emerson suggests.)

Another way of understanding the humanities is to consider that they are concerned not so much with making a living as with living a worthwhile life. James Still, the poet, novelist, and short story writer, observes that after we have food, shelter, and clothing, we begin to ask: "Then what?" He refers to the "then-what days," which constitute most of our lives. The humanities are concerned with the "then-what" days.

The humanities have to do with those things which make us specifically human. What are those things? Lanugage. Yes. What else? Jacob Bronowski, in *The Ascent of Man*, identifies something else in his distinction between biological and cultural adaptation. Every animal, plant, and insect, given enough time, is capable of making biological adaptations, Bronowski observes. But only human beings are capable of cultural adaptations, which involve choice, for only human beings have the freedom of choice.

This ability, this freedom, resides in what Bronowski calls the "power of anticipation," in the "forward-looking imagination" which is the ability, specifically human, to look at a situation, analyze it, and make choices that will affect our welfare at some future time. This power of anticipation manifests itself in the ability to draw conclusions, based on what we can see, and about what we can't see. We can see our cultural arrangements—the way we make a living, the way we relate to one another in society, as individuals and as groups. By observing these arrangements we can draw conclusions about what we can't see. This human ability works both forward and backward: we can examine our present and consider ways in which the present is a product of the past; we may discover in our present the seeds of our future.

Those things that we see every day, and therefore take for granted, are often the very things we may never really see at all. But what if we deliberately inspect what is ordinarily not examined and, by considering what we can see, draw conclusions about what we can't see—about our values and assumptions? This human activity we might think of as *doing* the humanities, much as scientists *do* science.

While we can distinguish between the different kinds of inquiry involved in the sciences and in the humanities, the doing of science and the doing of the humanities are ultimately compatible; indeed, they are commingled in every human, as Emerson suggests. Some of the best scientists have realized the compatibility of the sciences and the humanities, even their interdependence, and have expressed concern that the usefulness and legitimacy of the humanities are overlooked in our time. Alfred North Whitehead noted that, as a result of specialization, the celibacy of the medieval learned class has been replaced in the modern world by a "celibacy of the intellect which is divorced from the concrete contemplation of the complete facts." Whitehead's implication is that contemplation of the complete facts involves both the perspectives of the sciences and the humanities. J. Robert Oppenheimer thought that the great success achieved in the natural sciences by subsuming many particulars under a general order had made us "a little obtuse to the role of the contingent and particular in life"—in other words, a little obtuse to many of the things that are the subject of examination and inquiry in the humanities.

At Oak Ridge in the mid-forties, J. H. Rush and some of his associates, concerned with the implications of atomic energy on our traditional freedoms, began to be concerned with government and matters of public policy. Having been concerned with the questions of the scientist—Will it work? If so, how?—they began to consider questions posed by the perspective of the humanities: What to do, and why? Forty years later, the humanities are still inseparable from a consideration of our traditional freedoms—to such a degree that cultivation of the humanities, in the context of our democratic way of life, might be considered an investment in freedom.

We are accustomed to hearing that deficit spending and alien ideology are the only threats to our freedom. The connection between the humanities and the maintenance of freedom is rarely appreciated. The Russian dissident Alexander Ginzburg makes this connection vivid when he points out the importance of historical memory. In Russia, Ginzburg emphasizes in lectures, it was absolutely necessary for the revolution to "obliterate historical memory, so people could have no conception of any alternative to what the revolution offered."

Ginzburg and others who have lived in un-freedom appreciate the value of historical memory. Ginzburg's countryman and author of *The Gulag Archipelago*, Alexander Solzhenitsyn, quotes the Russian saying: "Dwell on the past and you lose one eye; forget the past and you lost both eyes." The proverb suggests how the humanities, through a study of the accumulated knowledge of the ages, provide us with vision; how they are a lens with which we inspect our lives, individually and collectively; how they permit us to examine the timely under the aspect of the timeless; and how, without them, we are blind to alternatives and possibilities in our lives.

Yet we Americans do not sufficiently appreciate the uses of history and historical memory. A brief exchange between two characters in the film, *Damnation Alley*, conveys the typically American view. Two men drive past a junkyard. The younger man remarks: "I never saw so many cars." The older man says: "That's your heritage, Billy." "What's heritage?" Billy asks. The answer comes: "What people leave other people when they find out it don't work." We associate this viewpoint with Henry Ford, who gave us the automobile. And although Ford didn't really say "History is bunk," that's how we choose to remember it—despite the historian Arnold Toynbee having pointed out that "Ford is history."

In countries that have no democratic traditions, or where freedom is only weakly established or recently won, the importance of historical memory is better understood and appreciated. Thus the historian Lutz Niethammer, writing on the value of oral history in his native West Germany, says: "a democratic future needs a past in which not only elites are audible." Our democratic future in America is not solely but to a great degree dependent on the kind of image we have of our national past, on the voices we hear from that past. Is the image we pass along accurate? Do we hear all the voices? Frances Fitzgerald, in *America Revised*, a study of the way American history has been presented in secondary school texts since the Civil War, maintains credibly that these texts have in many instances distorted our past, and in others entirely ignored significant parts of it. The humanities appropriately speak to this situation.

Our values and beliefs, our traditions and customs contain an image of ourselves as a people. That image may be thought of as our collective soul. This is the view of Archibald MacLeish, who writes:

> The soul of a people is the image it cherishes of itself; the aspect in which it sees itself against the past; the attributes to which its future conduct must respond. To destroy that image is to destroy, in a very real sense, the identity of the nation, for to destroy the image is to destroy the means by which the nations recognizes what it is and what it has to do.

The humanities—the texts, works of art and disciplines associated with the humanities: history, literature, philosophy, religious studies, art and music history—the humanities are the custodians of this cherished image of ourselves as a people. We can look to the humanities if we wish to sharpen the images of Americans as free people. And it is by *doing* the humanities, as scientists do science, that we can behave and think as free people, for it is in the humanities that we are encouraged to concern ourselves with issues and ideas free people are concerned with. When we start behaving and thinking as free people, *using* our freedom, we strengthen that freedom. (It is not only in athletic endeavors that you lose it if you don't use it.)

The American image has become blurred, MacLeish thinks, because we have not acted so much as re-acted (since World War II) to a perceived threat to our freedom, communism:

> A people who have thought of themselves for a hundred years as having purposes of their own for changing the world cannot learn overnight to think of themselves as resisters of another's purposes without beginning to wonder who they are.... A people who have been real to themselves because they were *for* something cannot continue to be real to themselves when they find they are merely *against* something.

Freedom, MacLeish says, was once something we used, but has now become something we *save*, something we put away and protect like other possessions, like a deed or a bond. But the "true test of freedom is in its use. It has no other test."

The humanities provide opportunities for us to prove to ourselves that while grappling with human problems does require technical, industrial, and scientific skills, the skills of technicians and scientists, great as they are, are not sufficient. They are all skills of means, skills that offer solutions to the question of how to do things. There are also skills that have to do not with means but with ends. These are the skills we employ when we do the humanities, when we clarify values, pose moral and ethical questions. Again, MacLeish: "...it is not the technical problem requiring special knowledge which stands in the way.... The real obstacle is the obstacle of ends, not means."

We deal with the obstacle of ends through the humanities. The humanities are the ground in which we can cultivate what we truly cherish, what we truly honor (it was Plato who observed shrewdly that what is honored in a country is cultivated there), in which we can cultivate the activity of thinking like free people— that is, about ends as well as means.

The connection between freedom and the humanities is suggested in a story related by Plutarch: A father asks the price of educating his son. The price, he is told, is a thousand drachmas. The father blurts an oath and declares, "Why, I can buy a slave for a thousand drachmas."—"Then you will have two slaves," comes the reply, "your son and the fellow you buy."

We can update the story for our own time. "Why, I can buy a tank for x amount, or a missile!—"Yes, but you have not thereby secured your freedom."

The heart of the matter lies beyond it, but the metaphor of the marketplace still helps us to understand: until the value of the humanities in the maintenance of freedom is appreciated, we are shopping for ignorance at bargain prices. To the degree that we think of education as mere training, as the acquisition of certain skills and their application in economic competition, we will prepare students to be tools, instruments in someone else's hands. We will not be putting students in full possession of their power and potential, which is to make them useful to themselves as well as to others.

J. H. Rush called his memoir of the years at Oak Ridge "Prometheus in Tennessee." His title refers, of course, to the Greek myth of the Titan who stole fire from the gods and gave it to mankind, and appropriately conveys his attitude about development of the atomic bomb. But we should remember that the mythological figure is referred to by an aptronym: *Prometheus* in the Greek is, literally, forethought, and means something closely akin to what Jacob Bronowski calls "the power of anticipation" and the "forward-looking imagination," the specifically human ability exercised not only in the sciences but in the humanities as well. And it is often overlooked that in the Greek story Prometheus (forethought) gave mankind fire *and* the arts. The story suggests that our science and technology, our arts and humanities are equally from the gods. J. H. Rush and his associates, who participated in the scientists' movement of 1945-47, and who organized the Federation of American Scientists, understood this as have many other members of the Oak Ridge community over the years. Whether we are farmers or physicists, homemakers or horticulturalists, we are all first human beings, and as Americans we are first of all free citizens of the only nation in history founded on an idea. Therefore it is especially important to us that not only our pipes but also our philosophy hold water.

THE POLITICS OF SCIENCE

James Overholt

Although Oak Ridge has come to symbolize the birth of the atomic age, the establishment of that community and those of Los Alamos and Hanford marked another, perhaps equally important, event in the development of American science. For the appearance of Oak Ridge signaled the end of a long tradition, a tradition in which the national government had for 150 years paid scant attention to scientists and their work. As one historian has noted, American science before 1940 had grown up "an orphan." It had been ill-funded and generally ignored. Only with the coming of World War II and the threat to national survival, did science finally receive government nurture. Only then was it harnessed to national purposes.

This might seem surprising in light of the beliefs held by the Founding Fathers 150 years earlier. For never had any group of men placed greater hope in science than those great statesmen of the eighteenth century. Thomas Jefferson, John Adams, Benjamin Franklin, and James Madison, to name but a few, believed profoundly that the hopes of human history and of America sailed upon the ship of science. They applauded the "splendid improvements in human society" made possible by science; and Jefferson wrote that "science has liberated the ideas of those who read and reflect.... Science is progressive, and talents and enterprise on the alert."

Yet those same men who extolled the virtues of science so

glowingly wrote a constitution and fashioned a nation that hindered for a century and a half government support of science. While in other nations science received handsome patronage, in America it received almost none. Part of this is explained by the American experience, which emphasized self-sufficiency and individualism. But probably more is explained by the Founding Fathers' deep fear of an intrusive government. Shaped deeply by the American Revolution and by the threat of distant monarchs, these men set about, above all, to form a government unable to intrude upon individual rights. To them, the scourge of their times was an intrusive, tyrannical government. When they formed their nation they specified a rigorous curtailment of the national government's role.

Clearly Madison, Jefferson, and others of their generation believed in science, but they believed in a limited government more. Freedom of the individual, they contended, came through a "division of powers;" and the national purpose was a reduction of the national government's role. Consequently, the notion of a national university devoted to the advancement of science (which was suggested during the Constitutional Convention of 1787), and national societies and institutes designed to promote technical knowledge died by the same hand that killed government interference in public assemblies, newspapers, and local government. Science, like other enterprises, would be left to fend for itself.

Even by the end of the nineteenth century, when America had become an industrial giant, government officials persisted in the notion of separating government from science. While the College de France, the Royal Institution of London, and the Pasteur Institute in Germany were being established in Europe, no comparative institutions were created in America. To be sure, the National Academy of Science was organized during the Civil War, but the American government never advanced its cause and soon allowed it to languish into insignificance. Whenever the suggestion of a national university or a central organization for science came up, Congress almost always turned a deaf ear. Because of their poor understanding of science, as well as their belief in limited government, congressmen of the nineteenth century found it almost impossible to promote the idea of government science.

This is not to say that the American government stayed aloof

529

entirely; it did support some forms of technology. It supported, for example, the survey of westward lands, the problems of navigation, internal improvements, and certain public health issues. But this, of course, came under applied science, which sometimes appealed to legislators. As for pure science and pure research—where teams of scientists explored possibilities in laboratories—that was almost never approved. As late as the 1920s, "the nation was spending a total of $200 million a year in the application of science, but only $10 million in pure research." As Herbert Hoover noted, America was appallingly inferior to Europe in the pure sciences.

Thus even with the twentieth century, when men like Hoover and Thorstein Veblen argued that "science was the key to rational progress" and asked that money be given to it, Congress remained unconvinced. It simply could not see how science could help the nation. As a result, it left research to others. In electricity, metallurgy, and chemicals, the research was almost always carried out at universities or at philanthropic foundations like the Rockefeller Institute or the Carnegie Institution. In fact, instead of these institutions looking to government for money, as one might think, there were actual cases where government agencies looked to them for money.

Compared to other nations, then, the American government remained blind to the relationship between pure scientific research and national purposes. While in Germany there were numerous state-supported universities thriving in an atmosphere of busy scientific research, there were almost no such universities in the United States. While scores of research chairs and graduate fellowships existed in Europe, in America there were only a few. While in Germany national organizations for the direction of science enjoyed government funding, in America none could be found.

A case in point was the National Research Council (NRC), which was organized during World War I. Although this organization was created to design better technical methods to win the war, the military paid almost no heed to it. Generalship and élan, it was believed, would win the war, not technology and the scientific method. Moreover, when the war ended, the NRC was left to depend entirely upon private support.

To be sure, the American political tradition of separation of science and government died hard. While Americans had always loved technology, the federal government had never taken "upon itself the role of fostering the creation of new knowledge." To have done so would have violated the concept of limited government. The argument was that it was unconstitutional, that government science violated the principles of democracy. Robert A. Millikan, professor of physics at the University of Chicago in the 1920s, voiced this view strongly. "Too much centralization," he contended, "even in the pursuit of science in this country, is a dangerous tendency." He requested instead "not a central Institute of Physics and Chemistry, but the stimulation of at least a dozen such creative centers scattered all over the country ... to be associated ... with effective educational centers."

World War II, though, changed all this. For the United States suddenly faced a two-front war against Germany and Japan. Not since 1812 had a foreign war cast such a long shadow over the American homeland. American scientists, in particular, sensed the threat and quickly approached President Roosevelt. They urged him to marshall science and technology to help win the conflict. And stunningly their efforts exceeded even their wildest hopes. From the president and Congress, there came a "vast infusion of federal funds" into weapons research. The figures alone underscore the extent of the change. In 1940, the federal budget for research and development stood at $74 million, most of that for agriculture; but by war's end the budget had increased to $1.59 billion. Overnight, the American government had discovered science, bestowing upon it financial and political support that knew no precedent in the American experience.

The scientist probably most responsible for convincing government to change its policy toward science was Dr. Vannevar Bush, an electrical engineer and a pioneer in computer design. An academician who knew the ropes of government, Bush had entertained thoughts of applying science and technology to war for some time. He was clearly the strongest link between government and science, with friends on both sides. He understood very well the need for science and government to work together to win the war. When Karl Compton informed him in May 1940 that uranium fission could have a "military significance," he immediately used his friendship with Harry Hopkins to approach President

531

Roosevelt with the idea. In this meeting, he convinced the president of the need for a national scientific organization; and on June 27 an executive order was issued, creating the National Defense Research Committee, which shortly became the Office of Scientific Research and Development (OSRD).

Even more important was the manner in which Bush convinced the president to set up the OSRD. For years scientists had been leery of government, almost as aloof toward it as it had been toward them, afraid that government patronage might compromise the integrity of their research. They had, in fact, been known to refuse grants and funds based on that fear. Thus when Bush approached Roosevelt, one of his prime concerns was to erect a protective barrier to prevent government intervention into scientific research. And considering the circumstances, Bush was prodigiously successful. The OSRD got an amazing degree of freedom.

First of all, the new organization consisted entirely of civilians and reported directly to the president, with Bush as its director and Dr. James Conant, another fellow scientist, its second in command. Moreover, it had the power to contract its research work to universities, which greatly assuaged scientists' fears of government intervention. Almost overnight, private institutions like the University of California, MIT, Harvard, and the University of Chicago received federal subsidies undreamt of a few years before, directing research in the areas of uranium, radar, and the electronic computer. All told, "over fifty universities and industrial firms received contracts of $1 million or more during the war." And all of this was directed by scientists who only a few months before had been ignored by government, by scientists who had had no authority whatever.

American science had gained what it had never known before: large budgets, institutional legitimacy, and the management of science by scientists. It is true that the atom bomb project fell under the jurisdiction of the War Department, with General Leslie Groves in command, and that there was much annoyance about security precautions and tension between Groves and the scientists; but the scientists still had an amazing degree of control over the project. The laboratories, after all, were run by civilian scientists, not by the military, and it was the scientists who made the final decisions on technical matters.

Dr. Vannevar Bush (L) and Dr. Karl Compton (R) consulting during the war years. Bush was the first director of the Office of Scientific Research and Development, an agency that represented the fusion of government and science.

Some of the scientists who worked on the atomic bomb and who received large budgets from the federal government. From left to right, Ernest O. Lawrence, Arthur Holly Compton, Vannevar Bush, James B. Conant, Karl T. Compton, and Alfred L. Loomis.

Conclusion

Thus the creation of Oak Ridge, along with other wartime facilities and organizations, marked the point in American history when science and government joined hands. Politicians by 1945 dreamt untold dreams for science, arguing that the nation could ill afford to do without it, that through the mobilization of science with federally funded research programs great achievements were in the offing. The war had taught them that science in the hands of state provided an awesome tool. They envisioned applying the methods of the Manhattan Project to such problems as poverty, education, housing, and transportation. To them, big science had lifted mankind to a new stage of human existence.

Problems did arise, however, and some of them resounded back to the founding principles of the nation. Already by the end of the war, serious constitutional questions had arisen when Bush and other scientists sought special treatment and favor for their research, arguing in 1945 that their work should be screened from congressional control. "Basic research," they contended, "could not be subjected to other conventional criteria of performance" when Congress voted on money bills. Understandably, the complexity of pure science made such a request likely; but still it was a request for "support without control." Even more important, however, was the enormous concentration of power that the union of science and government ensured. After the war, modern administrations, armed with all the appurtenances of scientific technology, had assumed so much power that it made the old pleas of the Founding Fathers for "division of powers" seem completely dated. To be sure, these governments could combat problems of disease and poverty, becoming the font for new frontiers, but they could also erect military systems so that the world might end up with what historian Walter McDougall calls today "the institutionalization of wartime methods."

Still, there was another dimension to government science, one that, ironically, gave it its strength and suggested its shortcomings. And that was the "blind veneration" that it tended to pay to the Future. For in the Future, state science seemed to invest so much of its vigorous labor and intellect. In looking almost wholly to what it could do Tomorrow, its achievements seemed endless, its discoveries always new, though its use of history quite spare—a point that has caused concern for more than a few social critics and historians.

During the eighteenth century, James Madison had spoken of the "blind veneration" that the sixteenth and seventeenth centuries had paid to antiquity, copying as they did the ideas and artistic expressions of the ancients. He had thought this a rather "unmanly spirit." The proudest boast he could make about Americans of his century was they had turned their backs on antiquity and were willing to experiment, to look to the future. This was in large measure the spirit of science asserting itself, and he welcomed it. But the point should not be carried too far. While Madison looked to the future, he also looked hard into the past. One merely need think of the summer of 1787 in Philadelphia to believe it. There, where Madison and other Americans had assembled to write a new constitution, he sat poring over the hundreds of history books that Thomas Jefferson had sent him from Paris—his "literary cargo" as Jefferson called them—trying to glean from them the lessons of ancient and modern confederacies that had failed and succeeded. This was a man not about to expel from his mind the wisdom of the ages, nor one whose hopes were tied solely to the future. He looked to the future, certainly, but did not dare do so without gazing long into the past. For him, the signposts for his age lay in the "lessons of the past."

One of the great achievements that communities like Oak Ridge have given modern society is a willingness to experiment, to look upon new frontiers, to shake the dust of old habits from its feet, but as Madison would probably have warned, they should never do so at the expense of paying "blind veneration" to the future. Just as he had feared that those ages before him had enslaved themselves to the past, so too would he have warned that our age—with its government science—can become too heavily dependent upon the future, and upon the technology that carries us into that future. A willingness to look forward, then, should never exclude an equal willingness to look back.

SELECTIVE BIBLIOGRAPHY

BOOKS

Baum, Willa K. and David K. Dunaway. *Oral History.* Nashville: American Association for State and Local History, 1984.

Beard, Charles A. and William Beard. *The American Leviathan: The Republic in the Machine Age.* New York: Macmillan, 1931.

Berman, Marshall. *All That is Solid Melts in Air: The Experience of Modernity.* New York: Simon and Schuster, 1982.

Bronowski, Jacob. *The Ascent of Man.* Boston: Little-Brown, 1974.

Brown, Anthony Cave and Charles B. MacDonald, eds. *The Secret History of the Atomic Bomb.* New York: Dial Press, 1977.

Campbell, Olive and Cecil J. Sharp. *English Folk Songs From the Southern Appalachians.* New York: G. D. Putnam Sons, 1917.

Davidson, Donald. *The Tennessee.* 2 vols. New York: Rinehart, 1946-48.

Dupree, A. Hunter. *Science in the Federal Government.* Salem, New Hampshire: Ayer, 1980.

Dykeman, Wilma. *Tennessee: A Bicentennial History.* New York: W. W. Norton, 1975.

Eller, Ronald D. *Miners, Millhands, and Mountaineers: Industrialization of the Appalachian South.* Knoxville: University of Tennessee Press, 1982.

Fitzgerald, Frances. *America Revised.* Boston: Little-Brown, 1979.

Glasstone, Samuel. *Sourcebook of Atomic Energy.* New York: D. Van Norstrand, Co., 1967.

Goodchild, Peter. *J. Robert Oppenheimer: Shatterer of Worlds.* New York: International Publications, 1985.

Greenberg, Daniel S. *The Politics of Pure Science.* New York: New American Library, 1967.

Groueff, Stephane. *Manhattan Project: The Untold Story of the Making of the Atomic Bomb.* Boston: Little-Brown, 1967.

Groves, Leslie R. *Now It Can Be Told: The Story of the Manhattan Project.* New York: Harper and Brothers, 1962.

Hawley, Gessner G. and Sigmund W. Leifson. *Atomic Energy in War and Peace.* New York: Reinhold Publishing, 1945.

538

Herken, Gregg F. *The Winning Weapon: The Atomic Bomb in the Cold War 1945-1950.* New York: Alfred A. Knopf, 1981.

Hewlett, Richard G. and Oscar E. Anderson, Jr. *The New World.* Vol. 1, 1939-1946. Washington, D.C.: United States Atomic Energy Commission, 1962.

_____ . *Atomic Shield.* Vol. 2, 1947-1952. Washington, D.C.: United States Atomic Energy Commission, 1969.

Hofstadter, Richard. *The American Political Tradition and The Men Who Made It.* New York: Vintage Book Edition, 1974.

Johnson, Charles W. and Charles O. Jackson. *City Behind a Fence: Oak Ridge, Tennessee 1942-1946.* Knoxville: University of Tennessee Press, 1981.

Kunetka, James W. *City of Fire: Los Alamos and the Birth of the Atomic Age, 1943-45.* Englewood Cliffs, N.J.: Prentice-Hall, 1978.

Laurence, William L. *Dawn Over Zero: The Story of the Atomic Bomb.* New York: Alfred A. Knopf, 1946.

Leyburn, James G. *The Scotch-Irish: A Social History.* Chapel Hill: University of North Carolina Press, 1962.

Loeb, Paul. *Nuclear Culture: Living and Working in the World's Largest Atomic Complex.* New York: Coward, McCann and Geoghegan, 1982.

McDougall, Walter A. *... The Heavens and the Earth.* New York: Basic Books, Inc., 1985.

Miller, Howard S. *Dollars For Research: Science and Its Patrons in Nineteenth-Century America.* Seattle: University of Washington Press, 1970.

Morland, Howard. *The Secret That Exploded.* New York: Random House, 1981.

Oppenheimer, J. Robert. *The Open Mind.* New York: Simon and Schuster, 1963.

Pettitt, Roland A. *Los Alamos Before the Dawn.* Los Alamos: Pajarito Publications, 1972.

Purcell, John. *The Best-Kept Secret: The Story of the Atomic Bomb.* New York: Vanguard Press, 1963.

Robinson, George O. *The Oak Ridge Story.* Kingsport, Tennessee: Southern Publishing, 1950.

Scarborough, Dorothy. *A Song Catcher in Southern Mountains: American Folk Songs of British Ancestry.* New York: Columbia University Press, 1937.

Smith, Alice Kimball. *A Peril and A Hope: The Scientists' Movement in America, 1945-1947.* Chicago: University of Chicago Press, 1965.

Smyth, Henry DeWolf. *Atomic Energy For Military Purposes.* Princeton, New Jersey: Princeton University Press, 1945.

Weller, Jack E. *Yesterday's People: Life in Contemporary Appalachia.* Lexington: University of Kentucky Press, 1965.

Wells, Herbert George. *The World Set Free.* Collins Clear-Type Press, 1956. (First pub. 1914.)

PERIODICALS

Devore, Robert. "The Man Who Made Manhattan." *Collier's* (October 13, 1945): 12ff.

Fallows, James. "America's Changing Economic Landscape." *The Atlantic Monthly* (March 1985): 47-68.

Jackson, Charles O. and Charles W. Johnson. "The Urbane Frontier: The Army and Community of Oak Ridge, Tennessee, 1942-47." *Military Affairs* (February 1977): 11.

James, William. "On a Certain Blindness in Human Beings." In *Talks to Teachers on Psychology: And to Students on Some of Life's Ideals.* New York: The Norton Library, 1958. (First pub. 1899.)

Lang, Daniel. "The Atomic City." *New Yorker* (September 29, 1945): 46-51.

MacLeish, Archibald. "The Contest of America." *The Atlantic Monthly* (March 1980): 35-42.

Miller, Jim Wayne. "The Last Bargain Left: The Humanities in the 1980s." *The Nebraska Humanist 5*, No. 1-2 (Spring-Fall, 1982).

Peele, Elizabeth, "A History of Segregation in Oak Ridge, 1943-1960." (unpub. Deposited in archives of Regional Appalachian Center of the Children's Museum of Oak Ridge.)

Rockwell, Theodore, III. "Frontier Life Among the Atom Splitters." *Saturday Evening Post* (December 1, 1945): 28ff.

Rush, J. H. "Prometheus in Tennessee." *Saturday Review* (July 2, 1960): 10-12.

Smyser, Dick. "City's Most Unique Neighborhood." *The Oak Ridger* (February 1981): 1 and 8.

West, Marvin. "Oak Ridge: The Atomic City." *Tennessee Valley Perspective* (Summer 1974):

Wickware, Francis Sell. "Oak Ridge." *Life* (September 9, 1946): 2ff.

DOCUMENTS

Agricultural Census Records, 1880s. Customs House, Knoxville, Tennessee.

Deed Book "V," Vol. 3, p. 322 and Deed Book "C," Vol. 4, p. 147. Anderson County Registrar of Deeds, Anderson County Courthouse, Clinton, Tennessee.

Fielder, George. "Historic Sites Reconnaissance of the Oak Ridge Reservation, Oak Ridge, Tennessee." ORNL/TM 5811.

General Leslie Groves Collection. United States Military Academy, West Point, New York.

Land Grant Number 20009, Box 19, p. 784; and Number 24704, Book 26, p. 55. Customs House, Knoxville, Tennessee.

Population Census Records, 1800s. Customs House, Knoxville, Tennessee.

Record Books of the Judiciary, 1800s. Customs House, Knoxville, Tennessee.

Will Books, 1800s. Anderson County Courthouse, Clinton, Tennessee.

U.S. Army Corp of Engineers, Segment G, 1944, Records of Acquisition, Manhattan Project. From Jack Newman, Procurements and Contracts, U.S. Department of Energy, Oak Ridge, Tennessee.

CONTRIBUTORS

JUNE ADAMSON, associate professor of journalism at the University of Tennessee, worked for ten years on the staff of *The Oak Ridger*. While at the paper she won several Tennessee Press Association awards for her work. She has also published articles in several magazines and journals. She came to Oak Ridge in 1944 and is currently working on a book about the Clinton school desegregation crisis of the 1950s.

JANE BARNES ALDERFER, resource coordinator/librarian for the Regional Appalachian Center since 1982, holds an M.A. in American Studies and an M.A. in Library Science. She worked in the indexing of *An Encyclopedia of East Tennessee* and in archival processing for An Appalachian Experience. She has held archival positions at Educational Testing Service (Princeton, New Jersey) and at the Chicago Historical Society.

MARION ALEXANDER, teacher in the Oak Ridge Schools for twenty years, came to Oak Ridge in 1952 with her husband and two sons. She was so impressed with the school system that she returned to college to earn her teaching certificate and was hired in 1964 to teach English.

MARILOU AWIAKTA (BONHAM THOMPSON), member of Leadership Memphis and the Arts-in-the-Schools, was one of twelve city leaders honored in 1985 by the National Conference of Christians and Jews. Of Cherokee descent, she has published several books, articles, and poems, many dealing with Oak Ridge. She was born in Knoxville and moved to Oak Ridge in 1945, at age nine.

CONNIE BOLLING, Appalachian folklorist, resigned after teaching for fifteen years and came to Oak Ridge in 1943 to work on the Manhattan Project. In 1973 he retired from his work in Oak Ridge, but has since kept busy writing about his experiences in and folklore about his native region for the *Coalfield Progress* newspaper in Virginia.

JUNE M. BOONE, freelance writer, came to Oak Ridge with her family in 1945 and graduated from Oak Ridge High School a year later. In her eleven years of writing she has had many short stories and articles published, including contributions to *An Encyclopedia of East Tennessee* and *The Appalachian Studies Teacher's Manual*.

RUTH CAREY, free-lance photographer and writer, moved from Knoxville to Oak Ridge with her husband in 1944. She joined the U.S. Atomic Energy Commission (which later became part of the

Department of Energy) in 1948. Retiring in 1983, she has done work for *The Oak Ridger* and the Oak Ridge Playhouse.

ERIC KENT CLARKE, psychiatrist, was born in Ontario in 1894. He graduated from the University of Toronto Medical School at the age of twenty-one. During World War I he was alternately a member of the British and Canadian armies. After moving to the United States in 1927, he served in the medical schools of both the Universities of Rochester and Minnesota. Between 1944 and 1946 he was chief psychiatrist for the Manhattan District, stationed in Oak Ridge. In 1946 he returned to Minnesota and founded the Minnesota Psychiatry Institute. He died in 1958.

CHARLES COUNTS, potter, author, and designer-craftsman, graduated from Oak Ridge High School in 1952. In 1957 he received an M.A. from Southern Illinois University and a year later founded Beaver Ridge Pottery. He is a life member of the Southern Highland Handicraft Guild and has written two books on pottery. He now lives in Atlanta, Georgia.

MARY K. COX, arrived in Oak Ridge in 1946 with a radio, a coffee table, two children, and her husband. Born in Ava, Illinois, she has been a private music teacher for many years and taught sociology and anthropology at Austin Peay State University for twelve years.

RUBY DANIEL, member of the Community Craft Center in Norris, has lived in Knox County for fifty-two years. She loves to quilt and work in crafts. She and her husband have one daughter and live very close to the location of her mother's first home place on Oak Ridge Highway.

BONNIE LEE DINGS, journalist, started writing in the 1960s. Since then she has written and edited numerous stories and essays, and has taught English and journalism. Recently she has worked as a technical editor and public relations consultant for scientific, commercial, nonprofit, and academic clients.

JOANNE S. GAILAR, equal opportunity coordinator for Martin Marietta Energy Systems, is a New Orleans native who came to Oak Ridge as a bride in 1945. Claiming writing as a hobby, she has written on such varied subjects as civil defense (both the U.S. and U.S.S.R. programs), Georgia Avenue in Oak Ridge, and Emily Dickinson.

CONNIE J. GREEN, graduate student in creative writing at the University of Tennessee, moved as a child from the coal-mining area of eastern Kentucky to Oak Ridge. She has taught in Oak Ridge, at

Roane State, and at the University of Tennessee. Her poetry, short stories, and articles have appeared in various regional and national magazines, and she is currently working on a novel.

ROBERT R. HENTZ, poet and fiction writer, worked in Oak Ridge as an analytic chemist during and shortly after World War II. After leaving Oak Ridge he earned a Ph.D. from Notre Dame in 1950, then went on to teach and work in science until 1975 when he retired to pursue other interests, particularly extensive reading and writing of fiction and poetry.

PATRICIA A. HOPE, journalist, photographer, and freelance writer, was born in Harriman and has written articles for many publications in East Tennessee and elsewhere. She has also written fiction and poetry, taught creative writing, and won numerous awards for her work.

JACINTA K. HOWARD, violin and viola teacher, came to Oak Ridge at the beginning of the city's history in the fall of 1943. The widow of Frederick T. Howard, a physicist at Oak Ridge National Laboratory, she is the mother of two children and a charter member of the Oak Ridge Symphony Orchestra.

THOMAS F. HOWARD grew up in Oak Ridge and graduated from Oak Ridge High School in 1963. He is a graduate of the University of Chicago and has been a student at the University of California, Berkeley studying anthropology and geography. He has worked as a journalist and researcher and now lives in Berkeley, but visits Oak Ridge regularly.

SUE ELLEN HUDSON, charter member of the East Tennessee Writers Association, returned to the area with her husband after being away for nearly a decade. In 1982 she was one of the fifteen national winners in a writing competition sponsored by *Guideposts*, and has had articles published in a variety of magazines.

JOHN RICE IRWIN, writer, historian, and a leading authority on the culture of southern Appalachia, was an educator and superintendent of the Anderson County Schools before founding the Museum of Appalachia in Norris. His work has earned him a national reputation, and among his writings are four books which have nationwide distribution.

HELEN C. JERNIGAN lived and worked in Happy Valley during the summer of 1944. After graduation from Tennessee Wesleyan, she became associate editor of *The Carbide Courier* and a librarian for the Oak Ridge Schools. She later became director and corporate secretary for Tennelec, Inc., and a columnist and special assignments writer for *The Oak Ridger*. She is currently Circuit Court Clerk of Anderson County.

LOIS KAUFMAN, freelance writer, has lived in East Tennessee and North Carolina since 1963. A graduate of the University of Oklahoma School of Journalism, she frequently writes about individuals in the East Tennessee area, including Oak Ridge residents employed at Oak Ridge National Laboratory. She has two children.

CHRIS KEIM, former division director of technical information at Oak Ridge National Laboratory, came to Oak Ridge in early 1944. With a background in mathematics, physics, and chemistry, he first worked for Tennessee Eastman in the Y-12 area. Since retiring he has devoted much of his energy toward Special Olympics Rowing, of which he is national director.

SARAH KETRON, retired educator, came to Oak Ridge in 1944 from Kentucky where she had served as vice principal of the high school in Frankfort. She served the Oak Ridge Schools as a teacher, counselor at Jefferson Junior High School, and, until her retirement in 1973, as director of Pupil Personnel Services. She also helped establish many local organizations and remains active in several of these.

CAROLYN KORSMEYER, philosophy professor at the State University of New York at Buffalo, lived in Oak Ridge from 1945 to 1962, when she graduated from high school. She has been on the faculty at Buffalo since 1971 and lives in that city with her husband and two sons.

JANE WARREN LARSON came to Oak Ridge in 1943 from Rochester, New York. She subsequently became head of the Y-12 Information Center for Union Carbide Corporation, leaving in 1951 to join Rand Corporation in Los Angeles. In 1957 she married Clarence E. Larson, a former Oak Ridger. Jane is the daughter of Dr. and Mrs. Stafford L. Warren who were based in Oak Ridge during the war. She has had a lifetime hobby of ceramics projects and is currently carrying out a public commission for three large ceramic murals on Wisconsin Avenue in Bethesda where they have their home.

THOMAS F.X. MCCARTHY, retired journalist and editor, came to Oak Ridge in May 1944 as a clerk in charge of Selective Service at the K-25 plant. After the war he became managing editor first of the *Oak Ridge Journal* (the city's government-subsidized weekly paper), then of the short-lived daily *Oak Ridge Times*, eventually moving to a position with Oak Ridge Associated Universities. He retired in 1979, but still does work for ORAU and book reviews for the *Knoxville News-Sentinel.*

DON MCKAY came to Oak Ridge as *The Oak Ridger's* publisher when it was started in 1949. Born in Pennsylvania, he worked his way up in the newspaper business, starting as an errand boy with an Olean, New York newspaper. A widower, he is the father of four children.

JIM WAYNE MILLER, professor at Western Kentucky University, was born in the mountains of North Carolina. In 1965 he received his Ph.D. from Vanderbilt University in both German language and American literature. Besides being an advocate of Appalachian studies, he is also a highly acclaimed poet.

K. D. NICHOLS, retired major general in the U.S. Army, served as district engineer of the Manhattan Project during World War II. His office at Oak Ridge was the administrative center of the wartime atomic energy activities. He is a member of the National Academy of Engineering and is presently completing his autobiography. He is the father of two children and the grandfather of four.

JAMES OVERHOLT, director of the Regional Appalachian Center of the Children's Museum, started work at the Center in 1982. A former high school teacher, he received his Ph.D. in history from Miami University of Ohio in 1981. After eight years in Ohio he returned to his native East Tennessee with his wife and two children.

SANDRA WHITTEN PLANT, chief of Public and Employee Communications for Oak Ridge Associated Universities, came to Oak Ridge in 1951 when she was nine years old. She has taught creative writing at Roane State, where for a time she also served as assistant director of public information. In 1981 she achieved her accreditation in public relations.

WILLIAM G. POLLARD, retired priest in the Episcopal Church, earned a Ph.D. in physics in 1934 and joined the Manhattan Project at Columbia University in 1944. After the war he became involved in forming the Oak Ridge Institute of Nuclear Studies, now renamed Oak Ridge Associated Universities. He moved to Oak Ridge in 1947.

LIANE RUSSELL and her husband, William Russell, have been successive heads of the Mammalian Genetics Section of Oak Ridge National Laboratory since its beginning in 1947. She has been head of the mutagenesis and teratogenesis section of ORNL's Biology Division since 1975. She holds an A.B. in chemistry from Hunter College and a Ph.D. in zoology and genetics from the University of Chicago. She has received many awards and was the first woman elected to the National Academy of Sciences. She and her husband are founders of Tennessee Citizens for Wilderness Planning.

KATHRYN SONNEN arrived in Oak Ridge in February 1947. Mother of three children, she has been a member of the Elm Grove PTA, League of Women Voters, and the Oak Ridge High School PTA in addition to the St. Mary's Home and School Association.

MARTHA C. SPARROW, archivist, came to Oak Ridge in September 1943 with her parents and her ten-day-old brother. In 1980 she received her M.A. in history, writing her thesis on a social history of Oak Ridge during World War II. She presently lives in northeast Mississippi with her husband and two children.

VALERIA STEELE, historian and playwright, graduated from Oak Ridge High School in 1977 and Berea College in 1981. A member of the Arts Council, she has directed some of her own plays in Oak Ridge, as well as Douglas Turner Ward's *Day of Absence.*

ELLISON H. TAYLOR, retired director of the Chemistry Division of Oak Ridge National Laboratory, came to Oak Ridge in 1945 after having worked on the Manhattan Project at Columbia University. He has also taught physical chemistry and done research in physical chemistry and chemical physics.

THOMAS W. THOMPSON, historian with the U.S. Air Force, has family roots that extend into the East Tennessee countryside. Graduating with a B.S. from East Tennessee State University, he has also earned an M.A. and Ph.D. in English history. He will have a book published in 1987. With his wife and three children, he lives in upstate New York.

MAISIE TUNNELL came to Oak Ridge with her husband in 1943. In addition to twenty-two years of teaching experience, she has also written many skits for school, church, and civic organizations. The Tunnells were one of the first families to buy a lot and build in Oak Ridge.

JOAN WALLACE came to Oak Ridge in 1947 at the age of seventeen years. She and her mother, Katherine Ratjen, moved to the city to join her father, Harold, who had worked in Oak Ridge during the war. Joan has been employed by *The Oak Ridger* since 1963 and served as assistant editor for ten years. She is a member of the First

United Methodist Church and the Altrusa Club.

ALVIN M. WEINBERG, scientist, writer, and administrator, was a member of the original group that developed the first chain reactors in 1941. He has been a director at both Oak Ridge National Laboratory and Oak Ridge Associated Universities. He has collaborated on a book about nuclear reactor theory and has had many of his essays collected in a book, *Reflections On Big Science*.

HORACE V. WELLS, JR., newspaper publisher, graduated from Vanderbilt University in 1930 and worked for the Nashville *Tennessean*, where he was state news editor. Seeking the opportunity for a newspaper of his own, he moved to Clinton in 1933 and started the Clinton *Courier*—later the *Courier-News*. A widower, Mr. Wells has four daughters, twelve grandchildren, and a great-grandchild on the way.

AMY K. WOLFE moved to the Oak Ridge area in 1983. An anthropologist at Oak Ridge National Laboratory, she studies the effects of technologies on social systems. She received her Ph.D. in anthropology from the University of Pennsylvania. Her dissertation examined perceptions of industrial risk in Oak Ridge and Rockwood.

INDEX

Prepared by Jane Barnes Alderfer
assisted by Anne Adamson

Because of the nature of the book, the index has been restricted to broad topics designed to lead the reader to sections of the essays dealing with these subjects. Proper names have not been cited except in a few instances (for example, Margaret Mead). The goal of the index has been to locate as many topics as possible within the constraints of time so that the reader might explore specific subjects.